To Pat

A good friend. Thanks
for your interest

Tom

Artistic Greatness

Artistic Greatness

A Comparative Exploration of Michelangelo, Beethoven, & Monet

Thomas McBurney

1999
Galde Press, Inc.
Lakeville, Minnesota, U.S.A.

Artistic Greatness

Printed in Canada

First Edition
First Printing, 1999

Library of Congress Cataloging-in-Publication Data
McBurney, Thomas, 1938–
Artistic greatness : a comparative exploration of Michelangelo, Beethoven, & Monet / Thomas McBurney. — 1st ed.
p. cm.
Includes bibliographical references.
ISBN 1–880090–78–3
1. Arts—Psychological aspects. 2. Creation (Literary, artistic, etc.) 3. Michelangelo Buonarroti, 1475–1564. 4. Beethoven, Ludwig van, 1770–1827. 5. Monet, Claude, 1840–1926. I. Title.
NX165.M43 1999
700'.92'2—dc21
[B] 99–22009
CIP

Galde Press, Inc.
PO Box 460
Lakeville, Minnesota 55044–0460

Dedication

To my wife Barbara
and my daughters Ann, Susan, Megan and Lesley
who provide so much of the
love and inspiration in my life

Contents

Acknowledgments and Thanks xv

Introduction xvii

Michelangelo Buonarroti (1475–1564) 1

Michelangelo's Times 1
The Renaissance 3
Historical and Political Overview 5
Florence and the Medici 6
Humanism 11
Religion: The Church 13
Additional Influences 18
Renaissance Art 19

Michelangelo's Life 23
Birth and Early Years in Florence 23
Bologna and Rome as a Young Man 25
In Florence, 1501–1505 27
Working for Julius II 30
In Florence: Working for the Medici 36
Political Events—Conflict and Problems 41
Rome: New Challenges and Frustrations 44
Old Age: Continuing His Work 48
His Final Years 50

Michelangelo's Personal Characteristics 53
Appearance 53
Family 53
Finances 59
General Relationships 60
Relations with Other Artists 62

Close Personal Relationships 65
Religious Beliefs 69
Personality 69

Michelangelo's Works 74
Sculpture 75
Painting 79
Architecture 84

Ludwig Van Beethoven (1770–1827) 91

Beethoven's Times 94
Europe in the 1700s 94
The Enlightenment 96
The French Revolution 98
Napoleon 100
Congress of Vienna 102
The City of Bonn 103
Vienna and the Hapsburgs 105

Musical Perspective 109
The Renaissance (approximately 1450–1600) 110
Baroque (1600–1750) 110
Pre-Classical 114
Classical 115

Beethoven's Life 127
Family Background and Birth 127
Youth in Bonn, 1770–1787 128
Musical Growth and Family Problems, 1787–1792 132
Early Years in Vienna, 1792–1800 136
Personal Crisis, 1800–1802 144
Fame, Creativity and Growth, 1803–1813 151
Crisis and Frustration, 1813–1820 165

The Final Years, 1820–1827 172

Beethoven's Personal Characteristics 180
Appearance 180
Habits and Lifestyle 181
Finances 182
Personality 184
Philosophy and Religion 187
Health 189
Inner Conflicts 190

Beethoven's Works 192
Stylistic Periods 192
Influences on His Work 193
Work Routine 194
Composing 196
His Output 198
His Legacy 206

Claude Monet (1840–1926) 211

Monet's Times 214
France and Europe—Mid-Nineteenth Century 214
France—Second Republic/Second Empire, 1848–1870 215
The Third Republic 216
The Last Decades of the Nineteenth Century 218
Dreyfus Affair 219
France—Early Twentieth Century 221
Paris—The City 222
Center of the Arts 223
Cafés and Social Life 224
Technology 225
Philosophical and Intellectual Trends 227

Artistic Environment and History 230
Neoclassicism 230
Romanticism 231
Realism 232
Corot 235
Other Influences 236

Impressionism 239
General Background 239
Characteristics of Impressionism 240
Chronology of the Movement 241
The Impressionist Painters 245

Monet's Life 255
Youth—Paris and Le Havre, 1840–1856 255
Early Development as a Painter, 1856–1862 256
Years of Growth and Struggle—The 1860s 261
Exile, 1870–1871 270
Argenteuil—The 1870s 271
Personal and Family Problems—The Late 1870s 277
Vétheuil—An Interlude 280
The Move to Giverny 283
Painting Excursions—The 1880s 285
Recognition and Involvement in Paris, 1889–1890 290
The Series Paintings of the 1890s 293
Personal and Family Change—The 1890s 299
The End of the Century 302
Focusing His Life and Work at Giverny 306
Monet in His Early Seventies 309
His Art at Giverny 312
Monet's Final Years 315

Monet's Personal Characteristics 320
Appearance 320

Family 321
Finances 322
Personality and Relationships 323
Interests and Beliefs 325

Monet's Works 327
General Approach 327
Out-of-Door Painting 328
Subject Matter 329
Composition 331
Building the Painting 332
Productivity and Output 335
Other Media 336
Monet's Influence and Legacy 337

Observations and Conclusions 341
Defining Artistic Greatness 341
Significant Parallels 344
Concluding Thoughts 354

Bibliography 357

Acknowledgments and Thanks

Support and advice along the way is important in completing a project like this. Many people offered much-appreciated encouragement. There were a few people who were particularly helpful.

Several times I received very useful criticism and editorial advice from my friend historian Rod Anderson. Partial readings and discussions of the book occurred at various points. Particularly helpful were the comments of Billie Young, Ann Pflaum and daughter Ann McBurney. Much of the typing and manuscript work was handled by the extremely efficient Ms. Shawn Hollembeak. Logistical, organizing and process help came from daughter Megan McBurney. Wonderful hospitality in Florence was provided by Cy and Paula DeCosse. The general advice and involvement of literary consultant Scott Edelstein was very important. He provided me with wise counsel and often-needed encouragement.

There were a number of artists and creative people who gave me insights into the inner workings of their art form. My thanks go to:

- Renowned international conductor Edo de Waart.
- The wonderfully innovative composer Libby Larsen.
- The brilliant American/Tuscan painter Patrice Lombardi.
- Versatile illustrator and sculptor Richard Boardman who guided me through the stone-cutting schools and the magnificent marble quarries of Carrara.
- And especially to the talented painter Mark Balma who welcomed me up on his scaffold as he executed some of his fabulous frescos.

I must also acknowledge the cheerful help I received from several people who made some of my research most unusual and enjoyable.

- The friendly, young Austrian woman who opened up an old farmhouse in the small village of Gniexendorf to show us where Beethoven lived and worked for several months in 1826 just before he died.

- The chatty old man who proudly showed us the ancient house where Michelangelo was born in the tiny Tuscan village of Caprese.
- The cheerful Catholic priest who escorted us through the inner sanctum of the Vatican so we could spend half an hour inside the "never open to the public" Pauline Chapel viewing Michelangelo's great last frescos.
- The efficient staffs of the archives and back rooms of the British Museum, the Louvre, the Uffizi Gallery and the Casa Buonarroti who patiently and carefully brought out the priceless originals of hundreds of Michelangelo's drawings.

Finally, I want to thank my wonderful wife, Barabara, who is herself a fine painter. Her support was terrific. I particularly appreciated her patience and understanding as I slowly worked my way through the conceptualizing, the research, and the writing of this book.

Introduction

When we stare in awe at the Sistine Chapel ceiling, or become enveloped by the sounds of a Beethoven symphony, or let ourselves be drawn into the sensuous world of Monet's water lilies, we sometimes wonder how a human being was able to create something so magnificent.

Of the many artists who have achieved fame and left behind works of lasting beauty, only a small number have been truly great. And of these, only a small fraction have not only opened up entirely new artistic paths, but set a standard which remains a driving influence decades or even centuries later. What made these few artists capable of such accomplishment? What forces, events and attributes made them and their work so influential?

In *Artistic Greatness*, I hope to explore these issues and to answer these questions by focusing on the lives and work of three of the greatest artists in the Western tradition.

Michelangelo Buonarroti (1475–1564)

Long proclaimed as the world's greatest artist, he lived at the end of one of the most active and fertile artistic periods in human history, the Italian Renaissance. His artistic output is spread across a number of art forms: sculpture, painting, architecture, drawing and design.

Ludwig van Beethoven (1770–1827)

His compositions are still considered the ideal of what great music can be. He, too, lived in a time and place of intense artistic activity. His work can be viewed as the culmination of a period of major creative output by a variety of important composers and the beginning of a new and more powerful direction in music.

Claude Monet (1840–1926)

Monet was the preeminent painter of the French Impressionist movement. He is passionately admired and widely acknowledged as one of the greatest of all painters.

Important for the validity of this exploration is the fact that these artists not only worked in different art forms but also lived in times separated by many years, in places separated by many miles, and in societies driven by very different forces.

For each of the three, we will begin by examining the historical, social and artistic forces that shaped their lives and work. We'll also look at each artist's personality and at important relationships and events in their lives. Then, with this knowledge, we'll examine each artist's creative output in terms of its artistic technique, its uniqueness, and its significance to the evolution of the entire art form.

Once we've explored these three artists individually, we will look at their commonalities, of which there are many. As we will see, these common elements appear not only in their approaches to their work, but in their temperaments, their upbringings, their personal relationships, the pivotal points in history in which they lived, and the aesthetic bent of their cultures.

Some of these similarities and parallels, such as the artists' attitudes toward their work, are very much what we might expect. Others, however, such as a cultural readiness for major aesthetic redirection, are less obvious and still others, such as the artists' attitudes toward money, are surprising indeed.

I hope to show that these commonalities are anything but mere coincidence. These common elements are precisely what distinguish great artists—those able to change the course of artistic history—from those who are merely highly accomplished.

Ultimately, I will identify a set of core qualities and influences that can be said to define artistic greatness or, at the very least, to engender and to nurture it.

Readers with no formal background in art, music or architecture need not fear that they will get lost or confused in this book. In all cases I have provided the necessary background information on each artist and on the culture and society in which he lived.

In short, this book is a tour of the lives of three of the world's greatest and most influential artists, as well as a walk through the labyrinths of culture, history, aesthetics, and the human mind. My hope is that readers will thoroughly enjoy both journeys.

THOMAS R. MCBURNEY

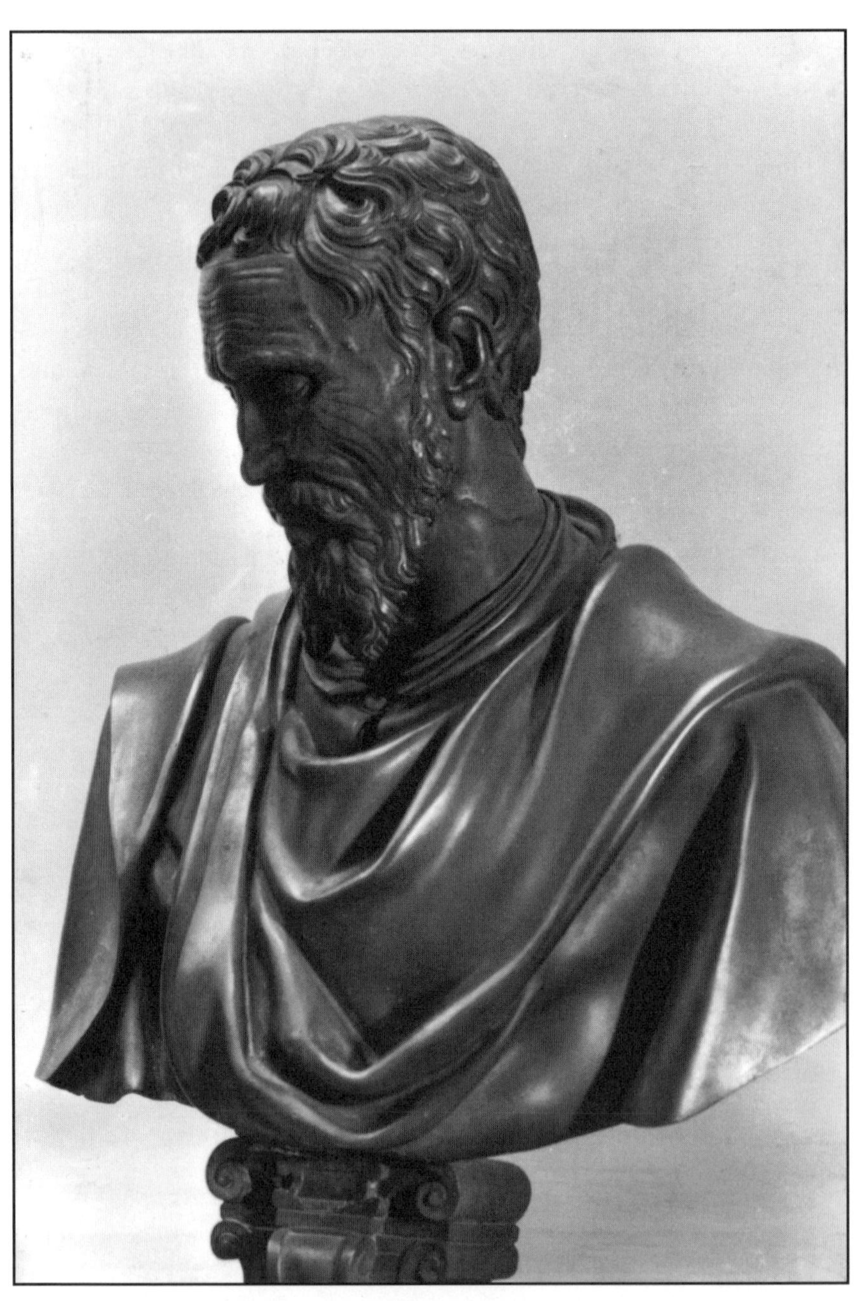

This bronze bust of Michelangelo is by his friend Daniele de Volterra. It portrays him in his eighties and captures not only his physical characteristics, but also his inner strength and control over his conflicting emotions.

Michelangelo Buonarroti (1475–1564)

Even in his own lifetime, Michelangelo was widely praised as the greatest artist who ever lived.

His fame came early, when he was only in his twenties. By the time he was forty, the famous Renaissance poet Ariosto had given him the title "Il Divino," setting Michelangelo apart from his contemporaries.

He gave us true masterpieces in sculpture, painting and architecture. In addition, he was one of the world's great draftsmen and a very good poet. His works reflect a powerful intellect steeped in Platonic philosophies, Roman antiquity, humanism, and deeply spiritual Christianity.

Still, his life was one of almost constant torment and stress. He was something of a loner and struggled with personal relationships. He was in constant conflict with his various patrons (mainly popes, the Medici, or the city of Florence); as a result, much of his work was left unfinished. His correspondence reflects constant haggling and complaining over finances, business plans and political intrigues. He was an extremely complex, driven, self-critical man with an atypical amount of psychological baggage.

He worked and thought of himself mainly as a sculptor of marble, particularly in his early years. He started work on (and occasionally finished) a number of works in that medium. However, he was equally renowned with the brush, even though he often had to be forced into working as a painter. He painted mainly in the then-popular and difficult fresco technique. His frescos in the Vatican represent some of the greatest artworks in history. Toward the end of his life he spent considerable time as an architect and city planner; these works exist today as examples of innovation and lasting excellence.

Michelangelo's life spanned the last years of the period known as the Italian Renaissance—approximately 1350 to 1550. He benefited from and built upon the intellectual ferment, and the tremendous artistic innovation and output, that had gone before him. His work brought everything up to a new level so that his contemporaries almost unanimously acknowledged him as the greatest artist ever.

He grew up in the north central part of Italy and spent most of his life working in either Florence or Rome. During these years, what we now call Italy was in almost constant conflict and turmoil. A series of confrontations among the city-states was followed by periods during which the armies of France and Spain marched back and forth across the peninsula, causing great unrest and damage.

Simultaneously, the Catholic Church, which played a central role in Michelangelo's life, went through major changes, most dramatically illustrated by the challenge of the Reformation from the north.

We are fortunate to have a variety of sources that provide reasonably accurate glimpses of this man and the period when he lived. First of all, there are his letters, of which nearly five hundred survive. These deal mostly with everyday affairs such as contracts, financial issues, family problems and travel plans. They give a fascinating look into Michelangelo as a person—how he thought, what he worried about, what he liked and didn't like. In addition, there are hundreds of pages of records that can be used to trace the nature and progress of many of his artistic projects. We also have copies of some three hundred of his poems, as well as two biographies written and published during his lifetime:

- Giorgio Vasari's *Lives of the Artists,* published in 1550 and updated in 1568.
- Ascanio Condivi's *The Life of Michelangelo*, published in 1553.

Both men knew and worked with Michelangelo, and it is believed that Michelangelo had some influence over both, especially Condivi. To some extent, therefore, their writings may reflect Michelangelo's desire to create his own public image. While their accounts of his life are in general agreement, they have some differences which are still being debated.

Michelangelo's Times

The Renaissance

The Renaissance, which can be loosely defined as the period from about 1350 to 1550, was not a piece of history marked by specific initiating and terminating events. Rather, it was more a movement, a way of thinking, an approach to life itself. It grew out of the Middle Ages and, in turn, was absorbed by the events and trends of the late sixteenth century. Its purest expression was in north central Italy (Florence and Tuscany), where it first took form in the early 1300s. Eventually the Renaissance spread to other parts of Italy and then north to the rest of Europe.

Renaissance, from the French, basically means "rebirth." And in the sense that much of its emphasis and motivation came from the rediscovery of Roman and Greek culture, it was a restatement of the best of those ancient societies. However, an even stronger part of the Renaissance was a new approach to our view of ourselves. The centuries-long belief of humankind as rather helpless players in God's big plan was slowly changed to a more human-centered view. It was an outlook that said we do indeed have some control and influence in our lives, that we can in fact play a role in helping ourselves and others. Religion and church continued to play a major role in people's lives, but there was a shift towards a more human-centered outlook on life.

During the Renaissance, dramatic changes occurred in many formal institutions and in the way society was organized. In commerce, for example, a basically capitalistic model became fairly widespread during these years. Major innovations took place in trading, banking, currency and insurance. Great fortunes were made by those with business acumen. Often this business success was a steppingstone to political power and provided an economic base for major patronage of the arts. Crude forms of democracy (though limited only to the upper strata) sprung up in many areas. Men talked more about rights and freedom, and there was continuous effort toward republican forms of government (i.e., where power is vested in a voting group).

Unlike in England or France, on the Italian peninsula there was no long-standing traditional political structure or major geographically centered power base. This allowed many city-states and regional powers to emerge. It was within these fairly autonomous political entities that much of the experiments in republicanism took place. It was also within these regional units that strong feelings of localism emerged. This resulted in both unique local traditions and many local wars throughout much of the Renaissance period.

For all its glories and its widespread and continuing influence, the Renaissance was basically an elitist movement. It occurred primarily among the nobles, the successful merchants, the well educated, the high clergy, and the major artisans. The vast majority of the people, the rural peasants and the urban working class, had little political power. They were frequently devastated by the wars, famine, disease and economic hard times that were regular parts of life during this period. Most likely there was very little knowledge (let alone appreciation) of the great artistic, philosophical and economic glories of the Renaissance among the struggling underclass. The benefits and the increased sense of self-worth were enjoyed mainly by the affluent in the rich cities of Venice, Milan, Rome and Florence. It was in these cities that the rich spent their fortunes patronizing artists and commissioning their works.

The Renaissance occurred in its strongest form in Florence, the main town of Tuscany on the Arno River. It rests on a flat plain, surrounded by hills and mountains, and in 1550 had some seventy thousand inhabitants.

Florence emerged as a vibrant economic and political force in the very early part of the Renaissance. It boasted a strong textile business (manufacturing, processing and dyeing) plus innovative and far-reaching financial and trading capabilities. Florentine woolen cloth was a dominant force in European commerce during much of the 1300s and 1400s. Its banking and financing operations reached out to many of the major population centers of Europe.

Florence and the other major cities developed an educated class that could manage these business ventures and create the political structures that would support them. Thus, there grew up a moneyed class of merchant families who were educated, proud, worldly, politically active and open to new ideas. This resulted in cities that aggressively controlled the surrounding territory and became increasingly jealous of each other's independence. Several, particularly Florence, had the economic power and relative political stability to become leaders in many areas of human endeavor.

In the early years of the Renaissance, Rome, where one would expect the rebirth and rediscovery of ancient cultures to be strongest, was a much smaller and less significant city. Rome had suffered economically and politically when the papacy moved to Avignon in the period from 1309 to 1377. It never had the commercial aggressiveness of Florence or other major cities. Only later in the Renaissance did Rome achieve a strong position as an economic, political and artistic center.

Historical and Political Overview

During the years leading up to 1454, the various city-states of the Italian peninsula warred frequently. Alliances were formed and broken. Mercenaries (condottieri) were routinely hired. There was constant intrigue and fighting as each state tried to enlarge and secure its borders and consolidate its power.

After the Treaty of Lodi was signed in 1454, there was a period of relative peace made possible by an elaborate system of alliances. Each state could then focus more of its energy and resources on its own internal interests, such as commerce, economic growth, artistic endeavors and political infighting.

This relative calm was shattered in 1494 when France, under the sword of Charles VIII, invaded from the north. France's main goal was the conquest of the kingdom of Naples. However, along the way it upset the fragile status quo. In Florence, the locally powerful merchant family, the Medici, was thrown out as rulers, and a republican government was set up in its place.

During 1494–1530 the armies of various countries of Europe moved in and out of the area, in a series of campaigns and battles fought with an ever-changing combination of alliances with the local powers. The foreign invasions did not unite the Italian states, as one might suspect. Instead, it divided them and increased internal power struggles and treacheries. The city-states occasionally tried to play off the great foreign powers against each other, but were generally not very successful. The main foreign protagonists were France (under a series of kings), Spain (under Ferdinand II) and the Empire (under Charles V), which brought together the realms of Germany, Spain and the

Hapsburgs. Spain eventually emerged as the dominant foreign power, holding influence over Italian affairs well into the 17th century.

The event that most stands out in this time of great violence is the sack of Rome in 1527. This was carried out with great brutality by Spanish-directed troops. It resulted in the loss of countless works of art, the destruction of Rome's political and economic infrastructure, and the rape of many of the nuns living in Rome. (The Pope, Clement VIII, locked himself up in the Castle St. Angelo until he could escape into the countryside.)

While all this was taking place, Michelangelo enjoyed some of his most productive years. He kept moving between Florence and Rome, and occasionally other locations, and was generally able to keep away from the action.

Things began to settle down around 1530. France renounced its claim on Italy in 1529. Spain and France continued their conflicts, but Italy was less frequently the battlefield. Their wars were finally concluded in 1559 by the Treaty of Câteau Cambrésis, and the French were at last driven from Italian lands. However, Spain (through Emperor Charles V) persevered and continued to exert its influence in Italian affairs for many years.

The foreign armies took back with them many of the ideas and innovations of the Renaissance. Thus, even as Italy was falling to the foreign sword, her civilization was gaining influence in much of Europe. The progress and innovation of the Italian Renaissance ultimately provided appealing models for other countries in the areas of arts, commerce and humanistic values.

Florence and the Medici

We need to look more closely at Florence during this period, as it was here that Michelangelo spent his early years. In the fifteenth century, Florence was one of the most civilized areas of Europe. It had achieved a remarkable degree of prosperity and cultural sophistication. Its governing and financial institutions and practices were innovative, generally successful and widely admired. And it was here that the heart of the Renaissance artistic movement beat.

Though republican in form, the real political power in Florence had for some time been in the hands of the leading merchant families, who had built up great wealth and influence. In 1434 Cosimo de' Medici became the unofficial leader of Florence. The years of his rule (1434–1464) and that of his grandson Lorenzo the Magnificent (1469–1492) are rightly seen as Florence's Golden Age.

The unique aspect of the rule of Cosimo and Lorenzo is that they exercised their strong leadership role unofficially with no specific office or title. Their indirect influence allowed them to retain the facade of private citizenship while being treated like princes and exercising despotic power in practice.

Cosimo's rule (1434–1464) was characterized by great expansion of commerce, relative peace and extensive patronage of the arts. Important artists such as the sculptors Donatello and Ghiberti, the painter Fra Angelico, and the architect Brunelleschi all thrived under his patronage.

In commerce, the Medici business interests were aggressively expanded by Cosimo and Lorenzo. Cosimo was basically a merchant banker, and under his leadership the Medici had branches doing business in not only the major cities of Italy, but also in Geneva, London and Bruges (in what is now Belgium). Cosimo also excelled as a statesman. He engineered a period of relative peace, mainly through an alliance with Milan, which allowed the arts and commerce to flourish in Florence in the mid-15th century.

Cosimo died in 1464. Power passed to his son Piero (the Gouty), who was sickly, bedridden and generally not very effective. He died after five years in power, and his son, twenty-year-old Lorenzo the Magnificent, took over. During Lorenzo's twenty-three-year rule, Florence experienced some of its most glorious years. But it also started to falter economically, as Lorenzo paid too much attention to politics and art patronage and not enough to family business interests. Under his watch, the London branch was closed and the Bruges branch was sold off. However, Lorenzo was a very successful diplomat who managed to keep the relative peace through alliances and understandings with Milan and Naples.

Lorenzo surrounded himself with a truly brilliant group of scholars. Great emphasis was placed on philosophical and intellectual matters. The humanistic approach to learning and living (humanism) flowered during this time. A strong school of Platonic philosophy flourished. There was much discussion and study of ancient Greece and Rome. High-quality poetry was written in both Latin and the native Tuscan language. Lorenzo himself was a distinguished poet, as well as a collector of fine coins and jewelry and, of course, a major patron of the arts.

The Medici palace in Florence became a vibrant center of learning and intellectual discussion. It was into this environment that Lorenzo brought the fourteen-year-old Michelangelo, providing him with the opportunity to learn from the best minds of the day, and exposing him to the great ideas from ancient Greece and Rome as well as to the basic tenets of humanism.

The period of Lorenzo's rule was generally free from major strife. However, in an incident indicative of the intrigue and brutality of the times, there was an attempt to assassinate him in 1478. With the support of Pope Sixtus IV, a rival family, the Pazzi, formed a conspiracy and attempted to kill Lorenzo and his brother Giuliano while they were attending Mass in the Duomo in Florence. The plot went awry and only Giuliano was killed; Lorenzo escaped to the adjoining sacristy with slight injury. The conspirators from the Pazzi clan rode through the streets trying to gather support but instead were arrested and quickly hanged from high on the Palazzo della Signoria for all to see. Lorenzo promptly regained control. Swift and brutal retribution followed on members of the Pazzi family and their supporters. Many people were tortured and killed. Lorenzo's position was strengthened, and he remained supreme until his death in 1492 at the age of forty-three.

After Lorenzo died, his eldest son, Piero, succeeded him at the age of twenty-one. (The second son, Giovanni, then seventeen, had been made a cardinal at the age of thirteen and was destined to become Pope Leo X.) Piero didn't have his father's talent, and his aggressiveness and conceit alienated many Florentines. In 1494, very shortly into Piero's reign, the French invaded. Piero went out to negotiate with the French as they approached Florentine territory. In trying to make peace with them and avoid violence, he surrendered Pisa (a key city near the sea) and several fortresses. This humiliation was too much for the citizens of Florence to take.

Piero and his family were expelled, thus ending sixty years of Medici domination and rule.

The Florentines' confidence was shaken as they saw their self- image of a virtuous, exemplary people shattered by the humiliating arrival of foreign troops. A new republican regime was set up, and a Grand Council of three thousand men was created as the sovereign body. They, in turn, were to elect the executive body of nine men—the Signoria. The Grand Council met in the Palazzo della Signoria in a new, spacious hall. Michelangelo and Leonardo da Vinci were commissioned to paint frescos to decorate this new hall and glorify past Florentine military victories. Unfortunately, neither fresco was ever completed.

Another man with real influence and power during the mid to late 1490s was a mysterious Dominican monk from Ferrara, Girolamo Savonarola. He became the prior of the Convent of San Marco in Florence in 1491. While he is said to have had contact with Lorenzo the Magnificent, his moral preaching stood in sharp contrast to the humanistic, intellectual and artistic interest of the Medici and their followers. A spellbinding orator, his sermons in the Duomo urged the citizens of Florence to repent their sins, live righteously and return to the spirit of early Christianity instead of pagan Greece and Rome. He criticized the Medici for destroying the liberty of the citizens of Florence. He urged reform of the corrupt papacy.

Many Florentines felt he was the true voice of God and that the French invasion was, as Savonarola claimed, punishment for their wicked ways. Savonarola exerted great influence on the new republican government and was responsible for the burning of many works of art. Soon, however, he pushed things too far. His moral preaching and generally disruptive activities turned the Florentines against him. He was excommunicated by Pope Alexander VI, and in May 1498 he was arrested, tried for heresy, hanged, and then burned along with several of his associates as thousands watched in the central Square, the Piazza della Signoria.

Michelangelo was in Florence during some of the period of Savonarola's influence. He no doubt heard his sermons, and very likely they influenced his young and active mind.

The new republic struggled on for eighteen years. In 1502 Piero Soderini was elected to the top job of gonfaloniere (standard bearer) for life, and he managed to hold things together until 1512. Florence made a number of attempts to recapture Pisa, and also had to fight off rebellions by some of the outlying Tuscan towns. In addition, there was a widespread movement to get rid of the French presence on the peninsula, and a number of battles were fought toward that end. Meanwhile, the papacy tried to build a powerful state in central Italy.

During this period, Michelangelo spent much of his time in Rome. However, when he was in Florence in the early 1500s, Michelangelo (then in his late twenties) was asked by the proud new republican government to create a statue that would symbolize the great civic spirit and values of the Florentines. From this commission came his famous *David,* which originally stood in the Piazza della Signoria and today is in the Accademia in Florence.

Eventually an alliance was built between the papal forces, Spain, Venice and England. In 1512 the French army withdrew from Italy, leaving pro-French Florence abandoned. Spanish troops advanced on Florence with the task of restoring the Medici. On their way they sacked and destroyed the city of Prato, eight miles to the northwest of Florence, sending a scared and demoralized Piero Soderini into exile. Soon a new government was set up. It contained some of the traditional republican institutions but was under the control of the Medici: first Lorenzo's second son Giovanni—soon to be Pope—and then several other family members. After Giovanni became Pope Leo X in 1513, most key decisions were made in the Vatican.

The Medici continued to rule in Florence up to 1527. During these years much of the political as well as the artistic activity shifted toward Rome. A series of strong popes had built up papal states through political arrangement and military aggressiveness. Two of the popes were from the Medici clan: Leo X (elected 1513, died 1521) and Clement VII (elected 1523, died 1534). During their reigns they exerted great influence over events in Florence and saw to it that their family interests were well served.

After the Medici restoration in 1512, Michelangelo continued to travel between Rome, Florence and the marble quarries in Carrara, on Italy's west coast. However, much of his time was spent in Florence working at the behest of the Medici popes on Medici family projects, such as the Medici tombs and the never-completed facade of the church San Lorenzo.

The sack of Rome in 1527 caused the citizens of Florence to rise up against the Medici and throw them out once again. A republic was set up. Rome's demise made the papacy of the Medici Pope Clement VII weak and ineffectual. After a time Clement VII was forced to come to terms with

Emperor Charles V, who agreed in 1529 to help restore the Medici in Florence.

Michelangelo was recruited to use his creative and architectural skills to design the fortifications for Florence's defense. In late 1529, Spain made its final assault upon Florence and its republican government. The city was put under siege, and after ten months it fell in August 1530. Spanish troops entered the starving city and restored the Medici. There was severe retribution in the forms of exile, confiscation of property and one-way trips to the scaffold.

Although the Medici were back in power, they had to acknowledge Charles V's sovereign rights over Florentine territory. The Signoria was abolished and Duke Allesandro de' Medici (great-grandson of Lorenzo the Magnificent) was proclaimed head of state. His role lasted only until 1537. His rude manners, severe authoritarian ways and blatant sexual escapades did not endear him to his fellow citizens. Allesandro was murdered by a distant cousin, the eccentric and thoroughly unwholesome Lorenzaccio de' Medici. This set the stage for the installation of Cosimo de' Medici from another branch of the family. He was chosen out of desperation—he was a long shot as he was only seventeen. But luck was with the Florentines this time, as he turned out to be one of the ablest rulers of the sixteenth century. He ruled over a stable city and society until 1574.

Michelangelo left Florence for good in 1534. Cosimo tried many times to get him to return, but he never did come back to the city of his childhood, his spiritual home.

Humanism

Interwoven into much of the Renaissance is humanism. Literally, *humanism* means "the study of the humanities"; that is, the human-oriented (as opposed to God-oriented) subjects of grammar, rhetoric, poetry, history and moral philosophy. All of this study is based on the reading of classical Greek and Roman authors. At its core it is an academic concept.

However, as interest in humanistic studies grew and broadened, humanism became a cultural force across the upper levels of society. What had started as mainly a scholarly and academic phenomenon developed into a wide-ranging movement that had penetrated into most areas of Italian civilization by the mid-1400s. Later it was to make itself felt in the rest of Europe.

During the Middle Ages, much of the ancient Greek and Roman literature and philosophy had been either lost or kept hidden away in monasteries. As this material was rediscovered, scholars grew appreciative of the ancient world and saw the ancients as models from which they could learn about art, politics, and life in general. This learning was passed on through the schools and in discussion so that eventually a large percentage of educated people were familiar with it. Those exposed to the humanist studies were to become the leaders and thinkers of the Renaissance—princes, churchmen, businessmen, poets, artists, jurists and the like. Hence, there emerged a more human-centered spirit and an increased openness to human potential. These both inspired and allowed people to try new approaches and look at things in a different way. Painting and sculpture, for instance, moved away from very religious and tightly-organized pieces toward more secular, realistic expression.

Beyond its academic base, humanism was a human-oriented view of life that emphasized values and the dignity of man. It was secular in nature—not pagan, not anti-religious. Humanists were concerned with human culture, values and society, not theology, as scholars had been in the previous centuries. It did not reject Christianity, only the medieval version of it. It called for people to broaden themselves and more actively participate in life's decisions. As a result of the growth of humanism, the intellectual climate changed significantly between the beginning of the Renaissance and its end.

Cosimo de' Medici and Lorenzo the Magnificent can both be considered humanists, particularly Lorenzo, who surrounded himself with humanist scholars. Humanism thus grew and spread along with the Medici influence.

In its later phase, humanism received a boost from the invention of printing. Although moveable type was invented in Germany about 1450, it was most quickly developed on a commercial scale in Italy, especially Venice. As a result, a large number of Greek and Latin classics were published and circulated in Italy in the late 1400s.

Michelangelo was surely deeply influenced by humanist thinking. As a part of Lorenzo's household (between 1490 and 1492), he no doubt heard of and studied humanistic subjects. Through all of Michelangelo's life, much of his work reflected the balancing of and conflict between his fundamental religious faith and his more modern humanistic beliefs.

Religion: The Church

The Catholic Church was a major force during this period, and its presence was felt by the Italian people in more pervasive and very different ways than it is today. In addition, much of the great art that was created during the Renaissance came about through church commissions and was greatly influenced by who was in power in Rome.

As the early stirrings of the Renaissance were beginning in central Italy, both the papacy and the Catholic Church in general found their power and influence at a low point. In the early 14th century, a series of French popes decided that they preferred to rule from their home territory instead of the historical seat in Rome; hence, the papacy was moved to Avignon during the years 1309–1377. This period came to be called the "Babylonian Captivity." With the power and all the accompanying activity in France, Rome disintegrated into a small town of some seventeen thousand people. The city was left to the ravages of time and nature. Cows and sheep grazed around the ancient monuments and took shelter inside the churches.

Even though they lived in Avignon, the French popes tried to keep their claim as the temporal rulers of Rome and the surrounding territories. However, local despots soon established rule over the so-called papal states (a large portion of central Italy running northeast from Rome to the Adriatic Sea and up to Venice) and the power of the Church reached a low ebb on the Italian peninsula during these years.

Pope Gregory XI brought the papacy back to Rome in 1377. He arrived to find a decayed and half-deserted town. Just a year later he died, and Urban VI was elected. Before things settled down, a breakaway group of cardinals elected a rival pope, Clement VII, who went back to Avignon. This period of rival popes (there were even three for a time), called the Great Schism, lasted for thirty-nine years, until 1417. It caused great disruption both in and outside of the Church, and represents one of the most confusing and stressful periods in the Church's long and spotted history.

The election of Martin V in 1417 ended the Great Schism. Martin began the task of recovering the lost influence and prestige of the Church. That task was pursued along two lines: (1) to regain temporal power in the papal states and be able to protect those states against their neighbors, and (2) to associate the papacy with the great artistic and literary forces of the times, and thus to build Rome into a great city.

After Martin V we see a series of Renaissance popes who became famous (or infamous) for their political skills, their military activity, their administrative ability, their ruthlessness, their intellectual interests and their patronage of the arts rather than their spirituality or religious practices. These men were generally worldly, corrupt and tough and often they lived decadent, avaricious lives. But they did restore the strength of the papal states, the prestige of the Church and the splendor of Rome.

The Church grew in power and influence up until about the late 1520s. Lands were regained, Rome was turned into a showpiece for the arts, and the Church continued to be involved in many aspects of life. However, as Church activities increased, a strong anticlerical attitude developed in many quarters. There was much criticism of the Church's extravagances, its worldliness, its heavy taxes and its general lack of spirituality.

In the 1520s two events shook the Church; eventually they would set it off in new directions. The first was the Protestant Reformation. The most notable aspect of the Reformation was Martin Luther's protest movement in the German states which started around 1517 and grew throughout the 1520s. He criticized the Church's worldliness, its immoderation, and especially Pope Leo X's excesses in the selling of indulgences in order to pay for the building of St. Peter's Cathedral. (While Lutheranism represents the most significant protest, it should be considered part of a series of movements dating back two centuries that were concerned with the Church's excess and lack of true spirituality.) The Reformation was most immediately disturbing and politically disrupting in the states of the north—England and the area we now call Germany. In Italy its effects were most strongly felt in the emergence of a strong reactionary movement, the Counter Reformation.

As part of the Counter Reformation, which began in the final years of the Renaissance, the papacy gradually changed from an institution concerned mainly with temporal affairs to one more interested in religious and spiritual matters such as Church dogma and doctrine. Because of the Church's widespread influence, similar changes in attitude and interest appeared among much of the general populace. One can broadly say that where the Renaissance had been characterized by open-mindedness, inquisitiveness and tolerance in intellectual and spiritual matters, the Counter Reformation was an influence for intolerance, close-mindedness and strictness. That part of humanism which tried to reconcile the ancient values of Greece and Rome with Christianity was pushed aside. The Church tried to bring itself and its flock back to true beliefs and strict rules, as laid down by the pope.

The major work of the Counter Reformation occurred over the period 1530–1570, approximately the last forty years of Michelangelo's life. The popes during these years were more stringent, less worldly. Reformers dominated the key positions of power. The Church emphasized pastoral work, saving souls and helping the poor. In 1540 the evangelical Jesuit order was established, and in 1542 the Roman branch of the Inquisition opened.

The Council of Trent was convened in 1545 to formalize the Counter Reformation and to put into effect a new set of rules and laws for the Church. These included greater discipline, training and lifestyle requirements for the clergy, and supreme authority for the pope on a variety of subjects. In artistic matters, the Church took on a censor's role and specifically dealt with the subjects of orthodoxy and the use of the naked human body. The nude was virtually eliminated. Censorship went to such extremes that one of the popes had artists paint loincloths on the nudes in Michelangelo's *Last Judgment*, which had been completed in 1541.

While the Reformation was a major blow to the Church, a more immediate disaster really shook it out of its proud splendor and loose ways. The sack of Rome by Spanish-directed troops in 1527 ended much of the free (and largely pagan) lifestyle of the clergy and the citizens. In some ways it marked the beginning of the end of the Renaissance.

Several of the Renaissance popes deserve special mention because of their general influence and the central role they played in Michelangelo's life.

Julius II (1503–1513). Julius was from the della Rovere family of Genoa and a nephew of Pope Sixtus IV (who built the Sistine Chapel). He took over the papacy after it had been dreadfully abused by the highly decadent Borgia Pope Alexander VI. A gifted military leader, an excellent administrator and a political manipulator of the first order, he reigned over a glorious period of artistic and literary excellence in Rome. He was ambitious and energetic and determined to strengthen the papacy and expand its role. Under his patronage, Raphael began a beautiful series of paintings in the Vatican, and the architect Donato Bramante started work on the new St. Peter's. However, the greatest works produced under his patronage were Michelangelo's paintings on the ceiling of the Sistine Chapel and the marble statuary for his papal tomb.

Julius had a strong love/hate relationship with Michelangelo. Both men had wills of iron, and they clashed often as the pope tried to harness Michelangelo's creative powers to glorify his papacy. Several times Julius called Michelangelo away from important work in Florence to come to Rome to work on special projects. It was Julius who coerced Michelangelo into undertaking the four-year project of the Sistine ceiling. Michelangelo's work on Julius's tomb continued to plague the artist long after the Pope's death. This tomb underwent a number of changes in its plan and was never really built at all.

Leo X (1513–1521). The second son (Giovanni) of Lorenzo the Magnificent was made a cardinal at age thirteen because of his father's influence. Cultivated, charming and shrewd, he maneuvered himself into the papacy in 1513 at the very young age of thirty-eight. On becoming Pope, he is said to have exclaimed, "Let us enjoy the papacy, since God has given it to us." And enjoy he did,in his passion for hunting, festivals, and good food. He also spent lavishly on the arts, commissioning major works by Raphael and continuing work on St. Peter's. It was his excessive sale of indulgences to pay for all of this that moved Luther to open criticism of the Church and eventually to rebellion.

Michelangelo had known young Giovanni de' Medici (both born 1475) when they were youngsters in the home of Giovanni's father, Lorenzo the Magnificent. During his papacy, Leo X used Michelangelo to glorify the

Medici in Florence. A series of projects was started, though some never got beyond the planning stage. Michelangelo spent his time during this frustrating period of 1513 to 1521 running back and forth between Florence, Rome and the marble quarries trying to fulfill commissions for the Medici in Florence and attempting to complete his work on the still-unfinished tomb for Julius II.

Clement VII (1523–1534). The illegitimate son of Lorenzo the Magnificent's brother Giuliano (killed in the Pazzi plot), and a cousin of Pope Leo X, Clement VII helped restore some of the financial stability of the Church caused by the excesses of his predecessors. His was a turbulent reign, as the Protestants continued to make headway in Germany and England and, closer to home, Spanish troops sacked Rome in 1527. During much of this time, however, he proved to be a discriminating patron of the arts. Michelangelo continued to be pulled between his desire to finish Julius's tomb and the desires of Clement VII to have him work on Medici glorification projects in Florence. It was during Clement VII's papacy that Michelangelo did most of his work on the Medici tombs and the new sacristy of San Lorenzo in Florence.

Paul III (1534–1549). The transition pope who made critical moves to accelerate and formalize the Counter Reformation, Paul became a cardinal at a young age because his sister had been a mistress of an earlier pope. Although he cannot be considered a prude (he fathered at least four illegitimate children), he was concerned about the excesses and general condition of the church.

He introduced stricter systems of administration and ordered his cardinals to adopt a more moderate lifestyle. Paul's major effort in Church reform was his summoning of the Council of Trent (1545–1563) that, after much debate, put many of the elements of the Counter Reformation into a formalized program.

In city planning and architecture, Paul did much to open up Rome and build grand streets and piazzas. Michelangelo was called on to take an active role in this work, and in 1549 Paul made Michelangelo supreme architect of St. Peter's. It was through Paul III's patronage that Michelangelo painted the colossal *Last Judgment* on the wall of the Sistine Chapel. He also completed two masterful frescos on the side walls of the small Pauline Chapel in the Vatican.

Beyond the papal trappings, the statesmanship, the politics, the intrigue and the patronage, there was a day-to-day social side to the Church that had a profound effect on most Italians. The Church was a pervasive, active and not always popular participant in everyday existence. It was involved in all the major events of a person's life including birth, marriage (both arranging and performing), education, commerce, sickness and death. The Church served as a social center where men came to talk (even during Mass) and often conducted their business. Religious festivals were an important part of the normal person's social calendar.

While most Church bishops were of noble birth and well educated, the vast majority of the rank and file clergy were uneducated and underpaid. Often they were not well trained in religious matters. Still, they had great influence, especially in the countryside, and were often resented for their crude ways and general interference in people's lives. The men and women of the religious orders (Franciscan, Dominican, Carmelite, etc.) were somewhat better trained and provided much of the spiritual backbone of many communities.

Even though most Italians held strong Christian beliefs during this period, there was an underlying feeling of anticlericalism. This feeling provided the impetus for much of the secularism in Renaissance thinking. (Eventually the quality, training and service role of the clergy were improved and formalized by the Council of Trent.)

Additional Influences

The voyages of Christopher Columbus (1492–1504) and his fellow explorers to the New World were of great historical importance. These discoveries and the subsequent exploitation of these new lands were big news in Italy during much of Michelangelo's adult life. The commercial exploitation of the New World by Spain, Portugal, and England caused an economic power shift in Europe, strengthening those countries' treasuries and political ambitions, while weakening the powers in the Mediterranean area. This opening up of geographical and commercial horizons fit well with the man-centered secular attitudes of the time, and probably served to reinforce them.

During the late 1400s and early 1500s, England was undergoing a time of great stress and transition. In 1485, Henry VII established the Tudor Dynasty, and during his reign many of the ideas and practices of the Italian Renaissance took hold in England. His son, Henry VIII, succeeded him in 1509. Henry VIII's reign was initially marked by England's increased involvement in European matters, as well as wars with France. A series of attempted divorces and annulments soon brought Henry VIII into sharp conflict with Rome. With the trends of Protestantism and Counter Reformation in the air, a breach occurred in 1533; England went off on its own, and the Church of England was born. Michelangelo was in Rome during much of this time and was no doubt aware of the threat to the Roman Catholic Church that he believed in so strongly.

Renaissance Art

The most visible and well-known influence of the Renaissance was its effect on the arts. This is a subject of immense complexity and unending example and detail. To aid in our understanding of Michelangelo, we must sketch out the major trends and the major artists of his time since, after all, they were what Michelangelo learned about and built upon.

The Renaissance artistic flowering really began back in the late thirteenth century with the Florentine painter Cimabue (c. 1240–1302). His early works reflect a Byzantine influence, while his later works start to show a solidity and monumentality that predict what is to come. Probably his greatest legacy, though, was his discovery of Giotto.

Giotto (1267 or 1277–1337). Giotto was born near Florence and worked as a shepherd boy before his discovery by Cimabue. He was the first western painter to capture a sense of human drama and penetrate human psychology. Giotto was extremely innovative, insightful and prolific, and his brilliant talent was recognized in his own lifetime. Giotto's works can be seen all over Italy (Florence, Rome, Assisi, etc.), but his real masterpieces are the frescos for the Arena Chapel in Padua. Giotto was also a designer/architect of some note who played a significant role in the building of the Campanile that stands next to the Duomo in Florence. He remains a reference point and, in a way, a starting point in the history of western painting.

After Giotto, there was a dearth of major artists until around 1400. While much was going on artistically, there were no giants who set the tone for those that followed. The reason for this interlude is not clear, but surely the great Black Plague of 1347–1352, in which 30 to 50 percent of the population died, reduced the likelihood of many great artists appearing.

However, shortly after 1400 an extraordinary group of artists emerged. They served as the artistic inspiration and set artistic criteria for the better part of the new century. That group was succeeded by a rich array of very talented artists. Together, these two groups made the fifteenth century in Italy one of the most artistically innovative and productive periods in history.

Three extraordinary men came on the scene in Florence in the early 1400s: the painter Masaccio, the sculptor Donatello, and the architect Brunelleschi. Their innovative works set the standard for the many talented men who followed, and they formed the artistic core for what we call the classic Renaissance style.

A brief word about each is appropriate, as all three had an influence on Michelangelo's life, and on his work as a painter, sculptor and architect.

Masaccio (1401–1428). During his brief lifetime, Masaccio broke new ground in painting. His works show a new rounded, three-dimensional aspect and a human reality that had not been seen before. This attention to perspective, his use of light and shadow (as opposed to simple line drawings), the solidness and humanness of his forms, and his sense of equilibrium served as the basics of Renaissance painting for nearly one hundred years. His frescos in the Church of Santa Maria de Carmine in Florence have served as a necessary instructional standard for hundreds of artists, including Michelangelo, over the years.

Donatello (1386–1466). A man of great versatility and skill, Donatello was the preeminent sculptor during this important period. He worked in marble and bronze and did both free-standing statues and numerous panels in relief. He broke away from much of the piety of earlier artists. His works represent many vital aspects of Renaissance life—the brutal, playful, active and serene. He worked mainly in Tuscany (Florence and Siena), but he also created a monumental equestrian statue in Padua. One of his principal patrons was Cosimo de' Medici.

His innovativeness and ability to capture and reflect his subject's inner spirit have given his works a timeless quality. His work formed the base on which Michelangelo built.

Brunelleschi (1377–1446). Filippo Brunelleschi is best remembered as the designer and architect of the great dome on the cathedral in Florence. This was an engineering miracle because of its size and unique shape, and it earned him everlasting fame. His other works in Florence—the churches of San Lorenzo and Santo Spirito, the Pazzi Chapel and the Innocenti Hospital—are also masterpieces of serene beauty, perfect proportion, functionality and innovation. These came to be looked on as classic examples of Renaissance architectural style. In addition, Brunelleschi's work in understanding perspective—representation of three-dimensional space on a plane surface—was a major influence on both his close contemporaries Masaccio and Donatello, and on many of the major artists over the next one hundred years or so.

The mid and late fifteenth century also brought forth a large number of other high-quality artists who labored throughout Italy but had their focus in Florence. The wealth and interest in the arts of the upper strata of Florentine society provided these artists with many commissions and projects. These ultimately formed the major part of what we call Renaissance art. Some of these artists were Ghiberti (sculptor, 1378–1455), Verrocchio (sculptor and painter, 1435–1488), Botticelli (painter, 1445–1510), Fra Angelico (painter, 1387–1455), Fra Filippo Lippi (painter, c. 1406–1469) and Domenico Ghirlandaio (painter, 1449–1494).

Many of these artists headed up schools (*bottega*) where the master did the major work, was responsible for overall quality, and took the credit. Much of the minor work and assisting was done by young apprentices. Often these bottegas offered a variety of artistic products, such as shields and chests to their patrons.

Michelangelo began his career as a thirteen-year-old apprentice in the bottega of Domenico Ghirlandaio, working on frescos in Florentine churches.

These men were essentially artisans who made their living doing commission work. Often they had relatively little input on subject matter and even on interpretation. Their patrons were rich families, cardinals, popes and city governments, all of whom generally knew what they wanted. It was only later that artists were able to gain more importance, independence and respect so that they could control their subject matter and their handling of it.

In essence, as they moved from the fifteenth to the sixteenth century, the leading artists progressed from artisans to something akin to the independent artist we know today. Michelangelo played a major role in this movement. As his genius was recognized, he was given considerable creative freedom.

Michelangelo's Life

Birth and Early Years in Florence

Michelangelo's father, Ludovico Buonarroti, came from a moderately prominent and noble family in Tuscany. His ancestors had been successful business people. But the family fortune and prestige, such as they were, had been severely reduced by the mid-1400s. Ludovico, by all accounts, was a proud, unambitious man of limited intelligence.

In early 1475 he served a six-month appointment as the mayor (*podestà*) of the small Tuscan village of Caprese, some fifty miles southeast of Florence. It was here, on March 6, 1475, that Michelangelo was born. His mother, Francesca, was twenty at the time. Michelangelo was the second of five sons.

The family soon moved back to their native Florence, and the infant Michelangelo was quickly put out to a wet nurse, a stonemason's wife in the nearby stone-cutting village of Settignano. This separation lasted about two years. To make things even more difficult on the young Michelangelo, his mother died in 1481 at the age of twenty-six, when he was only six.

Details of Michelangelo's early years in Florence are spotty, but he appears to have been an exceptionally bright and inquisitive boy. In 1485, when Michelangelo was ten, his father remarried and Michelangelo was enrolled in a local school. We're told that he didn't particularly care for the academics and was constantly going off to draw and watch other artists at work. Ludovico wanted his son to get an education and become a man of letters, thus enhancing his efforts to think of himself and his family as of noble birth. But Michelangelo had other plans for himself, and this became a source of strong and sometimes violent conflict between father and son.

In 1488, at age thirteen, Michelangelo was apprenticed to the shop of Domenico Ghirlandaio, one of the most successful Florentine painters of the day. At the time, Michelangelo was three years older than the average beginner. He must have possessed considerable skills for, instead of paying tuition, he himself received a small sum. During this brief apprenticeship, Michelangelo learned the techniques of fresco painting that served him in later years in the Sistine Chapel. Also at this young age, he spent many hours studying his Florentine artistic ancestors whose artworks filled the city. Still-existing drawings from the hand of the young Michelangelo in the years 1489–1490 show masterful renderings of the works of Masaccio and Giotto.

While still working under Ghirlandaio, Michelangelo was asked in 1489 to join a sculpture school in the garden of San Marco run by the aging master Bertoldo, under the patronage of Lorenzo the Magnificent. This was a turning point in young Michelangelo's life, as he was now regularly exposed to ancient works of art. This also gave him an opportunity to practice more formally the techniques of sculpture.

Michelangelo soon came into personal contact with Lorenzo the Magnificent, who was to have a strong, if brief, influence on his life. Michelangelo apparently made his first sculpture for Lorenzo. Condivi tells the story:

> ...Michelangelo got those master masons to give him a piece (of marble) and being provided by the same men with tools, he set himself to copy the head of a fawn with such attentiveness and zeal that within a few days he brought it to perfection In the meanwhile, the Magnifico appeared, wanting to see at what stage the building was, and he found the boy who was busy polishing the fawn's head; and drawing somewhat near to him, he first considered how excellent the work was, and having regard of the boy's age, he marveled greatly; then, although he praised the work, nonetheless teasing him as a boy, he said: "Oh, you have made this fawn old yet left him all his teeth. Don't you know that in creatures of that age some are always missing?"
>
> It seemed an eternity to Michelangelo before the Magnifico went on his way and he could correct his error; and when he was left alone he removed an upper tooth from his old fellow, boring into the gum as if it had come away from it with its root. And the next day he waited for the Magnifico very eagerly. When the latter arrived, having seen the boy's simplicity and goodness, he laughed over it a great deal. But then, pondering on how perfectly the work was done, and what the boy's age was, as the undoubted father of all the talents, he determined to help and favor such genius and to take him into his own house....

The incident brought Michelangelo into Lorenzo's household, where he became a favorite of Lorenzo and his intellectual entourage. The young Michelangelo, now only fifteen to sixteen years old, was exposed to the leading poets and philosophers of the day. The influence on him was profound and long-lasting. (Also in the household were the assorted Medici children, including two future popes.)

The picture we have of Michelangelo during these years is of a very bright, self-assured youth who was fast developing his artistic skills, as well as soaking up a tremendous amount of knowledge and philosophy in the heady environment of the leading household of the land.

But there also appears to have been an arrogant and unpleasant side to the young artist. One day Michelangelo and a fellow student named Torrigiano were studying and drawing from the Masaccio frescos at the Church of Santa Mana de Carmine when Michelangelo began to taunt and criticize the work of his fellow student. Torrigiano became so infuriated that he smashed and broke Michelangelo's nose, disfiguring him for life.

Lorenzo died in April of 1492. The young Michelangelo suffered a period of grief and moved back to his father's house. He continued to work on several small marble pieces as he recovered from the shock of Lorenzo's death. It was also at this time, in the mid-1490s, that he conducted his anatomy experiments. He had become familiar with the prior of the Church of Santo Spirito, who allowed him to dissect some of the corpses from the church's hospital. These experiments, which were illegal, provided Michelangelo with the knowledge of the human body that made his later artistic creations so powerful and realistic.

Michelangelo returned to the Medici household for a brief period at the invitation of Lorenzo's successor, his son Piero. However, things quickly got rather tense politically, with the general unpopularity of Piero, the stern preaching of Savonarola and the threat of French invasion. Michelangelo sensed trouble and in late 1494 fled to the north. This was the first of a number of flights from trouble or stress he was to make during his lifetime.

Bologna and Rome as a Young Man

After a brief stay in Venice, Michelangelo settled in Bologna for most of 1495. There he was befriended by a local nobleman, and he found work carving three small statues for the tomb of St. Dominico. He soon tired of

Bologna, however, and returned to Florence in late 1495, after Piero de' Medici had been expelled and a republic established.

The Florence of the late 1490s was an exciting and often frightening place. The new republic was proudly asserting itself but was being influenced by the strict, frightening preaching of Savonarola. Michelangelo wanted to get to Rome—closer to the source of ancient art, and possibly to better prospects for patronage.

The specific occasion for his going to Rome gives us some insight into the times and perhaps the artist. Michelangelo had carved a marble statue of a sleeping cupid. It caught the attention of a minor Florentine patron, who judged it of such high quality that he said, "If you can manage to make it look as if it had been buried under the earth, I will forward it to Rome and it will be taken for an antique and you will sell it much better." The patron sold it as an antique to a Cardinal Riario in Rome for two hundred florins but paid Michelangelo only thirty florins. When the cardinal discovered the fraud, it was necessary for Michelangelo to go to Rome to sort things out. He left Florence just before the plague broke out, while Savonarola was still ranting from the pulpit.

The Rome that Michelangelo arrived in during June of 1496 was a far cry from its ancient splendor. Still, it contained a wealth of ancient art that proved to be a source of wonder and inspiration for Michelangelo. He had several letters of introduction from friends in Florence and soon was settled in the home of a nobleman. His initial efforts were focused on carving a life-size *Bacchus* for a Roman gentleman. Following this, in 1497, Michelangelo received a major commission from a French cardinal for a *pietà*. It was this work (now in St. Peter's) that established Michelangelo as the preeminent sculptor of his time.

During early 1498 Michelangelo went to Carrara to oversee the quarrying of the marble for his *pietà*. This was the first of many trips to that city, which had provided marble for artists and artisans for thousands of years. Michelangelo seemed to get great pleasure and a sense of renewal from these trips. While there he lived a very simple life, mixed with the local workmen and became very close to the basic materials of his art.

The guarantor of the contract for the *pietà* said it would be "the most beautiful work of marble in Rome, one that no living artist could better" a prediction that was clearly fulfilled. A work of sublime beauty, and one of Michelangelo's greatest creations, it was completed when Michelangelo was twenty-four.

To ensure that he would be recognized as the artist, Michelangelo put his name on a band across the Virgin Mary's breast. After the praise and recognition he received for this masterpiece, it would no longer be necessary to sign any of his works.

In spite of this magnificent creation, Michelangelo's time in Rome from 1496 to 1501 was very difficult. His letters reflect his unhappiness and frustration, and speak of harsh living conditions, illness and very hard work—themes that would continue throughout his life. The money he made was used to help his family back in Florence.

In Florence, 1501–1505

In the spring of 1501, Michelangelo returned to Florence with a strong reputation and good prospects for challenging commissions. The next five years yielded both prolific artistic creation and relative personal stability for the still young Michelangelo. He worked on a number of commissions in several different media during this time, including a very special civic commission for a giant David.

A gigantic, odd-shaped block of marble had been acquired many years earlier as part of a project to adorn the main Cathedral. It had been lying in the yard of the Cathedral workshop when on August 16, 1501, Michelangelo was entrusted with the highly prestigious *David* commission. He was most secretive in his work, locking himself in his workshop and refusing to let anyone see it until it was finished. Michelangelo worked on it for over two years, completing it in early 1504. The results of his efforts were truly awe-inspiring to the citizens of Florence. After much debate, the colossal sixteen-foot statue was carefully transported to a place of honor outside the town hall, the Palazzo della Signoria. The statue, depicting great strength and pride in the young, nude, powerfully built David, took on great political significance for the young Florentine republic. Michelangelo's reputation was further enhanced by this effort, and from then on he was widely recognized as the greatest of all artists. His *David* stands today inside the Accademia.

The only rival Michelangelo had for that position of greatest of the great was the then-forty-eight-year-old Leonardo da Vinci. Leonardo, widely acclaimed for his painting, sculpture, architecture and drawing skills, as well as for his overall inventiveness, had just returned to Florence after an absence of eighteen years. As part of the Florentine republic's efforts to aggrandize itself, Leonardo had received a commission to do a giant fresco in the hall of the Grand Council in the Palazzo della Signoria. He was to depict a great moment in Florentine history, a battle between Florence and Milan fought in 1440. A year later, in 1504, Michelangelo was asked to paint an equally large composition on an adjoining wall in the same room. Michelangelo chose for his subject the battle of Cascina, depicting a heroic battle with Pisa in 1364. Thus, the two great artistic giants of the late Renaissance faced off in a contest that at times showed serious antipathy.

Both frescos were to have been over sixty feet in width, and both had definite symbolic messages of propaganda and glorification of the Florentine republic. But what could have been the greatest artistic contest ever held ended up coming to nothing. While Michelangelo was finishing the drawings for his work, Leonardo was struggling with the application of the paint to the wall, using a new fresco technique. He made some technical mistakes and the paint blistered off the wall. He gave up in anger and frustration, and nothing is left of it.

Michelangelo continued to work on his wall drawings for the giant fresco. It was evidently a true masterpiece, said by some to be among the best things he ever did. His drawings depicted a mass of male figures caught in every conceivable pose at a key point before the battle. He depicted the nude male body with great strength, action and beauty, as he was to do in so many subsequent works. But before he had finished the wall drawings he was forced to abandon the work.

For a while the drawings served as examples for other artists. Benvenuto Cellini called them "a school for all of the world." The drawings were soon cut into sections, and eventually all the pieces disappeared. All that remain

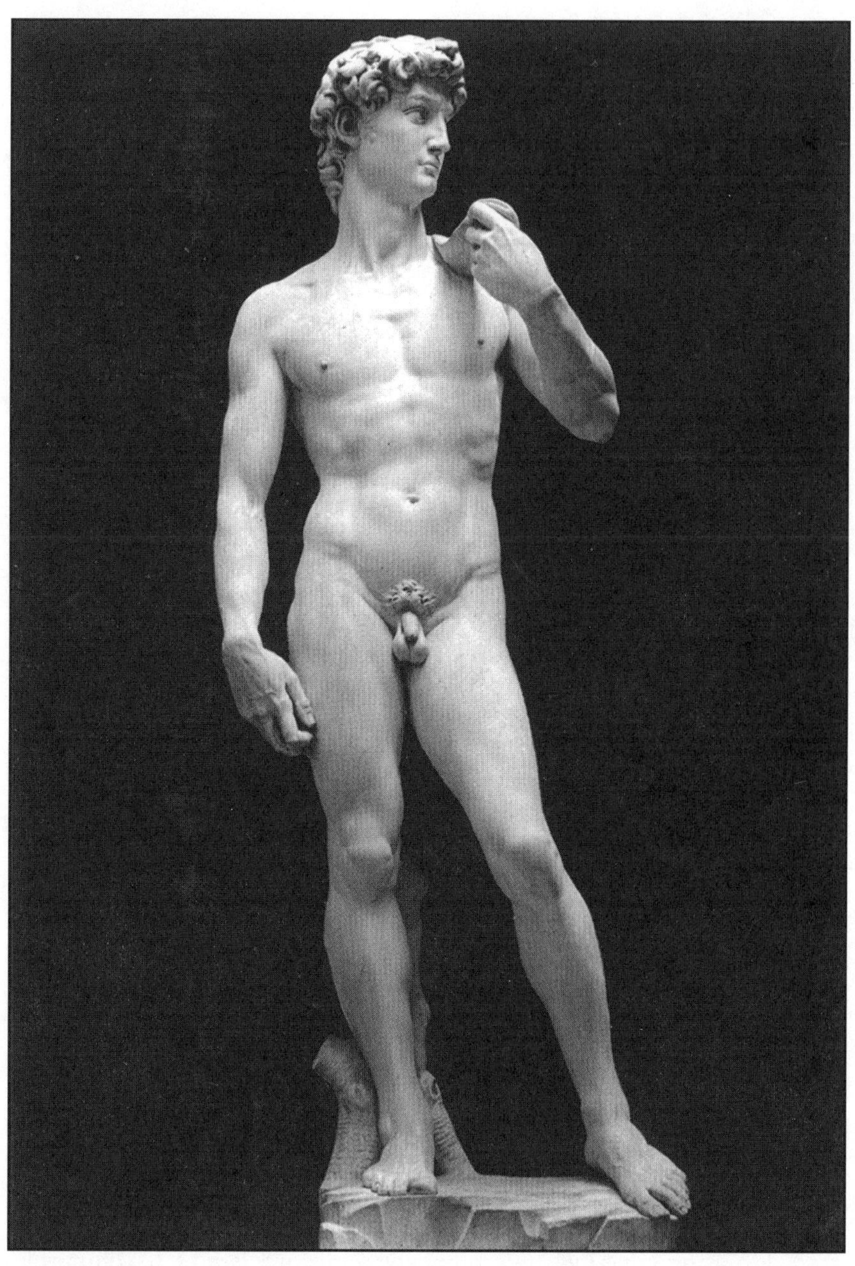

The giant-sized David was carved by the young Michelangelo between 1501 and 1504. The depiction of the youthful and powerful nude had great significance for the young Florentine republic.

are some studies that show the amazing anatomical knowledge and rendering talents of Michelangelo.

Nevertheless, these five years in Florence were indeed productive ones for the not-yet-thirty-year-old genius. His reputation was such that he was in great demand. In addition to the works mentioned above, he did a variety of commissions for a number of the leading families of the area. Four of these works were Madonnas, which he seems to have worked on more or less simultaneously. One was a painting depicting the holy family. Two were marble reliefs (left unfinished) showing Mary, Jesus and John. All three of these works are in the round (*tondo*) form. The fourth *Madonna* was a complete statue of Mary and Jesus that is now in Bruges. He also received a major commission to carve the Twelve Apostles for the Cathedral. He started one of these, St. Matthew, but never completed the commission.

It was at the height of all this activity that Michelangelo received a summons from Rome that changed his life forever. In March of 1505, the egotistical and demanding Pope Julius II commanded that Michelangelo come to Rome to work on his tomb.

Julius II found an outlet for his gigantic ego and megalomania in his patronage of the arts. He surrounded himself with men of great talent—Michelangelo, Bramante, Raphael—and had them work on colossal projects. His personal energy, along with the papal treasury, marked him as one of the most demanding and notable patrons of the entire Renaissance.

The call to Rome began a stormy relationship between Julius and Michelangelo, a relationship that would result in great frustration for the young artist and in some of the greatest works of art in history.

Working for Julius II

Soon after arriving in Rome, Michelangelo received approval for a design for Julius's tomb. It was to be huge and complex—a freestanding monument 26 by 36 feet, three levels high and containing some forty figures. In committing himself to finish it in five years, Michelangelo showed one of his weaknesses—a tendency to overestimate optimistically the amount of work he could produce in a given time.

With the plan approved, Michelangelo left for Carrara in mid-1505 to select marble for one of the greatest sculptural commissions in history. He stayed there about eight months, leading a sparse life with the workmen. It was a time of great excitement and inspiration. Condivi writes:

> And while there, one day seeing all those places from a mountain which overlooked the sea coast he formed the wish to make a colossus that would be visible to mariners from afar. In this he was encouraged especially by the available mass of rock. And he certainly would have done it, if he had had enough time and if the enterprise which had brought him there had permitted it; and I once heard him complain sadly about this.

Michelangelo's return to Rome from Carrara began a period of great frustration and disappointment. There were transportation problems with the marble, and Michelangelo was delayed in getting started. Concurrently, the Pope had a radical shift in priorities. As his plans for his tomb were finalized, it became clear to Julius that he needed a bigger church to hold it. The Pope decided that a new St. Peter's should be built and entrusted the huge project to the prominent architect Bramante. Thus, for both artistic and financial reasons, Julius's priorities changed and he lost interest in the tomb. Michelangelo's access to the Pope declined, and he left Rome in great anger in April of 1506. Thus ended the first part of what Condivi calls the "tragedy of the tomb."

Michelangelo would continue to intermittently work on Julius's tomb for the next forty years. It existed as a source of conflict and anguish through much of his working life. A letter from Michelangelo to a friend, written after he had gone back to Florence, gives us insight into this tense situation, and into the sensitivity and paranoia of the temperamental artist:

> As to my departure, the truth is that at table on Holy Saturday I heard the Pope say to a jeweler and to the Master of Ceremonies, to whom he was talking, that he did not wish to spend one *baiocco* more either on small stones or on large ones. At this I was much taken aback; however, before leaving I asked him for some part of what I needed to continue the work. His Holiness told me to return on Monday and I returned on Monday, and on Tuesday, and on Wednesday, and on Thursday as he was aware. Finally, on Friday morning I was turned out, in other words I was sent packing, and the fellow who turned me away said that he knew who I was, but that such were his orders. And this,

> having heard on the said Saturday the said words, and seeing their effect I was overwhelmed with despair. But this was not the one and only reason for my departure; there was something else besides which I do not want to write about—it is enough that I had caused to think that if I remained in Rome, my own tomb would be sooner made than the Pope's. This then is the reason for my sudden departure.

Back in Florence, Michelangelo no doubt reflected with great anger and frustration on the lost opportunity to create a marble structure of truly monumental grandeur. However, his paranoia showed through, as he imagined that Bramante was behind the Pope's change of heart. This hostility toward his perceived artistic rivals reared its head often in his life.

Soon Julius desired to have Michelangelo back in his service. The egotistical pontiff promised the headstrong young artist immunity from punishment if he would return. Communications went back and forth between Florence and Rome. Michelangelo, playing his cards cleverly, even threatened to go to work for the sultan in Turkey. The Pope grew more insistent and sent a series of briefs formally summoning Michelangelo back to Rome. Pressure was put on the government of Florence to expedite Michelangelo's return. Finally the pressure got to be too much and Piero Soderini, the ruler of Florence, told Michelangelo that he would not go to war with the Pope on his account. To help, Piero gave Michelangelo a very complimentary letter that indicates clearly how people viewed Michelangelo at the time:

> The bearer will be Michelangelo the Sculptor whom we send to please and satisfy his Holiness. We certify that he is an excellent young man and in his own art without peer in Italy, perhaps even in the Universe. It would be impossible to recommend him more highly. His nature is such that he requires to be drawn-out by kindness and encouragement; but if love is shown to him and he is well treated, he will accomplish things that will make the whole world wonder.

So Michelangelo left for Bologna in November of 1506 to make amends with the Pope. (Julius had just conquered Bologna as part of his campaign to restore the lost territories of the papal states.) The rather tense reunion of the aggressive, egotistical pope and the young, idealistic artist was a memorable one. As Condivi recounts it:

> ...Michelangelo...was conducted to his Holiness who was at the table in the Palace of the Sixteen. And once he saw him in his presence, the Pope turned to him with a look of rage and said "You are supposed to come to find us, yet you waited for us to come to find you." He wished to make it understood that His Holiness had come to Bologna, a place far nearer to Florence than to Rome. Michelangelo, kneeling, in a loud voice, asked for his pardon, making the excuse that he had erred not from ill will but from being enraged as he had not been able to bear being chased away in the way that he was. The Pope looked about himself with lowered head without saying anything, when a certain Monsignor in order to recommend and make excuses for Michelangelo, interrupted and said "Your Holiness, pay no regard to his error, because he has erred from ignorance. Painters, except for their art, are all just as ignorant." The Pope was enraged at this and said: "You are abusing him and we are not. It is you who are ignorant and you're a miserable wretch, not him. Get out of my sight and bad luck to you." And when he did not move, the Monsignor, as Michelangelo used to recall, was driven outside by the Pope's servants with a hail of blows.

Soon Michelangelo received a commission to execute a larger-than-life bronze statue of Julius. This was not what Michelangelo wanted, but he was not about to defy the Pope again. So he stayed on in Bologna during 1507, working on the huge statue and leading a life of misery and frustration. He wrote to his father:

> ...I'm living here in the greatest discomfort and in a state of extreme fatigue; I do nothing but work all day and night and I have endured and am enduring such fatigue that if I had to do the work over again I do not believe I should survive, because it has been a tremendous undertaking and had it been in anyone else's hands it would have been a disaster.

In fact, the first casting was unsuccessful and he had to do it again. He completed the statue in early 1508, then returned to Florence.

Within four years the statue was no more. When the previous ruling family returned to Bologna in 1511, the statue was torn down, brought to a foundry, melted and made into a giant gun (sarcastically called "la Julia") to be used in the future wars against Pope Julius II himself.

After just a few months in Florence, Michelangelo once more received a call from Pope Julius to come to Rome. The project this time was again something Michelangelo didn't particularly want to paint the ceiling of the papal chapel in the Vatican known as the Sistine. The Chapel had been built by Julius II's uncle Pope Sixtus IV in 1473. It is a large, rather barn-like structure measuring some 132 feet by 45 feet. Its ceiling is an impressive 50 feet above the floor. It is not a freestanding building, but is joined to and part of the total Vatican structure.

Some uncertainty and intrigue surrounds the commission. Michelangelo claims to have told the Pope that painting was not his art and he didn't want the commission. Concurrently, it seems Bramante told the Pope that he doubted Michelangelo's ability to paint foreshortened figures. But again, Julius had his way and on May 10, 1508, the thirty-three-year-old Michelangelo contracted to paint the ceiling. Thus began a project that produced perhaps the single greatest artistic effort in human history.

The four years that Michelangelo worked on the Sistine ceiling involved intense productivity and extreme personal hardship. The original commission was to paint the Twelve Apostles on the twelve pendentive like areas on the ceiling. This idea was soon dismissed, and the Pope released him from the original project, letting Michelangelo do what he wanted. Michelangelo received the help of a theologian or two in designing this ceiling from an iconographical standpoint. The challenge to fill this vast ceiling with biblical figures in an appropriate and artistic manner was considerable.

Michelangelo's mastery of the massive effort began with his designing and then building the unique scaffolding system that would allow him to do his work relatively safely at great heights. Even though he had some experience with fresco painting as a youth, working with Ghirlandaio, he had much to learn in basic techniques. Early on he made mistakes and even had to redo one of the sections because his plaster surface had been too damp.

He worked with a relatively small group of assistants and did most of the actual painting himself. The assistants helped with the mixing of paints and the preparatory work, and they did some of the painting of the decorative detail. When they did actually paint, it was under the strict control of the master. Partway through he sent some of his helpers back to Florence and toward the end worked mostly by himself.

It's important to get a feel for the mammoth size and the complex theological aspects of the work. It covers over 8,000 square feet and is composed

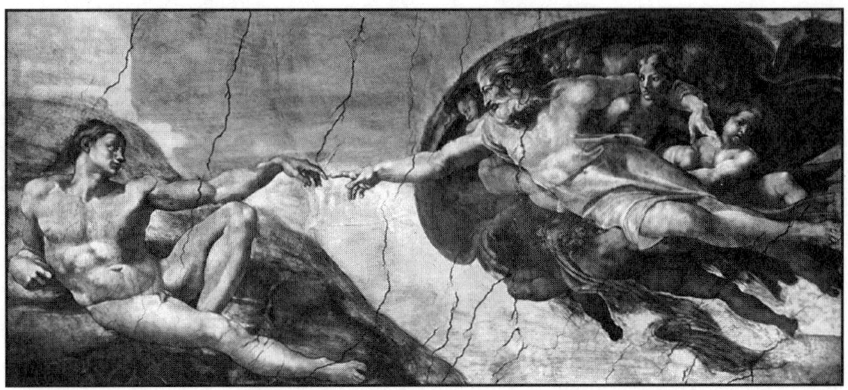

The famous fresco of the creation of Adam on the ceiling of the Sistine Chapel was completed when Michelangelo was in his mid-thirties. The work demonstrates his ability to convey movement and emotion and also shows his fascination with the nude male body.

of over 350 individual figures. The nine main panels depict the story of the creation and fall of humankind, starting with the separation of light from darkness and going all the way to the drunkenness of Noah. Each section is a masterpiece in itself, both in terms of the theological insight and the masterful representation of the human body. There are also twelve spectacular depictions of various prophets and sybils that are sculpture-like in their appearance; these clearly demonstrate the emerging monumental aspect of the High Renaissance.

The work was difficult and intense. Michelangelo painted for hours in an awkward, bent-back position that gave him great pain. Letters to his family during these years talk about his unhappiness, his loneliness, his poor health and the hard work.

In August 1510, Julius became impatient to see the work and ordered Michelangelo to take the scaffolding down so he and others could view it. There was also a break of some six months during which Michelangelo had to go to Bologna twice to get funds from the Pope so he could continue the project. He started work again in January of 1511. The break gave him time to assess his work; as a result, the second half of the ceiling is executed in an even grander manner.

The uncovering of the completed ceiling occurred in late October of 1512. It was immediately recognized as one of the greatest artistic achievements of all history, this further enhancing Michelangelo's reputation as the world's greatest artist.

Interestingly though, Michelangelo's letters to his father that October still speak of his miserable existence and his great anxiety. He ends his comments on his great accomplishment with a low key, "I have finished the Chapel I have been painting, the Pope is very well satisfied."

Soon after the completion of the Sistine ceiling, Michelangelo returned to work on the tomb of Pope Julius. The situation changed promptly, though, when Julius died in February of 1513. Michelangelo quickly entered into negotiations with Julius's heirs. A new design for a slightly more modest, non-freestanding tomb was agreed upon, and a new contract was signed only four months after Julius's death.

In Florence: Working for the Medici

The new pope, Leo X (son of Lorenzo the Magnificent), found the work of Michelangelo's perceived rival Raphael more to his liking. Thus he made no demands of Michelangelo for a couple of years, and Michelangelo was able to get back to his first love, sculpture. He moved the marble for the tomb to a sturdy house in Rome on the Marcel di Covi (on the site of the current Victor Emmanuel monument), where he lived and worked until his death. There followed two years of intensive work in which he produced three masterful figures, all designed to be part of Julius's tomb—two *Slaves* and *Moses.* All three show an evolving mastery that captures great inner emotion and expresses it with unforgettable strength and beauty. Only the *Moses* ended up on the final memorial to Julius. (The *Slaves* are now in the Louvre.) Squeezed into his intense working schedule were several trips to Carrara for more marble.

The year 1516 brought abrupt change in Michelangelo's artistic efforts. The della Rovere family (heirs to Pope Julius II) fell out of favor with the current pope, Leo X, and hence, for economic and political reasons, yet another contract for the tomb was negotiated. It was signed in July 1516 and called for a greatly reduced tomb (twenty-two figures instead of the original forty),

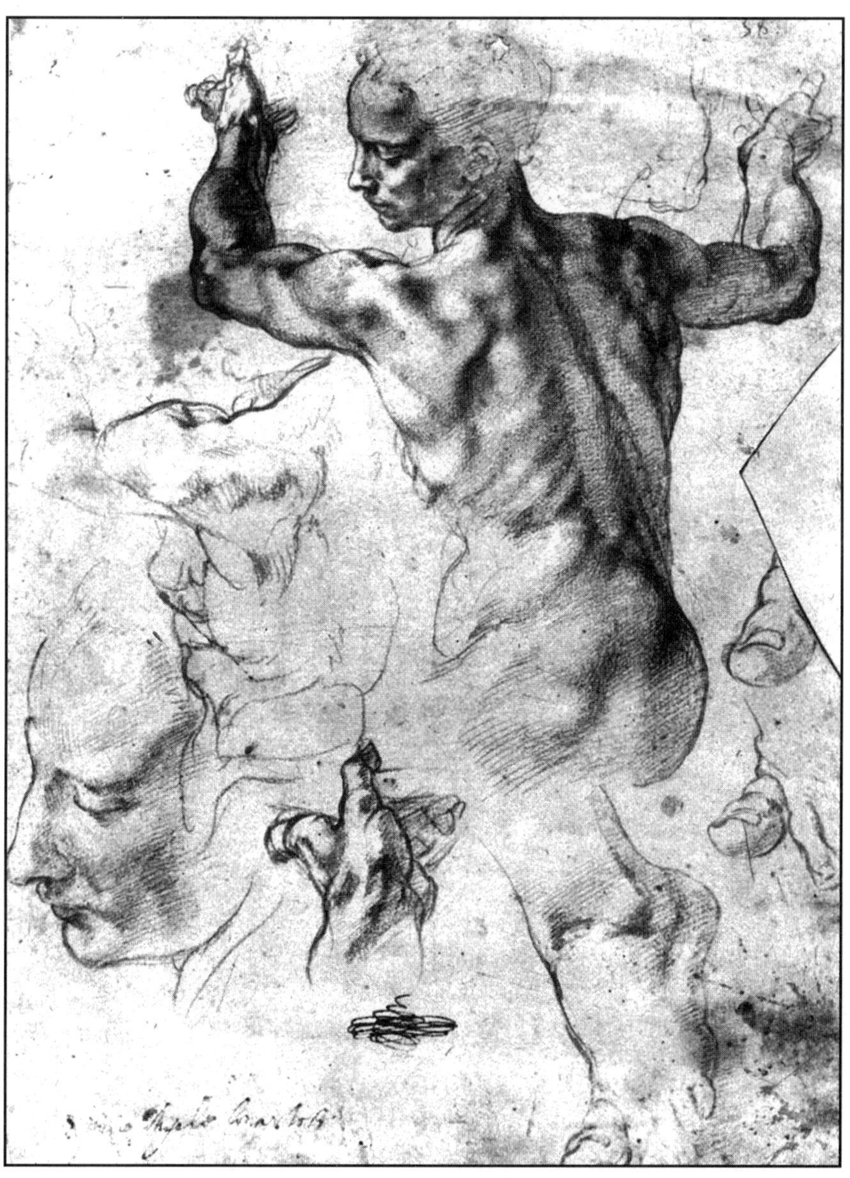

This drawing for the Lybian Sybil was done in 1511 as part of the preparation for the Sistine ceiling. It demonstrates Michelangelo's spectacular ability to do both insightful rough sketches and very refined and accurate drawing.

and the completion time was extended to nine years. Also in 1516, Michelangelo got a huge new commission, which was to be an additional source of great frustration for him in the years ahead.

With the papacy now in Medici hands and the Medici family back in power in Florence, there was an effort to glorify and strengthen the family's native city. Pope Leo X wanted to symbolize all this by beautifying the Medici Church of San Lorenzo. The church itself was already an architectural masterpiece by Brunelleschi, but the facade had never been completed. There was the usual intrigue surrounding who was to get this prestigious commission. By late 1516 Michelangelo had lobbied for and landed the job and was at work on the model. Michelangelo boasted that the facade would be "the mirror of architecture and sculpture in all of Italy." He produced a unique design that, though never executed, had an influence on architecture for years.

Michelangelo's contract was to run for eight years, but after four years of frustration and problems, the contract was canceled by Leo X in March of 1520. What should have been a period of great triumph and creativity was filled with problems and occupied by long, frustrating periods of attempting to acquire marble. Michelangelo learned he could no longer deal exclusively with Carrara but was ordered to develop the new Tuscan quarries at Pietra Santa. He spent many months constructing new roads in order to get the marble out. No real work was done on the facade itself. Michelangelo's frustration was summed up in a letter from Pietra Santa in April of 1518:

> The workers whom I brought from Florence know nothing on earth about quarrying or marble. They have already cost me more than 130 ducats and haven't yet quarried me a chip of marble that's any use, and they go round bamboozling everyone into believing that they have made great discoveries and are seeking to execute work for...others at my expense. I don't know what support they're getting, but the Pope shall hear all about it. Since I've been here I've thrown away about 300 ducats and haven't as yet got anything out of it for myself. In trying to tame these mountains and to introduce the industry into these parts, I've undertaken to raise the dead; for if, over and above the marbles, the Guild of Wool Merchants were to pay me 100 ducats a month for doing what I'm doing, they would do badly, without failing me over the concession.... The barges I hired at Pisa have never arrived. I think I've been gulled, and so it is with everything I do. Oh cursed a thousand times be the day I left Carrara. It's the cause of my undoing....Today it's a crime to do right.

Meanwhile, Michelangelo was under pressure from the della Rovere heirs to make progress on Julius II's tomb. In early 1519 he promised four sculptures in the near future. He was unable to fulfill his promise, but it appears he conceived and possibly started work on four figures of prisoners during this busy and frustrating time. He continued to work on these four figures intermittently over the next four to five years, and today they can be seen in their unfinished state in the Accademia in Florence.

Shortly after the contract for the facade of San Lorenzo was canceled, Pope Leo X commissioned Michelangelo to design a new sacristy for the Church of San Lorenzo. This structure was to be a family funeral chapel to hold the tombs of four Medici: Lorenzo the Magnificent; his brother Giuliano (murdered in the Pazzi Conspiracy in 1478); Giuliano, Duke of Nemours (died 1516); and Lorenzo, Duke of Urbino (died 1519). This building, along with the sculptures that were to fill the sacristy, occupied most of Michelangelo's artistic efforts for the next fourteen years of his life — until he left Florence for the last time in 1534.

The foundation work was in its early stages when Michelangelo got involved. The new sacristy to the right of the main altar was to be a counterbalance to, and be based on, the old sacristy designed by Brunelleschi, which is to the left of the main altar. Michelangelo was involved in the building of the new sacristy, which was designed with the Medici tombs in mind. The original design for the four tombs was a rather massive, freestanding affair. As the project progressed, however, it became evident that the design was too large for the interior space, and it was progressively scaled down into small, individual wall tombs—eventually for only the two younger Medici dukes.

Michelangelo again went to Carrara to look after the quarrying of the marble. But when Pope Leo X died in December of 1521, things came to a halt.

Leo X was replaced by a dour Dutchman, Adrian Dedel of Utrecht, who arrogantly kept his name and became Pope Adrian VI in January of 1522. He didn't care much for artistic endeavors, and things calmed down for a while. By September of 1523 he was dead (probably of poison), and Michelangelo was back in business working on the Medici tombs.

Adrian's replacement was Leo X's cousin Giulio de' Medici, the illegitimate son of the murdered Giuliano. He chose the name Clement VII and was to reign—as the last Medici pope—until 1534. He, too, was committed to glorifying the Medici in Florence, and he chose Michelangelo to be his chief instrument in doing so. Consequently, the period 1520 to 1527 was taken up mainly by work on the Medici tombs, with some continuing work on Julius's tomb, and by a new Medici project, an architectural commission for a library.

When Michelangelo had gone to Rome to congratulate the new pope in 1523, he was asked to submit a drawing for a library to hold the famed Medici collection of manuscripts. In 1524 Clement VII decided that the library (the Laurentian) would be built in the upper story of the Cloisters of San Lorenzo. Work progressed over the next few years on Michelangelo's elegant and beautiful design. His ideas were inventive, and the interior stairway is unique in all of architectural design. But economic problems for the Vatican, and then the horrible sack of Rome, brought this effort to a halt. A bit more work on the library was done in 1533 before Clement VII died. After Michelangelo finally left for Rome, the library was worked on from time to time and finally completed sometime around 1560.

All the work for the Medici in Florence—the never-completed facade of San Lorenzo, the new sacristy and the Medici tombs, and the Laurentian library—were huge undertakings, requiring great organizational and leadership skills. Michelangelo actively involved himself in all aspects of the work, not just the design of the buildings and the carving of the statues, but also the hiring of workers, decisions on their salaries, supervising, planning and logistics. In 1525 he had over one hundred people on his payroll, and during the eighteen years of work on the San Lorenzo projects he employed over two hundred workers.

During the mid-1520s the della Rovere heirs were at him again—rightly so, as he had made very little progress on his obligations under the second contract for Julius's tomb, signed in 1516. There were threats of a lawsuit and charges of fraud, as Michelangelo had already received considerable payments for not much progress. Michelangelo, who claimed he wanted to work on the tomb but couldn't, was frequently upset and frustrated. Lengthy negotiations took place and new designs were submitted, but, because of changing political circumstances, the signing of a new contract didn't occur until 1532. The frustration, uncertainty and stress continued.

Political Events—Conflict and Problems

From 1527 to 1530 political issues, not artistic ones, dominated Michelangelo's life. Pope Clement VII found himself at odds with the new emperor, Charles V, because of his alliance with the French. Charles's forces, with the help of German troops (many of whom were of the new Protestant persuasion), attacked Rome in May of 1527, and the infamous sack of Rome began. Michelangelo's patron, Clement VII, barricaded himself in the Castle St. Angelo and eventually escaped to Orvieto, broke and humiliated.

With the Medici pope rendered helpless, the populace in Florence rose up, expelled the Medici, and reestablished the republic of Florence. Michelangelo was now in a most awkward position, having existed under the Medici patronage for many years but also having definite republican tendencies and thus sympathy for the new regime.

Michelangelo soon found employment in the new republic, both as a sculptor (to create a giant Hercules, never completed, as a companion piece to the David) and as a designer of the fortifications of Florence. The newly revived republic had to quickly raise and train an army, as Clement VII soon made peace with Charles V and began to plan the conquest of Florence and the re-establishment of the Medici. In October of 1529, Michelangelo was named Superintendent of Fortifications for the Republic of Florence. He was also appointed a member of the nine-man policy-making military council.

Over the next year or so, he focused his creative energies on designing imaginative and unique fortifications for the expected siege of Florence by the troops of the papal/Spanish alliance. A number of his design sketches for the fortifications survive. These attest to his ingenuity and understanding of military and engineering principles and demonstrate the broad range of Michelangelo's creative skills. During these years he also visited the fortifications of other Italian cities, including Pisa, Leghorn (Laverno) and Ferrara.

Understandably, things became very tense in Florence as the day of attack approached. Espionage and suspicion were in the air. Michelangelo sensed trouble. Fearing for his own safety, in September of 1529 he fled Florence in a panic. His initial destination was Venice, and he had thoughts of then going on to France. He stayed in Venice only two months and while there made a design for the now famous Rialto Bridge.

But Florence wanted him back. After negotiations ensuring his clemency, Michelangelo returned to Florence in November of 1529. The siege of Florence had already begun, and it was to last until August of 1530.

The republic fell, the Medici were back in power, and Michelangelo was again in a most uncomfortable and precarious position. Anti-Medici activists were rounded up; some were imprisoned and some were hanged. Michelangelo, living in great fear, went into hiding for several months. A recently discovered small room under the Medici Chapel is the likely location of his concealment.

Pope Clement VII felt betrayed by Michelangelo's willingness to work for the Florentine Republicans. However, he soon forgave Michelangelo and enticed him out of hiding in late 1530 so that he could get back to work on the Medici Chapel.

The year 1531 brought further frustrations and grief to Michelangelo. Early in the year his father, Ludovico, died at age 87. Even though Michelangelo had an often frustrating and contentious relationship with his father, he constantly kept in touch with him and was forever trying to please him. Ludovico's death put Michelangelo into a state of great despair. He lost himself in his work, and his friends were gravely concerned for his health.

The work on the Medici Chapel figures was his main focus during this time, but he also had other artistic demands made on him. Things got so stressful for Michelangelo that in November of 1531 Pope Clement VII issued a brief forbidding the artist to work on anything other than the Pope's projects and the still-unfinished tomb of Julius II. He backed this up with threats of excommunication.

The issue of the unfinished tomb of Julius still hung over Michelangelo's head. It seemed a never-ending source of frustration. After protracted negotiations and a strong hand from Pope Clement VII, a new contract was signed in April of 1532. It obligated him to complete a scaled-down wall tomb (including six figures by his own hand) within three years. As Michelangelo had already received a lot of money from the project, he agreed to assume all the future expenses. The contract allowed him to spend up to two months per year in Rome working on the tomb.

In addition to his weak health, his father's death, and his frustrating artistic demands, Michelangelo also had real problems with the newly appointed Medici rulers of Florence. In 1531 the Pope had appointed his illegitimate son Alessandro to rule Florence and made him Duke of Florence in May of 1532. Alessandro was tyrannical, eccentric and mentally unstable. He also had an irrational dislike of Michelangelo.

The years 1532 to 1534, as Michelangelo moved back and forth between Florence and Rome, were not good times for the fifty-seven-year-old artist. He continued working on the Medici Chapel and on the Laurentian Library, but he had lost much of his initial enthusiasm for these projects. The Medici, while back in power, were still the disturbing symbol of anti-republicanism for Michelangelo. He genuinely feared the unstable and hostile Alessandro. In addition, the members of the Medici family to whom he was closest were now gone. Fortunately, there was at least one positive aspect to his life during these years. On one of his Roman visits in 1532, Michelangelo met a handsome young nobleman named Tommaso di Cavalieri. Michelangelo was smitten; his life took on new meaning, and he lived with greater purpose and enthusiasm. A series of letters and drawings attest to his fascination and infatuation with the young Roman. Finally all this came together and Michelangelo moved to Rome for good in 1534.

When he left Florence, both the Medici Chapel sculptures and the Laurentian Library were unfinished. The Chapel stands today as the greatest ensemble of Michelangelo's works. It contains two wall tombs of three figures each as well as the beautiful, serene and strong Medici *Madonna.*

When he departed in 1534, much remained to be done, and the statues were simply left on the Chapel floor. It was years before everything was put together as we see it today.

Rome: New Challenges and Frustrations

Within days after Michelangelo's arrival in Rome, Clement VII died. Michelangelo, finally freed of the Medici, whom he had served for nearly forty-five years, felt that now he could at last concentrate on finishing the tomb of Julius II. It had been almost thirty years since he had first started working on it.

But the new pope, Paul III, had other plans. He said he had been waiting for thirty years for the opportunity to have Michelangelo work for him.

For the next fifteen years Michelangelo became closely tied to the artistic interests and desires of the elderly pontiff. Work on Julius's tomb was pretty much put on hold, and Paul III told the della Rovere clan they would eventually have to settle for an even smaller tomb. Just to make sure that Michelangelo worked only for him, Michelangelo was given the title of Chief Architect, Sculptor and Painter to the Vatican and a handsome salary.

The Pope's first project for Michelangelo had actually been discussed in late 1533 with Pope Clement VII. The plan was to paint the huge altar wall of the Sistine Chapel with a rendering of the resurrection of Christ. Paul III quickly changed the subject matter to the Last Judgment, and work got under way. Hundreds of preparatory drawings were made, wall drawings were executed and the actual painting (in fresco) was begun in May of 1536.

The *Last Judgment* is huge (56 feet high by 44 feet wide) and very complex, containing hundreds of figures. It is an amazing masterpiece of great dynamism and movement. It portrays a strong, beardless, nude Christ in the middle, and a swirl of saints and sinners rising in triumph or descending into hell. It reveals a complex, intricate design of nude figures in a wide variety of poses expressing a broad range of human emotions. It is a truly monumental work of great theological and artistic significance.

Michelangelo was an old man when he painted the *Last Judgment.* It was hard work and he took a fall off the scaffold partway through. But after five years the work was unveiled in 1541, twenty-nine years after he completed the famous Sistine ceiling overhead.

At the unveiling it is said that Pope Paul III fell to his knees and cried out to the Lord in praise. Nevertheless, the work soon became the subject of continuing criticism. The strictness of the Counter Reformation gave voice to some who were offended by the nudity. The controversy went on for some years, and eventually (after Michelangelo's death) some of the figures were given loincloths or wholly repainted.

During the late 1530s, Michelangelo had several close relationships that brought special meaning to his generally austere and difficult existence. There was, of course, Tommaso di Cavalieri. In addition, however, in 1536 he was introduced to one of the outstanding women of the Renaissance, Vittoria Colonna. He was sixty-four and she was forty-six at the time. She was the widow of a Marchese and a well-educated, headstrong, cultured and very religious woman. She and Michelangelo became deeply devoted friends and she assumed an important role in his life. They visited often and exchanged letters.

Also during this time, Michelangelo started what was to become a long and involved correspondence and relationship with his nephew, Lionardo Buonarroti, son of his deceased younger brother, Buonarroto, who had died of the plague in 1528. He took a very paternal, and at times overbearing, interest in the young man. He seems to have been the only family member left about whom Michelangelo really cared.

Their relationship continued, mainly by letter, until the time of Michelangelo's death.

The seven-year period after the completion of the *Last Judgment* was one of great creative output for the aging Michelangelo. Soon Pope Paul III had him working on major frescos for the side walls of his recently completed private chapel in the Vatican, the Pauline, located fewer than one hundred yards away from the Sistine Chapel. The two paintings, *The Conversion of Paul* and *The Crucifixion of Peter*, occupied most of Michelangelo's artistic energies to the end of the decade. They are works of great spiritual insight that reflect the aging Michelangelo's increasing concern with his own fate, as well as the increasingly strict effects of the Counter Reformation. The paintings are rather austere and lack the sensuality and anatomical energy of his earlier works. They were his last paintings, having been completed in 1550, his seventy-fifth year.

The 1540s were again a period of anguish and unhappiness for Michelangelo in spite of his continuing creative productivity. He fell seriously ill several times. He often had great trouble urinating and suffered from kidney stones. He became increasingly concerned with his old age and his death. A letter to a friend in Florence in 1547 sums up his thoughts:

> I am an old man and death has robbed me of dreams of youth may those who do not know what old age means bear it with what patience they may when they reach it, because it cannot be imagined beforehand.

The death of two old and dear friends caused further pain. In the fall of 1546 Luigi del Riccio died. Luigi had served as Michelangelo's business manager and general advisor since 1540 and had taken care of him several times when he was gravely ill, nursing him back to health. Luigi had planned to publish a volume of Michelangelo's poetry. Then, just four months later, his close and spiritual friend Vittoria Colonna died. Michelangelo went into a period of profound grief. His still busy artistic energy no doubt provided a relief to his pain and suffering.

In early 1547, the Pope asked Michelangelo to take on additional duties and appointed him architect of the new St. Peter's in 1549. This architectural challenge, which Michelangelo resisted, opened up new outlets for his unending reserve of creativity and occupied him until the time of his death. Through his hard work, unusual creative approaches and unbending will power, he produced designs for and made progress on some of the most beautiful and significant architectural masterpieces in Rome.

The busy 1540s also finally saw the completion of the seemingly neverending tale of the tomb of Julius II. After much argument, strife and negotiations, a fourth (and final) contract was agreed upon in August 1542. It called for only three figures by Michelangelo: the *Moses* (probably finished nearly thirty years earlier in 1516) and two side statues, *Rachel* (representing active life) and *Leah* (representing contemplative life). He finally finished these last two statues, and his work was essentially completed in 1544. His assistants did three rather uninspiring statues for the second level of the tomb, and all was finished in early 1545. Thus, forty years after Michelangelo had enthusiastically started work on the colossal forty-statue freestanding tomb to be set in St. Peter's, the project had ended up as a modest wall tomb containing only three works by Michelangelo and resting in the Roman church of St. Pietro in Vincoli. The project had brought Michelangelo years of grief, frus-

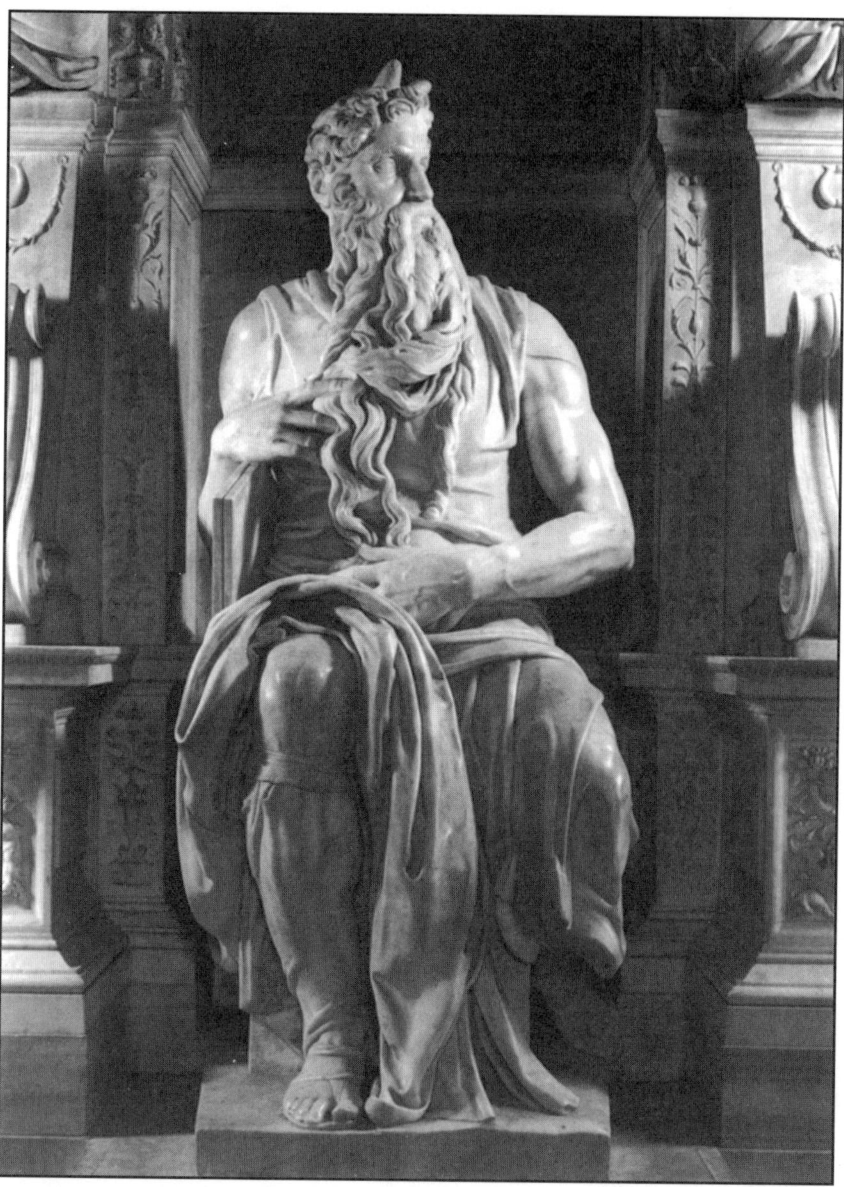

The Moses, carved around 1515, was to have been part of the huge tomb of Pope Julius II. It demonstrates Michelangelo's supreme ability to show both detailed exterior features and express inner feeling and tension.

tration and guilt, and precious little praise or satisfaction. And the final irony is that Julius never was buried in the finished tomb. He continues to lie in St. Peter's beside his uncle Sixtus IV.

Old Age: Continuing His Work

By 1550, Michelangelo was indeed an old man of seventy-five who was concerned about death and constantly complaining about his problems and his ill health. He still had nearly fifteen years of life ahead of him, however, and while he had to slow down, he continued to create and to be heavily involved in major artistic projects until the very end. His letters show an increasing crotchetiness and sensitivity, but his mind remained sharp as his body continued to fade.

During these years, Michelangelo worked intermittently on a complex, larger-than-life, four-figure *Pietà* that was to be for his own tomb. Begun in 1547, it shows Jesus, his mother, Nicodemus and one of the Marys in a scene of great passion and sorrow. This work gave Michelangelo an outlet for his first love, sculpturing marble. But, like most of his projects, it was also a source of frustration. In 1555 Michelangelo found a flaw in the marble of the nearly finished statue and became so angered that he lost patience and started to smash the work. Fortunately, one of his assistants talked him out of it and the masterpiece was saved. It was in the Florence cathedral for years but now sits in the Museum of the Opera of the Duomo in Florence.

Michelangelo served four popes during his last fourteen years. His great beneficiary, Paul III, died in November of 1549. He was replaced by Julius III, who reigned for five years. Julius continued to support Michelangelo in his work as chief architect of St. Peter's, often overruling court intrigue and quashing political scheming against the architect.

Julius III died in 1555 and was followed by Pope Marcellus II. His puritanical approach to life and his lack of interest in the arts did not bode well for Michelangelo. He considered moving back to Florence but felt obligated to continue his crucial role in the building of St. Peter's. Luckily, Marcellus II died after only three weeks in power. He was followed on the throne by the seventy-nine-year-old Paul IV, who supported Michelangelo in his work at St. Peter's.

During Paul IV's reign there was a threatened attack on Rome by Spain. Remembering the horror of 1527, the Romans negotiated and the siege was lifted after only five to six months. During part of the siege, the work on St. Peter's was suspended and Michelangelo fled to Spoleto at age eighty-one but soon returned to continue his work.

During these years his surviving correspondence is dominated by family affairs, mainly with his nephew Lionardo. He gives much advice on choosing a wife, buying a house and choosing a career. The birth of a son for Lionardo and his wife in 1554 brought Michelangelo great joy.

His letters also trace the work in St. Peter's and his loyalty to the project. Although he had the support of the Pope, there were constant efforts by Michelangelo's rivals to discredit and displace him as the head of the project. Still he persevered, and in a letter to Vasari from Rome in May of 1557 he wrote about St. Peter's:

> But through lack of money the work has been retarded and is being retarded, when it has reached the most toilsome and difficult part, so that if I were to abandon it now, it would result in nothing but the uttermost disgrace and loss of the whole reward for the pains I have endured for the love of God during the said 10 years.

During the time he worked on St. Peter's he refused to take any payment.

Pope Paul IV died in August of 1559. His successor was Pius IV, who reigned until a year after Michelangelo's death. He, too, was most supportive of the great and revered artist, even issuing a brief forbidding any changes in Michelangelo's plans for St. Peter's after the artist's death. (The brief was subsequently ignored.)

Through these last years, Cosimo, the Duke of Florence, tried to entice Michelangelo to return to his native city. There was a genuine desire on the part of the Medici duke and the citizens of Florence to have the aging master spend his last days in Florence. Michelangelo felt honored by the request and even seemed to consider the idea from time to time. However, he decided that he didn't want to undertake such a major change at such an old age. Probably most important, though, was his desire to stick with the St. Peter's project, to which he felt he had an almost sacred duty. His letter of May 1557 to Duke Cosimo describes his desire to continue the work in Rome:

> ...I could not yet leave the fabric of St. Peter's without causing great damage to the fabric and bringing the greatest disgrace upon myself.

His Final Years

Still productive in his eighty-fifth year, Michelangelo completed the model for the dome of St. Peter's. However, his health continued to decline. In 1561 he had a seizure but recovered fairly quickly, and he continued to work on architectural designs for various other projects in Rome. Surprisingly, he kept up a regular stream of correspondence, much of it to his nephew Lionardo, telling him how to run his affairs, thanking him for gifts of wine and cheese, and complaining about his old age and health. His cantankerous nature shows itself in a letter written in 1563, at age eighty-eight:

> Lionardo I see from your letter that you are lending credits to certain envious rascals who, being unable either to manage me or to rob me, write you a pack of lies. They are a lot of sharks and you are such a fool to lend credence to them about my affairs, as if I were an infant. Spurn them as envious scandal mongering low living rascals.
>
> As regards allowing myself to be looked after, about which you write me, and about the other thing—I tell you, as to being looked after, I could not be better off; neither could I be more faithfully treated and looked after in every way. As regards my being robbed, which I believe you mean, I assure you I don't need to worry about the people I have in the house, whom I can rely upon. Therefore look after yourself and don't worry about my affairs, because I know how to look after myself, if I need to, and I am not an infant. Farewell.

While most of his creative energies were focused on architectural design projects, Michelangelo did keep working with marble up to the very end. Shortly after attempting to smash his four-figure *Pietà* in 1555, Michelangelo had acquired another block of marble to work on a small piece that already had some figures roughed out. Over the next nine years he worked on this piece, evolving it into a very rough but moving statue of Mary and Jesus in a moment of deep sorrow, as the dead Christ is taken down from the cross. The unfinished work is rather abstract, but the deep emotional tie between mother and son is clear, as their bodies are entwined and almost fused into one. Contemporaries record that Michelangelo was still working on this piece six days before his death. This strange work, now called the *Rondanini Pietà* (from the Roman palace where it once stood), is now in the Sforza Castle in Milan.

A review of his correspondence during the last years reflect his moods and concerns:

In 1555 (at age eighty) he wrote to Vasari:

> My dear Messer Giorgio, I know that you realize from my writing that I am at the eleventh hour and that I conceive of no thought in which death is not engraved. God grant that I may keep him waiting for another year or so.

And in a sad and touching letter to his nephew Lionardo in 1556 he wrote:

> Lionardo I did not acknowledge the *trebbiano* (wine), as I was pressed when I received it…that is to say 36 flasks. It's the best you've ever sent me, for which I thank you, but I'm sorry you put yourself to this expense, particularly as I've no longer anyone to give it to, since all my friends are dead.

A year later, in 1557, he again wrote to Lionardo about his health:

> As regards my physical state, I'm ill, that is to say with all the ills to which old men are prone with the stone, so that I cannot urinate, with the colic, with the backache, so that often I am unable to walk up stairs, and worse still I'm full of worries, because if I leave the conveniences I have here for my ills, I should not survive three days.

And in a brief letter to Vasari, in 1557, he ironically said:

> My brain and my memory have gone to await me elsewhere.

In his final letter in December of 1563, just a month and a half before his death, he expressed some of his moods and concerns:

> Lionardo I had your last letter with 12 most excellent and delicious marzolini cheeses, for which I thank you. I'm delighted at your well being; the same is true of me. Having received several letters of yours recently and not having replied, I have omitted to do so, because I can't use my hand to write; therefore from now on I'll get others to write and I'll sign. I think that's all. From Rome on the 28th day of December 1563.

His death came on February 18, 1564, after a week's illness. He died surrounded by a physician and several of his remaining friends, including Tommaso di Cavalieri. He left no written will, saying only that he left his soul to God, his body to earth and his material possessions to his nearest relative (Lionardo). At the end he asked his friends to recall to him the sufferings of Christ.

Michelangelo had expressed a desire to be buried in his native Florence. Similarly, Duke Cosimo de' Medici desired to bring the body back to Florence. To avoid conflict, Michelangelo's remains were smuggled out of Rome by some merchants, concealed in a bale, disguised as a piece of merchandise.

Much ceremony and mourning soon followed in Florence. The city grieved the loss of the man they considered the greatest artist ever. After preparation of a special funeral book and the delivery of prestigious funeral orations, Michelangelo was finally buried in the church of Santa Croce, in his old neighborhood. Vasari, his friend and biographer, designed the tomb where he now rests.

Michelangelo's Personal Characteristics

Thus far we have explored the historical and social forces that provide the backdrop for Michelangelo's life, as well as traced the major events and experiences of his eighty-nine years. Let us now go back into that life and examine in more detail some of the most important aspects of the man, his personality, and his relationships with others.

Appearance

Both Condivi and Vasari are consistent in their descriptions of Michelangelo. He had been somewhat delicate and sickly as a child, but for most of the rest of his life he was relatively healthy, evidently being very disciplined in avoiding excessive drink, food or sexual activities. He was of medium height and had broad shoulders, a slender, well-proportioned body and a rather round face. Its distinguishing characteristics were the famous squashed nose (from the blow by his youthful artistic rival), a well-formed chin, and thin lips, with the lower one projecting out a bit. His eyes were small, brown in color with flecks of yellow and blue. His hair was black (turning gray in his later years), and he wore a thin, short-forked beard. Several sketches and busts still in existence give us a good sense of how he looked. Michelangelo also included rough self-portraits in several of his own works. These renditions give him a leathery, worn, serious appearance.

Michelangelo was conscious about his appearance, and he generally dressed well. His records show that he kept track of the fabrics he purchased and the specific items of clothing he had made from them. He tended to dress in black, which mirrored the aristocratic fashions of the time and no doubt reflected Michelangelo's social aspirations.

Family

Throughout his life, Michelangelo was closely involved with his family and their affairs. These complex and stressful relationships were sources of tension and guilt that he rarely escaped.

Possibly the absence of a strong relationship with his mother had a great influence on Michelangelo. You will recall that shortly after he was born, Michelangelo was separated from his mother for approximately two years. This separation deprived him of the love and nurturing that are so important to a child's emotional development. Michelangelo returned to his mother and father at around age two, and he became a small part of a large family household (his parents were then living with his father's brother's family). Francesca's energies over the next four years were occupied mainly by bearing three more sons. She died after having the last one in 1481; Michelangelo was six at the time. Thereafter he remained with his father and brothers as part of the large Buonarroti two-family household. Thus we see a child growing up without a close mother/son relationship and, as we shall see, a distant and difficult relationship with his father.

A yearning for a close mother/son relationship appears as a significant theme in many of Michelangelo's works. One of his earliest pieces, *The Madonna of the Stairs* (completed in 1491), shows a Madonna who is rather stiff, unloving and unresponsive to her child. This rendition is very unlike the traditional depiction of the maternal, warm and caring mother of Christ that we see in other Renaissance paintings and sculptures. This feeling of the Virgin's separateness and detachment from Jesus is characteristic of the many Madonnas and pietàs that Michelangelo created over the next sixty years.

Michelangelo was the second of five brothers. Only one of them ever married. The eldest, Lionardo, was two years senior to Michelangelo. Not much is known about him except that he became a Dominican friar in 1491 and a follower of Savonarola. He died around 1510, at which point Michelangelo assumed the role of eldest son. The fourth brother, Giovan Simone (1479–1548), appears to have been intelligent and quite emotional. He and Michelangelo had a number of conflicts over financial matters and over Giovan Simone's treatment of their father.

The youngest Buonarroti son was Sigismondo (1481–1555). He was a bit of a ne'er-do-well, serving time in various mercenary armies and finally settling down on the family farm. As Michelangelo's reputation grew and he became more status conscious, Sigismondo became a source of embarrassment to him. In a letter in 1546, Michelangelo wrote to his nephew regarding Sigismondo:

> ...I have always striven to resuscitate our house, but I have not had brothers worthy of this. So strive to do what I tell you and get Sigismondo to return to live in Florence, so that it should no longer be said here, to my great shame, that I have a brother at Settignano who trudges after oxen....

It was Buonarroto (1477–1528), the third son, to whom Michelangelo was closest. He was a capable man who made his living in the wool trade. Michelangelo helped him in his business ventures with both money and advice. He also had plenty of thoughts for him regarding his choice of a wife:

> ...You tell me that this fellow wants to give you one of his daughters to wife; but I tell you that all the offers he makes will be unfulfilled, except for the wife once he has foisted her on you, and you will have more of her than you want....

Buonarroto was the only son to marry. Two of his children (Lionardo and Francesca) survived and were sources of affection and objects of attention for Michelangelo as he grew older.

Michelangelo's brothers were important to him and he corresponded with them regularly. He gave them advice, stuck his nose into their affairs and helped them financially. He even set two of them up in the wool-trading business. The relationships, however, appear to have been filled with stress, and Michelangelo was often rather martyr-like in letting them know the sacrifices he was making for them. In 1509 he wrote to his brother Giovan Simone from Rome:

> ...For 12 years now I have gone about all over Italy, leading a miserable life; I have borne every kind of humiliation, suffered every kind of hardship, worn myself to the bone with every kind of labor, risked my life in a thousand dangers, solely to help my family; and now, when I begin to rise up a little, you alone must be the one to confound and destroy in one hour what I have accomplished in so many years and with such pains....

It was with his father, Ludovico (1444–1531), that Michelangelo had his most intense and difficult relationship. Early on Ludovico realized Michelangelo's intelligence and pushed him to follow a path of academic training that would lead to a prestigious lifestyle and thus help restore the Buonarroti family name. Ludovico felt life as an artisan would be a disgrace to the family, and Michelangelo received beatings from his father and his uncle in their attempt to force him not to pursue his artistic inclinations. Nevertheless, the parent/son relationship was strong, and over the years Michelangelo constantly helped his father and tried to please him. Michelangelo sent his father regular payments for his living expenses and was his sole source of support for his final three decades. But there was constant bickering and argument between them. Several of Michelangelo's letters express the frustration and lack of satisfaction in the relationship. From Rome in 1512 he wrote to his father:

> ...For I lead a miserable existence and reck not of life nor honor—that is of this world; I live wearied by stupendous labors and beset by a thousand anxieties. And thus I have lived for some 15 years now and never an hours happiness have I had, and all this have I done in order to help you, though you have never either recognized or believed it—God forgive us all. I am prepared always to do the same as long as I live, provided I'm able.

A letter in 1521 shows great emotion and pleading:

> ...for I'm certain that never to this day, since the day I was born, has it ever occurred to me to do anything, either great or small, opposed to your interests; and all the toils and troubles I've continually endured, I've always endured for your sake.... I've always taken care of you and you know that I have assured you that what I have is yours....I beg of you to forgive me...for it matters more to me than you think. After all I am your son....

Toward the end of Ludovico's life, things evidently got a bit better, and father and son seemed to express themselves with less frustration. Ludovico wrote to Michelangelo in 1531, just a few months before he died at age eighty-seven:

> May God be thanked for His grace in having inspired you to be so charitable towards me, that I remain alive without having to beg or borrow, and if in truth I have been saved from hunger, it is thanks to God and then to you, who have shown me such kindness. May God reward you in this world and the next.

After his father died, Michelangelo expressed great sorrow and wrote a very moving poem in his memory.

We can see some very poignant expressions of this intense, conflict-filled relationship in Michelangelo's work. It shows up in the relationship between Noah and his sons in the *Drunkenness of Noah* on the Sistine ceiling and in his depiction of the father carrying his dead son in the *Deluge* panel, also on the Sistine ceiling.

I have already outlined Michelangelo's close relationship with his nephew, Lionardo (1519–1599). Lionardo was only nine when his father, Buonarroto, died during the plague of 1528. From that point until his death, Michelangelo took a strong and very paternal interest in Lionardo and, to a somewhat lesser extent, in his sister Francesca. Over two-thirds of Michelangelo's last three hundred personal letters are addressed to him. The nephew served both as the link to Michelangelo's past (as his father and brothers died off) and as the sole hope of carrying the Buonarroti name forward.

Their relationship, carried on mainly by correspondence, involved Michelangelo's moving into most aspects of Lionardo's life. He was very much a part in helping the young nephew choose a wife. His advice reflects both his values and a sense of frustration. He wrote to Lionardo from Rome in 1550:

> About your taking a wife—which is necessary—I've nothing to say to you, except that you should not be particular as to the dowry, because possessions are of less value than people. All you need have an eye to is birth, good health and, above all a nice disposition. As regards beauty, not being, after all the most handsome youth in Florence yourself, you need not bother overmuch, provided she is neither deformed nor ill favored. I think that's all on this point....

Throughout his contacts with Lionardo, Michelangelo continued the stressful and conflict-filled behavior that characterized his relations with his brothers and his father. He would give material support and lots of advice, but would also make sure Lionardo was aware of the sacrifices he was making. He often berated Lionardo, further expressing the frustrating and unsatisfactory nature of the relationship. Two letters in 1546 illustrate:

> ...And don't write to me anymore; because every time I get a letter from you, I'm thrown into a fever, such a struggle do I have to read it. I do not know where you learnt to write. If you had to write to the biggest ass in the world, I believe you'd write with more care. So there's no need to add to my vexations, because I've enough of them already....

And again a few months later:

> Lionardo—you've written me a long rigmarole about a trifle which only annoys me. About the money of which you write, telling me how you have to spend it, decide between yourselves and spend it on what you need most. I don't think there's anything else, and I've no time for writing either.

Michelangelo was constantly unsure of Lionardo's feelings for him, and this insecurity often crept into his letters. From Rome he wrote to Lionardo in 1546:

> As to your having come to Rome in such a rush, I don't know whether you would have come so quickly had I been starving and in want. It suffices that you throw away money you haven't earned, so great is your anxiety not to lose this inheritance. And then you say that you are under an obligation to come, because of the love you bear me. Cupboard love! If you have loved me, you would now have written to me, saying "Michelangelo, spend the 3,000 scudi there on yourself, because you have given us so much that it's enough for us. We care more for you than for your possessions."
>
> You have all lived on me for 40 years now and not so much as a kind word have I ever had from you.

Their affinity ebbed back and forth, with both care and frustration on both sides. Still, Michelangelo continued to write to Lionardo up to his last days. When news of his uncle's impending death reached him, Lionardo hastened to Rome to be at Michelangelo's side. He arrived several days after his uncle's death, to discover that Michelangelo had left his entire estate to him.

The strong feelings that Michelangelo had for his family, and the lack of satisfaction in those relationships, reveal several underlying themes:

- The lack of a strong, loving mother figure in his life
- The constant conflict with his father, and his continuous and generally unsuccessful efforts to please him
- His strong desire to re-establish the reputation of the Buonarrotis as a prestigious and noble Tuscan family
- The self-appointed responsibility of taking care of his family, resulting in his giving them much of the money he earned, along with lots of

advice and meddling, but always making sure they knew about the sacrifices he was making for them

- A long-lasting final attempt to hold on to the happy family he never had, and a desire to ensure the continuation of the Buonarroti name through his strong and conflict-filled relationship with his nephew Lionardo

Finances

Michelangelo's relationships with his family evolved as they did partly because of economics. Michelangelo supported most of his family for many years. He did this not only because he felt a duty to do so but because he was financially able. While he often pleaded poverty and generally lived a simple life, he was, in fact, fairly wealthy for most of his life.

Michelangelo often said "business is not my profession," and he would feign ignorance in commercial matters. However, he was a knowledgeable and wise administrator of his financial affairs. He handled many of his investment, negotiating, banking and money transfer decisions himself. He would also, when the need arose, get advice from friends on more complex business matters. In his later years he had business managers, including his friend Luigi del Riccio.

He was generally well paid for his artistic efforts, although he would occasionally claim he made very little money on certain projects. Later in his life he received a regular salary from the Vatican—part of which came from being assigned the rights to the revenues from a ferry across the Po River near Piacenza.

His investments were primarily in real estate, and at one time in 1534 he owned eleven properties. Many of these investments were made through his family after detailed and often contentious correspondence. His principles of real estate investing, taken from several of his letters, are quite insightful and would serve us well today:

- Buy good value—in a good location (not too close to the Arno because of flooding)

- Buy in the right part of town
- Make sure the title is good
- Think about what needs to be done to fix up the new property
- Don't quibble over just a little money on the price
- Negotiate well—don't let them know you're too interested
- Go slowly

Because of his movements between Florence and Rome, there was often a need to transfer money and negotiate contracts through the mails. Michelangelo's letters to his family and various business contacts reveal his desire for secrecy in financial affairs and his inclination to get involved in the details. We see that over the course of the years, he chose to use at least twenty-one different Roman and Florentine banks to handle his remittances and transfers.

His general financial activity shows him to have been a person who paid his bills on time, expected to be paid what he was owed, and had at least the normal concern about being secure in his old age. While historians, and often Michelangelo himself, have given us a picture of a poor, struggling artist, the facts show a man with substantial financial resources for most of his life. There were times early in his career when he no doubt was poor, and he often recalled them. For most of his life, though, he lived comfortably, with adequate housing, ample food, several servants and sound investments.

But in spite of his relative affluence, material possessions don't appear to have mattered much to Michelangelo. What drove him was his work, and when he was engaged in a project, very little else mattered. During those times he focused on creating, and in fact lived a life of intensive, all-absorbing work that left him little time to enjoy his financial successes.

General Relationships

The image of Michelangelo as an irascible loner with few friends has some basis in fact. But that image is not completely accurate. The broad issue of Michelangelo's relations with others is, like most aspects of his life, much more complex.

Because of his overriding, single-minded focus on his art, he often simply didn't have much time for developing close relationships. Still, like many truly great artists, he had an insecure side that caused him to need friendships and admiration. Over the years he developed meaningful and satisfying friendships with a variety of men, including assistants, other artists, business managers, civic leaders, clergy and the like. In later years he often corresponded with them in warm terms. As Michelangelo's fame grew, many of these associations evolved into relationships where the person's principal desire was to serve Michelangelo. Luigi del Riccio wrote to him in 1542, "How much I desire to serve you is known to everyone acquainted with me."

In times of stress Michelangelo particularly needed relationships, and he would express an almost childlike happiness when time with friends went well. In 1525, after a period of hard work and depression, he wrote to a friend:

> Yesterday evening our friend Captain Cuio and several other gentlemen kindly invited me to go and have supper with them, which gave me great pleasure, as I emerged a little from my depression, or rather from my obsession. I not only enjoyed the supper, which was extremely pleasant, but also, and even more than this the discussion which took place.

Still his paranoia, sensitivity and lack of trust would occasionally show through, and he was quick to take offense at perceived insults or slights. And outside of his circle of friends, he often had sarcastic, cutting comments for those not in his favor. Vasari relates several of these comments:

> A painter once earned a great deal for a work which had cost him a considerable amount of time and effort. When he was asked what he thought of the man as an artist, Michelangelo replied, "So long as he wants to be rich, he'll stay poor."
>
> On seeing an acquaintance all decked out like a pilgrim and saying mass, he exclaimed, "Oh, you do look fine! It would be good for your soul if you were as good within as you seem on the outside."
>
> And in a letter writing about an unpleasant, sanctimonious woman trying to foist her daughter on his nephew, Michelangelo writes, "...She has written me a long rigmarole, together with a sermon urging me to live a good life and to give alms. She says she has been urging you to live like a Christian and has probably told you she was inspired by God to give you the said girl. I maintain she would do much better to attend to her spinning and weaving than to go around professing so much sanctity. It seems to me she is trying to be another Sister Domenica, so don't trust her."

For a man of such intense artistic focus, Michelangelo was fortunate to have a number of people around him who really cared. He appears to have appreciated their devotion, and in most cases he returned their feelings and established meaningful friendships that were important to him, particularly in his old age.

Relations With Other Artists

Relationships with other artists took a different slant. Here we see some of Michelangelo's basic insecurity and paranoia. He had a tendency to see most other artists as rivals. Unless they became admirers of his work, and assumed a subservient and supportive role, he found them to be threats, and spoke of them with utter disdain.

In Michelangelo's mind, his most significant rivals were probably Leonardo da Vinci and the Raphael/Bramante clique in Rome.

Leonardo had already acquired a prestigious reputation for his artistic and intellectual exploits when he returned to Florence in 1500 at age forty-eight. Where Leonardo was refined and gentlemanly, and took great care in studying and depicting nature and landscapes, Michelangelo was more emotional and rough in his manners, and focused his art on the human soul as expressed through the beauty of the male body. On occasion, insults were hurled between the two artists as the cocky, younger Michelangelo sought to put down the older and more versatile Leonardo.

Raphael arrived in Rome in 1508 at age twenty-five. He was something of a protégé of the great architect Bramante. Pope Julius II quickly recognized his talent and commissioned him to paint the walls of the papal apartments in the Vatican, the Stanza. Widely acclaimed and very successful, he represented a threat to Michelangelo both artistically and in terms of the attention and patronage of the Pope. Michelangelo felt it was the Bramante/Raphael group that convinced the Pope to stop work on his tomb and begin work on the new St. Peter's Cathedral. There are also stories of members of this group insinuating that Michelangelo did not have the ability to handle the difficult task of painting the Sistine ceiling. Michelangelo's paranoia and vulnerability undoubtedly played a role in gaining credence for these stories. However, through fact or perception, a rivalry did develop in Michelangelo's mind, and he referred to it regularly over the years. Raphael lived elegantly and attracted others with his gentlemanliness, polished ways and pleasant manner. Michelangelo was, of course, the opposite and here, no doubt, lay some of the causes of their rivalry.

Interestingly, though, Raphael was influenced artistically by Michelangelo. While working in Rome, his style developed toward the more classic style of Michelangelo, with clear emphasis on muscles and complex poses of the body. After sneaking in to see Michelangelo's great work on the Sistine ceiling (still in progress), Raphael was so impressed that he painted a Michelangelo-type figure into the famous work he was completing in the Pope's apartments just a few yards away in the Vatican.

After Julius's death, the urbane and talented Raphael became the favorite artist of the new pope, Leo X. He was chosen architect of St. Peter's after Bramante's death in 1514. His presence in Rome during these years, until he died in 1520, was a continuing annoyance to Michelangelo. Michelangelo did, however, get in the last dig when years later, in 1542, he wrote to a cardinal documenting his side of things and implying his artistic influence over his rival who had died some twenty-two years earlier:

> ...All the discords that arose between Pope Julius and me were owing to the envy of Bramante and Raphael of Urbino; and this is the reason why he did not proceed with the Tomb in his lifetime, in order to ruin me. And Raphael has good reason to be envious, since what he knew of art he learnt from me.

Despite the ever-present perception of competition and rivalry, Michelangelo did work closely and relatively harmoniously with a number of other artists. These were men of considerable talent who were anxious to further themselves by working with the master. He was comfortable with this as long as they acknowledged his preeminence and saw things as he did. The most famous of these artists— Sebastiano del Piombo (painter, 1485–1547), Jacopo Pontormo (painter, 1494–1556) and Daniele da Volterra (painter and sculptor, 1509–1566)—were all first-rate talents in their own right and had well-earned reputations when they came under the influence of Michelangelo. He worked with these men, often providing drawings for them to execute in full paintings. He even took a hand in trying to secure for them selected commissions.

Often Michelangelo would use one of these protégés as a surrogate in his battle with his various rivals in the Bramante/Raphael clique in Rome. Eventually, though, his relationships with Sebastiano and Pontormo came apart. It was Daniele da Volterra who ended up serving his master in the most lasting way. He created a memorable and insightful bust of the aging Michelangelo that is one of the best records we have of him. Daniele also had the dubious task, at the behest of some of the official Counter Reformation prudes, of painting over the sexual organs of the many nudes in Michelangelo's *Last Judgment,* after his death.

Unlike many artists of the time, Michelangelo never had a typical workshop (*bottega*) of apprentices who came to him for training and played a major role in executing commissions. He generally did not provide products or services that such businesses usually produced, i.e., banners, shields, wedding chests, frescos for small family chapels, etc. He was popular enough to receive more major commissions than he could complete.

To help him, he employed the necessary assistants and collaborators, depending on the nature of the project. He worked essentially alone on the David but had five assistants on the bronze statue of Julius II, thirteen for most of the work on the Sistine ceiling, and over one hundred for the architectural work in Florence in the 1520s. Some of the men Michelangelo employed were friends of many years and had specific skills that he needed. They were never men of great talent, but several did go on to become influential in major artistic projects throughout Italy in the sixteenth century. By all accounts Michelangelo was an involved and often difficult taskmaster.

While he was universally respected and literally worshiped by many, there were others who found him an unpleasant rival and too strong a force in their artistic environment. Thus we see continuous bickering and maneuvering, driven by the jealousy of his artistic rivals and by the principled arrogance of Michelangelo himself. Vasari touches on this jealousy when he describes several incidents that occurred surrounding Michelangelo's work on St. Peter's:

> When the Pope was pressing him to accept the position of chief architect he (Michelangelo) said to them (his rivals) openly one day that they should enlist the help of their friends to do everything in their power to prevent his being put in charge. For if he were, he went on, he would refuse to allow any of them to enter the building. These words, spoken in public, were taken very badly, as may well be imagined; as they explain why they conceive for Michelangelo a bitter hatred which grew daily more intense (as they saw him change all the plans inside and out) till they could scarcely bear to let him live. Everyday, as will be described, they thought out various new ways to torment him.

In 1551 there was another confrontation involving the followers of a rival architect, Sangallo. Vasari describes an incident where the pope had set up a meeting with a number of cardinals and the competing architects:

> So after they had all assembled the Pope told Michelangelo that the deputies alleged that the hemicycle would have little light.
>
> Michelangelo said, "I would like them to speak for themselves."
>
> Cardinal Marchello declared, "Here we are."
>
> Then Michelangelo said to him: "My Lord, above these windows in the vault, which will be made of travertine, are to go three more."
>
> "But you never told us that," the cardinal remarked.
>
> And then Michelangelo announced: "I'm not and I don't intend to be obliged to discuss with your Eminence or anyone else what I ought or intend to do. Your duty is to collect the money and guard it against thieves and you must leave the task of designing the building to me."

Close Personal Relationships

Though Michelangelo was generally a loner, because of his intense and relatively solitary working habits, he from time to time had a few deep and consuming personal relationships. The most significant and famous of these was, of course, with Tommaso di Cavalieri. They met in Rome in 1532, when Michelangelo was fifty-seven and Tommaso was twenty-three. Tommaso was described as having great physical beauty, grace, charm and intelligence. He came from an aristocratic background and in all ways represented the classic ideal male that was such a strong, driving force in Michelangelo's philosophy, his work and (evidently) his fantasies. Tommaso became the center of Michelangelo's affection, and their friendship evolved over the remainder of

Michelangelo's lifetime. Throughout the relationship was a strong theme of Michelangelo's desire to humbly serve the young man.

In a series of passionate and personal poems, letters and very symbolic drawings, Michelangelo expressed his strong feelings of affection for the young nobleman. From Rome in 1533, early in the relationship, Michelangelo wrote:

> ...Far from being a mere babe, as you say of yourself in your letter, you seem to me to have lived on earth a thousand times before. But I should deem myself unborn, or rather still born, and should confess myself disgraced before heaven and earth, if from your letter I had not seen and believed that your lordship would willingly accept some of my drawings. This has caused me much surprise and pleasure no less.

Several years later from Florence he wrote:

> My dear lord—Had I not believed that I had convinced you of the immense, nay, boundless love I bear you, your grave apprehension shown by your letter that I might have forgotten you, as I have written you would seem to me neither strange nor surprising.—But be that as it may, I realize now that I could as soon forget your name as forget the food on which I live—nay I could sooner forget the food on which I live, which unhappily nourishes only the body, than your name, which nourishes body and soul, filling both with such delight that I'm insensible to sorrow or fear of death, while my memory of you endures....

Evidently Michelangelo's feelings for Tommaso were returned, and Tommaso's letters to Michelangelo express his gratitude for having so great a man as Michelangelo show interest in him. He assures Michelangelo of his desire for their friendship.

The deep emotions and fantasies sparked by his attraction for Tommaso must have been a source of great stress and conflict for Michelangelo. His strong Christian and platonic beliefs, his artistic and intellectual fascination with the classical ideal male, and his strong will must have conflicted with his guilt-ridden physical desires to sexually consummate the relationship. There is no clear evidence to enlighten us on the existence, the extent, or the lack of any physical relationship. Most scholars feel that had they become sexually intimate, the guilt Michelangelo would have felt, and his resulting behavior, would have shown up in his letters or other records. My own guess is that the relationship was one of intense emotions and attraction, but was not sexual in nature. Tommaso eventually married, had two sons, and remained a close friend of Michelangelo. He was at Michelangelo's bedside when he died in 1564.

In addition to Tommaso, Michelangelo had a series of close relationships with a number of other young men throughout much of his life. Again, it's not clear whether any of these were at least partly sexual in nature. (Homosexuality was outlawed and officially frowned upon during the Renaissance. However, it was openly acknowledged and accepted in some quarters, particularly in artistic circles. There are records of either gossip or official charges against such artists as Leonardo da Vinci and Botticelli. There was even a well-known and highly regarded artist whose sexual proclivities earned him the working name of "Il Sodoma." In spite of his known sexual preferences, he received papal commissions from Pope Leo X.)

Regardless of whether or not there was a physical element to these relationships, Michelangelo seems to have gotten pleasure from—and, no doubt, had some inner need filled by—having handsome young men around him. They often served as assistants to him. In later years they would recall the almost paternal interest he took in them.

It is clear that throughout his life Michelangelo existed almost entirely in a world of men. Some might say that the rejection by his mother or the conflict with his father may have affected him. Certainly his idealization of the male nude, his interest in ancient myths with homosexual overtones and his belief in the popular Neoplatonic philosophies were consistent with his desire for close male relationships. The exact nature and intensity of these relationships is not known. Although one can conclude that Michelangelo was attracted to other men and may in fact have had sexual relations with some of them, I believe it would be more accurate to portray those relationships as mainly platonic in nature and driven by Michelangelo's emotional and spiritual attachment to the ideal male. Sexually, Michelangelo's life was probably one of mostly sublimation and abstinence.

Michelangelo's one close relationship with a woman came at a time of great personal change and spiritual need. Having left Florence for good in late 1534, Michelangelo soon was at work on an intense and stern religious painting, the *Last Judgment.* He met Vittoria Colonna in Rome during this time, and they immediately became spiritual soul mates and developed a deep admiration and affection for each other.

Vittoria came from a noble heritage and had been married early to a prestigious Marchese who spent most of his time off fighting in the wars. Widowed at age thirty-five, she devoted much of the rest of her life to spiritual and moral matters, often living in convents. She was greatly admired for her knowledge, her spiritual strength and her commitment to the then-reforming Catholic Church. Though not particularly beautiful or even feminine, she struck a chord of need in Michelangelo's life during a very stressful period.

In this relationship as well he humbly expresses a desire to serve her. His letters to her reflect a sense of worship and reverence. In return, she gave him religious and spiritual guidance during a difficult period when Michelangelo was struggling with the balance between his Christianity and his humanism, a balance that was being challenged by the stricter practices of the Counter Reformation. She moved him toward a more deeply religious belief in his later years, particularly toward a focus on the passion of Christ. This was to be expressed in the deeply moving pietàs that he worked on in the 1550s and 1560s.

Their friendship was at times intense, and it provided inspiration and pleasure for both of them. It was, though, of an intellectual and spiritual nature, with no evidence of any physical intimacy. Condivi expresses its importance to Michelangelo:

> ...and she would come to Rome for no other reason than to see Michelangelo; and he in return loved her so much that I remember having heard him say that what grieved him above all else was that when he went to see her as she was passing from this life, he did not kiss her brow or her face but simply her hand. Through her death, he many times felt despair, acting like a man robbed of his senses.

Michelangelo had only a few other relationships with women during his lifetime. All were minor friendships of a more everyday nature. Several of these were with women who had been part of the households of men in Michelangelo's life (i.e., the maidservant of his father and the wife of one of his long-time assistants). Michelangelo showed great compassion and interest in the well-being of these women and made sure that they were taken care of in their old age.

Thus we see that while Michelangelo was often difficult to be around, he had the need for friendship—and he even occasionally would let his emotions out and plunge into deep commitments that filled a real need in his life.

Religious Beliefs

Basic to Michelangelo's character and his values were his strongly held religious beliefs. While he was constantly having to balance his fundamental Christianity against his humanistic tendencies, underneath it all he was a devout member of the powerful Catholic Church. Hence he probably had to deal with some of the conflicts that went along with that faith. While he observed the basic Catholic forms of worship and had a very real hope of heaven, he also no doubt had the guilt of his sins, homosexual instincts and spiritual shortcomings. His faith remained basically firm throughout his life, and in his later years he became more concerned with death and the salvation of his soul. His working life was almost entirely filled with understanding and then depicting, in stone or in paint, the tales of the Bible and the intense drama of Christ and the holy family.

Personality

Michelangelo was often described during his lifetime as having the quality of *terribilità*. Scholars give various meanings to this term, but words like "frightening," "powerful," "unpredictable" and "awesome" give a fairly accurate picture of what the term means. Pope Leo X, who had known Michelangelo for many years, expressed his hesitancy in working with the artist when he said, "He is too violent; one can't deal with him."

As we've seen, Michelangelo was very sensitive, and once offended either flared up or withdrew. He would call people unreliable, swindlers, scoundrels and deceitful, but after a time would resume his relationship with them. He had the well-earned reputation of an often quarrelsome and very private man. However, close examination of his letters and comments by his contemporaries reveals a person who was often considerate and sensitive to the feelings of others. And, importantly, he appears to have had great personal insight into his own vulnerabilities and character. Probably most revealing is a statement attributed to Michelangelo (by a contemporary named Giannotti) when he was declining an invitation to dine with friends:

> You must know that I am, of all men who were ever born, the most inclined to love persons. Whenever I behold someone who possesses any talent or displays any dexterity of mind, who can do or say something more appropriately than the rest of the world, I am compelled to fall in love with him; and then I give myself up to him so entirely that I am no longer my own property, but wholly his...if I were to dine with you...each of you would take from me a portion of myself...and instead of being refreshed and restored to health and gladness...I should be utterly bewildered and distraught, in such ways that for many days to come I should not know in what world I was moving.

His letters show a number of examples of his humanitarianism. He often instructed his family in Florence to give some of the money he sent to them to charities or those in need. And several times he donated funds to poor families for their daughters' dowries so that they could be married off in a reasonable manner. In most of these instances he preferred that his gifts be made quietly, with no public acknowledgment.

At times he also showed very touching consideration for the feelings of others. One rather pithy letter illustrates this as he tries to fire an assistant without hurting the feelings of the boy or his family:

> ...Besides all the other worries I have, I've now got this dung hill of a boy who says that he does not want to waste time, that he wants to learn....But they are good for nothing and have one end in view and nothing else. Please will you have him removed out of my sight because I am so disgusted I can bear it no more. Tell the father to send for him....but if he does not send I will send him away. If you speak to the lad's father tell him kindly about the affair; say that he is a good lad, but that he is too refined and not suited to my service and that he must send for him.

While he often did favors for those in need and was prone to look after those who were down on their luck, there was an always-present hard side to this complex man. He had an underlying distrust of institutions and people that often shows up in his correspondence. In a letter to his nephew in 1545, referring to an investment he was thinking about, he wrote:

> ...I meant buying something, like land belonging to Niccolo della Bucca, or anything else you thought suitable, and not depositing it in a bank at all, because they're all fraudulent.

And again to his nephew, discussing the possible forming of a company:

> But because today there are nothing but frauds, and one can trust nobody, I advise you to proceed slowly....

And in a particularly angry moment, asking his nephew to find him a maid-servant:

> ...and if, in the meantime you could find me a maidservant who is clean and respectable—which is difficult, because they are all pigs and prostitutes—let me know. I pay ten julians a month; I live poorly but I pay well.

His sarcasm could be cutting even to members of his family whom he truly cared for. In an ungrateful letter to his nephew in 1540 he wrote:

> Lionardo—I received three shirts together with your letter, and am very surprised that you should have sent them to me, as they're so coarse that there's not a peasant in Rome who wouldn't be ashamed to wear them. Had they been finer, however, I shouldn't have wanted you to send them, because when I need any I'll send the money to buy them.

Underneath all his emotional ups and downs, Michelangelo was basically a man of great integrity and principle. Although he earned large sums for his work, he was always very careful that he received only what he thought he was worth, and would at times take lesser amounts if his conscience or circumstances so indicated. He went to great lengths to make sure that people didn't think he had overcharged for the work on Julius's tomb. He even worked the last years at no pay, as it had been determined that he had already received enough.

There were occasions when he would forego a salary if he felt it was the right thing to do. During the sack of Rome and the resulting financial problems for Pope Clement VII, he offered to continue work on the Medici projects at no pay. When appointed to be the master architect of St. Peter's (an appointment he resisted), Michelangelo refused to receive any payment, as he felt it was his sacred duty to perform the work, and he didn't want any of his rivals to question his motives. A letter to his brother Buonarroto in 1518 sums up his feelings on the subject of his personal integrity. Writing from Pietra Santa, he said:

> About the business of the road here, tell Jacopo that I'll do whatever his Magnificence pleases and that he'll never find himself cheated over anything he entrusts to me, because in matters of this kind I do not seek my own advantage, but the advantage of my patrons and of my country.

Michelangelo's artistic integrity was strong and uncompromising. He had a clear view of what art should be and the role it should play. He had little time and few positive comments for the opinions or the work of those who disagreed with him.

One interesting side to Michelangelo's character is shown in his increasing status consciousness, particularly in his later years. As he grew older he talked more about the noble background of his family, even to the point of considerable exaggeration. He was very conscious of his appearance and of having the kind of possessions (i.e., a horse instead of a mule) and property that would indicate his high status. He did not want to be looked at as just another artist or artisan. In this vein, much of his advice to Lionardo about buying a house involves prestige and family honor:

> About buying the house, I reaffirm the same, that is, that you should seek to buy an imposing house for 1,500 or 2,000 *scudi* if possible in our quarter...I say this, because an imposing house in the city redounds much more to one's credit, because it is more in evidence than farmlands, since we are, after all, citizens descended from a very noble family.

Early in his career, he signed his letters Michelangelo Scultore. A letter to his nephew in 1548 shows his changed thinking on this:

> Tell the priest not to address me anymore as 'Michelangelo Sculptor' because here I'm only known as Michelangelo Buonarroti, and that if a Florentine citizen wants to have an altar-piece painted he must find a painter—and that I was never a painter or a sculptor like those who set up shop for that purpose. I always

> refrain from doing so out of respect for my father and brothers; although I have served three popes, it has been under compulsion.

Michelangelo was a complex man of huge ego, intense focus, deep beliefs, brilliant intellect, considerable psychological problems, not much patience, normal needs and a concern for his family and his fellow human beings. Above all else, though, what shine through are his strong will power and sense of self. These are most clearly seen in his artistic integrity and his commitment to pursuing his artistic vision in an uncompromising way. But it shows up, I think, in a more everyday kind of way when, in 1549, he writes to his nephew about some business affairs and his choice of a wife. He concludes the letter:

> I think that's all. Reply when you've come to a decision, *and never dance to anyone's tune if it doesn't entirely content you.*

Michelangelo's Works

Michelangelo was the unrivaled and acknowledged master in three arts: sculpture, painting and architecture. He brought the same high degree of intensity, intellect, creativity and demand for perfection to all three art forms. It is this amazing breadth that has made Michelangelo such a significant and pivotal figure in the history of art. His friend and biographer, Vasari, captured the wide scope of his talents:

> —he who transcends and eclipses every other, is the divine Michelangelo Buonarroti, who takes the first place, not in one of these arts only, but in all three. This master surpasses and excels not only all those artists who have well nigh surpassed nature herself, but even all the most famous masters of antiquity, who did, beyond all doubt, vanquish her most gloriously: he alone has triumphed over the latter as over the earlier, and even over nature herself.

Like all great artists, as Michelangelo grew and matured, his work continued to change. Looking across his nearly seventy-five years of creative output, we can see him both as the culminating and leading artist of the High Renaissance and as the innovating father of the more stylistic, imaginative and emotional approach to painting and sculpture known as Mannerism. This in turn led to the Baroque period of the 1600 and 1700s, when art became even more extravagant, dynamic and ornate. He was truly an innovator and was not at all afraid to move beyond the greatness that preceded him and explore new approaches and new styles that then served as the standard for future generations.

Michelangelo's works have been an important inspiration for hundreds of prominent artists over the past 450 years ranging from the leading Baroque architect Bernini, to the innovative English painter J.M.W. Turner, and even to the versatile twentieth-century master Henri Matisse. Perhaps most importantly, though, was the influence Michelangelo had on the preeminent French sculptor Auguste Rodin (1840–1917). Rodin traveled to Italy early in his career and was overwhelmed and motivated by Michelangelo's works. He used several of them as direct inspirations for some of his greatest works—

specifically his *Gates of Hell* (from *Last Judgment*) and his The Age of Bronze (from Michelangelo's *Dying Slave*).

His technical skills appeared at an early age, as the young boy was constantly drawing and making renditions of the masterful works that surrounded him in Florence. He continued to draw throughout his life and considered it a basic skill that had to be mastered if one was to create great art. His inventiveness and creativity evolved over time, but he always felt it was necessary to constantly develop his basic technical skills or, as he said, "to learn the alphabets of his profession." The drawings Michelangelo made, in fact, constitute a body of work that could stand alone as a major artistic achievement. They were mainly sketches done in preparation for his various sculpture or painting projects, but there are also several very detailed and sensitive drawings that are complete in their own right. He was undoubtedly one of the great draftsmen of all time.

After early training in drawing and fresco painting, Michelangelo turned to sculpture. This continued as the core of his artistic work throughout his life. During several long periods he focused his efforts almost exclusively on major painting commissions, and during his later years he spent considerable time on architectural projects. But he always returned to his first love, carving stone.

Sculpture

Michelangelo claimed that his passion for carving stone came about because as an infant he was put out to nurse with the wife of a stonecutter in the village of Settignano. Vasari claims that Michelangelo told him jokingly:

> Giorgio if my brains are any good at all it's because I was born in the pure air of your Arezzo countryside, just as with my mother's milk I was sucked in the hammer and chisels I used for my statues.

He was exposed to the stonecutter's trade as a youth in Florence, and by fourteen he was part of the Medici household and working under the aging sculptor Bertoldo. A work from this period, *The Madonna of the Stairs,* clearly shows the influence of the earlier Renaissance master Donatello—just ten years later, at age twenty-four, after the completion of his first pietà, he was widely recognized as the leading sculptor in Italy.

Michelangelo's thoughts on the supremacy of sculpture as an art form are summed up in a letter he wrote to the Florentine scholar and critic Benedetto Varchi in 1547:

> ...I admit that it seems to me that painting may be held to be good in the degree in which it approximates relief (sculpture), and relief to be bad in the degree in which it approximates to painting. I used therefore to think that painting derived its light from sculpture and that between the two the difference was as that between the sun and the moon.—By sculpture I mean that which is fashioned by the effort of cutting away, that which is fashioned by the method of building up being like unto painting....If he who wrote that painting is nobler than sculpture understood as little about the other things of which he writes—my maid servant could have expressed them better.

He approached his work in an intense and straightforward manner. He generally started by making studies of his subject in the form of drawings, or sometimes rough wax or clay models. After his thoughts were visualized, he would begin to sculpt the marble. Here his conceptual approach was unique. He attacked the stone and cut away the excess material that surrounded and encased the subject, which he visualized as inside the block of marble. His was a process of "freeing" what he felt to be the figure inside the stone. In contrast, most of the sculptors before him (including Donatello and Ghiberti) had approached sculpture as more of a building-up process.

Benvenuto Cellini described the process Michelangelo used this way:

> The best method ever was used by the great Michelangelo; after having drawn the principal view on the block, one begins to remove the marble from this side as if one were working a relief and in this way, step by step, one brings to light the whole figure.

Vasari describes the method by comparing Michelangelo's process to pulling a figure up out of the water, slowly revealing the parts as they emerge. Starting from the front, Michelangelo would chip away the stone and the figure would emerge and be "liberated" from inside. His statues thus tend to have a main front view, even though many of them are freestanding and can be viewed from all sides.

The tools of the sculptor were relatively simple but difficult to master. There was a series of chisels that became increasingly refined as the artist needed more detail. These were struck with a rough hammer or mallet as the artist chipped away at the "excess" material. In most cases assistants were employed to rough out the figure with a punch or a flat chisel. (Michelangelo probably used assistants for some of this preliminary work, but to a lesser degree than most other artists of the time.) In the later stages, tooth or clawed chisels were used for more detailed work. A bowed drill was also used to cut out pieces from the marble and to form hair curls or patterns as necessary. Later in the process, files and abrasives were used to smooth the stone and achieve the desired finish. It was tough work. There was danger involved, both from the strength and sharpness of the tools that were used and from the massive weight of the material itself.

Michelangelo's work habits were legendary. Being somewhat of a loner anyway, he would retreat to his studio and work furiously for hours on end. Vasari gives us a picture of the artist's dedication and intensity:

> For example as a young man he would be so intent on his work that he used to make do with a little bread and wine, and he was still doing the same when he grew old, until the time he painted the *Last Judgment* in the chapel, when he used to take his refreshments in the evening after the day's work was finished, but always very frugally.—This sober way of life kept him very alert and in want of very little sleep, and very often, being unable to rest, he would get up at night and set to work with his chisel, wearing a hat made of thick paper with a candle burning over the middle of his head so that he could see what he was doing and have his hands free.

Even in his old age he kept up an amazing pace. A visitor reported that:

> Michelangelo, even in frail health, could hammer more chips out of very hard marble in a quarter hour than three young stone carvers could do in three or four, which has to be seen to be believed, and he went at it with such impetuosity and fury that I thought the whole work must go to pieces, knocking off with one blow chips three or four fingers thick, so close to the mark that, if he had gone slightly beyond, he ran the danger of ruining everything.

Many of Michelangelo's sculptures remain unfinished. There has been much speculation and theorizing as to the reasons for this. Most of the works he did finish were done in his early years (e.g., *Bacchus, Roman Pietà, David*) and a few more were completed as parts of larger projects—e.g., Julius's tomb and the Medici Chapel. The rest were left in various stages of partial completion. Vasari says:

> For Michelangelo used to say that if he had had to be satisfied with what he did, then he would have sent out very few statues, or rather none at all. This was because he had so developed his art and judgment that when on revealing one of his figures he saw the slightest error he would abandon it and run to start working on another block, trusting that it would not happen again.

A few writers have argued that some of the works were meant to be left "unfinished" and that they were in fact complete works of art as they appear. I believe there are more practical reasons to explain the phenomenon. In several instances Michelangelo was simply pulled off a project and coerced to work on other things, as when Julius II called him from Florence to come to Rome in the early 1500s. On other occasions Michelangelo was in such demand that he simply never got around to finishing a work, which was nevertheless happily accepted by his grateful patrons.

Regardless, these unfinished works give us insight into Michelangelo's working techniques and his rare and powerful expressive skills. On a number of the unfinished works one can see examples of the various stages of the sculpting process, as he uses more refined chisels to bring increasingly greater finish and detail to the work. More interesting still, though, is the powerful sense of emotion that comes from the works that are only crudely roughed out. For example, the *St. Matthew* (started in 1503 and never completed) and *The Four Slaves* (started around 1520) show these roughed-out figures literally struggling to escape from their encasement in the marble. Even in this unfinished state, Michelangelo was able to convey movement and power.

Today there are approximately forty known sculptural works of Michelangelo in existence, though there is some controversy over a few of them. Many of the statues are massive works that took years to complete. There were probably another five or so major works that have either been lost or destroyed. Together they constitute a truly colossal output, especially when considered in the light of Michelangelo's work in other media.

The vast majority of his works depict religious, biblical or mythological figures. Eight of them include Christ and his mother, five of the Christ child and Mary (called Madonnas) and three of the dead Christ and Mary (called pietàs). The depth of Michelangelo's religious beliefs, and the nature of his patrons' commissions, clearly drove the choices of subject matter. Most works were highly symbolic and were intended by the patron as an expression of a particular thought or message.

His works consistently reflect his knowledge of anatomy and the intricate structure of the human body. In closely examining the details of the hands and limbs of the *David,* the *Moses* and the *Louvre Slaves,* one can almost feel the power of the muscles and the inner workings of the body. Michelangelo's fascination with the classical nude male is also a common theme which runs through many of his works. In these pieces he evokes a sensuality and power that is absent from his female statues, which are often colder, more distant and somewhat stiff in nature.

All artists from the sixteenth century on have had to work in Michelangelo's shadow. His innovations in depicting inner strength, powerful emotions and larger than life human qualities were a rich source of inspiration for those that came after him. People were in awe of his sculptures during his lifetime, and today experts and layman alike still see them as unmatched in their profound quality.

Painting

Michelangelo is famous for telling Pope Julius II that painting was not his art and that he didn't want to paint the Sistine Chapel ceiling. Nonetheless, Michelangelo did in fact paint at certain periods of his life, and to this art form he brought outstanding creativity and technical skills.

Most of Michelangelo's painting was done during a few intense and highly productive periods. The vast majority of his work as a painter was done in fresco on three major projects: the Sistine ceiling, the *Last Judgment* and the two frescos in the Pauline Chapel. All of these are within several hundred yards of each other in the Vatican in Rome. Each was a monumental effort, both in the startling quality of the outcome and the incredible amount of work required.

Michelangelo seldom worked in media other than fresco. Only two or three non-fresco paintings have survived, including the powerful *Doni Madonna*, now in the Uffizi Gallery in Florence (painted in tempera), and the still controversial and partially completed *Entombment* (painted in oil) that is in the National Gallery in London. Both of these paintings show strong sculpture-like figures. This individualizing of style, or "manner," eventually became the central theme of the emerging artistic movement that became known as Mannerism.

Since Michelangelo's greatest paintings are frescos, however, let us turn our attention to this art form. Fresco is a technique of painting with pigments dissolved in water on freshly laid plaster. As plaster and paint dry they become completely integrated.

The specific technique of fresco involved covering an area of masonry with a preliminary layer of plaster. This was just rough enough to provide a bond for a final layer of very fine plaster, which would be added later. Then either a freehand sketch of the whole composition was drawn on the wall or a full-scale cartoon prepared and its outline transferred to the plaster by pressing through it with a knife. Another method, called pouncing, involved blowing charcoal dust through holes pricked in the paper. Next, over the initial layer, enough of a final thin layer of plaster (the *intonaco*) was applied to contain a day's work. The artist then set to work with water-based pigments while the plaster was still damp; this allowed the colors to sink in before the plaster became dry and fixed. All the paint in all the necessary colors had to be put on that particular section before the plaster dried because once it had dried with the absorbed paint in it, the paint could not be removed. (It was possible, however, to put further details or additions on the work by applying dry paints on top of the unabsorbed plaster.)

Thus Michelangelo had to plan his work very carefully, having all the preliminary drawing done, the cartoons made and the colors prepared so that he could complete each section of the work in a single hectic painting session. Fresco painting is an unforgiving medium that allows for few mistakes or hesitation. It requires sustained energy, as the artist works constantly during the ten to twelve-hour period before the plaster dries. Vasari commented on this difficult medium:

> The fresco painter has to do in one day what the sculptor does in one month, otherwise time exposes the reworking, the patching, the touching up, colors added or reapplied in a dry state, which is ignoble.

Needless to say, fresco work was extremely difficult. Michelangelo employed relatively few assistants to grind the pigments for his paints, mix the plaster, hold up the cartoons for the pouncing and do some of the simple decorative painting. The physical strain was significant, particularly when working on the Sistine ceiling, where he stood bending back, paint dripping in his face for hours on end. In a poem written at the time, he satirically described the situation:

> My belly's pushed by force beneath my chin
> My beard toward heaven, I feel the back of my brain
> Upon my neck, I grow the breast of a harpy;
> My brush, above my face continually
> Makes it a splendid floor by dripping down.
> My loins have penetrated to my paunch,
> My rump's a crupper, and as a counterweight,
> And pointless to the unseen steps I go.
> In front of me my skin is being stretched
> While it flows up behind and forms a knot,
> And I am bending like a Syrian bow.

The work on the Sistine ceiling took four years (1508–1512). It was the largest mural ever commissioned, and it took Michelangelo over five hundred actual painting days (not counting doing the drawings and other preparations) to complete the work. It is monumental in concept, amazingly rich in detail and almost beyond belief in the variety of characters and experiences that are portrayed. The whole work ties together Michelangelo's skills in architecture, sculpture and painting. Many of the figures are almost monuments themselves. (The recent restoration of the ceiling has further revealed the superb quality of the masterpiece. We can now appreciate Michelangelo as the great colorist that he was. It is filled with rich and unique greens, blues, reds and golds, making up a glorious mosaic of startling beauty.) Vasari perhaps captured the feeling best when he wrote:

> When the work was thrown open, the whole world came running to see what Michelangelo had done; and certainly it was such as to make everyone speechless with astonishment. Then the pope, exalted by the results and encouraged to undertake even more gracious enterprises, generously rewarded Michelangelo with rich gifts and money.

The Sistine ceiling frescos were the most influential work of art since Giotto came on the scene some two hundred years earlier. The leading artists of the time, including Raphael, Leonardo and the Venetian master Titian, immediately started making drawings from it. The work soon became an academy of drawing for artists of the world. It has been a source of wonder and inspiration to artists and the public ever since.

Twenty-four years later, in 1536, Michelangelo began painting again, this time on the seven-year project of the *Last Judgment* to be painted on the altar wall of the same Sistine Chapel. Michelangelo had tried to avoid the commission, but he was coerced into it by Pope Paul III. He began the work when he was sixty-one years old.

Michelangelo cuts significant new ground with this work. Gone are some of the aspects of proportion, harmony and perspective that we see in his earlier work. The *Last Judgment* gives a picture of a disturbed, less beautiful human race. This is probably a reflection of the worry and discontent in the artist's life. However, Michelangelo is at this time more confident working in the fresco medium. We see more experimentation and more additions that were applied after the plaster had hardened.

Again, the recent restoration has revealed beautiful colors. The blue sky is unusually rich, and generally the colors are warmer than on the ceiling. This is probably a reflection of Michelangelo's exposure to the Venetian school of painting when he visited that city some years before.

From correspondence at the time, we see that the work was very difficult for the aging Michelangelo. It was particularly hard for him to climb up and down the scaffolding that covered the immense wall. There was some interruption of the work in 1539 and 1540, but he was almost continuously at work on the huge project for the full seven years. Working from a vast number of drawings, he painted nearly four hundred individual figures.

The unveiling occurred in late 1541. Vasari gives us a sense of how it was received:

> When the *Last Judgment* was revealed it was seen that Michelangelo had not only excelled the masters who had worked there previously but had also striven to excel even the vaulting that he had made so famous; for the *Last Judgment* was finer by far, and in it Michelangelo out stripped himself....All these details bear witness to the sublime power of Michelangelo's art, in which skill was combined with a natural, inborn grace. Michelangelo's figures stir the emotions even of people who know nothing about painting, let alone those who understand.

Even before the *Last Judgment* was completed, and while Michelangelo was trying to finish the work on Julius's tomb, Pope Paul III was making plans for another painting project for Michelangelo. Paul wanted him to paint two frescos on the side walls of the small, newly built Pauline Chapel in the Vatican. The first fresco, *The Conversion of St. Paul* was begun in 1542 and completed in 1545. A year later he began the second work, *The Crucifixion of St. Peter*, and completed it in 1550 at age seventy-five. The works show a unique sense of composition and depict great energy and emotion. Again, Vasari gives us a glimpse of how a contemporary viewed the works:

> ...Michelangelo painted *The Conversion of St. Paul* with Jesus Christ above and a multitude of nude angels making the most graceful movements while below dazed and terrified Paul had fallen from his horse to the ground The other scene contains *The Crucifixion of St. Peter* who is depicted in a figure of rare beauty fastened naked upon the cross....Here too there are many remarkably judicious and beautiful details. As has been said elsewhere, Michelangelo concentrated his energies on achieving absolute perfection in what he could do best. So there are no landscapes to be seen in these scenes nor any trees, buildings or other embellishments and variations; for he never spent time on such things, lest perhaps he should degrade his genius. These scenes, which he painted at the age of seventy-five, were the last pictures he did; and they cost him a great deal of effort, because painting, especially in fresco, is no work for men who have passed a certain age.

Architecture

Michelangelo's work in architecture began with his attempts to design structures to hold his sculptural works. With his supreme self-confidence, he moved easily into more complex projects and eventually into comprehensive and complete architectural commissions. His work reflects his inventiveness and a proclivity to move beyond the old rules.

Renaissance architecture had evolved from, but still closely followed, tenets set down by the ancient Roman Vitruvius. He expounded the concept of decorum—fitting architectural solutions to the requirements of function and type. He spoke of the importance of utility, strength, beauty, symmetry and the modular relationship of the parts to the whole. This rationality and orderliness appealed to the Renaissance architects and was the basic doctrine behind much of their work. The great structures of Brunelleschi (1377–1446) that were built throughout Florence were the supreme examples of this pure Renaissance architecture.

Michelangelo was influenced by all this but moved beyond it and broke the rules. He produced designs and finished works that were less rational, more soaring, more inspiring and often more beautiful than what had been created before. This originally, in turn, allowed others that followed to move off in new directions. Vasari captures this important point in discussing Michelangelo's work on the new sacristy for San Lorenzo in Florence:

> He wanted to execute the work in imitation of the old sacristy made by Filippo Brunelleschi but with different decorative features; and so he did the ornamentation in a composite order, in a style more varied and more original than any other master, ancient or modern, has ever been able to achieve for the beautiful cornices, capitals, bases, doors, tabernacles, and tombs were extremely novel, and in them he departed a great deal from the kind of architecture regulated by proportion, order, and rule which other artists did according to common usage and following Vitruvius and the works of antiquity but from which Michelangelo wanted to break away.
>
> The license he allowed himself has served as a great encouragement to others to follow his example; and subsequently we have seen the creation of new kinds of fantastic ornamentations containing more of the grotesque than of rule or reason; thus all artists are under a great and permanent obligation to Michelangelo, seeing that he broke the bonds and chains that had previously confined them to the creation of traditional forms.

Michelangelo's main architectural efforts can be looked at in two major groupings: the work for the Medici in Florence (1516–1534) and the variety of projects he undertook in Rome after moving there in 1534.

It was Pope Leo X's desire to glorify his own Medici family that brought about Michelangelo's series of architectural commissions in Florence. The first project involved building a facade on the Medici Church of San Lorenzo in Florence. This was a most prestigious commission, and the fact that it would likely include major sculpture made it an appealing challenge to Michelangelo. The facade was never built, but Michelangelo's design for it shows his emerging skill as an architect. His model for this facade is still in existence; it is his first complete architectural design, and it shows Michelangelo already moving beyond the classical practices of his predecessors.

The Medici soon had Michelangelo working on another family project, the Medici Chapel (the new sacristy attached to San Lorenzo). Here Michelangelo, for the first time, got involved in the design and building of the complete structure. The basic design was modeled after Brunelleschi's old sacristy on the other side of the church. But since this new structure was to hold Michelangelo's sculptures of the dead Medici princes, he built in an innovative mezzanine for a greater feeling of spaciousness. The result is a structure that is based on Brunelleschi's tradition but is filled with innovative concepts that give it a freshness and feeling of unity, making it one of the true gems of Renaissance architecture.

Michelangelo's final work for the Medici was to be his most unusual and most creative: the Laurentian Library. In 1524 Pope Clement VII asked Michelangelo to submit the design for a library to hold the famous manuscripts that had been collected by the Medici. This was an unusual project from the start, as a letter from Michelangelo to his agent in Rome shows:

> I learned...that his Holiness...wishes the design for the library to be by my hand. I have no information about it nor do I know where he wants to build it....I will do what I can, although it's not my profession.

Work progressed with major interruptions until Michelangelo left for Rome in 1534. It was only finished years later, when Michelangelo was an old man in Rome. He never saw the completed structure.

The library is part of the upper story of the Cloisters of San Lorenzo. There are really two interconnected parts to the work. The reading room is an unusually beautiful long hall, with special desks that are part of the overall design. Walls and windows are a perfect complement to the desks, and the entire room is pulled together by the elaborate terra cotta floor and the sturdy but ornate ceiling.

However, it is the vestibule and the staircase leading up to the library that really make this one of Michelangelo's most unusual creations. The staircase underwent a number of revisions in the course of the project, and each of these changes shows Michelangelo's great inventiveness and willingness to try something new. The final design, which Michelangelo sent from Rome, is truly unusual, even bizarre. There are actually three parallel staircases—the outer ones having no railing. There is a curving gracefulness about the inner stairway that gives the whole design a strange beauty. Though not very practical by normal standards, the stairway broke new ground, both in its uniqueness and in its use as a structural feature in the architectural design. The grand staircases of the late Baroque period owe much to this unusual work.

Michelangelo's Roman architectural activities began in 1538. His initial assignment came from Pope Paul III, who asked him to design a new civic center for Rome on the ancient Capoline Hill. This hill (the Campidoglio), which had been the ceremonial focal point in ancient Rome, had fallen into disrepair. It contained several buildings but was generally nonfunctional, as well as aesthetically nondescript. Michelangelo's design for the area involved a completely new plan, including a uniquely patterned surface for the piazza, an innovative design for the facade of one of the existing buildings, and a great external double staircase for another. The center of the piazza was built upon the then-unusual form of the oval. (Michelangelo invented a compass for use in drawing the oval patterns. It is these patterns that give the entire space a feeling of openness and at the same time provide a focus for the equestrian statue of Marcus Aurelius that once stood at the center.)

The overall conception and design of the piazza mark a major turning point in city planning. The beautiful and intimate details of the individual parts fit perfectly into the grandeur of the entire space. It remains today as a fitting symbol of the power of Rome. Nevertheless, very little of Michelangelo's design was executed while he was alive. Work was done intermittently, partially with the help of Tommaso di Cavalieri, and was finally completed in the mid-seventeenth century.

In 1546 Michelangelo won the competition for the completion of the facade for the Farnese Palace, the largest in Rome. Over the next four years, with the help of an assistant, Michelangelo designed an unusual upper cornice for the external facade and made major innovations in the inner courtyard of this important palace. His inventiveness on this project demonstrated once again his willingness to move beyond existing practices and create new solutions.

Work on the new St. Peter's was started in 1506 by one of Michelangelo's rivals, the architect Bramante, under orders from Pope Julius II. After Bramante's death in 1514, there was a series of successors, including Raphael. The last of these, Sangallo, was chief architect for twenty-six years. Little progress was made, however, mainly because of a lack of funds. Toward the end of that period (estimated 1540–1546) a large model was built and quite a lot of work was done, building upon the earlier construction by Bramante.

When Sangallo died in 1546, Pope Paul II asked Michelangelo to take over as architect of St. Peter's. This was a significant honor for Michelangelo, but it was also a major new responsibility for the aging artist. Michelangelo initially resisted the Pope's request, as he was already seventy-one years old. He finally agreed but insisted he would only work without salary. This, he said, was for his spiritual good, but it also made him less vulnerable to his jealous rivals.

He quickly indicated his dislike of Sangallo's model and started to pull down much of what Sangallo had built, thus starting a long-running feud with a group of Sangallo followers who remained loyal to the earlier plan. A letter in 1547 is particularly rich in revealing Michelangelo's thoughts at the time:

> Messeur Bartolommeo, dear friend—one cannot deny that Bramante was as skilled in architecture as anyone since the time of the ancients. He it was who laid down the first plan of St. Peter's, not full of confusion, but clear, simple, luminous and detached in such a way that it in no wise impinged upon the Palace. It was held to be a beautiful design, and manifestly still is, so that anyone who has departed from Bramante's arrangement, as Sangallo has done, has

> departed from the true course; and that this is so can be seen by anyone who looks at his model with unprejudiced eyes.
>
> He (meaning Sangallo), with that outer ambulatory of his, in the first place takes away all the light from Bramante's plan; and not only this, but does so when it has no light of its own, and so many dark lurking places above and below that they afford ample opportunity for innumerable rascalities such as the hiding of exiles, the coining of base money, the raping of nuns and other rascalities, so that at night, when the said church closes, it would need twenty-five men to seek out those who remain hidden inside, whom it would be a job to find. Then, there would be this other drawback—that by surrounding the said composition of Bramante's with the addition shown in the model, the Pauline Chapel, the offices of the Piombo, the Ruota and many other buildings would have to be demolished; nor do I think that the Sistine Chapel would survive intact. As regards that part of the outer ambulatory that has been built, which they say cost 100,000 *scudi,* this is not true, because it could be done for 16,000, and little would be lost if it were pulled down, because the dressed stones in the foundations could not come in more useful and the fabric would be 200,000 *scudi* to the good in cost and three hundred years in time. This is as I see it and without prejudice—because to gain my point would be greatly to my detriment. And if you are able to persuade the pope of this, you will be doing me a favor, because I'm not feeling very well. P.S. If Sangallo's model is adhered to, it also follows that all that has been done in my time may be pulled down which would be a great loss.

When Michelangelo took over in 1547, much of the inner central part of the church was already built. Michelangelo quickly produced an innovative design for the exterior of the church and for the colossal dome that was to be the crowning glory to this most important church in Christendom. He also simplified the interior by cutting out some of the excess peripheral areas and was able to save significant costs. He simplified the earlier designs and provided an exterior structure that is at the same time fittingly grandiose, architecturally innovative, inspirational and practical.

The dome he designed was originally based on the beautiful dome of Brunelleschi on the cathedral in Florence. The drum (inner part) was finished in 1557. Michelangelo then had a wooden model made of the dome, which was to be hemispherical in shape. It had pairs of exterior columns supporting the bottom sections with the curved surface leading up to a large and elaborate lantern structure on top. This design was modified during construction to the more pointed shape we see today. The main construction on

Michelangelo's designs occurred after his death, with the dome being completed in 1590 and the lantern in 1593. The dome is widely acclaimed as the best and most monumental ever built. It became the model for St. Paul's Cathedral in London, for the U.S. Capitol in Washington, D.C., and for countless other buildings of public importance.

The church we see today is different from what Michelangelo envisioned. In the early 1600s a long nave and accompanying side bays were added to the central basilica part that Michelangelo constructed. This addition does take away some of the grandeur of the huge dome as one approaches it from the front across St. Peter's Square.

Michelangelo continued working on this project up to his death at age eighty-nine. It is one of his most significant legacies.

Michelangelo's other architectural efforts in his later years were of less significance than the three I have discussed. However, each of these demonstrated his capacity to innovate and create unique designs that have inspired architects ever since.

Michelangelo's work in architecture has been one of his major contributions to the arts. His creations were not just beautiful and functional; they expressed his sculptor's feel for volume and mass, and hence have a feeling of solidness, monumentality and scale. Bernini, the seventeenth century architect, respected Michelangelo's architectural skills and works above all his other creations saying that "Since architecture is pure design, Michelangelo was a divine architect."

In looking at the breadth of Michelangelo's work, across all his art forms—sculpture, painting, architecture and drawing—one senses the unique coming together of extraordinary creativity and profound insight. He knew the basics of his art—the material, the technique, the history—and he developed his technical skills to near perfection. To this knowledge and skill base he brought a self-assured sense of innovation and psychological knowledge of humanity. Out of all this came works that are as awe-inspiring today as they were nearly five hundred years ago.

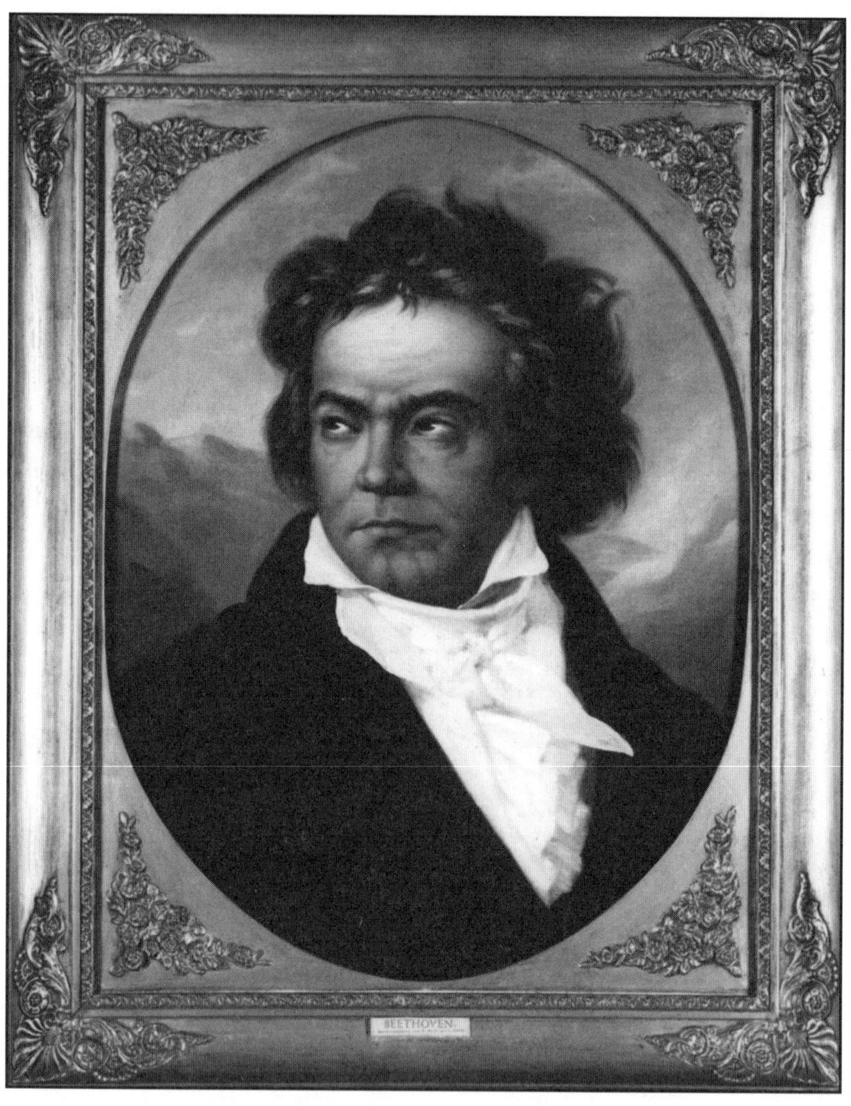

Beethoven at about the age of forty-eight. During this period he is deeply involved in legal battles over his nephew and is working on his Ninth Symphony.

Painting by Ferdinand Schimon
By permission of the Beethoven-Haus Bonn

Ludwig van Beethoven (1770–1827)

The fifty-six years of Ludwig van Beethoven's life took place during a period of major turmoil and change on the European continent. He lived in a time of great intellectual and philosophical ferment, of major political upheaval, of intense and brutal military activity and of significant social and economic rearranging. The flow of events stemming from the liberating thinking of the Enlightenment, the drama of the French Revolution, the ensuing Napoleonic Wars and the famous Congress of Vienna, give this period special historical significance.

For the people of the time, though, the period was one of confusion, terror, upheaval, military campaigns, sometimes lifted spirits and often dashed hopes.

Musically, this period was also one of important change. The very nature of music moved from the structured, well-defined and elegant Classical style to the more personal, expressive and emotional Romantic style. During these years the venue for performance moved from the salon and private residence toward the concert hall, thus expanding the audience and opening the way for music to become more of a business. Concurrently, the publishing of music for commercial purposes grew, influencing composer decisions on what kind of music to write. In addition, the roles of musician, performer and composer moved from being mainly dependent on the desires of wealthy patrons toward a more independent status.

Beethoven was deeply affected by these historic changes taking place around him. In many ways he was a participant in them, for the underlying intellectual and philosophical forces that drove much of the political change were also the foundation for many of Beethoven's beliefs and his outlook on life.

This complex man played a central role in changing the very direction of music. He was the right man in the right place at the right time. In hindsight, we can see him as the key transitional figure in the move from the great Classical tradition of Mozart and Haydn into the period of Romanticism and such composers as Berlioz and Brahms, who dominated Western music for the next hundred years.

While change and turmoil swirled around him, Beethoven was almost constantly dealing with a seemingly endless chain of problems and frustrations in his personal life. Although he possessed great musical powers, had many friends, was generally well off financially and enjoyed wide acclaim, his life was basically one of struggle. As a youth he had a series of family troubles. He suffered from poor health most of his life, had an erratic temper that affected his friendships, and while in his thirties essentially lost his hearing. He never did have a satisfying relationship with a woman and was constantly dissatisfied with his living arrangements. In his later years he became tragically involved in an ugly and lengthy battle over the guardianship of his nephew.

Even in his composing, Beethoven struggled. He was extremely committed to his work, but it did not come easily. Unlike Mozart and others who tended to get it right the first time, Beethoven was constantly doing sketches, drafts, revisions and last-minute changes to properly capture his unique musical vision.

From this complex and unusual genius, who lived in such extraordinary times, has come some of the greatest, most innovative and uplifting musical creations ever written. His large body of work shows mastery of many musical forms: symphony, opera, concerto, song, religious mass, chamber pieces and solo instrumental works. His large creative output continues to provide a standard of excellence and inspiration nearly two hundred years later. Almost forgotten now is the fact that Beethoven was a highly acclaimed pianist, regarded in his day as one of the world's best.

Beethoven spent most of his adult years in Vienna, the seat of the once-powerful Hapsburg Empire. Vienna was then the music capital of Europe. He moved in high circles and often depended on the noble class for his livelihood. But, unlike many of his musical predecessors, he felt himself to be someone special, entitled to be viewed as noble in his own right. He had a huge ego and was often outspoken regarding the extent of his musical genius; and, hence, his personal importance. His lofty ideals and belief in his own destiny resulted in a high but sometimes inconsistent level of artistic and personal integrity.

Over the years something of a Beethoven myth has grown up around this principled, brooding and strange musical genius. The facts of his life have been well researched, and there are numerous books and articles that analyze him from many different angles. We are fortunate to have a rich and varied array of source material available to us that helps to reveal not only the facts but also the thoughts and feelings of this complicated man.

Beethoven was a prolific but not very elegant letter writer. He didn't particularly like to write. "I would rather write 10,000 [musical] notes than one letter of the alphabet," he wrote in 1820. Nevertheless, over fifteen hundred of his letters survive. Some of these were written by others and signed by Beethoven when he was ill. The letters provide a wealth of factual information and give us a glimpse of his thinking and character. They deal with personal and family issues, provide insight into business negotiations with publishers, and sometimes give us a look into his musical thoughts. Occasionally, his rather wild and often coarse sense of humor shows through.

Also of great importance in understanding Beethoven are his so-called "conversation books." After about 1818, because of his deafness, he used notebooks to communicate with his friends and acquaintances. He would carry these books with him, and people would write out their comments or questions. Beethoven would often reply verbally, so reading these conversation books is often like listening to one end of a telephone conversation. Still, they are a very valuable resource in understanding the everyday life of Beethoven. They are filled with talk of the daily musical life of Vienna, gossip, occasional personal notes and even shopping lists.

There is also a variety of other surviving documents. Beethoven kept a memorandum book, much like a diary, during several key periods of his life. These books contain information on personal expenditures and travel as well as emotional and philosophical thoughts that give us great insight into his mind during particularly troubling periods. We also have some very special and significant letters from Beethoven's own hand that mark major turning points in his life.

Beethoven's Times

Beethoven lived during an extraordinary time in history. The period encompassed two great revolutions (American, 1776–1783 and French, 1789–1799) that changed forever humankind's outlook on how people should be governed. For nearly fifteen years after the last of these revolutions, Napoleon led his armies back and forth across Europe in the name of glory, liberty, equality, fraternity and reform. Yet he turned out to be an egomaniacal dictator who brought defeat and disaster to his country, humiliation to himself, and death to hundreds of thousands of people.

Underlying much of this revolutionary call for reform and the longing for a more equal and just society was a school of thought and a view of humankind known as the Enlightenment. These enlightened ideas served as the base for much of the intellectual and philosophical debate of the eighteenth century. They also led directly to many of the demands for change in the political systems.

All of this was, of course, heavily influential on Beethoven.

Europe in the 1700s

Europe in the eighteenth century was very different from the Europe of today and even from that of fifty years ago. Germany, for instance, was a loose association of some three hundred petty sovereignties ruled by secular or ecclesiastical princes. Together they made up the Holy Roman Empire, which was overseen by the Hapsburgs from their court in Vienna. In fact, as Voltaire observed, it was neither Holy, Roman, nor an empire. (Rivaling Austria for ultimate control over the German lands was Prussia, centered in Berlin, with its severe and militaristic traditions.)

These small Germanic sovereignties were quite autonomous, and their rulers built up independent courts and cultural lives that reflected their own interests. Many became thriving centers of artistic life that provided a welcoming atmosphere and a decent living for artists and musicians. It was into such a small sovereignty (the Electorate of Cologne, centered in Bonn) that Beethoven was born in 1770.

France during the 1700s was still a Bourbon monarchy burdened with generally dissipated and luxury-loving rulers, outmoded institutions and a dwindling treasury. Significantly, though, it was home to some of the great thinkers of the century. It was the French philosophers who were to develop, and eventually write of, enlightened ideas about human rights and about the importance of reason and rationality. This enlightened body of thought would lead to the great revolutions at the end of the century.

To the east, Russia opened itself up to progressive western thought and practices under Peter the Great (1672–1725). Throughout the century, while always retaining its strict authoritarian rule and its Slavic separateness, Russia would play an increasing role in European affairs.

England during this time was moving toward a stronger parliamentary system, greater industrialism and a broad-based tax system. It also had a fairly healthy treasury. Its concerns centered around making sure no one power on the continent grew too strong.

Relations between the large countries were largely driven by a desire for a balance of power. Each of the major nation-states was afraid of domination by any other state or group of states. Thus they applied some of the rational thinking of the times to their diplomacy. In some ways this "system" worked fairly well, and the independence of all countries (even the smaller ones) was generally safeguarded. However, since each country had its own resource needs, ambitions and ruler, the inevitable disputes often ended in war. Thus, during the 1700s we see a complex series of wars over controversies of disputed territories, trade and royal succession. Though these wars went on for much of the eighteenth century, they were mostly local and relatively controlled in terms of weapon power and casualties. The real violence would come later with the huge armies of Napoleon.

An understanding of the intricacies of European political and military activity in the years before the French Revolution is not necessary for our purposes. It should be noted, though, that this was a period of intense diplomatic activity and much contact between different societies and cultures. This in turn led to a rather cosmopolitan atmosphere that was to exert a very strong influence on the arts.

A major force at work outside of Europe during this time was the series of disputes over colonial empires in the New World. France, for instance, lost a good part of her North American possessions to England in the Seven Years War (1756–1763), known in America as the French and Indian War. Also, intervention by France and the Dutch helped America break away from England and thus weaken British economic and military power.

The foreign event that most influenced Europe during the last part of the eighteenth century was the American Revolution. Here was a live example of people breaking free from the old ways and ancient regimes of Europe. The spirit and ideals of the revolutionary Americans were based on the ideas of the Enlightenment. The revolution for liberty and freedom by Americans had great influence on the events leading to the French Revolution thirteen years later. It also provided a shining example to those moved by the issues of human freedom.

Such weighty thoughts were deeply influential on Beethoven and served as an inspiration for some of his important works.

The Enlightenment

The eighteenth century has become known as the Age of Enlightenment. During this period a more rational, anti-tradition, pro-liberty, human-rights line of thinking was developed, written about and eventually used in stimulating change and reform. It grew out of the scientific revolution of the seventeenth century, and quickly was at odds with the absolute authoritarianism epitomized by France's Louis XIV (died 1715).

Early in the eighteenth century there was a feeling among the educated in Europe that they were emerging from a long period of twilight into an age of progress and optimism. A group of philosophers and writers, centered mainly in France, developed a loosely defined set of ideas (or ideals) that called for action based on rational thought and scientific reasoning—as opposed to royal authority, tradition or religious teaching. Central to the Enlightenment were the idea of progress based on its benefits to humankind, and the importance of individual freedom. It was believed that if one could apply reason and scientific thinking, then progress could be made and society's most significant problems could be solved. Enlightened thinking stressed practical morality over the Church or supernatural religion. It emphasized common sense and applied science over traditional beliefs and superstition. It favored individual freedom and equal rights over privilege and divine right. It was essentially secular in nature and in time led to the Church's loss of much of its prestige and leadership.

Many of these ideas were unpopular and a threat to the ruling and privileged classes. Hence, the propagation of enlightened thought often took the form of drama or literary criticism and was often circulated underground. Still, the ideas took hold and captivated the minds of many of the influential people of the times.

There even developed a group of enlightened rulers—men who retained their divine right to rule but attempted to focus their regimes on "serving" the people and advancing the cause of progress toward the common good.

The whole concepts of human progress, rationality, human rights and the centrality of humanity were essentially new ideas in the late seventeenth or early eighteenth century. True, some two to three hundred years earlier the humanist thinkers of the Renaissance had developed a somewhat similar school of thought. They emphasized the importance of worldly matters and a human-centered perspective rather than the God-centered, religious outlook of the Middle Ages. But the humanists of the Renaissance took their inspiration from history and strove to emulate the glories of ancient Greece and Rome. The enlightened thinkers of the eighteenth century, on the other hand, did not look to the past and took their inspiration from contemporary people's inherent abilities to use reason and the scientific approach.

France was the center of the Enlightenment. It was here, in the first half of the eighteenth century, that a group of men emerged who became known as the "philosophers." Their debates and writings provided the basis for enlightened thought. Montesquireu (1689–1755), Rousseau (1712–1778) and Voltaire (1694–1778) were perhaps the most influential authors in spreading the thinking of the Enlightenment. The publication of the *Encyclopédie* in 1751 (edited by Diderot) was a key event. The work was a comprehensive alphabetical dictionary that had entries on political and religious terms. It was based on the belief that universal knowledge would lead to enlightened thought and rational behavior.

Enlightened thinking and the resulting drive for political reform provided the foundation for much of the progress and change that was made during the eighteenth century. In Prussia, for instance, Frederick the Great (who reigned 1740–1786) practiced a form of enlightened rule in his promotion of religious tolerance and his generally humane and just ways of dealing with his subjects. In Austria, Emperor Joseph II (who reigned 1765–1790) had an ambitious agenda for reform. He improved education and administration, abolished serfdom, introduced civil marriage and increased toleration and equality for all citizens and minorities. Both of these rulers were strong admirers of the Enlightenment writers.

The themes and ideas of the Enlightenment were central to Beethoven's values and outlook. He grew up around a small court in Bonn where these thoughts were discussed and sometimes practiced. As we'll see, his exposure to them proved to be a lasting influence on him in both his personal relations and his work.

Ironically, it was in France, where this enlightened intellectual ferment was strongest, that reform and progress were slowest in coming. The Bourbon monarchy continued down its tradition-bound autocratic and corrupt path even as the philosophers were spreading ideas about human rights, liberty and equality. These ideas were to eventually lead to the upheaval in 1789 that changed Europe forever and set in motion a series of events that would affect the lives of most Europeans for many years to come.

The French Revolution

France in the late eighteenth century was the leading country of Europe—economically, politically and culturally. Parisian life for the well-to-do was rich in dramatic and musical performance and social pleasures. However, among the noble classes and the monarchy there was a social blindness and a desire not to deal with the implications of the powerful ideas of the Enlightenment. As France approached the end of the 1780s, its substructure was being weakened by a combination of an unpopular and feeble monarchy, a parliament that favored the privileges of the nobility, a growing group of reactionary forces and a disgruntled peasantry. The country also had a huge public debt, caused partially by French support of America in its Revolutionary War.

Out of this problematic and volatile situation arose the French Revolution. It started with the calling of the Estates General in May of 1789. The initial goals of the revolution were accomplished with relative ease and peacefulness. Specifically, a Declaration of the Rights of Man was adopted in August 1789, guaranteeing property rights. In addition, feudalism was abolished, taxation was equalized, church lands were seized and a Constitution was drawn up in 1791. However, as the Revolution progressed from crisis to crisis, it lost sight of its original goals and became more extreme. Before long, it turned violently against the royal family, and after repeated humiliations, King Louis XVI was executed in January of 1793.

These events, particularly the decline and eventual fall of the monarchy, had major repercussions across the continent. Other European countries joined forces in defense of the old regimes, and war broke out in 1792. In France, the fear of foreign invasion, as well as internal politics and paranoia, soon led to the formation of a radical Committee on Public Safety.

A reign of terror followed during 1793 and 1794. In effect, the Committee abolished the very freedoms that the revolution had originally espoused. Soon the leaders of the Terror (Danton and Robespierre) were consumed by their own fanaticism and, like thousands before them, were sent to the guillotine. By late 1794 some semblance of rationality had returned, and the revolution was essentially over.

The lasting effects of the revolution are still not clear. The period following 1795 saw France still in financial trouble and a long way from being a land of political liberty or equality. In reality, not much had changed to improve the life of the peasant. Still, there was some progress. The absolute monarchy was abolished, arbitrary arrests were curbed, the Church was separated from the state and feudalism was weakened. These changes were eventually to have long-lasting effects on other regimes in Europe. In addition, some administrative and economic systems were introduced that paved the way for later progress.

Probably most important, though, was the spiritual heritage left by the events in France. The original idealistic concepts of liberty and equality that inspired the rebellion against the old regime in turn inspired and powerfully affected succeeding generations. This overthrow of the most powerful and best-established monarchy in Europe became a spiritual inspiration to all those concerned with their fellow humans and their rights. In spite of its excesses and shortcomings, the French Revolution was thus the most significant event in Europe since the Reformation.

Its effect on the intellectuals and the artists of the day was enormous. To young idealists such as Beethoven, the ideas of the Enlightenment and the events in France were of great importance, influencing how they viewed themselves, their fellow human beings and their work.

Napoleon

As France regrouped from the turmoil of the revolution, its people became fascinated by the brilliant military exploits of a young Corsican named Napoleon Bonaparte. His fame came from his victories for the revolutionary government during campaigns in Italy and Egypt. With corruption and inflation raging at home and foreign armies still a threat, the calculating Napoleon overthrew the French government in October 1799. He set up a consulate with himself as the first counsel, with executive powers. He then set off a frantic period of military conquests, political and social reform and personal aggrandizement. During the next fifteen years there was a constant series of military campaigns that saw his armies in combat in areas as widespread as Spain, Italy, Prussia, Austria, Holland and Russia. At one time he was virtually in control of all of Europe. He saw himself as the "new Charlemagne," and in 1804 had himself crowned as Emperor.

In addition to his military successes, Napoleon used his dictatorial powers to institute a wide range of reforms. The educational system was strengthened, the French Academy reorganized, government finance reformed and a stronger currency introduced. He concluded a concordat with the Pope, restoring some of the former rights and prestige of the Church. Probably most significant were his legal reforms contained in the famous Code

Napoleon. It embodied many of the enlightened concepts of the revolution; i.e., equality before the law, religious liberty and human rights.

Even though he retained strict dictatorial powers and exercised strong censorship, Napoleon's reforms and his glorious military victories captured the imagination of a large number of people, both inside and outside France. For many, including Beethoven for a while, he became a Romantic hero, a champion of the rights of human beings and the crowning triumph of the original goals of the revolution. In time, though, his personal ambition drove him to military overexpansion and the establishment of a family dynasty. Consequently, his success and popularity faltered.

The effects of his military activity were consequential and widespread. Millions died or were wounded in his campaigns, and whole countries were reshaped. For example, his victories and the subsequent restructuring in the German lands reduced the some three hundred minor principalities down to a handful: Austria, Prussia, the Confederation of the Rhine and a few smaller territories. In the course of his various triumphs, and the resulting treaties and alliances, many territories were transferred from one great power to another. In 1806, as a major gesture reflecting his supremacy, he decreed an end to the anachronistic Holy Roman Empire.

Napoleon occupied Vienna twice—in 1805 and again in 1809. These two events injected the stress of war and the weakness of the Hapsburg monarchy into the lives of a rather isolated Viennese society. Beethoven was part of that social milieu, and he too was affected by these events.

After years of almost constant victory and glory, Napoleon's invasion of Russia in 1812 ended in disaster. His retreat turned into a rout as many of his conscripts deserted. A broad alliance of Prussia, Russia, Austria and Sweden defeated the Napoleonic armies in 1813, and his troops were forced to flee back to France. His other enemies—Spain, Holland and England—joined together, and an allied army entered Paris triumphantly in 1814. Napoleon abdicated and was exiled to the island of Elba.

By the time of his downfall in 1814 (and, subsequently, after his brief and failed comeback in 1815), Napoleon had lost much of the aura and mystique that had made him such an inspirational hero to many Europeans. In spite of the positive legacies of the Napoleonic Code and other reforms, enthusiasm for him had turned to resentment. There was a desire to settle things down, sort problems out and allow countries to regain some control over their own destinies. This significant task was taken up by the leaders of the European countries when they gathered at the extraordinary Congress of Vienna.

Congress of Vienna

The Congress was convened in September 1814 and lasted until June 1815. Some two hundred political entities sent delegations. They in turn were accompanied by their families and assorted assistants, chamberlains, consorts, ladies in waiting and the like. Together, some ten thousand of these self-important dignitaries descended on the imperial capital.

Emperor Franz I of Austria played host, and most of the crowned heads of Europe attended. The major players, who met behind closed doors and made all the major decisions, were Austrian Foreign Minister Prince Metternich, British Foreign Minister Castlereagh, Tsar Alexander I of Russia and the great chameleon of that political age, Prince Talleyrand of France. He was a true opportunist, as he had previously served the revolutionary government, survived the Terror, then served Napoleon and was now working for the restored Bourbon government of Louis XVII.

The Congress was a big event for Vienna and its citizens and a social planning nightmare for the Emperor's staff. The task of hosting, feeding and entertaining thousands of foreign dignitaries placed great strains on the monarchy's finances and its logistical capabilities. Since most of the attendees really had very little to do, the Viennese had to provide a constant flow of entertainment and diversions.

Thus, during the Congress Vienna was indeed a lively place. A special festival committee was appointed, and it produced a dazzling and expensive series of banquets, concerts, balls, operas, ballets, parades, hunts and expeditions. Beethoven was pulled into this activity. He gave a number of concerts, appeared before numerous royalty, wrote some special music for the occasion and even had an audience with the Empress of Russia.

By the end of the Congress, however, Vienna was a nearly impoverished city, and still under the rule of the creaking Hapsburg dynasty.

The Congress essentially restored much of the old system and established a new balance of power. However, there was an underlying trend away from the old social and political order. The ideas of social and economic progress, the importance of freedom and equality, and the legitimacy of national aspirations had taken hold and would continue to grow in the years ahead.

Following the Congress, Europe went through a period of relative peace as the major powers sought to preserve the conservative rearranging they had accomplished in Vienna. A more Pan-European outlook emerged, and as part of their plan to hold on to their power, the major governments held a series of conferences dealing with problems of mutual concern. As a result, the period following 1815 was free of major wars, and the ruling classes were able to focus on suppressing internal movements that advocated greater rights and freedom. Thus the political atmosphere of Beethoven's final years was characterized by a peaceful atmosphere on the broader European scene but continuing issues of freedom and rights for the individual at home.

The City of Bonn

Beethoven was born in Bonn and lived there for twenty-two years until he departed for Vienna in 1792. His early emotional, intellectual and musical development was strongly influenced by the artistic, political and cerebral environment in this pretty little town on the lower Rhine.

Since the thirteenth century, Bonn had been the official seat of the Archbishop of Cologne. It owed its allegiance to the Hapsburg monarchy in Vienna, which was the seat of the Holy Roman Empire. Its rulers were generally princes (often of the Hapsburg family), who combined their ecclesiastical and secular duties under the title of Elector. (This meant they were eligible to participate in the "election" of the Holy Roman Emperor.) The Elector, of course, was appointed by the Hapsburgs in Vienna. Bonn, like the other electorates, operated fairly autonomously; hence, its intellectual and social life reflected the interests of the current Elector.

During Beethoven's life, Bonn was a town of about ten thousand people. It had very little commerce or functions other than being the seat of the Elector/Bishop of Cologne. Most of its citizens depended on the Elector for their livelihood in one way or another. (One of the locals of the time summed up their dependency by saying, "All Bonn is fed from the Elector's kitchen.") The population for the most part lived within the city walls. Compared with many larger cities of the area, it was a picture of neatness and comfort. A visitor in 1780 described the city this way:

> Bonn is a pretty town, neatly built and its streets tolerably well paved, all in black lava. It is situated in a flat near the river. The Elector of Cologne's palace faces the south entry. It has no beauty of architecture and is all plain white without any pretensions.

Beethoven lived under two Electors. Maximilian Friederich became Archbishop /Elector in 1761 and ruled until he died in 1784. He encouraged a wide range of cultural activities, especially theater and opera, and promoted the dissemination of enlightened literature. Three generations of Beethoven family musicians served on his court musical staff—including the young Ludwig.

In 1784, Maximilian Franz, the younger brother of the Hapsburg Emperor Joseph II, was appointed Elector at Bonn. Following the enlightened beliefs and practices of Joseph II in Vienna, Max Franz made Bonn a little Vienna on the Rhine. The ideas of the Enlightenment became the dominating principles of Max's rule. Intellectual freedom was encouraged, and the court library contained the most up-to-date writings of the Enlightened thinkers. Importantly, in 1785 the Bonn Academy was upgraded to University status and staffed with intellectuals and philosophers with strong Enlightenment views. During these years various societies formed which promoted progress through reason and provided forums for enlightened discussion. Many friends and associates of Beethoven participated in these groups. This open-minded and inquisitive thinking also influenced artistic affairs and nurtured major activity in music and drama, including works by Gluck, Salieri and Mozart.

Beethoven was involved with the court as a musician by the time he was only eight years old. He was able to see and hear the great works of the time while he himself was developing his musical talents. Simultaneously, over the years he was exposed to the ideas of the Enlightenment that were so strongly a part of Max Franz's court. He had the good fortune to be part of one of the most progressive courts of the time, and it was in this atmosphere of enlightened ideals and respect for the arts that Beethoven's social and cultural principles and attitudes were formed.

Vienna and the Hapsburgs

The Hapsburgs established their rule in the area of central Europe now known as Austria in the late thirteenth century. Vienna (Wien), an eastern outpost city for Europe on the Danube River, remained the center of Hapsburg power into the twentieth century. For most of these years the Hapsburg emperors were the titular heads of the Holy Roman Empire. Over the centuries, through conquest or dynastic marriages, the Hapsburg influence expanded and the Austro-Hungary land became a major participant in the European balance-of-power game. As it conquered additional countries and ethnic groups and absorbed some of their cultures, Vienna took on a very cosmopolitan atmosphere. Also, because of its eastern location, the Hapsburg Empire had several major conflicts with the Turks. These had a lasting effect, socially and culturally, on the Viennese. Thus Vienna was a city of varied racial and cultural heritage that provided its citizens an amazingly wide variety of artistic, culinary and sensual pleasures.

In spite of all these cosmopolitan influences, however, Vienna remained a Catholic city. Unlike many of the Germanic territories in the north, which broke away from the Catholic Church during the Reformation, Vienna and the Hapsburgs supported Rome's Counter Reformation.

Vienna did have its share of wars, rebellions, pestilence and famine, but all in all the Hapsburgs provided Vienna with relative stability and economic well-being. Its rulers generally encouraged the arts, particularly music. In fact, many of the Hapsburgs were musicians themselves. Thus there was a rich musical tradition in Vienna as it entered the last half of the eighteenth century.

In 1740 Maria Theresa succeeded her father on the throne. As Archduchess of Austria (and later Queen of Hungary and Queen of Bohemia), she became one of the great rulers of the Hapsburg Empire. Pugnacious and determined to exert her influence, she had an ongoing rivalry with the Prussians for dominance in central Europe. Her reign saw a series of wars that kept central

Europe in nearly constant turmoil. At home she was a stern, rather prudish, but eventually respected ruler. She bore five sons and eleven daughters—one of whom, Marie Antoinette, married King Louis XVI of France.

From an artistic standpoint she encouraged theater, spectacles and a wide variety of musical activities. It was at one of these royal musical performances that the seven-year-old prodigy Mozart jumped up on Maria Theresa's lap and gave her a kiss. Later she would remark that the Mozarts were "useless people, running around the world like beggars."

Maria's husband, Franz, died in 1765. Their eldest son, Joseph, became co-ruler of Austria with his mother, and after her death in 1780 he became Emperor. Joseph II was one of the enlightened rulers of the late eighteenth century who worked to implement policies that in some ways reflected the enlightened beliefs of progress, reform and human rights. He gave freedom of worship and civil equality to non-Catholic Christians, improved the conditions of Jews, freed the peasants from serfdom and made improvements in public education and health. Still, he was essentially an autocratic person who tended to centralize most decisions. It was during his reign that the great masters of Classical music, including Mozart and Haydn, thrived. He died in 1790 believing he had lived as a guardian and a servant of the state. (Because of these reforms and his enlightened beliefs, Joseph has become something of a Viennese folk hero.)

Joseph was succeeded by his younger brother Leopold II, who was not of the same philosophical mode. He quickly moved to rescind many of Joseph's reforms and promised to restore some of the previous conditions in the Hapsburg lands.

Leopold's sudden death in 1792 brought his son Franz II to the throne. Frightened by the overthrow of the monarchy in France, Franz continued the reactionary policies of Leopold and increased repression and political surveillance. His regime was devoted to preservation of the monarchy and the privileges of the noble class. It became the classic example of a police state, including a controlled press, censorship of reading material, restricted travel and a network of spies.

Surprisingly, there was very little resistance to these oppressive policies. Most Viennese accepted things as they were and assumed a relaxed attitude, showing very little opposition or rebellion. Many of the business and trading classes found their commercial interests tied up with those of the monarchy and thus, generally, decided to go along with things as they were.

For those of the middle and upper classes, life was quite pleasant. There was plenty to eat and drink for most people. The nobility kept up their grand lifestyles and indulged in lavish parties and active patronage of the arts. A wide variety of entertainment existed, including high-quality operas, concerts, dance halls and brothels. Morals were loose, and life took on a rather superficial tone, with great energy put into parties, gossip, court intrigue and general enjoyment. Interest in music was especially strong. Performers and composers alike found a thriving market for their skills.

Over the next twenty years, as the Napoleonic Wars raged across Europe, the importance of Vienna and the Hapsburgs started to decline. But on the surface, life generally remained pleasant for the Viennese, and the people were, on the whole, indifferent to political events.

However, the two occupations by the French, in 1805 and 1809, were difficult. Many had to leave the city. There were shortages of food, and the regime suffered serious financial problems.

After the defeat of Napoleon and the exciting but financially draining Congress of 1814–1815, Vienna took on a different feeling. Many of its nobility lost their fortunes, and patronage of the arts became more difficult. Fortunately, there was a concurrent rise in prosperity among the financial and business classes, who to some extent were able to provide additional patronage for the many musicians who lived and worked there. In spite of its problems and its declining fortunes, Vienna did retain its leading role as one of the great cultural centers of Europe.

Emperor Franz I continued to rule through the end of Beethoven's life (1827) and eventually died in 1835. His last years were taken up by a continuing series of political problems resulting from the arrangements made at the Congress of Vienna.

The Vienna Beethoven moved to in 1792 contained some two hundred thousand people. Like most cities in Europe, it had clear class distinctions. At the top were the monarchy, the nobility and the high aristocracy, committed to enjoying their privileged lives and holding on to power. Next, underneath the nobility, were the state bureaucrats, the professionals and the minor aristocrats. They rendered service to the state and the noble classes, engaged in finance and commerce and aspired to move into the top levels of society. Many of Beethoven's friends were of this lesser aristocrat class. At the bottom were the artisans, unskilled workers and, in the country, the peasants. They were, of course, poor and quite oppressed, and they accounted for well over half of the Austrian populace. Their occasional uprisings were always met with firm repression.

Life among the middle and upper classes was focused more on social life and family than on matters of politics or philosophy. Outside observers had the impression that the Viennese were more dedicated to entertainment than to enlightenment, to escapism rather than involvement in the affairs of state. Much of the everyday social life revolved around the coffee house and the tavern. For those of the noble class or the sub-aristocracy there were frequent parties, concerts and assorted diversions in their elegant townhouses. During the summer, much of the activity moved out of the city to country estates, where the parties and concerts continued.

Physically, Vienna was a city pleasant to the eye and conducive to an enjoyable lifestyle. Wide avenues for the many carriages and strollers were lined with well-stocked shops. The imperial household and government offices were centered in the Hofburg castle area. Just outside the city stood the imposing Schönbrunn Palace, where the royal family and court moved during the summer. Throughout the city were the palaces of the aristocracy. Often quite large, they served as places of amusement and musical performance for the nobility and their friends. There were also a number of theaters in the city that offered a wide variety of performances of drama, opera and concerts. Among the most important in Beethoven's time were the Theater an der Wien, the University Festsaal and several theaters within the royal castle area. Concerts could also be heard in a number of restaurants.

It was in this cosmopolitan and relatively prosperous environment of Vienna that Beethoven lived, performed and composed. Yet he was a man of greater depth and intensity than most of the Viennese. Indeed, as he developed and his music became well known, part of the musical life in Vienna took on a deeper, more emotional and more meaningful tone.

Musical Perspective

Music, like other art forms, has evolved at an uneven pace over time. The period during Beethoven's life was unusual for serious music, as many trends came together and true change occurred. There were significant alterations in the very nature of music: how it sounded, who heard it, where they heard it, the influence it had and the roles of the performer and composer. This metamorphosis was, of course, the culmination of trends that had been underway for some time.

Beethoven was blessed with a musical heritage that came out of a society where the nobility generally valued and enjoyed music, and were willing to pay for it. During the eighteenth century a number of outstanding composers achieved their fame producing works for major and minor nobility in the various states of Europe. They relied on this patronage for their livelihood, as there were relatively few "public" concerts. Life for many of the composers of the 1700s thus consisted of being in the service of either the Church or a musically inclined noble. In the latter cases, it also meant doing his bidding in terms of writing music, organizing performances, participating in the concerts and often giving lessons. There were exceptions to this, of course, but generally it was not until the end of the eighteenth century that musicians or composers (often the same) had some degree of economic independence and creative freedom.

A number of related and interacting trends caused this move away from the restricted, small-scale performances for a limited audience toward the more accessible, large public concerts that became popular in Beethoven's later years. In addition, there were important changes in the instruments, the musical forms and the composing techniques that were employed.

Historical perspective is important here. A look at these trends and a brief examination of the dominant musical styles and the major composers before Beethoven will therefore be helpful.

It must be noted, of course, that these musical periods were not discrete blocks of time. Rather, we should look on them as part of an evolution of overlapping periods that have some common musical characteristics and practices.

The Renaissance (approximately 1450–1600)

Much of Renaissance music was performed in churches. It was largely for the human voice and was polyphonic in nature; that is, it was many-voiced and consisted of a series of equally important interwoven vocal lines, composed in a way that the various parts were in counterpoint to each other. The separate, melodic parts would blend and harmonize. Renaissance secular music was similar, though often flutes, guitars or simple keyboard instruments were added for harmony. The compositions were generally tightly constructed and had a calm but detached nature to them.

Toward the end of the period, musicians started to experiment with new forms, and they created works with more contrast and greater emotion. Concurrently, instrumental music started to break away from its primary role of supporting and supplementing the human voice. Generally, serious music, both religious and secular, became more popular. Its growth and dispersion were helped by the invention of printing.

While there was a lot of secular music written, the majority of high-quality works were religious, and the most-renowned composers during the period worked mainly for the Church. The most famous were Palestrina (1525–1594) in Rome, Orlando di Lasso (1532–1594) in Munich, Giovanni Gabrieli (1557–1612) in Venice, and Josquin des Prez (1440–1521) in Italy and France.

Baroque (1600–1750)

Music took a new direction early in this period. Instruments were added to the sacred music, and composers found that the polyphonic counterpoint didn't always suit the instruments. They started to replace the long, overlapping lines of melody with shorter groups of chords and harmonies. These "pieces" of sound could then be varied and repeated, giving a richer, more complex sound. Thus, the music became more systematic and structured while still providing the listener with superb melodies.

Opera was invented in Florence in the 1590s and quickly spread across Europe. This called for a more exact blending of instrument and voice as the music accompanied the drama. As instrument usage increased in both the church and the theater, the quality and variety of the instruments and the abilities of the players improved. As a result, there was a marked increase in the amount of instrumental music composed, as people wanted to enjoy the pleasures of these sounds outside the church or the stage. Composers invented new musical forms to utilize these instrumental groups and please their patrons.

Some of these new forms provided the early building blocks for the future. *Suites* were popular, originally as groups of independent dance tunes and eventually as more structured pieces with the parts connected and common melodies pulling a whole composition together into a single mood. We also see in this period the emergence of the *sonata* form; this would evolve into a major element of musical structure for the next two centuries. In its earliest form the *sonata* was a tightly organized work in several movements that followed a standard order (i.e., slow, fast, slow, fast). Its simplest, most basic characteristics of exposition of a theme, development, and then recapitulation were modified and expanded over time. It served as one of the basic musical forms for Beethoven and for most composers since his time.

During the Baroque period we see the beginning of a trend away from the equal-voiced polyphony and vocal counterpoint of the Renaissance. While this counterpoint continued to play a very important role (especially in the music of Johann Sebastian Bach), there was a move towards homophony, in which one part (either vocal or instrumental) carried the melody and was supported by chords in an accompaniment that was subordinated to the melody. This supporting accompaniment evolved into the concept of the *basso continuo,* where the bass part took on a greater prominence and eventually played both a harmonic and sometimes a melodic role. The *basso continuo* was one of the key characteristics of Baroque music. It was played by two kinds of instruments—either a keyboard instrument such as an organ or harpsichord, or a more melodic instrument such as a cello, bass or viola da gamba.

As harmonies became more important, the whole concept of tonality took on a greater role, and music sounded richer and more extravagant. Also in this period, we start to see composers striving to communicate greater emotion through the use of tempo indications: e.g., *allegro* (fast), *adagio* (slow) and dynamic markings: e.g., *forte* (loud) and *piano* (soft).

During this period, the church and the homes of the aristocracy started to decline as the centers of musical life. While most composers were still dependent on them, a few, like Handel, made some of their livelihood directly from the public.

Two exceptional composers emerged toward the end of this period—Bach and Handel. Their work summed up and perfected much of the development that had come before them. The music they composed has been extremely important in the evolution of Western music, and has taught and inspired many of the major composers over the last nearly three hundred years. Beethoven was very familiar with, and a great admirer of, the works of both of these men.

Johann Sebastian Bach (1685–1750). J. S. Bach came from a long line of musicians who had worked in the Protestant northern German lands. He earned his living in a series of positions, serving churches and courts throughout Germany. He was a first-class organ virtuoso as well as a versatile composer. His various jobs required him to write music for the Lutheran Church and for a variety of nobles. As a result, his prolific output encompasses works in virtually all of the musical forms of the day except opera.

While working for churches, he composed organ pieces (toccatas, fugues, etc.), chorales, cantatas and hymns, as well as his most monumental works, the B Minor Mass and the St. Matthew Passion. During his years of patronage from secular princes, his output was mainly instrumental works—concertos, suites, solo keyboard works and sonatas for various instruments. His own greatness comes from perfecting these forms, not in expanding them or in inventing new forms.

His music was able to utilize many of the styles that were then in use and bring into exquisite balance the opposing principles of counterpoint and harmony. He was, of course, a master of both. His compositions have an almost scientific structure to them and a sense of order and technical perfection. They are characterized by driving rhythms and an elaboration of ideas through the use of inventive polyphony and counterpoint. To the listener, his music has a beautiful, almost flawless completeness, a balance, and a rich intensity.

Bach looked on himself as a hard-working craftsman. He was well respected by his colleagues but during his lifetime was not particularly well known across Europe. By Beethoven's time, however, his reputation was such that Beethoven, who greatly admired his keyboard works, is said to have suggested that he should not be called Bach ("brook" in German) but "ocean."

It was not until the 1820s that Bach's works became widely known and respected resulting in the reputation for mastery that he enjoys today.

George Frederick Handel (1685–1759). Handel is a good example of the international, or cosmopolitan, nature of music during the Baroque period. He was born, raised and taught his basic skills in Germany. In his early twenties he spent four years in Italy absorbing much from the active musical life there, and composing a number of operas. Then, after a brief stint as the musical director for the court in Hanover, he moved to London, where he worked until his death. As a youth he studied counterpoint and learned to play a variety of instruments, including violin, oboe, harpsichord and organ. Very soon he had a reputation as a very talented organist. His intense musical education also involved learning the music of German and Italian composers by copying their scores.

In London he enjoyed the patronage of the royal family and various other nobles. Much of his time was taken up composing and producing Italian-style operas that were popular with the English; during his life he wrote over forty. He also wrote a wide variety of chamber music for aristocratic gatherings. And for the royal family he wrote suites designed for special occasions. He was quite a popular figure in society and did well financially.

In his later years, as the popularity of Italian opera waned, he turned to a new kind of composition: the *oratorio,* with words in English. These could be produced less expensively than operas, and there was a wider middle-class audience available for them. These were large works for chorus and orchestra, which drew their inspiration from Italian opera and the choral traditions in England. They dealt with sacred subjects, but, unlike Bach's big choral works, were not intended for the church service. Handel turned out a large number of oratorios during the 1730s and 1740s, writing thirty in all. They were generally very popular and brought him fame and financial success. The most famous of these, *Messiah,* was first performed in 1742 in Dublin. It was a popular staple from then on. The public performances of these oratorios were, in a way, a prelude to the more popular public concerts that started to thrive in Vienna in Beethoven's time.

Handel became blind in his old age, but he continued giving concerts until he died in 1759. He was a famous man at the time of his death and was honored by a huge service in Westminster Abbey.

Handel was an acknowledged master of choral music, as well as most of the other forms of Baroque compositions. But his works represent a movement toward a new style and away from the highly refined counterpoint of Bach. His musical flow is less continuous, less based on the moving lines of polyphony. Instead, it is structured around vertical chords that give very rich, brilliant and complex sounds. Many of his works show a clearer sense of melody than was typical among his predecessors. The emotionalism and dramatic effects of his oratorios had great appeal to a wide audience. Handel's works had great influence on Beethoven, who often called Handel his favorite composer.

Pre-Classical

Musical historians speak of a brief period around the mid-1700s as pre-Classical. There was, in fact, a traditional style that followed the Baroque and preceded what we now call the Classical period. While no clear lines of distinction can be made, significant changes of style and form took place roughly from 1740 through 1770. The trend away from counterpoint toward homophonic texture was accelerated. The *basso continuo* was less frequently used, and a variety of new instruments emerged. During this brief period the so-called Rococo style emerged in France. Also known as the style *Gallant,* it was lighter and more elaborate and had more ornamentation than much of the heavier, grandiose Baroque music. In Germany this style was known as *Empfindsamer Stil.* It was highly emotional and expressive and had at least some intellectual and emotional connection to the literary *Sturm und Drang* (storm and stress) movement. Several of J. S. Bach's sons were important composers in this style.

Classical

The term *Classical* is often used today to refer to serious music from any number of historical periods. For our purposes, we will use the musical history definition; that is, the period from about 1770 to the late 1820s.

The Classical period is seen today as a culmination of the many trends in and around the world of Western music and as a high point in the development of the art form. It brought together the rigor and structure of northern German music with the vocality and melody of Italian.

The period coincidentally corresponds with the time of Beethoven's life, and most music scholars agree that the Classical era ended with Beethoven's death. Beethoven can thus be said to be the key transitional figure who moved music beyond the Classical style into the Romantic.

While there are many exceptions and much overlap, we can clearly see the existence of a number of general characteristics that set the Classical period apart from earlier times and made it so significant in the history of Western music. It was during this period that secular music became more important than sacred music and that instrumental music became more dominant than vocal works. The forms of music written during this period had their antecedents in the Baroque but were actually more formal with definite movements. There was generally a purity of structure where one section or movement ended and the next began. There were pauses between these movements, and themes were rarely carried over from one movement to the next. The music had a high degree of clarity and precision.

In terms of texture, the music was generally homophonic, with a single melodic line accompanied by less melodic material to provide the harmony. It had a voicelike emphasis on the individual melody, reflecting the accent on the individual in Enlightenment thought. The melodies, or themes, were typically made up of short (full measure) phrases, and after being introduced were varied and developed within a movement. This was in contrast to the longer, continuous melodic lines of the Baroque.

The music was accessible, was written for the enjoyment of the listener, and existed in and of itself. Very little of it aimed to convey specific meanings or associations with non-musical subjects. It was characterized by elegance, restraint, formality and, at least to the casual listener, a feeling of simplicity and naturalness.

The popular musical forms were the rondo, overture, theme and variations, and several forms associated with the sonata concept. As mentioned earlier, this concept is a basic plan of instrumental composition usually consisting of three to four contrasting sections characterized by introduction of a theme, then development and recapitulation. It is now a widely used and loosely defined term that applies to both the overall structure of an entire piece of music and to the substructure of a particular movement (often called *sonata allegro*). The most important of these sonata forms are the symphony, concerto and various types of chamber music (duets, trios, quartets, etc.). In addition, solo keyboard music reached new heights during this period.

The symphony as we know it today was developed, and some say perfected, in the late eighteenth century. It is one of the most significant and lasting contributions of the Classical period. The symphony evolved from the *sinfonia,* a term for the overture to an Italian opera. It grew from a three-section structure to the Classical four-movement works, such as in the later symphonies of Mozart and Haydn. These usually consisted of a fast first movement (*allegro*), followed by a slow, melodic second movement, then a dance-like *minuet,* and finally a fast and exciting finish. These were written for a small orchestra (twenty-five to thirty-five instruments) typically made up of strings and one or two flutes, oboes, bassoons and horns. Later, clarinets, trumpets and timpani were added.

By Beethoven's later years, orchestras had grown much larger. (He himself preferred about sixty musicians.) Strings were given the dominant role, with the first violins usually carrying the main thematic material and the second violins and violas assigned the harmonic role.

The symphony became the base for further growth and innovation not only for Beethoven but for most of the major composers of the nineteenth century. Beethoven composed nine symphonies—the first several conforming closely to the Classical form, the latter ones being very innovative in terms of structure, length and orchestration.

The popular solo *concerto* of the Classical period grew out of a generally similar form in the Baroque. In the hands of masters like Mozart, Haydn and Beethoven it became an extremely popular platform for some of the great virtuosi of the period. The typical concerto was written for one (but occasionally two or three) instruments and orchestra. It had three movements and a fast-slow-fast structure. The first movement, usually in sonata form, had the main thematic/melodic material introduced by the orchestra and then developed by the soloist. There was an exciting dynamic and contrast between orchestra and soloist that gave this musical form a unique power and a sense of conflict and eventual resolution. Toward the end of the first movement there was usually a *cadenza,* which gave the soloist a chance to improvise and show off his technical skills. The second movement of a concerto was almost always slow and lyrical, with less direct tension between soloist and orchestra. The final movement usually had a lively tempo and a strong uplifting finish.

In the Baroque period, concertos were written for a wide variety of instruments or groups. The concerto of the Classical period, however, focused mainly on the piano and violin—although some composers, such as Mozart and Haydn, composed concertos for the flute, horn, clarinet and occasionally other instruments. (Beethoven's concerto compositions include five for piano, one for violin and one triple concerto for violin, cello and piano.)

Chamber music for small groups was a significant part of the musical life of the Classical period. The pieces were written for ensembles of a few players. A loosely defined group of musical forms such as serenades and divertimentos were written for informal entertainment. They were usually lighter and less refined than symphonies and often included dances, marches and minuets.

A more formal and important medium was the string quartet. This group consisted of two violins, a viola and a cello. The works were usually in four movements, much like a symphony, and represented some of the most intense and sophisticated output of the major composers of the Classical period. In addition, various combinations of small groups of instruments were employed in trios, quartets and quintets, depending on the desires of the patron, the impulses of the composer and the availability of musicians.

Compositions for solo piano or harpsichord had been popular for years, particularly during the pre-Classical period. This form was further developed by Mozart and Haydn; by Beethoven's time, the piano sonata and piano variations were major forms of musical expression. The sonata for piano and violin also took on an important role in these years. The piano was often the dominant instrument, with the violin performing accompaniment.

While this period is known mainly for its instrumental music, there was also significant growth and development in the fields of opera and religious choral music. Opera, in fact, played an important role in the musical life of the times.

The center for operatic excellence and tradition always had been Italy. The dominant form during the late Baroque was the *opera seria*, which was characterized by vocal virtuosity and a formal structure. It typically consisted of three acts, a heroic plot drawn from Greek or Latin sources, and a series of arias and duets loosely connected by commentary or recitations. The vocally dominated musical structure took precedence over the dramatic aspects of the work. There were almost no choruses, and the orchestra was used mainly to accompany the singers.

During the early and mid-1700s the opera seria underwent reforms, and its rigid formalized structure started to loosen up. Choruses were often used for musical and dramatic effect, and the orchestra took on a more important and expressive role. The lead singers were used more flexibly as part of the drama, not just in loosely connected arias. The works showed greater concern for the dramatic aspects of the story and paid less attention to vocal virtuosity.

The central figure in this reform was Christoph Willibald Gluck (1714–1787). German by birth, he studied in Italy and worked in both Paris and Vienna. His reform operas tied the music and drama together in a stronger, more unified way. Gluck's operas were influential and popular across Europe, and his work forms a foundation for the major operatic composers of the Classical period. However, the operas of Mozart represent the best of the period, as they stand out for both the rich quality of the music and the superb sense of drama achieved by the integration of all the elements.

Strictly religious music played only a minor role during the late eighteenth and early nineteenth centuries. Works ostensibly written on religious themes were often actually quite secular. Masses and oratorios were operatic in nature, with solo voices, choruses and orchestras combined for dramatic effect. Many of the composers of church music also wrote operas and used many of the same elements in both media. Even though they are best remembered for other works, the great composers of the Classical period did some of their best work in these semireligious forms. Mozart wrote fifteen masses including his last work, the Requiem in D Minor. Haydn wrote fourteen masses plus a number of oratorios, including *The Creation* and *The Seasons.* Beethoven wrote one oratorio, *Christ on the Mount of Olives* and several masses, including his powerful *Missa Solemnis.*

Paralleling the development and increasing sophistication of musical forms were the improvement and innovation in musical instruments that were available. There was a major change in the quality of wind instruments as different valves were added to give more range and control. The clarinet was developed during the eighteenth century and became a regular part of the orchestra by the Classical period. The flute, oboe and bassoon were improved and with the clarinet formed the woodwind section, which became an integral part of the Classical orchestra. Various horns, trumpets and trombones were modified and took on added importance as the orchestra became a more balanced and less string-dominated ensemble.

By far the most important instrumental development of the time, however, was the emergence of the pianoforte (or piano, as we know it today) as the dominant keyboard instrument. Its name comes from the Italian *piano* (soft) and *forte* (loud), which refer to the ability of the player to produce louder or softer tones by varying the touch or pressure on the keyboard. This control had not been possible with earlier instruments such as the clavichord or harpsichord. By moving away from the plucking of the strings on the harpsichord and the broader vibrations of the clavichord, the pianoforte developed greater exactness, power and versatility. By the 1780s it was exceedingly popular with performers and composers alike. It became a favorite with the traveling virtuosi of the time as they astounded audiences and earned their living traveling from one city or court to another. The major composers all wrote extensively for this new, technically superior instrument.

Most Classical period composers struggled to make a living. Finding steady employment from a patron was still the typical and desired path, but the pattern changed fairly dramatically toward the end of the eighteenth century. As economic strength and musical interest grew among the developing middle class, there was a greater market for more popular music. Composers operated more on their own and, working through publishers or participating in public concerts, were able to earn a respectable living. There still were no pure composers as such, as they all performed and gave lessons. But out of all this independent activity there emerged a freer, less-patronized musician who had greater freedom to respond to a broader marketplace and compose what he wanted.

Haydn was really the last major composer who worked primarily for a patron. (Haydn was in the service of the Esterházy family for over thirty years.) However, in his later life he was independent, working in London for a while and doing quite well financially. Mozart spent most of his life looking for a permanent patron. He did operate on his own for most of his short adult life but with only mixed success.

Beethoven showed greater independence than most of his predecessors. While he did have patrons, they were usually for short periods, for specific purposes or of a generally non-confining nature. It was his independence in this regard that sets him apart from historical trends and from many of his predecessors.

Music publishing was also changing, contributing to the growth and popularity of music during the Classical period. For a major composer like Beethoven, working with publishers was an important and frustrating part of life. There was a significant increase in the amount of music published during these years, especially in Vienna. Generally, when a new work was completed, the composer hired a professional copyist to put the work in clear and legible form for the publisher. Over time, printing costs came down, and as the public market expanded, the number of publishers grew in most European cities. It was a legitimate commercial business driven by what would sell in the marketplace and characterized by much negotiating between publisher and composer. Royalties such as we have today didn't exist; the composer usually received a single fee, and the publisher maintained exclusive rights to the first edition. These rights were usually protected by law, but generally for only one country. As a result, pirate copies were often made. Composers would occasionally sell original rights to publishers in different countries—or even on occasion to two publishers in the same country.

In order to fully understand this Classical period and to grasp Beethoven's unique role in it, we will briefly look at the two greatest Classical composers that preceded him.

Franz Joseph Haydn (1732–1809). Haydn is now generally regarded as the most purely Classical of the great Classical composers. He is remembered mostly for instrumental works, but like many musicians of his time, his versatility is demonstrated in the large number of operas, oratorios and masses that he wrote.

Haydn's most significant contributions are his symphonies and string quartets. He excelled in these genres, giving them the form and structure that provided the base for subsequent development.

Born in lower Austria into a non-musical family, he possessed a beautiful singing voice. At age eight he joined the famous choir at St. Stephen's church in Vienna. At seventeen his voice broke, and he was out on his own, trying to make a living playing in small instrumental groups and giving lessons. His musical education was very informal. He did take a few lessons in composition, but mostly studied on his own. He gradually gained a musical reputation in Vienna, and in 1759 he obtained a position as music director for Count Morzin in Bohemia. It was here that he wrote his first symphony.

Things took a very positive turn in 1760 when Haydn gained employment with the Esterházy family, one of the richest and most influential in Europe. Working in the splendid isolation of their vast country estates southeast of Vienna, he composed an impressive volume and variety of works. Duties as Kapellmeister for the Esterházy, in addition to composing, included being in charge of an orchestra, a brass band, opera singers and a chapel choir, well over a hundred people. When the prince was in residence, the weekly schedule included two orchestra concerts, two operas, three Sunday services, a play or two, plus a number of chamber music concerts. In spite of, and probably because of, all these musical requirements and responsibilities, Haydn produced hundreds of works of extraordinarily high quality.

Even though he was technically a servant and his contract was rather restrictive, the situation was perfect for Haydn. As he himself said:

> My prince was pleased with all my work, I was commended, and as conductor of an orchestra I could make experiments, observe what strengthened and what weakened an effect and thereupon improve, substitute, omit, and try new things; I was cut off from the world, there was no one around to mislead or harass me, and so I was forced to become original.

Gradually his reputation spread across Europe and he became quite famous. On his trips to Vienna he occasionally met with Mozart, and the two developed a warm and respectful relationship. Haydn early on recognized the genius of the younger Mozart and said to Mozart's father:

> I tell before God and as an honest man, that your son is the greatest composer I know, personally or by reputation; he has taste and apart from that the greatest possible knowledge of composition.

The respect Mozart in turn had for Haydn was expressed in the six string quartets he dedicated to Haydn in 1785.

In 1790 the Esterházy prince Nicholas died and Haydn was finally free to leave their service and expand his horizons. At age sixty he moved to Vienna and finally got a home of his own. But he was soon convinced to go to London by the impresario and violinist Johann Peter Salomon. His two stays in England (1791–1792 and 1794–1795) were very successful. He was widely acclaimed, was entertained by the aristocracy, received an honorary degree from Oxford and made a lot of money. Many of his concerts featured the performance of some of his twelve London symphonies, written especially for these occasions. He was tempted to stay on in London but decided to return to Vienna, where he re-entered the services of the Esterházys; but this time he retained much greater freedom to work and live where he wanted.

During his first London trip, Haydn stopped in Bonn and met the young Beethoven, who evidently impressed him. Beethoven then went to Vienna and briefly studied with Haydn until Haydn left for London again in 1794.

Haydn spent his last years in Vienna primarily writing choral works, the most famous being two oratorios, *The Creation* and *The Seasons.* These were inspired by Haydn's hearing of Handel's *Messiah* in London some years before. In 1797 he wrote out a simple melody that was to become the Austrian national anthem, and was later adopted by the Germans as "Deutschland, Deutschland Über Alles."

In 1808, on his seventy-sixth birthday, Haydn was honored at a great concert in Vienna that featured his oratorio *The Creation.* Conducted by Salieri, with many aristocrats in the audience, Beethoven was so moved that he bowed and kissed the hand of his old teacher.

When Haydn died in 1809, Vienna was occupied by the French. To show respect for the great master, Napoleon had an honor guard posted at Haydn's house, where the composer was lying in state.

Haydn's work played a major role in the growth and development of Western music. He took much from the late Baroque and blended in elements of both the French *Gallant* style and the more emotional German *Sturm und Drang* movement. He was continually experimenting, and his late symphonies and string quartets, composed in the 1790s, represent the perfected Classical mode. An extremely versatile composer, he created music characterized by a blend of sophistication, purity, directness and often humor. His output was truly monumental—one hundred four symphonies, twenty four concertos, eighty three string quartets, over one hundred fifty trios for various instruments, fifty two sonatas, dozens of serenades and *divertimentos,* twenty operas, thirteen masses, six oratorios and various works for solo voice.

Haydn's influence on his contemporaries and those that came later was profound. Mozart perhaps best summed it up when he said:

> There is no one who can do it all—to joke and to terrify, to evoke laughter and profound sentiment—all equally well, except Joseph Haydn.

Wolfgang Amadeus Mozart (1756–1791). Mozart's tragically short life was filled with travel, frustration, a broad musical education, financial problems and, above all, a prolific outpouring of over six hundred compositions. Despite the ups and downs in his life, his music consistently displays his great gift for melody, rhythm and dramatic content. He mastered all the techniques and forms of the Classical period and brought the piano concerto and opera to new heights.

His father, Leopold, was the assistant Kappelmeister to the court in Salzburg and a renowned violinist and composer. By the time his last child, Wolfgang, was age three it was clear the family had a most unusual youngster on their hands. By age four he was quickly learning and playing complex works on the keyboard. At five he began composing, and by his ninth birthday he completed his first symphony. His first oratorio came at age eleven and an opera at twelve.

Such amazing talent was quickly commercialized by father Leopold, who felt it was his duty to make his son's God-given gifts known to the world. He became both coach and career manager and soon took the young prodigy to the capitals of Europe, beginning in 1762. During the next ten years, until he was sixteen, Mozart spent over half his time traveling and performing in the palaces, salons and concert halls of Europe. He was a virtuoso on the clavier and also an accomplished violinist and organist. He became famous for his wide variety of musical skills, and at times the family even made a fair amount of money.

During these travels Mozart came into contact with all of the musical styles that were being written or performed in Europe. His active mind absorbed everything, and his compositions reflect the variety of music that he heard. He built upon the various styles, and thus his music has a unique cosmopolitan quality. He particularly liked the beautiful, light melodic music of Italy, which he visited several times in the 1760s and 1770s.

In 1771, at age sixteen, he obtained work in the musical entourage of the Archbishop of Salzburg. This position allowed him to continue to travel and gain fame and occasional commissions in Paris, Italy and the capitals of southern Germany. These trips, and the accompanying elation and excitement, were in sharp contrast to the rather dreary life in provincial Salzburg, where he was looked on as basically a servant whose job it was to compose music on demand for the local nobility. During these travels he attempted to secure a better position in several cities, but was unsuccessful.

In 1781 Mozart moved to Vienna, where he hoped to have an independent career as a composer, performer and, if need be, teacher. He had some initial success with a few operas, some instrumental works and his performances. He continued to struggle financially, however, mainly because of overspending rather than lack of sufficient income. The court appointment he always hoped for never materialized.

During his ten years in Vienna, through good times and bad, Mozart composed some of the most beautiful and brilliant music in history. He developed his own Classical style that somehow uniquely combined what he had learned in his travels with his own special genius. He also became friends with Haydn and absorbed some of his musical ideas.

In 1782 he became acquainted with the music of J.S. Bach and in turn incorporated some of Bach's techniques and textures into his music. Work continuously flowed from his pen in the form of concertos, symphonies, quartets, piano sonatas and operas (i.e., *The Marriage of Figaro, Don Giovanni,* and *Così fan tutte*). He also composed a variety of serenades and *divertimentos* for specific social occasions.

In 1787 he came into contact with the young Beethoven, who had just arrived from Bonn for a short stay. Their relationship was brief, but after Beethoven played for him he predicted a great future for the seventeen-year-old pianist. Mozart's music stands on its own, by its own rules, and is not written for other external purposes.

In Mozart's music we find little trace of the difficulties and desperation in his life. For instance, during a period of extreme financial need and frustration, Mozart composed his three greatest and most glorious symphonies (nos. 39, 40 and 41). He also wrote seventeen beautiful melodic and inventive piano concertos during these years that offer little, if any, insight into his personal problems.

There were periods of relative financial success, but neither Mozart nor his wife were good at managing his affairs. He did receive a minor appointment as court composer in 1787 but at a nominal salary. He often needed money and had to turn to friends for help. Still, the composing continued and he was writing the Requiem in D Minor when he died on December 5, 1791. At the time he was deeply in debt. The funeral at St. Stephen's

Cathedral in Vienna was attended by a few close friends; he was buried in an unmarked grave.

As the wealth of his output attests, Mozart was an extremely agile, versatile and prolific composer. His composing methods amazed his contemporaries. He would work out musical ideas in his head in great detail, often while he traveled or engaged in some other activity. The ideas would then be transferred to paper and into the musical structure that he had already worked out. While doing this writing he could talk or joke, and thus to his friends his composing looked easy. The music seemed to just flow from his hand in near perfect form. There was very little going back and revising, as was common with most composers.

His six hundred works were categorized by the German L. von Köchel in 1862, and his works today are always identified with the Köchel, or "K," number.

In Mozart's music we hear the brilliant, technical perfection of the Classical style. The sheer beauty and emotive nature of his music were inspirational to the young Beethoven and made Mozart a hero to the more emotional Romantic composers that followed in the 1800s.

Beethoven's Life

Family Background and Birth

Beethoven's grandfather (also Ludwig) came from a family of modest means in Belgium. He received early musical training on the organ and other keyboard instruments. By age twenty-one, in 1733, he had made his way to the court in Bonn, where he found employment as a singer in the choir. Shortly after his arrival, he married Maria Josepha Poll. An aggressive and active man, he soon established himself as a wine merchant and a money lender, in addition to his main job as a singer.

In 1761 he obtained an appointment as court Kapellmeister in charge of music in the theater, concert hall and ballroom, as well as in the chapel. He held this post until his death in 1773, and by all accounts he performed his duties well. But he was only a performer and an organizer, not a composer.

Ludwig's marriage was not a happy one. His wife Maria had three children, but only one, Johann (Beethoven's father, born in 1740), survived. Maria suffered from alcoholism and some time after 1761 was committed to a cloister, where she remained until her death in 1775. Thus Ludwig the elder lived without a wife. He focused his attention on his musical duties, his business interests and his only child, Johann.

Johann, it seems, did not do well in school but did exhibit some musical talent. By age twelve, his father had placed him in the court chapel as a soprano. From his father he learned to play the clavier and the violin. By age seventeen his voice had changed, but he continued as an average performer in the electoral choir until his retirement years later.

Johann's life was dominated by his strong-willed father. The elder Ludwig taught him music, chose his profession, secured his employment and generally controlled his life. The father was convinced his son would not amount to much, and on occasion was quite open in sharing this opinion.

Young Johann was quite submissive to his father's control. His major act of defiance was his marriage in 1767. The elder Ludwig opposed Johann's marriage to Maria Magdalena Keverich, age twenty-one and the recent widow of a court valet. She was the daughter of the chief cook at the Elector's summer palace, and below the social level Ludwig wished for his son. Maria's family wasn't all that pleased either, and the couple married in Bonn rather than the bride's hometown. Ludwig refused to attend.

The young couple set up housekeeping in central Bonn. Father Ludwig moved in just down the street, where he continued his domination over his son.

Johann's career was one of little distinction and only average accomplishment. He earned a modest salary as a court musician and supplemented this by giving classes and voice lessons to the children of nobility. His inclination toward heavy drinking eventually became a significant problem.

His wife, Maria, turned out to be a somber, very serious person. She was said to be clever, capable of good conversation, well liked and respected. It appears that she was not a happy woman, though, and her marriage was a disappointment. She advised young ladies to stay single and once described her life as a chain of sorrows.

It was into this less-than-blissful family situation that Ludwig was born on December 15/16, 1770. The couple's first son, Ludwig Maria, had died after living six days in April of 1769. Maria later had five more children, and of these only two survived: Casper Anton Carl (born April 1774) and Nicholas Johann (born October 1776). The other three died as infants, with the last one, Maria, dying in late 1787 at the age of eighteen months, when Ludwig was seventeen years old.

Youth in Bonn, 1770–1787

The youthful Beethoven became quite attached to his paternal grandfather, who was also his godfather. The elder Ludwig died in late 1773, when Beethoven was only three, but he remained a revered and important figure in Beethoven's life.

It was not long before the young Ludwig became involved in music. His father started to instruct him at age four or five. Once Johann's domineering father was dead, Johann used the teaching of his own son to establish his role as the real head of the household.

Clearly the Beethoven family had a very gifted young child, and the father tried to make the most of it. However, his instruction methods featured violence, threats and punishment instead of guidance and encouragement. Witnesses in later years would recall the visible suffering of the young Louis (Ludwig). One remembered that he "saw the little Louis van Beethoven in the house standing in front of the clavier and weeping." And another recalled:

> Beethoven's father used violence when it came to making him start his musical studies, and there were few days he was not beaten in order to compel him to set himself at the piano.

Beethoven received instruction in both piano and violin. On occasion he would be taught by friends of his father, including one of his drinking pals. It is recorded that the adults would return from their boozing late at night, wake up the young Ludwig and make him play the piano until the next morning.

Johann was proud of his extremely talented son. He invited people to come and hear the young boy play the piano, and in 1778 he presented him in concert. However, his pride did not extend to encouraging the violin and clavier improvisations that young Ludwig liked to invent. He wanted Ludwig to stay on the narrow path of mastering the instrument by playing the notes as written. Once, when his father walked in on the young Beethoven, he said:

> What silly trash are you scraping away at now? You know that I can't bear that; scrape according to the notes; otherwise your scraping won't be of much use.

Beethoven's formal non-musical education was quite limited. In accordance with the custom of the time, he did not progress beyond elementary school—only a few of the noble class, and/or the very gifted, went on to the Gymnasium. He wasn't much of a student, and years later friends and classmates would recall that he learned very little in school. This lack of formal education troubled Beethoven throughout his life as he continued to struggle with writing, punctuation and simple arithmetic.

Beethoven's life focused mainly on music. In spite of the pressure from his father, he was happiest when he was alone practicing. His musical education took a significant upturn in 1779 with the arrival in Bonn of the German conductor, composer and organist Christian Neefe. Neefe, who became the musical director of the Elector's theater company, quickly recognized Beethoven's genius and began teaching him composition in 1780 or 1781. He was his only significant instructor for the next ten years.

Neefe also trained Beethoven as a concert organist, and by 1782, when Beethoven was not yet twelve years old, he left him temporarily in charge of musical affairs when he left town. Neefe also gave his young student the position of cembalist (harpsichord), which meant he directed the orchestra and had to play the scores from sight. In recognition of Beethoven's emerging composing skills, he arranged for publication of his early works. Neefe wrote the first public notice about Beethoven in March 1783 in the local *Magazin der Musik*:

> Louis van Beethoven, a boy of eleven years and of most promising talent. He plays the clavier very skillfully and with power, reads at sight very well...so far as his duties permitted, Herr Neefe has also given him instruction in thorough bass. He is now training him in composition and for his encouragement has had nine variations for the pianoforte written by him on a march by Ernst Dressler—engraved at Mannheim. This youthful genius is deserving of help to enable him to travel. He would surely become a second Wolfgang Amadeus Mozart were he to continue as he has begun.

Beethoven's life was difficult during these early years of his musical development. The character and behavior of his father prevented any kind of closeness or nurturing relationship. While he felt affection for his mother, her unhappiness in the marriage, plus her loss of four of her seven children, eventually made a close mother-son relationship impossible. In later years Beethoven would speak of his mother with great respect and love, but there is little evidence of the kind of closeness that a young boy needs and craves—especially in a household headed by an insecure, domineering, heavy-drinking father whose career was marked by mediocrity and frustration.

The young Beethoven was a rather shy, lonely, withdrawn child. He had few social skills, was often ill-humored with others and was distinguished by a sloppy appearance. He was a bit of a dreamer, and contemporaries remember him staring out at the hills across the Rhine from Bonn.

He seems to have gotten much of his social nourishment from families other than his own. The Beethovens moved around a lot, and in 1777 they started living in an apartment of the Fischer family. Here the young Ludwig was able to be a part of a more normal and collegial family situation.

In about 1783 Beethoven was befriended by the von Breuning family. They had a number of children, and their house became a second home to him. He was exposed to a warm and cultured environment that was not part of his own family routine.

He spent many hours with the von Breunings, and it was here that he received his first exposure to German literature and poetry, the Enlightenment thinkers, and the Greek and Roman classics. The circle of the von Breunings' extended family brought Beethoven into contact with a broader group of acquaintances and provided him with many of his earliest and most meaningful friendships. One of these, Franz Wegeler, became a life-long friend and eventually a biographer of Beethoven after his death. It was also in the von Breuning circle that Beethoven first met Count Ferdinand von Waldstein. The Count was well connected and close to the Elector. He quickly recognized the talents of the young Beethoven, became his first real patron and exerted a strong influence on his early career development.

As Beethoven reached his midteens, the pace of his musical life quickened. He took on additional responsibilities with the court, started to give lessons, further developed his piano virtuosity and spent more time composing. By the early 1780s he knew he was the equal of his father in music, and his self-confidence and appreciation of his own unique talents grew. The breadth of his musical skills widened; he became proficient on the violin, viola, organ and assorted keyboard instruments.

His compositions from his very early years reflect both the skill and the commitment of the young prodigy. In 1782 he wrote a set of variations on a march, in 1782–1783 he composed three sonatas for piano, in 1784 he began a piano concerto and in 1785 he wrote three quartets for piano and strings. Several of these, along with some songs he wrote, were published, and he started to gain recognition. While not everybody accepted his skills—one tart critic likened his first published works to "those of a third or fourth form student"—Beethoven developed a group of music lovers who ardently believed in him. Neefe felt so strongly about his skills that he proposed that Beethoven should travel to broaden his outlook and to receive more training and exposure. Funds were raised (probably from the Elector), and in the spring of 1787, still not seventeen years old, Beethoven set out for Vienna, the musical capital of Europe.

Musical Growth and Family Problems, 1787–1792

It was hoped that the young pianist from Bonn could play for and possibly take lessons from Mozart, who was then enjoying great fame and some prosperity in Vienna. Shortly after his arrival, however, Beethoven learned that his mother's health had deteriorated, and he was asked to come back to Bonn immediately. His stay in Vienna lasted only two weeks and was, on the whole, a failure. As the Elector pointed out, Beethoven brought back "nothing but debts."

Beethoven did meet Mozart during his brief stay. He had an opportunity to play for him, and his improvising evidently impressed Mozart so much that he is reported as saying, "Keep an eye on him; someday he will give the world something to talk about."

Beethoven's arrival back in Bonn in May of 1787 commenced a period of extreme stress and difficulty for the sixteen year old. His mother died of consumption in July, and Beethoven was very deeply saddened and depressed. Four months later his baby sister, Maria, died. The condition of Beethoven's father continued to decline as he drank heavily and his voice became "stale," thus jeopardizing his position in the court choir. Beethoven in effect became head and supporter of the family. By 1789 his father was retired, and Beethoven petitioned to get half of his father's salary in order to insure the support of his two younger brothers.

As his family responsibilities increased, Beethoven continued to grow intellectually and expand his knowledge base. In addition to his exposure to the learned discussions at the von Breunings', he found in Christian Neefe something of a moral mentor. Neefe exposed Beethoven to his own moral and ethical beliefs based on his interest in the Enlightenment and the German *Sturm und Drang* movement. Beethoven found additional intellectual stimulation in taverns near the university that were frequented by students, professors and the radical thinkers of the area. He came into contact with the most enlightened and best minds of Bonn, and in 1789 he even enrolled in the university for a short period.

His real intellectual growth, however, came through self-education, conversation and exposure to others. He was a great reader, devouring the works of the major thinkers of history. In later life he recalled,

> Yet from my childhood I have striven to understand what the better and wiser people of every age were driving at in their works.

It was during these years that Beethoven developed his basic outlook and values, which were such strong parts of his character and personality. His commitment to virtue and service to humanity developed at this early age. In later years he would say:

> Never, never will you find me dishonorable. Since my childhood I have learned to love virtue and everything beautiful and good. From my earliest childhood my zeal to serve our poor, suffering humanity in any way whatsoever by means of my art has made no compromise with any lower motive.

Musically, the late 1780s and early 1790s were periods of tremendous growth and learning for Beethoven. The musical life of Bonn during this period was rich in its array of opera and instrumental music, combining the evolving Classical style and works from earlier periods. Beethoven often played viola in the court orchestra and was thus deeply immersed in the works of Gluck, Salieri, Neefe, Mozart and many others. The instrumental music of the outstanding composers of the day was available in published form, either for sale or in the Elector's court library. The richness of Bonn's musical life, much like a scaled-down Vienna, provided Beethoven with knowledge and artistic nourishment.

Playing the piano was Beethoven's main focus, and he developed great skill and a widening reputation for his virtuosity. On a trip with the court musicians in 1791 he astonished a well-known pianist with his amazing sight-reading and improvising abilities. Later in the trip, after he had played in Mergentheim, one of the locals wrote:

> The greatness of this amiable, lighthearted man, as a virtuoso, may in my opinion be safely estimated from his almost inexhaustible wealth of ideas, the

> altogether characteristic style of expression in his playing, and the great execution which he displays. I know, therefore, no one thing which he lacks, that conduces to the greatness of an artist. Even the members of this remarkable orchestra are, without exception, his admirers, and all ears when he plays. Yet he is exceedingly modest and free from all pretension.

Beethoven's compositions during these years—his late teens and early twenties—show him exploring and working in the conventional musical forms of the times. He wrote a variety of piano pieces, including five sonatas and several sets of variations. In the chamber music genre, he wrote a number of quartets and trios using various combinations of piano, violin, cello and wind instruments. There were also *lieder* (songs) and some incidental music for a ballet.

Undoubtedly, the most impressive part of his output was a set of cantatas: the *Cantata on the Death of Emperor Joseph II* (completed in March 1790, after the Emperor's death in February), and its companion piece *Cantata on the Elevation of Leopold II to the Imperial Dignity* (completed in the fall of 1790). For various reasons, neither work was performed in Beethoven's lifetime.

His most significant work of the time was the *Joseph* Cantata. Here we see the existence of motifs and musical ideas that recur in a number of his later works. We also for the first time get a feeling for the heroic and transcendent nature of Beethoven's music that was to form the basis for much of his later style.

While Beethoven's work gained him considerable recognition around court musical circles, he was by no means universally acclaimed. A mid-1791 listing of court musicians, for example, fails to mention him as a composer.

Socially, life for Beethoven improved somewhat in these years as he widened his circle of friends and gained self-confidence and social skills. Especially important to him was the comradeship he found with members of the court orchestra. He continued to stay close to the von Breunings, and the widow Frau Helene von Breuning became something of a surrogate mother for him. She was able to exert a positive influence over him, both in urging him to do his duties and in restraining him from his tendency toward vanity and obstinacy.

Beethoven's role as head of the Beethoven household grew as his father Johann became an increasingly senile alcoholic and a source of worry and embarrassment. On occasion Beethoven and his younger brothers would be obliged to get their father out of jail after one of his drinking bouts. The family was poor but certainly not impoverished. The income from the Elector was supplemented by Beethoven's teaching. They were able to employ maids and had a housekeeper to look after the younger children.

Personally, young Beethoven continued to have his struggles. To Frau von Breuning he spoke of his passionate moods and his obstinacy. To others he spoke of his melancholia. He was often irrational. He had difficulty with women and was unable to establish any kind of loving or intimate relationship during these years. He would typically become infatuated with a woman who was already involved or pledged to another, and he would end up disappointed and frustrated.

In 1792 an event took place which started Beethoven on a path away from the active but still provincial musical life in Bonn and toward a new career in Vienna. In December of 1790 the venerable and famous Josepf Haydn had stopped in Bonn on his way to his first concert season in London. He had been greeted with great fanfare by the Elector and the leading local musicians, including Beethoven. On the return trip from London in mid-1792, Haydn again stopped in Bonn. This time Beethoven showed the old master one of his cantatas, and Haydn was impressed enough to accept Beethoven as a pupil in composition. At the urging of Count von Waldstein, the Elector granted Beethoven a leave of absence and funded him with salary and expenses. By fall he was ready to go.

In October of 1792, as Beethoven was preparing to leave, Waldstein prophetically wrote to him:

> Dear Beethoven, You are now going to Vienna in fulfillment of a wish that has for so long been thwarted. The genius of Mozart still mourns and weeps the death of its pupil. It has found a refuge in the inexhaustible Haydn, but no occupation; through him it desires once more to find a union with someone. Through your increasing diligence, receive Mozart's spirit from the hands of Haydn. Your true friend, Waldstein.

On November 2 he left, traveling with a companion. The journey was a thrilling one, as drastic events, both political and military, had started to close in on the lower Rhine. In April of 1792 war had broken out between the Hapsburgs and the new republic of France. By early October French troops reached the city of Mainz, just a few miles upstream from Bonn. The Elector Max Franz was forced to temporarily leave the city. (In 1794 the Elector left for good, and within three years the electorate was annexed by the new French republic.) The first part of Beethoven's journey was a fast ride right through the assembling armies. They were almost cut off by French troops in Limburg. But, after arriving safely in Frankfurt, the rest of the journey went without incident.

Early Years in Vienna, 1792–1800

Beethoven's arrival in Vienna in November of 1792, as he was just turning twenty-two, marked the beginning of one of the few happy periods in his life. Like many other youths, he came to Vienna with the intention of developing his musical skills and finding an outlet for his talents in order to make a living. His original intention was to go back to Bonn after a short time and resume his musical activities there. But he never did return, and in fact spent the better part of the next thirty-five years in and around Vienna.

Things did start out on a negative note, though. After just a month in the city, Beethoven received word of his father's death. There is very little record of his reaction, and he did not return to Bonn for the funeral.

At the time of his move to Vienna, Beethoven was described as a "small, thin, dark-complexioned, pockmarked, dark-eyed, bewigged musician of twenty-two years." As inauspicious as his entry into Vienna was, he soon became an active participant in the rich musical life of the Hapsburg capital. He arrived with letters of introduction from the well-connected Waldstein; these, along with his invitation to study with the famous Haydn, guaranteed reception into the right social circles. Thus he quickly gained access to the palaces and salons of the nobility and the houses of the musical connoisseurs.

Records of his early activities show him setting himself up in a small apartment and getting a piano, buying clothes appropriate for his new role, looking for a wig maker and inquiring about a dance teacher. As might be expected, he quickly ran into financial problems and in his early years had to procure loans—at least on one occasion from Haydn.

In his first years in Vienna, Beethoven was regarded primarily as a piano player. The great Mozart had died in December 1791, and there was no clear pianistic champion presiding over the Viennese musical scene. There were, though, many excellent pianists around, engaged mostly in giving piano lessons to the children of the wealthy families.

Beethoven soon established himself as a major virtuoso and looked with distrust upon the other leading pianists as rivals and competitors to be beaten and insulted. He even referred to some of them as his sworn enemies.

Initially, the primary venues for his performances were the salons of the aristocrats. After 1795, however, he began playing at public concerts, which were starting to become popular in Vienna. He had a strong style, and played with power and imagination. This often contrasted with the more delicate and softer style of some of the earlier virtuosos. Comments from some observers of his performances and from his rivals give a good picture of Beethoven's extraordinary skills. His pupil Karl Czerny later recalled:

> In whatever company he might chance to be, he knew how to produce such an effect upon every hearer that frequently not an eye remained dry, while many would break out into loud sobs; for there was something wonderful in his expression in addition to the beauty and originality of his ideas and his spirited style of rendering them. After ending an improvisation of this kind he would burst into loud laughter and banter his hearers on the emotion he had caused them. "You are fools," he would say—"Who can live among such spoiled children?" he would cry.

Czerny also reported the downcast comments from one of Beethoven's pianistic competitors, Abbe Gelinek, after one of their piano-playing contests:

> Oh, I shall think back on the last night many a time. That young fellow was full of the very devil. Never have I heard such playing! He improvised on a theme I had given him as I have never heard Mozart himself improvise. Then he played compositions of his own which are in the highest degree astonishing and grandiose and he displayed difficulties and affectionate piano beyond anything of which we might have dreamed.

It was as a composer, though, that Beethoven had come to Vienna to study with Haydn. Within a month the lessons had begun. They lasted for only a year and proved a disappointment for both Beethoven and Haydn. They were often in conflict with one another and had different temperaments and expectations for the relationship. The young Beethoven was opinionated, mistrustful, strong-willed and often obstinate. He expected Haydn to teach him composing techniques such as counterpoint, and he wanted Haydn to be strict about it. The sixty-year-old Haydn seemed too paternal and relaxed, as well as condescending and possessive, to the intense Beethoven.

The lessons with Haydn were not enough for Beethoven, and he began to look elsewhere for instruction. In early 1794 Haydn left for his second trip to London, and the lessons ended. Even though Beethoven was to dedicate specific works to Haydn in later years, he refused to officially acknowledge on any of his works that he had been Haydn's pupil.

One incident gives us some glimpse of the character of the two men in these years. Early on, Beethoven was having trouble financially, and he went into debt. He asked Haydn to write to the Elector of Bonn on his behalf, hoping to get an increase in his subsidy. Haydn wrote to the Elector in November 1793, enclosing five musical pieces, "compositions of my dear pupil, Beethoven," who he predicted would in time become one of Europe's great composers. He then pointed out to the Elector that the young composer's subsidy of one hundred ducats was quite inadequate and that he should increase it substantially. The Elector's response reflected poorly on Beethoven, as it is clear that he had misled the trusting Haydn. In his reply the Elector pointed out that four of the five pieces had been composed and performed in Bonn before Beethoven left for Vienna. In addition, he informed Haydn that Beethoven was in fact receiving considerably more than the hundred ducats, and he saw no reason why the amount should be raised. The perturbed Elector concluded:

> I am wondering if he would not do better to begin his return journey, in order to resume his duties here; for I very much doubt whether he will have made any important progress in composition and taste during his present stay, and I fear he will only bring back debts from his journey, just as he did from his first trip to Vienna.

The lives of the two great composers continued to intersect on occasion, but the relationship remained one of respect but little warmth.

Beethoven still felt the need for additional instruction, as his thirst for musical knowledge was immense. He studied for a while with Johann Schenk but was careful to conceal the fact from Haydn. Probably the most important instruction he received was from Johann Albrechtsberger, a stern pedagogue and the Kapellmeister of St. Stephen's. He was reputed to be the best teacher of counterpoint in Vienna. Beethoven studied with him for several years, and he proved to be a conscientious and disciplined teacher. The instructions were valuable to Beethoven, and in later years he would return to them for self-study. Beethoven also purused vocal writing with Antonio Salieri, the Imperial Kapellmeister.

His relations with his instructors always included some elements of conflict, as his teachers were torn between their admiration for Beethoven's considerable skills and their resentment of his strong will and stubborn nature. Ultimately, Beethoven could learn only so much from others. He felt he had to move ahead on his own and learn from experience as a composer if he were going to fulfill the expanding musical desires and ambitions that were within him.

Beethoven also continued to develop his skills with and knowledge of instruments. He took violin lessons for a while and developed a real attachment to the instrument even though he had no special talent. He of course constantly worked on piano playing but also became interested in the mechanics of the instrument, constantly looking for pianos of greater range and tone.

His total commitment to his art form moved him to acquire musical input from a wide variety of sources. He was constantly listening to, studying and often criticizing the music of his contemporaries. He tried to learn from others, and his inquisitive mind made him receptive to new ideas. But he was not a follower or an imitator. Musical ideas from others were considered and then merged into his own strong and maturing beliefs.

It was during these early years in Vienna that a group of supporters started to gather around Beethoven. For many of the aristocratic families of Vienna, music was the preferred expression of their wealth and a socially desirable reflection of their culture and social status. Their devotion to music was far greater than that of their counterparts in the other major cities in Europe. Many of them kept chamber groups or instrumental soloists, and a few even had resident opera companies. Their salons were the primary performance venues for the musical activities of the day.

Beethoven was quickly brought into this active circle. He developed close, and, in some cases, long-lasting relationships with some of the leading families. Many of them became his patrons when they recognized the brilliant skills of the young, intense and often moody musician. He soon became the recipient of a flattering array of gifts, money and invitations. Some of his patrons in these early years in Vienna were:

• Prince Joseph Lobkowitz. He had a private orchestra that Beethoven often used. For a time he gave Beethoven an annual annuity.

• Count Andreas Razumovsky. A music lover, amateur violinist and Russian Ambassador to Vienna, he supported a string quartet and commissioned many works by Beethoven.

• Count Moritz von Fries. A wealthy head of a banking firm, he commissioned numerous pieces by Beethoven. Occasionally he acted as intermediary for Beethoven with publishers.

• Baron Gottfried van Swieten. A friend of Mozart and Haydn, and a leading musical connoisseur, he sponsored important concerts and received the dedication of Beethoven's first symphony.

Beethoven's leading patron of these years, though, was Prince Karl Lichnowsky (1756–1814). He and his wife, Princess Christiane, hosted a series of musical parties where many of Beethoven's works were initially performed. It was also in their home where Beethoven became acquainted with many of the young musicians who would become his friends. Two particularly important friendships were formed during these sessions. One was with the prince's brother, Count Moritz Lichnowsky, and the other was with Baron Nikolus von Zmeskall, an official of the Hungarian embassy, an amateur cellist, and a minor composer. He became Beethoven's lifelong friend and would often perform small services for him, such as providing quill pens, which Beethoven could never cut properly.

Beethoven became very close to the Lichnowskys and even moved in with them for several years. According to the account of an associate, Lichnowsky treated Beethoven "as a friend and brother and induced the entire nobility to support him." The princess became something of a second mother to him.

His close association with the Lichnowskys amplified some of the conflicting feelings Beethoven was having about his relationship with his patrons. Beethoven wanted their affection, their praise and, of course, their commissions and financial support. But his pride, strong will and stubborn independence put him on guard against any form of control, patronizing behavior or condescending remarks. Beethoven's friend Wegeler recalled that on one occasion Prince Lichnowsky directed his serviceman that if ever he and Beethoven should ring at the same time, the latter was to be the first served. Beethoven heard this remark and the same day engaged a servant himself. On another occasion, when Beethoven was learning to ride horseback, the prince offered Beethoven the use of his stable. Beethoven, afraid of the feelings of dependency, went out and bought a horse of his own.

Even though he desired and probably needed the family-like closeness the Lichnowskys provided, particularly the princess's maternal concerns, he often felt stifled in the relationship. He frequently ate away from the family as an expression of his independence. Once he expressed to a friend, "The dinner hour at the Prince's was 4:00. Am I supposed to come home every day at half past three, change my clothes, shave and all that? I'll have none of it."

Beethoven was also very touchy about being made to perform if he felt he was being exploited or put on display. On occasion he would simply refuse to play, and a number of times he stomped out of a salon when he felt he was not being treated with proper respect as a person and an artist. Yet in spite of his contradictory feelings about his patrons and his often foolish behavior, most of his supporters came to accept his unusual personality as part of his genius.

The nature of these relationships with his patrons, and the financial support he received, were important parts of his struggle to establish his position as an independent artist. During these early years in Vienna he went through a period of significant transition from both an economic and an artistic standpoint. By the late 1790s, he had made the change from being an almost completely dependent court musician of the Elector of Bonn to being a fairly independent composer and pianist. He now received commissions and considerable financial aid from a variety of enthusiastic patrons in Vienna. He also made some money giving public concerts and, occasionally, lessons.

From time to time throughout his life, Beethoven seemed determined to go back to the security and status of a permanent position in a major court. But his desire to be his own master always led him down the path of increasing financial and artistic independence.

By the mid-1790s, the focus of Beethoven's life was clearly in Vienna. Bonn had been occupied by French troops, and his subsidy from the Elector stopped in March of 1794. There was no longer a plan to return to Bonn. By the end of 1795 both his brothers had moved to Vienna—Casper Carl becoming a music teacher and Nicholas Johann going into business as an apothecary. Some of his boyhood friends arrived as well. The three von Breuning brothers arrived, along with Franz Wegeler.

Thus, by his twenty-fifth year, Beethoven was set up and doing quite well in Vienna. He was head of his small, parentless family, had a growing reputation as a pianist and composer and had an array of well-to-do patrons and friends. Life generally looked good.

Nevertheless, there were several aspects of his life that were indicative of the unrest and turmoil that continued inside him. Beethoven showed a need to constantly change his living arrangements. He rarely stayed in any place for more than a year or so. He was frequently dissatisfied, and evidently wasn't a very pleasant renter, as he generally lived with an amazing amount of disorder and messiness.

Beethoven's desire for a meaningful female relationship was another source of frustration. We see the beginnings of a pattern of fascination and infatuation that very quickly ends in rejection and disappointment. He proposed to a singer in 1794 but was rejected, supposedly because he was "ugly and half crazy." There were several other women, almost always above him socially, in whom he was interested. He seemed to spend a lot of time falling in and out of love with women who either had no interest in him or were already married or engaged.

He would sometimes dedicate one of his compositions to them, but no lasting romantic relationship developed. This desire for closeness and his failure to obtain it became a continuing pattern in Beethoven's life for many years. (As for merely sexual encounters, Beethoven—at least in these early times—seems to have been wary of prostitutes. To his brother Nicholas Johann he wrote, "Do be on your guard against the whole tribe of bad women.")

As Beethoven became more involved in Viennese musical life, his output of compositions increased. Much of his work during these years was written for performance in the salons of his patrons and was often dedicated to them. He wrote extensively for the piano, composing a large number of sets of variations, plus assorted sonatas. There were also works for stringed instruments as well as chamber works for winds. The late 1790s also saw the completion and performance of his first two piano concertos, written in the typical Classical style, but showing clear indications of the new direction Beethoven was taking. Public concerts were becoming more important, and the performance of these works, often with Beethoven playing the solo parts, was enhancing Beethoven's reputation as well as his pocketbook.

Knowledge of Beethoven's skills as a virtuoso had reached other major cities in Europe by the mid-1790s. There now appeared to be a broader market for his talents. A tour was arranged, and in February of 1796 Beethoven, accompanied by Lichnowsky, set out for Prague. He was a hit. He wrote back to his brother Johann:

> My art is winning me friends, renown and what more do I want? And this time I should make a good deal of money.

From there it was on to Dresden, where he played before the Elector of Saxony. The trip then culminated in Berlin. He stayed there for over a month and played several times before the King of Prussia (Frederick Wilhelm II). In deference to the cello-playing king, Beethoven wrote two cello sonatas and performed them with the resident cellist. The King, in appreciation, gave Beethoven a gold snuffbox that Beethoven proudly said was "no ordinary snuffbox, but such a one that might have been customary to give to an ambassador."

Later that same year, Beethoven made a brief trip to perform in what is now Bratislava. In the fall of 1798 he again went to Prague, where he gave two public concerts, playing his first and second piano concertos, plus other piano works. The Bohemian composer Johann Tomasek, who had heard all the great pianists of the time, was in attendance. Later he wrote:

> Beethoven's magnificent playing and particularly the daring flights of his improvisations stirred me strangely to the depths of my soul; indeed I found myself so profoundly bowed down that I did not touch my pianoforte for several days.

Tomasek felt Beethoven was the greatest pianist of all time.

As the eighteenth century drew to a close, Beethoven could look with pride on his status and his accomplishments. He was aware of, and strongly committed to, developing his unique musical abilities, and he had a group of ardent patrons supporting him. He no longer had major financial problems, and his personal life, while still stressful and somewhat chaotic, was at least not interfering with his work. He was still shy and not particularly social, but he had made some friends and was interacting with women, even though not making much progress in forming an intimate relationship. Overall, his first eight years in Vienna had gone well.

There were, though, clouds on the horizon. There is some evidence that he had a serious illness in 1796 and 1797. But of most concern, and to his great horror, he had begun to realize in his late twenties that he was having serious hearing problems. The very thought deeply frightened him. Thus, around the turn of the century he entered a period of severe depression while at the same time making great progress artistically and achieving considerable fame as a composer.

Personal Crisis, 1800–1802

The year 1800 was an important turning point for Beethoven. In April of that year he put on the first public concert for his own benefit. It was a big affair, and it put Beethoven on a par with the greatest of his predecessors. A look at the program gives us a feeling for the musical life in Vienna.

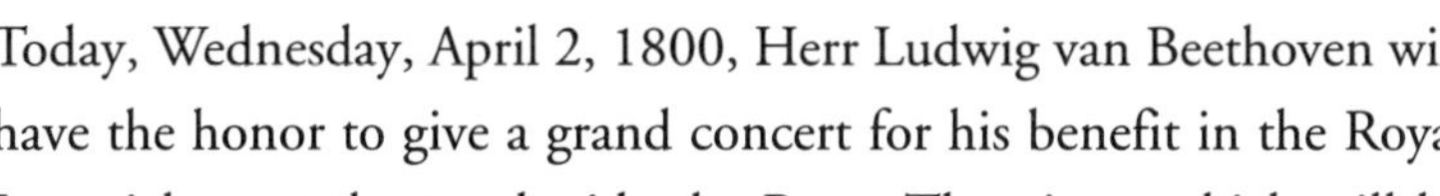

Today, Wednesday, April 2, 1800, Herr Ludwig van Beethoven will have the honor to give a grand concert for his benefit in the Royal Imperial court theater, beside the Burg. The pieces which will be performed are the following:

1) A Grand Symphony by the late Kapellmeister, Mozart.

2) An aria from *The Creation*, by Princely Kapellmeister Herr Haydn, sung by Mlle Saal.

3) A Grand Concerto for pianoforte played and composed by Herr Ludwig van Beethoven.

4) A Septet most humbly and obediently dedicated to Her Majesty the Empress, and composed by Herr Ludwig van Beethoven for four string and three wind instruments.

5) A Duet from Haydn's *The Creation* sung by Herr and Mlle Saal.

6) Herr Ludwig van Beethoven will improvise on the pianoforte.

7) A new Grand Symphony with complete orchestra composed by Herr Ludwig van Beethoven.

—

Tickets for boxes and stalls are to be had of Herr van Beethoven at his lodging in the Tiefen Graben no. 241, third floor, and of the box keeper.

—

The admission prices are as usual.

—

The start is at half past 6.

———✦———

Later that year Beethoven was granted a small annuity by Prince Lichnowsky, which gave him greater financial independence and some relief from having to accept all commissions or publishers' offers.

This period of the early 1800s was marked by the completion and publishing of his first set of string quartets. These signified the move away from his primary concentration on composing for the piano. They also enabled him to make a mark on this complex genre which, along with the symphony, was to be among the dominant musical forms during the nineteenth century. Additionally, in 1801 his score for the ballet *The Creatures of Prometheus* was completed. It was a huge success, being performed over twenty times in two years and bringing him further fame. It was also during this time that foreign publishers began to bid for his works, enabling Beethoven to broaden his base of prestige and income potential.

But underneath this outward appearance of productivity and success, Beethoven was torn by inner conflicts and worries. His contradictory feelings are reflected in a letter to his friend Wegeler, written in June of 1801:

> You want to know something about my present situation. Well, on the whole, it is not all bad...My compositions bring me in a good deal; and I may say that I am offered more commissions than it is possible for me to carry out. Moreover, for every composition I can count on six or seven publishers, and even more, if I want them; people no longer come to an arrangement with me, I state my price and they pay. So you see how pleasantly situated I am—
>
> But that jealous demon, my wretched health, has put a nasty spoke in my wheel; and it amounts to this, that for the last three years my hearing has become weaker and weaker. The trouble is supposed to have been caused by the condition of my abdomen, which, as you know, was wretched before I left Bonn, but has become worse in Vienna where I have been constantly afflicted with diarrhea and have been suffering the consequences from an extraordinary debility.—For almost two years I have ceased to attend any social function, just because I find it impossible to say to people I am deaf. If I had any other profession I might be able to cope with my infirmity; but in my profession it is a terrible handicap. And if my enemies, of whom I have a fair number, were to hear about it, what would they say? In order to give you some idea of this strange deafness, let me tell you that in a theater I have to place myself quite close to the orchestra in order to understand what the actor is saying, and that at a distance I cannot hear the high notes of instruments or voices. As for the spoken voice, it is surprising that some people have never noticed my deafness; but since I have always been liable to fits of absent-mindedness, they attribute my hardness of hearing to that. Sometimes, too, I can scarcely hear a person who speaks softly; I can hear sounds, it is true, but cannot make out the words. But if anyone shouts I can't bear it. Heaven alone knows what is to become of me. Vering (a doctor) tells me that my hearing will certainly improve, although my deafness may not be

completely cured. Already I have cursed my Creator and my existence. Plutarch has shown me the path of resignation. If it is at all possible, I will bid defiance to my fate, though I feel that as long as I live there will be moments when I shall be God's most unhappy creature. Resignation, what a wretched resource! Yet it is all that is left to me.

Just several days later he wrote to another friend, Karl Amenda:

How often would I like to have you here for me, for your B(eethoven) is leading a very unhappy life and is at variance with nature and his Creator. Many times already I have cursed Him for exposing His creatures to the slightest hazard so that the most beautiful blossom is thereby often crushed and destroyed. Let me tell you that my most prized possession, my hearing, has greatly deteriorated. When you were still with me, I already felt the symptoms, but I said nothing about them. Now they have become very much worse...You will realize what a sad life I must now lead, seeing that I am cut off from everything that is dear and precious to me…I must withdraw from everything and my best years will rapidly pass away without my being able to achieve all that my talent and my strength have commanded me to do. Sad resignation, to which I am forced to have no recourse. Needless to say, I am resolved to overcome all this, but how is it going to be done?

By the fall of 1801 his spirits had picked up a bit. He found a doctor whom he liked, and some optimism returned to his outlook. In November 1801 he wrote again to Wegeler:

True enough, I cannot deny it, the humming and buzzing is slightly less than it used to be, particularly in my left ear where my deafness really began…But so far my hearing is not a bit better...I am now leading a slightly more pleasant life by mixing more with my fellow creatures—for some time now, my physical strength has been increasing more and more and therefore my mental powers, also. Every day brings me nearer to the goal which I feel, but cannot describe...I will seize Fate by the throat; it shall certainly not bend and crush me completely.

Also in this letter to Wegeler, Beethoven talks about a "dear charming girl who loves me and whom I love." He was referring to the seventeen-year-old Countess Giulietta Guicciardi, one of his piano students. He was infatuated with her, but like his other "loves," nothing came of it and she married another composer closer to her age. Beethoven did give her a place in history, though, as he dedicated his famous *Moonlight* Sonata to her.

For some months in late 1801 and early 1802, Beethoven led an active and productive life. His composing continued and he spent time with his friends. To his delight, more of his old companions from Bonn arrived in Vienna. Of particular importance to Beethoven was his close friendship with Zmeskall, whom he saw regularly in addition to engaging in amusing and witty correspondence. (He addressed his friend as Baron MuckDriver, or Plenipotentiary of Beethoven's Kingdom.) He also spent more time with his brother Casper Carl, who helped Beethoven in some of his business dealings.

By the spring of 1802, Beethoven's depression had returned. In April of that year he moved out of Vienna to the nearby country village of Heiligenstadt for the summer. Over the years these summers in the country were particularly important to Beethoven, as he seemed to find inspiration and relaxation during his long walks in the woods. Beethoven's 1802 stay in Heiligenstadt was longer than usual and was probably taken on the advice of his doctors—or perhaps he just wanted to get away from the stress of dealing with his hearing problems in society. He continued his composing there, but his mood swings and general depression continued. One of his students, Ferdinand Ries (son of his Bonn neighbor Franz Ries), later recalled an incident that gives us insight into Beethoven's moods and behavior:

> I called his attention to a shepherd who was piping very agreeably in the woods on a flute made of a twig of elder. For half an hour Beethoven could hear nothing and though I assured him that it was quite the same with me (which was not the case), he became extremely quiet and morose. When occasionally he seemed to be merry, it was generally to the extreme of boisterousness; but this happened seldom.

Late in the fall his spirits hit the depths. His thoughts and the extent of his despair were expressed in the famous "Heiligenstadt Testament," written in October 1802. He addressed it to his two brothers (but curiously left out the name of Johann). He never sent it, and it was discovered after his death.

> For My Brothers Carl and ________ Beethoven
> Oh, you men who think or say that I am malevolent, stubborn, or misanthropic, how greatly do you wrong me. You do not know the secret cause which makes me seem that way to you. From childhood on, my heart and soul have been full of the tender feeling of goodwill, and I was ever inclined to accomplish great things. But, think that for six years now I have been hopelessly afflicted, made

worse by senseless physicians, from year to year deceived with hopes of improvement, finally compelled to face the prospect of a lasting malady (whose cure will take years or, perhaps, be impossible). Though born with a fiery, active temperament, ever susceptible to the diversions of society, I was soon compelled to withdraw myself, to live life alone. If at times I tried to forget all this, oh how harshly was I flung back by the doubly sad experience of my bad hearing. Yet it was impossible for me to say to people, "Speak louder, shout, for I am deaf." Ah, how could I possibly admit an infirmity in the one sense which ought to be more perfect in me than in others, a sense which I once possessed in the highest perfection, a perfection such as few in my profession enjoy or ever have enjoyed.—Oh I cannot do it; therefore forgive me when you see me draw back when I would have gladly mingled with you. My misfortune is doubly painful to me because I am bound to be misunderstood; for me there can be no relaxation with my fellow men, no refined conversations, no mutual exchange of ideas. I must live almost alone, like one who has been banished; I can mix with society only as much as true necessity demands. If I approach near to people a hot terror seizes upon me, and I fear being exposed to the danger that my condition might be noticed. Thus it has been during the last six months which I have spent in the country. By ordering me to spare my hearing as much as possible, my intelligent doctor almost fell in with my own present frame of mind, though sometimes I ran counter to it by yielding to my desire for companionship. But what a humiliation for me when someone standing next to me heard a flute in the distance and I heard nothing, or someone heard a shepherd singing and again I heard nothing. Such incidents drove me almost to despair; a little more of that and I would have ended my life —it was only my art that held me back. Ah, it seemed to me impossible to leave the world until I had brought forth all that I felt was within me. So I endured this wretched existence—truly wretched for so susceptible a body, which can be thrown by a sudden change from the best condition to the very worst.—Patience, they say, is what I must now choose for my guide, and I have done so—I hope my determination will remain firm to endure until it pleases the inexorable Parcae to break the thread. Perhaps I shall get better, perhaps not; I am ready.—Forced to become a philosopher already in my twenty-eighth year,—oh it is not easy, and for the artist much more difficult than for anyone else.—Divine One, thou seest my inmost soul; thou knowest that therein dwells the love of mankind and the desire to do good.—Oh fellow men, when at some point you read this, consider then that you have done me an injustice; someone who has had misfortune may console himself to find a similar case to his, who despite all the limitations of Nature nevertheless did everything within his powers to become accepted among worthy artists and men.—You, my brothers Carl and ________, as soon as I am dead, if Dr. Schmidt is still alive, ask him in my name to describe my malady, and attach this written document to his account of my illness so that so far as is possible at least the world may become reconciled to me after my death.—At the same time, I declare you two to be the heirs to my small fortune (if so it can be called); divide it fairly; bear with and help each other. What injury you have done me you know was long ago forgiven. To you, brother Carl, I give special thanks for the attachment you have shown me of late. It is my wish that you may have a better and freer life than I have had. Recommend virtue to your children; it alone, not money, can make them happy. I speak from experience; this was what upheld me in time of misery. Thanks to it and to my art, I did not end my life by suicide—Farewell and love each other—I thank all my friends, particularly Prince Lichnowsky and Professor Schmidt—I would like the instruments from Prince L. to be preserved by one of you, but not to be the cause of strife between you, and as soon as they can serve you a better purpose, then sell them. How happy I shall be if I can still be helpful to you in my grave—so be it.—With joy I hasten to meet death.—If it comes before I have had the chance to develop all my artistic capacities, it will still be coming too soon despite my harsh fate, and I should probably wish it later—yet even so I should be happy, for would it not free me from a state of endless suffering?—Come when thou wilt, I shall meet thee bravely.—Farewell and do not wholly forget me when I am dead; I deserve this from you, for during my lifetime I was thinking of you often and of ways to make you happy—please be so—

Ludwig van Beethoven
Heiglnstadt, (Heiligenstadt)
October 6th, 1802

For my brothers Carl and ________ to be read and executed after my death.
Heiglnstadt, October 10, 1802
Thus I bid thee farewell—and indeed sadly.—Yes, that fond hope— which I brought here with me, to be cured to a degree at least—this I must now wholly abandon. As the leaves of autumn fall and are withered—so likewise has my hope been blighted—I leave here—almost as I came—even the high courage—which often inspired me in the beautiful days of summer—has disappeared—Oh Providence—grant me at last but one day of pure joy—it is so long since real joy echoed in my heart—Oh when—Oh when, Oh Divine One—shall I feel it again in the temple of nature and of mankind—Never?—No—Oh that would be too hard.

There is some controversy regarding Beethoven's seriousness about his talk of suicide. But taken as a whole, the Heiligenstadt Testament is a significant and genuine outpouring of Beethoven's deepest feeling and his basic unhappiness. The statement cites his deafness as the primary cause of his discontent, and certainly it was the major problem in Beethoven's life. But his life had never been one of real happiness or contentment. Even back in Bonn, those who associated with him were aware of his moodiness, obstinacy and tendency to pull back from others. So we must see this extraordinary document not just in reaction to Beethoven's deep depression over his loss of hearing but also as a crying out about a whole set of deep anxieties and frustrations.

Amazingly, very little of this anguish is reflected in Beethoven's work during this time. His bright and lively second symphony was completed in 1802, and by November he was already negotiating with publishers on two sets of new and innovative piano variations. It was during these years that Beethoven's composing also started to be more innovative, and he talked of a "new path."

Fame, Creativity and Growth, 1803–1813

Over the course of his life, Beethoven had periods of great creativity and productivity after times of crisis and depression. He would immerse himself in his work, turning his focus away from his personal problems toward the significant artistic challenges he had set for himself.

Following his years of despondency in 1801 and 1802, Beethoven entered a period of relative personal stability, high creative achievement and considerable international fame. During these years his reputation grew in a number of countries. He was particularly revered in England, where his major works could be heard regularly by the early 1800s. And across all of Europe, the publication of Beethoven's works continued to spread. (France was somewhat of a different story, as there were only a few public performances of his works in Paris. In reaction, Beethoven said, "The French find my music beyond their power of performance.")

Shortly after moving back to Vienna from Heiligenstadt, Beethoven accepted an offer to write an opera. As part of the deal, he and his brother moved into the Theater an der Wien, where Beethoven could work. This was a real opportunity for Beethoven, as there was a thriving market for the heroic operas then popular in Paris that were being imported into Vienna. Lack of a finished libretto delayed the beginning of work for several months, and by the end of the year only the first scene had been completed. Beethoven eventually decided he didn't like the libretto at all and stopped the project. It was only later that he began working on his one successful opera,

Leonore/Fidelio, which was to go through many revisions and permutations before it was finished some ten years later.

Part of his arrangement at the Theater an der Wien was the opportunity for Beethoven to give a concert. Beethoven quickly wrote an oratorio, *Christ on the Mount of Olives,* for the occasion. It was performed in a grand concert on April 5, 1803, along with his first and second symphonies and his third piano concerto (with the composer as soloist).

It is fair to say that at this point Beethoven and the aging Haydn were the leading musical figures of the time.

While all this other activity was going on, Beethoven was working on a grand new symphony that was to take him and the symphonic form in drastically new directions. The composing of Beethoven's third symphony took place mainly in the summer and early fall of 1803 while Beethoven was staying in the village of Oberdöbling, just outside of Vienna. It was an immense undertaking, and the final work was the result of many revisions and sketches. The work is monumental and complex in scale and runs some fifty minutes in length—nearly twice as long as most symphonies up to that time. It is filled with rich themes and musical ideas, violent contrasts, and periods of great audio suspense that are woven into a masterful whole. The piece was previewed at a private performance at Prince Lobkowitz's in late 1804. The first public performance was held in April 1805. It met with mixed reviews. (A man in the audience hollered out, "I'll give another *Kreutzer* (money) if only the thing will stop.")

Beethoven originally titled the symphony *Bonaparte,* in tribute to the revolutionary leader of France, who then was still thought of by many as the heroic embodiment of Enlightenment ideals. This idealization changed for Beethoven when in March of 1804 Napoleon, first counsel of France, proclaimed himself Emperor. On hearing the news, Beethoven flew into a rage and cried out:

> Is he then, too, nothing more than an ordinary human being? Now he, too, will trample on all the rights of man and indulge only his ambition. He will exalt himself above all others, become a tyrant!

He angrily scratched out the original. The work was subsequently given the title *Heroic Symphony* (*Eroica*) when it was published in 1806.

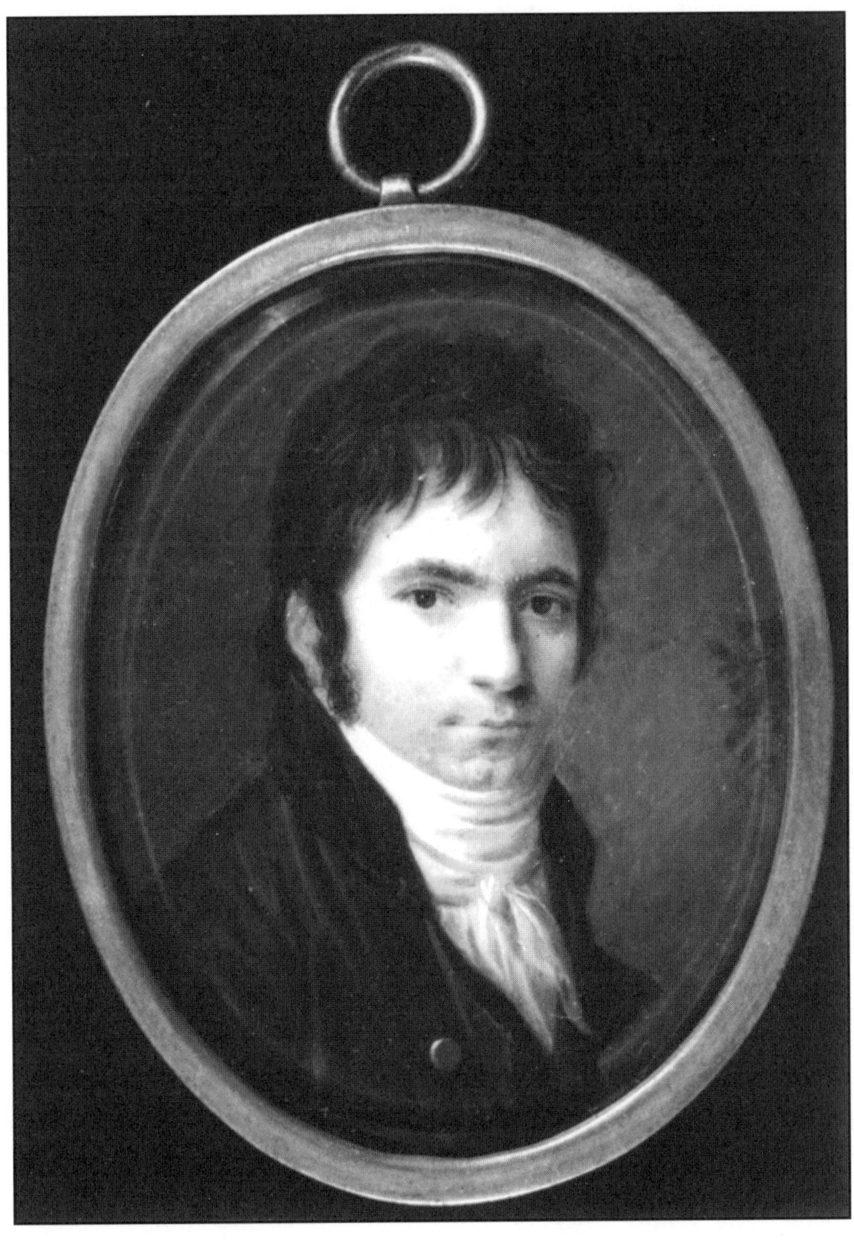

Beethoven at the age of thirty-three (1803), the year he composed the Eroica *Symphony.*

Portrait by Christian Horneman

By permission of the Beethoven-Haus Bonn. Collection H. C. Bodmer

Beethoven continued to hold the values of the Enlightenment—love of human beings, justice and reason. For many years he had had something of a love-hate relationship with France and had even considered moving there for a while. Beethoven would frequently express great displeasure with France and Napoleon. After one of Napoleon's victories, Beethoven supposedly said, "It's a pity that I do not understand the art of war as well as I do the art of music. I would conquer him." Still, friends of Beethoven could detect in him admiration for Napoleon's accomplishments and his rise from humble beginnings.

In spite of the French occupation of Vienna in late 1805 and 1806 and the general political and intellectual upheaval of the time, the mid-years of the first decade of the nineteenth century were extremely productive for Beethoven. This period resulted in pieces that reflected elements of the French "grand style," emotionally conjuring up heroism, grandeur and the triumph of reason and justice in the affairs of humanity. During the years 1804–1808 he completed an astonishing array of masterpieces, highlighted by his fourth, fifth and sixth symphonies, fourth piano concerto, a violin concerto, a triple concerto, three string quartets and a series of smaller pieces, including the *Waldstein* Sonata, dedicated to his early patron and friend from Bonn.

While this outpouring of instrumental works was taking place, Beethoven was struggling with an opera. His original attempt to write one for the Theater an der Wien had been abandoned in late 1803. In the meantime, he had found a libretto more to his liking– "Léonore ou l'amour conjugal" by the Frenchman J.N. Bouilly. It was the story of a political prisoner rescued by his wife, and it was supposedly based on an actual incident in the French Revolution. It appealed to Beethoven because of its heroic qualities and because it gave him an opportunity to write a "rescue" opera of the type that was so popular at the time. Further, Beethoven could identify with the helpless hero. Beethoven felt powerless because of his deafness and could feel empathy with the devoted wife Leonore (disguised as Fidelio), who symbolized the ideal woman Beethoven could never find. The work was Beethoven's major effort during much of 1804–1806. It was in fairly complete form by the summer of 1805 and scheduled for performance that fall.

Because of its revolutionary undertones, however, it ran into trouble with the censors. This problem was shortly resolved, but in early November

French armies occupied Vienna, and most of the nobility and many patrons fled the city.

On November 20, when *Leonore* opened, the sparse crowd included a number of French officers. Beethoven directed the performance from the piano. There was applause from the small audience, but it was not a good night. Performances on the following two evenings played to very small and unenthusiastic audiences. The opera was withdrawn.

As Beethoven's friends returned to the city in the months that followed, there was interest in a revival. Many felt the work was too long and a bit slow in parts, so Beethoven, with great reluctance, made significant changes. The opera's name was also changed from *Leonore* to *Fidelio.* It was performed two more times in the spring of 1806, to a slightly better reception. But then Beethoven got into a quarrel with the theater director and withdrew his score.

It was not until 1814, after further revisions, that the opera was again performed. The work is now part of the regular repertoire of opera houses around the world. Wonderful by-products are the four different overtures that Beethoven composed for the various revisions. The most famous are *Leonore no. 3* for the 1806 performance, and *Fidelio* for the 1814 version.

While musically Beethoven continued to grow, innovate and produce an astonishing variety of work during these years, his private life remained filled with conflict and travail. In 1804 he became involved with one of his piano students, Countess Josephine von Brunsvik. She was the young widow of a recently deceased nobleman and had four small children. True to pattern, Beethoven fell in love with her, and an intense relationship developed between them—more intense for Beethoven than for the young countess. Though she was close to him and concerned for his happiness, and though she admired his ideals and artistic skills, she evidently did not want more than a close friendship. She claimed it was concern for her young family that prevented more intimacy. But her reluctance was surely strengthened by Beethoven's lack of social standing and his irregular habits. They soon drifted apart, and by 1810, when she married a baron, Beethoven's affections had moved on to another.

Beethoven's volatile nature also caused conflict with his friends, which added to the general stress of his life. In 1804 a change in ownership of the

Theater an der Wien caused Beethoven to move to new lodgings with his old friend from Bonn, Steven von Breuning. Shortly thereafter, Beethoven caused a quarrel, and he moved to Baden, five miles south of Vienna. By fall he and von Breuning had made up, but a letter in November of that year by the loyal and understanding von Breuning gives us insight into Beethoven's condition:

> You would not believe—what an indescribable and, I might say, ghastly effect the loss of hearing has had on him. Imagine to yourself what the feeling of being a victim of misfortune can do to his vehement character, namely reserve, mistrust, often towards his best friends, and indecision in many things. On the whole with only a few exceptions when he gives expression to his original spirit, to be with him is truly an effort, wherein one can never trust oneself—

Beethoven also fought with his patrons on occasion, and his temper sometimes caused significant problems. Things came to a head with his major patron Prince Lichnowsky when he asked Beethoven to play for a group of French officers he assembled in his home during the occupation in the fall of 1806. Beethoven got angry and refused what he termed "menial labor." He and the prince almost came to blows. Chairs were raised in anger and Beethoven stomped out. On arriving home, he smashed the bust of his patron on the floor. Again, relations were patched up, and the prince remained a loyal and understanding friend.

Financial matters also troubled Beethoven during this period. In spite of all his success and spreading fame, Beethoven still had no steady and dependable source of income. He was making quite a good living by marketing his works to publishers and by selling some of them to noblemen, who would receive a dedication and initial performance rights. He also continued to receive an annuity from Lichnowsky until around 1806—possibly stopped after the chair-raising incident mentioned above. Beethoven was able to cut back considerably on his teaching and was freed from composing the standard little contra dances and minuets that had been economically necessary in his earlier years. Still, he was worried by the lack of dependability of his income. He often longed for a permanent position where he could work without worry. The memory of Mozart dying in poverty no doubt hung over him. In 1807 he petitioned to the Royal Imperial Court Theater for a contract that would provide him a fixed annual income of 2,400 florins in return for composing an opera every year, as well as other works. He also asked for use of a theater once a year for a benefit concert for himself. In his written petition he hinted that he might have to leave Vienna if he were turned down. The application was not accepted, and his request for a benefit concert for 1807 was also turned down.

He did, though, finally get the use of the Theater an der Wien for the night of December 22, 1808, and he arranged an enormous concert, or Akademie. It turned out to be one of the strangest concerts in musical history. Drawing on his recent productivity, he programmed a concert of four hours. Many of the pieces were new to the Viennese audience. The program consisted of first performances of the fifth and sixth symphonies and the fourth piano concerto (with Beethoven as soloist); movements from a recently completed Mass in C Major; an aria written much earlier; and some improvisations. It concluded with a hastily written choral fantasy for piano, orchestra and chorus. There was very little rehearsal time, and the orchestra had a dispute with Beethoven stemming from an earlier concert. Things did not go well. The orchestra broke down in the middle of the fantasy and the piece had to be restarted. In addition, Beethoven had quarreled with the original soprano, and the substitute that had been found wasn't up to the task. Furthermore, the theater was extremely cold. One audience member said,

> There we sat from six to ten-thirty in the bitter cold and found by experience that one might have too much even of a good thing.

The concert proved to be difficult for performer and listener alike. The monetary results, while not specifically known, were no doubt disappointing, and Beethoven continued to worry about his financial security.

Throughout these years Beethoven would occasionally complain about Vienna and the Viennese. Several times he threatened to leave the city, and in early 1809 he received an offer that would allow him to do so. The offer came from Napoleon's younger brother Jérôme, who had just been set up as King of Westphalia. Beethoven was asked to come to Kassel and become Kapellmeister of his court. Deep down, Beethoven didn't really want to leave Vienna, but he used the offer as a bargaining tool. Over the course of several months in early 1809, through several intermediaries, he negotiated with three young nobles who felt it very important to keep the now-famous Beethoven in the beleaguered Hapsburg capital of Vienna. The agreement exceeded the Kassel offer and guaranteed Beethoven the sum of four thousand florins annually. Beethoven agreed to remain in Austria though, surprisingly, the agreement did not require Beethoven to compose any particular number of works or perform any specific duties. He also bargained for the title of Imperial Kapellmeister, but without success. The guarantors who signed the contract were Prince Lobkowitz (seven hundred florins), Prince Kinsky (one thousand eight hundred florins) and Archduke Rudolph, younger brother of the Emperor (one thousand five hundred florins). These nobles wrote:

> As it has been demonstrated that only one who is as free from care as possible can devote himself to a single department of activity and create works of magnitude which are exalted and which ennoble art, the undersigned have decided to place Herr Ludwig van Beethoven in a position where the necessaries of life shall not cause him embarrassment or clog his powerful genius.

Thus by his thirty-ninth year, Beethoven had attained an unprecedented degree of security and independence. In theory he was no longer subservient to the desires of individual patrons or forced to sell himself and his music to the general public. It was a major turning point for him, both financially and mentally.

After several years, however, the agreement ran into trouble, first because of the war-induced currency devaluation and later, due to the deaths of Kinsky in 1812 and Lobkowitz in 1816. But things were eventually resolved in Beethoven's favor, and he retained a high degree of security.

One of the signatories, Archduke Rudolph (1788–1831), played an important and positive role in Beethoven's life. Rudolph was the highest ranking and most noble of Beethoven's patrons, and the two men had a genuine respect and affection for each other.

Beethoven had taken on the young prince as a piano student in 1803 or 1804. Rudolph had considerable skills as both a player and a composer, and he was essentially Beethoven's only student in composition.

The prince, eighteen years younger than Beethoven, continually treated him with understanding, had great admiration for his work, and was generally accepting of his moods and temperamental nature.

Beethoven was devoted to Rudolph and valued his friendship, even though he would often try to beg off giving him lessons. Beethoven dedicated more works to Rudolph than to any other person. Some of the most famous are the fourth and fifth piano concertos, the *Archduke* Trio and a major late work, the *Missa Solemnis.* Particularly touching was a programmatic piano sonata (Sonata no. 26 in E-flat Major, *Les Adieus*) Beethoven wrote to express his feelings about Rudolph's forced departure from Vienna during the 1809 French occupation, and his eventual return. The warm relationship between the two men continued without interruption until Beethoven's death.

The 1809 French occupation lasted only two months, but it was a miserable time for Beethoven. Many of his friends fled, and he took up refuge with his brother Casper Carl, his wife and their two-year-old son, Karl. During the bombardment he would go into the cellar and cover his ears with pillows. His despair was poured out in a letter of July 1809:

> You are indeed mistaken in supposing that I have been very well. For in the meantime we have been suffering misery in a most concentrated form. Let me tell you that since May 4th I have produced very little coherent work, at most a fragment here and there. The whole course of events has in my case affected both body and soul...the existence I had built up only a short time ago rests on shaky foundations...what a destructive, disorderly life I see and hear around me: nothing but drums, cannons, and human misery in every form—.

Following the French withdrawal and the return of his friends and patrons, Beethoven experienced several years of relative normalcy—that is, significant creative output along with his ongoing problems of ill health, worsening deafness, disputes with publishers, periods of depression and disappointment in love.

Early in 1810 Beethoven began work on a commission to write the incidental music to Goethe's play *Egmont.* This was an exciting prospect, as Beethoven had long been an admirer of the great German poet. The heroic plot, dealing with self-sacrifice and the triumph of the Dutch over their oppressors, no doubt appealed to Beethoven. The work was quickly completed and performed in June of that year. He also wrote songs for other Goethe writings that spring.

His contact with Goethe was made initially through Bettina Brentano, a charming woman he had met several years earlier. Beethoven and Goethe developed great respect for each other. Their communication was carried on initially through their intermediaries and eventually in a direct exchange of letters. They finally met in July of 1812 at the Bohemian spa of Teplitz. Their impressions of one another are revealing. Goethe writes to his wife shortly after meeting Beethoven:

> I have never before seen a more comprehensive, energetic or intense artist. I understand very well how strange he must appear to the outside world.

Several months later, in a letter to a friend, he said:

> I met Beethoven in Teplitz. His talent astounded me; but unfortunately he is a quite intractable person, which in fact is not unjustified if he finds the world detestable; but as a result, of course he does not make things more enjoyable either for himself or for others. He is much to be forgiven and also to be pitied, since he can hear nothing. This is perhaps less harmful to the musical than to the social part of his life. And being by nature laconic, he feels his defect twice as much.

Beethoven wrote:

> Goethe delights far too much in the court atmosphere, far more than is becoming in a poet.

The difference between the two great artists is captured in the story about Beethoven and Goethe walking on a path in a garden. As a group of noblemen approached, Goethe moved to the side to bow. It is reported that Beethoven walked straight ahead, not willing to move aside for any man, noble or not.

During that week in July the artists saw each other numerous times, but after that summer they never met again. Beethoven set additional Goethe works to music, but his fervent desire to provide music for Goethe's *Faust* was never fulfilled.

Beethoven's love life continued to be a source of often intense emotion and frustration. His infatuation with the not-yet-twenty-year-old Therese von Malfatti elicited from him a marriage proposal in 1810 that was promptly turned down. The once-again-rejected Beethoven expressed his feelings somewhat defensively to a friend:

> I can therefore seek support only in my own heart; there is none for me outside of it. No, nothing but wounds have come to me from friendship and such kindred feelings—So be it then: for you, poor B(eethoven), there is no happiness in the outer world, you must create it in yourself. Only in the ideal world can you find friends.

Depression continued to plague Beethoven as he struggled with his health and personal problems. In mid-1810 he wrote to his old friend Wegeler:

> Yet I should be happy, perhaps one of the happiest of mortals, if that fiend had not settled in my ears—if I had not read somewhere that a man should not voluntarily quit his life so long as he can perform a good deed, I would have left this Earth long ago—and, what is more, by my own hand. Oh, this life is indeed beautiful, but for me it is poisoned forever.

A year later, after a period of especially poor health, he decided to spend the summer of 1811 at Teplitz, taking the cure. Here he found some respite from his troubles and was able to spend time with friends. Teplitz was a popular summer meeting spot for many dignitaries and officials as it served as a neutral territory during these years of the Napoleonic Wars. Amidst the socializing Beethoven continued his work. At the request of a royal patron he composed incidental music for two stage works (*King Stephen* and *The Ruins of Athens*) to celebrate the opening of a new theater in Pest (now part of Budapest). Somewhat rested and reinvigorated, he returned to Vienna in the fall and immediately began work on his seventh symphony. This turned out to be a lively and vibrant work. It was completed in the spring of 1812, and he continued on without a break to his eighth symphony.

Pleased with his increased output and the apparent positive effects on his health, he decided to return to Teplitz in 1812. The summer was an eventful one. Besides his visits with Goethe, Beethoven reached an emotional turning point in his difficult history with women. It was from Teplitz on July 6–7 that Beethoven wrote his famous "Immortal Beloved" letter that was found in his papers after his death.

The intended recipient of the letter has been a subject of much historical debate. It was addressed to an unnamed person and never mailed. The famed musicologist and Beethoven specialist Maynard Solomon has done the most extensive research and drawn the most convincing conclusion as to whom Beethoven was writing. According to Solomon, the woman was Antonie Brentano, a Viennese aristocrat who had married a Frankfurt businessman, Franz Brentano. (Franz was the brother of Beethoven's friend, Bettina Brentano.) Antonie, who was ten years younger than Beethoven, had known him since early 1810, when the Brentanos had come from Frankfurt for a stay in Vienna. Although she was married and the mother of a ten-year-old daughter, she was extremely devoted to Beethoven and his work, and a very warm and affectionate relationship had grown between them. Antonie and Beethoven were in the same general vicinity during the summer of 1812 and apparently were together for several days in Prague in early July. It was just after that, when he was in Teplitz and the Brentanos had gone on to Karlsbad ("K" in the letter), that Beethoven wrote this three-part letter:

> LETTERS TO THE IMMORTAL BELOVED
>
> July 6, in the morning
>
> My angel, my all, my very self—Only a few words today and at that with pencil (with yours)—Not till tomorrow will my lodgings be definitely determined upon—what a useless waste of time—Why this deep sorrow when necessity speaks—can our love endure except through sacrifices, through not demanding everything from one another; can you change the fact that you are not wholly mine, I not wholly thine—Oh God, look out into the beauties of nature and comfort your heart with that which must be—Love demands everything and that very justly—thus it is to me with you, and to you with me. But you forget so easily that I must live for me and for you; if we were wholly united you would feel the pain of it as little as I—My journey was a fearful one; I did not reach here until 4 o'clock yesterday morning. Lacking horses the postcoach chose another route, but what an awful one; at the stage before the last I was warned not to travel at night; I was made fearful of a forest, but that only made me the more eager—and I was wrong. The coach must needs break down on the wretched road, a bottomless mud road. Without such postilions as I had with me I would have remained stuck in the road. Esterházy, traveling the usual road here, had the same fate with eight horses that I had with four - Yet I got some pleasure out of it, as I always do when I successfully overcome difficulties—Now a quick change to things internal from things external. We shall surely see each other soon; moreover, today I cannot share with you the thoughts I have had during these last few days touching my own life—If our hearts were always close together, I would have none of these. My heart is full of so many things to say to you—ah—there are moments when I feel that speech amounts to noth-

ing at all—Cheer up —remain my true, my only treasure, my all as I am yours. The gods must send us the rest, what for us must and shall be—

Your faithful Ludwig

Evening, Monday, July 6

You are suffering, my dearest creature—only now have I learned that letters must be posted very early in the morning on Mondays— Thursdays—the only days on which the mail-coach goes from here to K.—You are suffering—Ah, wherever I am, you are with me—I will arrange it with you and me that I can live with you. What a life!!! thus!!! without you—pursued by the goodness of mankind hither and thither—which I as little want to deserve as I deserve it - Humility of man towards man—it pains me—and when I consider myself in relation to the universe, what am I and what is He—whom we call the greatest—and yet—herein lies the divine in man—I weep when I reflect that you will probably not receive the first report from me until Saturday—Much as you love me—I love you more—But do not ever conceal yourself from me—good night—As I am taking baths I must go to bed—Oh God—so near! so far! Is not our love truly a heavenly structure, and also as firm as the vault of Heaven?—

Good morning, on July 7

Though still in bed, my thoughts go out to you, my Immortal Beloved, now and then joyfully, then sadly, waiting to learn whether or not fate will hear us—I can live only wholly with you or not at all—Yes, I am resolved to wander so long away from you until I can fly to your arms and say that I am really at home with you, and can send my soul enwrapped in you into the land of spirits—Yes, unhappily it must be so—You will be the more contained since you know my fidelity to you. No one else can ever possess my heart—never—never—Oh God, why must one be parted from one whom one so loves. And yet my life in V(ienna) is now a wretched life—Your love makes me at once the happiest and the unhappiest of men—At my age I need a steady, quiet life—can that be so in our connection? My angel, I have just been told that the mail-coach goes every day—therefore I must close at once so that you may receive the l(etter) at once.—Be calm, only by a calm consideration of our existence can we achieve our purpose to live together—Be calm—love me—today—yesterday—what tearful longings for you—you—you—my life—my all—farewell.—Oh continue to love me—never misjudge the most faithful heart of your beloved

L.

ever thine
ever mine
ever ours

The depth of these emotional outpourings is significant. For possibly the first time we see evidence of a woman returning Beethoven's love and accepting him as a lovable man. Still, there are feelings of ambiguity in the letter as Beethoven writes about the difficulties of their relationship and his need to live for himself. He failed to mail the letter, and there is no evidence of any further passion or pursuit.

The relationship was obviously very important to Beethoven and represents a watershed in his unhappy emotional life. He had come close to a real commitment, yet once again it did not work. This time, however, he could not entirely blame overwhelming creative demands or insurmountable social problems for the failure. He now had to face the reality that he was probably incapable of being part of a lasting close relationship or having a normal family or sexual life.

Soon after he wrote the "Immortal Beloved" letter, Beethoven joined the Brentano family in Karlsbad for a while, then stayed in touch with them after they moved back to Frankfurt in the autumn of 1812. Both Antonie and her daughter received dedications of important works in later years.

Beethoven, now forty-two, had fourteen more years to live. During that time he had no romantic relationships. As he abandoned his quest for marriage, he became more defensive and negative about the whole subject. His thoughts were summed up in a comment by some friends in 1817:

> As far as his experience went, he did not know a single married couple who on one side or the other did not repent the step he or she took in marrying; and that, for himself, he was excessively glad that not one of the girls whom he had passionately loved in former days had become his wife.

The subject was a painful one for Beethoven, and periodically he would confide to friends his sadness at never establishing an intimate family relationship.

More stress was added to Beethoven's life when, on the way back to Vienna, he stopped in Linz to visit his brother Nicholas Johann. He soon was involved in his brother's life. Johann, who had become a successful apothecary, was having an affair with his housekeeper, one Therese Obermayer, and had thoughts of marriage. Beethoven was against the relationship and was soon attempting to get the local bishop and civil authorities to evict the girl. Johann would have none of this and foiled Beethoven's plan by marrying Therese on November 8, 1812. The angry Beethoven returned to Vienna in defeat.

Crisis and Frustration, 1813–1820

The summer of 1812 was a turning point for Beethoven. The emotional crisis involving his "Immortal Beloved" letter and his failed attempt to control his brother's life marked the beginning of a long period of general depression, reduced musical output, declining health and family problems.

He seems to have fallen into a state of severe depression during most of 1813. He spoke of suicide to his friends, and there is some indication he may have made an attempt at it. His emotional stress is revealed in a letter to Archduke Rudolph in late December, 1812:

> I have been ailing, although mentally, it is true more than physically.

Just a month later he wrote to Rudolph again:

> As for my health, it is pretty much the same, the more so as moral factors are affecting it and these apparently are not very speedily removed.

That spring friends described him in a deplorable state—withdrawn, dirty and very sloppily dressed. Certainly he was still struggling with the reality of his final failure at building an intimate relationship. In addition, his brother Casper Carl almost died from consumption that April, causing Beethoven to become involved in that family's financial well-being. He wrote virtually nothing of lasting musical value during these months.

Things picked up a bit later in the year as a result of Beethoven's contact with a musical inventor and entrepreneur named Johann Nepomuk Mälzel, who contrived a mechanical organ called the panharmonium, which imitated the sounds of an entire orchestra. (Mälzel later invented the metronome.) His idea was to collaborate with Beethoven on a piece of program music to celebrate Wellington's victory over the French in the battle of Vittoria (June 1813). Viennese patriotic fever was high at this time as the tide had turned against Napoleon. The project was a blatant attempt to cash in on the feelings of nationalistic pride.

The result was the so-called *Battle* Symphony or *Wellington's Victory.* It is a rather bombastic and absurd piece of music featuring the sounds of cannonade, much tympany, loud playing and several variations of "God Save the

King." The Viennese loved it, and it received four successful performances in the winter of 1813–1814. Beethoven included the first performance of his seventh and eighth symphonies in the concerts. His popularity, as well as his finances, grew to new heights.

Spurred on by his commercial success, Beethoven became very productive once again for the next year. Continuing to play on the patriotic mood of the day, he wrote a series of vocal works marking special occasions. They were quite popular and brought Beethoven additional fame. But compared to much of his earlier work, they were shallow and basically motivated by opportunism and the mood of the time.

A more important result of Beethoven's increased popularity was a call for the revival of his opera *Fidelio,* which hadn't been performed since 1806. Beethoven reworked much of the opera and wrote yet another overture for it. It opened in May to great acclaim and was repeated regularly throughout the year.

In the fall of 1814 the leaders and royalty of Europe gathered in Vienna to celebrate the victory over Napoleon's France and to plan the future of the continent. Much music and many festivities surrounded the Congress, and many of the royalty were treated to performances of *Fidelio* in the early fall.

Beethoven used the Congress as an opportunity to write more "occasion" music. The first of these was a short choral work welcoming the sovereigns to the Congress. Later he wrote a cantata celebrating the "glorious moment" at this turning point in European history. These were heady times for Beethoven, as he was able to compose for and have his music performed for the aristocracy of Europe. He enjoyed the praise and fame, and was especially pleased when he was made an honorary citizen of Vienna in 1815.

The year 1814 also occasioned the end of Beethoven's career as a performing pianist. In April of that year he participated in the first public performance of the *Archduke* Trio that he had completed in 1811. Fellow composer Ludwig Spohr commented on the event:

> On account of his deafness there was scarcely anything left of the virtuosity which had formerly been so greatly admired. In forte passages the poor man pounded on the keys till the strings jangled, and in piano he played so softly that the whole group of notes were omitted, so that the music was unintelligible.

Ironically, it was at this time of high general popularity that Beethoven's fortunes began to reverse. As the long Napoleonic Wars came to a close, the Viennese returned to a more conservative, stable existence, and their musical taste started to tend more toward entertainment rather than meaningful musical expression. In addition, Beethoven's creative juices had slowed, and his output during 1813–1815, while often initially popular, lacked the depth and quality of his earlier years.

His work was sporadic during late 1814 and 1815. It ranged from the rather bland *Namesday* Overture, written in honor of the Kaiser, to some quite intricate chamber works. His days of intense productivity and innovative creativity seemed to be over. His patrons and friends still supported him, but his reputation was now based primarily on the works written some years before. One of his contemporaries wrote:

> In opposition to his admirers, the first rank of which is represented by Razumovsky, Apponyi, Kraft, etc.—who adore Beethoven, is found an overwhelming majority of connoisseurs who refuse absolutely to listen to his works hereafter.

Adding to his problems was the fact that a number of Beethoven's supporters were no longer around. Kinsky had died in 1812, the steadfast Lichnowsky passed away in 1814 and Lobkowitz was to go in 1816. The palace of long-term patron Razumovsky burned in December 1814, and the prince moved back to Russia, taking some of his musicians (who were friends of Beethoven) with him. Others drifted away for various reasons.

In essence, the Viennese musical establishment that had supported the likes of Mozart, Haydn, and Beethoven had for the most part faded away. The days of aristocratic salons and palaces with their own orchestras were gone.

Starting in late 1815, family problems caused Beethoven the most grief and continued to deplete a good part of his physical and emotional energies over the next ten years. Beethoven's brother Casper Carl had been in ill health for some time. When he was close to death in 1813, he signed a will appointing Beethoven guardian of his son Karl (born 1806). This was, of course, rather unusual considering that the young boy's mother, Johanna, was still alive and married to Casper Carl. Beethoven had originally opposed the marriage of his brother Carl to Johanna in 1806 but, like his later attempt to break up his brother Johann's relationship in 1812, it was all for naught and resulted only in alienating his future sister-in-law as well as his brother.

Casper Carl's health deteriorated rapidly in the fall of 1815. Just a day before his death he signed a codicil to his will that stated his desires regarding the future of his nine-year-old son Karl. Its purpose seemed clear but at the same time unrealistic, as it made the boy's mother and the possessive Beethoven co-guardians. In the document he states:

> —that I by no means desire that my son be taken away from his mother, but that he shall always and so long as his future career permits remain with his mother, to which end the guardianship of him is to be exercised by her as well as by my brother—for the welfare of my child I recommend compliance to my wife and more moderation to my brother. God permit them to be harmonious for the sake of my child's welfare. This is the last wish of the dying husband and brother.

Thus a battle was started that, in effect, lasted until nearly the end of Beethoven's life in 1827. Beethoven took his new responsibilities seriously and became rather fanatical in his desire to become, in effect, young Karl's father. A long, complex and emotional series of conflicts and legal battles followed that ended with Beethoven's gaining full responsibility for Karl. This was followed by another six years of Beethoven attempting to raise the rather rebellious boy. It was a draining ordeal for the composer, whose actions bordered on the mean and irrational.

A detailed examination of the intricacies of the many court hearings, arguments and ugly episodes is not necessary for our purpose. However, a brief summary of some of the conflict gives us insight into Beethoven's feelings and the significant role this issue played in his life for over ten years.

• Within a week of his brother's death, Beethoven moved quickly to claim guardianship over the only child of the three Beethoven brothers. He appealed to the Royal Landrecht (Court) to give him sole guardianship, justifying his appeal with the claim that the mother was unfit. His attempt to discredit her was based on a rather questionable charge of embezzlement made against her four years earlier. By January 1816 Beethoven had won and was legally appointed guardian. Karl was promptly removed from his mother and sent to boarding school. (This initial victory by Beethoven triggered continuing arguments before the court for the next four years.)

• Beethoven's actions toward Johanna alternated between extreme hostility and occasional episodes of thoughtfulness and empathy. He often implied she was a prostitute, calling her "Queen of the Night," after the character in Mozart's *The Magic Flute.* At other times he expressed sympathy for her plight. There was even rumor that he was secretly in love with her.

• Beethoven's relations with Karl were also volatile and ambivalent. He professed a deep love for the boy but was often very severe with him, and at times beat him. Other periods were marked by affection and pride. Generally, though, he was very possessive and controlling, and there appears to have been no real comfortableness or intimacy between them. For much of the time Karl was sent to a boarding school. When Beethoven tried to set up a normal household and have the boy live with him, generally chaos followed.

• During one of the court hearings in December of 1818, when Johanna was trying to gain some influence in her son's life, Beethoven made a statement that was to cause him considerable grief. The litigation in the case had always been carried out in the Landrecht, or Royal Court, based on the assumption of Ludwig van Beethoven's supposedly noble background. (The Dutch *van* was equated with the German/Austrian *von*, signifying nobility—something nobody questioned in a man of Beethoven's stature.) During testimony Beethoven said of Karl, "Or if he was but of noble birth—."

• The court pursued the issue, and it soon became clear that the Dutch-descended van Beethovens had no proof of their nobility. (Beethoven pointed to his heart and head and said, "My nobility is here, and here.") The whole case was thus dismissed from the jurisdiction of the noble court and transferred to the Magistrat, the civil court which had jurisdiction over cases for the common citizen. The episode was humiliating for the proud and egotistical Beethoven and caused him to become even more depressed. He was described as being "deeply mortified" and said it was the grossest insult he had ever received.

• In 1819, Johanna was given temporary custody of her son, and Beethoven was no longer the guardian. But he persisted, and in his final legal assault he brought great pressure on the court through his many contacts, including Archduke Rudolph. Finally, in the spring of 1820 Beethoven won, and the court approved him and a friend as guardians of Karl. Johanna appealed to the Emperor. She was turned down, and by the end of July 1820 the case was closed, thus ending four and one-half years of accusations, legal battles, intrigue, bad behavior and draining emotional stress.

• Following the legal victory, Karl and Beethoven continued to have a difficult relationship. The boy would spend some of his summers with Beethoven and occasionally served as his assistant of sorts. But as the boy grew into a young man and started to develop his own life, Beethoven became even more possessive and domineering. There were very few periods of tranquility and affection.

This whole series of events dealing with Karl was very complex from a psychological standpoint. Beethoven's unfulfilled desires to be part of a real family and have a loving, domestic relationship, coupled with his own dissatisfying family situation as a child, seemed to have brought a frantic intensity to his dealings with his nephew and his sister-in-law. Beethoven's deep and complex fear, insecurity and unhappiness caused him to behave in irrational and cruel ways. His actions were often contrary to the ethics and values that he so strongly professed. There is evidence that he was aware of these contradictions: on occasion he would profess guilt, then justify his actions as the result of his deep love for his nephew and surrogate son.

Much has been written regarding Beethoven's subconscious motives and desires throughout this whole difficult affair. The theories range from a Freudian view that Beethoven was angrily acting out his repressed sexual feelings for Johanna, to a theory that Beethoven had a complete ethical breakdown. What seems clear is that Beethoven once again was reaching out for family and love but acting in ways that prevented any meaningful relationship from developing. One senses, though, that these years brought significant emotional growth as well as frustration and pain. Beethoven was forced to deal with concrete issues of family relationships and intense feelings for a considerable period of time. At least occasionally he had to look at his own emotions and shortcomings. His writings during this period expressed both his hope for family and his own self-doubts and guilt over some of his actions.

Beethoven's creative output was quite meager during the early years (1815–1817) of problems with his nephew. He wrote a few minor vocal works and some revisions of smaller, earlier works, but nothing of real significance. He did start some larger serious pieces, but they were never completed. The occasional concerts of his music that he conducted (he no longer could perform as a pianist in public) were not well attended and met with little enthusiasm. His style of music was no longer popular with the Viennese public, and he often grew despondent at the artistic changes he saw around him. To a visitor in 1816 he complained:

> Art no longer stands so high above the ordinary, is no longer so respected, and above all is no longer valued in terms of recompense.

His popularity did remain high in England. There was talk of a tour, and in 1817 he was invited to write two grand symphonies. The tour never took place (for health reasons) and the symphonies were not begun.

His health continued to deteriorate, especially his hearing. By 1818 he was almost completely deaf. It was during this time that Beethoven started using his Conversation Books to record what others wanted to communicate to him.

As he approached his fiftieth year, Beethoven had gained the reputation of a mad genius. His behavior around friends was often rude and sullen, followed by periods of warmth and reconciliation. Out in public, street urchins often made fun of the slovenly figure as he walked about, singing and humming. He would often speak out against the government and people of status, seemingly unaware of the possible consequences in the police state in which he lived. (Metternich's secret police generally left him alone, believing he was a bit touched in the head.) It was overall another very low period in his life.

Late in 1817, however, Beethoven characteristically started to pull himself together and push himself creatively in new directions. The first real evidence are the early sketches for his gigantic and innovative four-movement piano sonata, the *Hammerklavier,* which was commenced in the autumn of 1817 and completed in the early fall of 1818. He also started early sketches for his ninth symphony. In 1819 he began work on his great religious masterpiece, the *Missa Solemnis.* It was to be dedicated to his long-time loyal patron and friend Archduke Rudolph, who had been appointed Archbishop of Olmütz.

Thus by the end of 1820 we see Beethoven emerging from a very stressful, and not particularly productive, five-year period. The legal battles surrounding his nephew were mostly behind him, though many of the emotional issues remained. While his public popularity had declined, he still maintained his circle of respected musical friends, who supported him and gave him the love and sympathy he needed. He was popular abroad, and his works continued to be published.

The Final Years: 1820–1827

The last years of Beethoven's life can be characterized as a period of declining health, increasing eccentricity, continuing conflict with his nephew, renewed popularity and, above all, prolific musical output. His creative powers ignited in a burst of energy and innovation that was to propel him into new areas. With much of his deep emotional crisis behind him, he threw himself into his work. A historian in Vienna in 1822 described him as "one of the most active men who ever lived." He would often miss meals and regularly work late into the night.

He had undertaken two major projects, the gigantic ninth symphony and the *Missa Solemnis*, as well as a number of other works. There were other offers of commissions that he either turned down or accepted but never started. By early 1824 he had completed the *Missa Solemnis*, the ninth symphony and the *Diabelli* Variations for piano. They are all works of supreme quality and innovation that reflect Beethoven's renewed energy.

Symphony no. 9 in D Major is considered by many to be Beethoven's greatest work. In it, Beethoven brought together a number of artistic ideas that had been germinating in his mind for many years. During his last days in Bonn, Beethoven had expressed a desire to do a vocal setting of Schiller's "Ode to Joy," and he had made sketches of the idea from time to time. The 1817 request from the London Philharmonic Society for two more symphonies had given him the impulse to write a new and different kind of work. The ideas for these two symphonies were merged into one, and by early 1824 the massive work was finished, complete with the unique choral finale.

The *Missa Solemnis* was written for the Archduke Rudolph's elevation to Archbishop which occurred in March of 1820. Beethoven was late, as was often the case, and the piece was completed in early 1823. The writing of the work became an emotional and passionate undertaking for Beethoven. Although he was not a traditionally religious man, he expressed his deepest spiritual feelings in this work. Beethoven considered the *Missa Solemnis* one of his greatest creations.

The work became quite controversial in the commercial marketplace. Beethoven offered it to a wide variety of publishers and also sold it to various crowned heads of Europe. In spite of these financial manipulations, which sullied Beethoven's reputation and cost him several friendships, the work must be considered one of Beethoven's greatest accomplishments.

The third great masterpiece from the early 1820s was the *Diabelli* Variations. In 1819 the Viennese composer and publisher Anton Diabelli invited fifteen composers to write piano variations on a simple waltz tune he had written. His intention was to publish an album of all the entries. Among those composers submitting entries were Franz Schubert and the eleven-year-old Franz Liszt. Beethoven didn't think much of the tune but took it as a challenge. He composed not one but thirty-three variations. They were so stirring in their beauty and originality that Diabelli proclaimed them a successor to Bach's famous *Goldberg* Variations, and he published them as a separate work. Beethoven thought so much of them that he dedicated them to Antonie Brentano, probably his "Immortal Beloved."

Just as Beethoven's composing was reaching new heights, his ability to conduct was declining. His last attempt ended in disaster. In the fall of 1822 his opera *Fidelio* was enjoying a revival. Beethoven attempted to conduct the dress rehearsal. A Madame Schroder described the scene:

> The last rehearsals were set, when I learned before the dress rehearsal that Beethoven had asked for the honor of conducting the work himself in celebration of the day—With a bewildered face and unearthly inspired eyes, waving his baton back and forth in violent motions, he stood in the midst of the performing musicians and didn't hear a note!—The inevitable happened: the deaf master threw the singers and orchestra completely off the beat and into the greatest confusion, and no one knew any longer where they were.

When Beethoven realized what had happened, he called for his friend, Anton Schindler, who convinced him to give up and go home. Schindler later wrote:

> Once there he threw himself under the sofa, covered his face with his hands and remained thus until we sat down to eat. During the meal not a word passed his lips—

In spite of this disappointment, Beethoven's music started to again become more popular, after six or seven years of some neglect. His symphonies and several of his choral works were often part of a series of concerts given by various groups in Vienna in the years 1820–1823.

His career reached a peak at a historic concert held in May 1824. By then Beethoven had completed his ninth symphony and the *Missa Solemnis.* He was still unsure of Viennese musical taste, and he considered taking the new works to Berlin for their premiere. Word of this got out, and an appeal was drafted and signed by thirty prominent musicians and musical personalities. The touching message read, in part:

> Do not withhold longer from the popular enjoyment, do not keep longer from the oppressed sense of that which is great and perfect, a performance of the latest masterworks of your hand—We know that a new flower glows in the garland of your glorious still unequaled symphonies —Do not longer disappoint the general expectations.

Beethoven was deeply moved and agreed to hold a special concert in Vienna at the Kärntnertor Theater on May 7, 1824. It consisted of a recent overture he had written in 1822 (*Consecration of the House*); the Kyrie, Credo, and Agnus Dei from the *Missa Solemnis*; and the ninth symphony. The theater was crowded and the audience enthusiastic about hearing these new creations of the great and strange master. Beethoven assisted in the performance mainly by setting the tempo, but of course he could hear nothing. There was a great ovation at the end of the ninth symphony. The deaf Beethoven, facing the orchestra, was unaware of it until one of the singers, a Madame Unger, pulled on his sleeve and pointed to the audience behind him. Beethoven turned and bowed.

The profit for the concert was not up to expectations. Expenses had gotten out of hand, and Beethoven was frustrated. After the concert he got into a big row and accused management and one of his friends of cheating him.

The major part of the concert was repeated on May 24. It was held at noon on a sunny day. Attendance was poor, and Beethoven was again disappointed at the financial results.

During the 1820s, Beethoven was concerned about money, as he had been throughout most of his life. He was by no means poor, but his expenses always tended to run beyond his income. Since he was not receiving much from concerts, commissions or publishing fees in these years, Beethoven started to go into debt. He borrowed from friends and received advances on works not yet begun. This, of course, put a strain on both his friendships and his emotions.

Despite his financial concerns, his driving work schedule and his often irrational behavior, Beethoven continued to attract a large number of friends. While many of his older companions had died or moved away, he was constantly making new and often younger friends. Many of them were quite in awe of Beethoven and were most anxious to serve him in various ways. Some came from the Viennese musical establishment; others were journalists and editors. Many were just people he had dealt with in his struggles regarding his nephew Karl.

During his last years, very few, if any, of Beethoven's close friends were women. He no longer seemed to need the close friendship and confidence of women that he had required earlier in his life. His last intense exchange of letters with a woman had been with Nanette Streicher, whom he confided in and asked for advice from during the crisis with Karl. This correspondence had ended in 1818.

He did, of course, have contact with women and would still occasionally lament the fact that he had never married. His sexual desires were fulfilled by prostitutes and casual acquaintances—or, evidently, once in a while the wife of one of his friends. But there is no evidence of any emotional relationships taking place during these years.

Beethoven enjoyed and needed companionship. He took pleasure in gathering friends around him and spending time in taverns, discussing matters both profound and trivial. Of course, most of these conversations were carried on with the aid of his Conversation Books. An observer from the time, one Friedrich Rochlitz—editor of a Leipzig paper—gives two separate accounts that provide us with insight into Beethoven's character and behavior during this period:

> His talk and actions were one long chain of eccentricities, some of them most peculiar. Yet, they all radiated a truly childlike amiability, carelessness and confidence in all who approached him. Even his barking tirades, such as those against his Viennese contemporaries, were only explosions of his fanciful imagination and his momentary excitement. They were uttered without any haughtiness, without any feeling of bitterness or resentment, simply blustered out lightly and good-humoredly—He often showed—that to the person who had grievously injured him, or whom he had just most violently denounced, he would be willing to give his last thaler, should that person need it.

> I found a seat from which I could see him and since he spoke loud enough, also could hear nearly all that he said. It could not actually be called a conversation, for he spoke in monologue, usually at some length, and more as though by hapchance and at random. Those about him contributed little, merely laughing or nodding their approval. He philosophized, or one might say politicized, after his own fashion. He spoke of England and the English, and how both were associated in his thoughts with a splendor incomparable—which, in part sounded tolerably fantastic. Then he told all sorts of stories of the French, from the days of the second occupation of Vienna. For them he had no kind words. His remarks all were made with the greatest unconcern and without the least reserve, and whatever he said was spiced with highly original, naive judgements or comical fancies. He impressed me as being a man with a rich, aggressive intellect and unlimited, never resting imagination.

Beginning in mid-1824, Beethoven turned his creative energies to the medium of the string quartet. He had not composed one since 1810. Now that he was through with his massive orchestral and choral works, he devoted his remaining years to breaking new ground and reaching new heights in this complex musical genre. Over the next three years, he composed five of them and expanded the long, complex final movement of one of them into a separate piece called the "Grosse Fugue." All are considered masterpieces, and they are among his most arduous and challenging works.

At no other time in his life did Beethoven concentrate so exclusively on one musical form. He worked on them constantly, with occasional breaks due to health problems. He even acknowledged the recovery from one of his illnesses by inscribing a melody in one of the quartets "Hymn of Thanksgiving to the Divinity, from a Convalescent, in the Lydian Mode."

The quartets were innovative and in many ways difficult pieces for musicians and audiences of the time. They triggered mostly favorable reactions, but occasionally their complexity and uniqueness would inspire comments such as the one in a Leipzig review that called the "Grosse Fugue" "incomprehensible, a sort of Chinese puzzle."

In these works, Beethoven had again pushed himself and the traditional Classical forms beyond traditional boundaries. His innovation in musical texture, tempo and form gives some of the works a sense of extreme complexity and discontinuity. But the underlying structure of the quartets shows a unity and coherence that mark these as perhaps Beethoven's most daring compositions.

While this intense musical creation was going on, Beethoven was still dealing with family matters. Nephew Karl spent most of the years 1820–1823 attending the Blöchlinger Institute and living apart from Beethoven. The relationship was fairly calm for this period, with Karl occasionally assisting Beethoven on personal and business matters. Karl also spent several summers and an occasional weekend with him. But when Karl transferred to the University, he came back to live with Beethoven, and the quarreling became intense once more. Karl tried to exert some independence, and Beethoven became even more suspicious and demanding. It was even rumored that Beethoven had one of his friends spy on his nephew. His letters and conversations with Karl were marked by accusations, recriminations and then a profession of deep love and reconciliation. Still wanting to be the father, Beethoven just could not let go and treat the now nearly twenty-year-old man as an adult.

Beethoven's overbearing and suffocating behavior put great pressure on Karl, and in July of 1826 he shot himself in the head. He was not successful in his suicide attempt and, when discovered, he asked to be taken to his mother. After his recovery, it was decided that he should go into the army. Arrangements were made, and after spending a final few, and apparently peaceful, months with Beethoven, he left to join his unit in January 1827—two months before Beethoven died.

Beethoven's last years also included a change in his relationship with his only other close relative, his brother Nicholas Johann. He had had very little contact with Nicholas Johann since trying to break up his marriage in 1812. His brother, in the meantime, had grown quite wealthy as a pharmacist in Linz. In 1819 he purchased a country estate in Gneixendorf, northwest of Vienna in the hills above the Danube. In 1822 he took a residence in Vienna. Beethoven and his brother renewed their relationship, and Beethoven, in typical fashion, emotionally expressed his hope that:

> God grant that the most natural bond, the bond between brothers, may not again be broken in an unnatural way.

He also assured his brother that he had nothing against his wife.

Beethoven took up lodgings adjoining Nicholas Johann's house, and the two brothers became quite close, with Nicholas Johann taking a role in Beethoven's business dealings, even lending him money. Before long, though, Beethoven was again interfering in his brother's affairs and objecting to his wife's friends. Beethoven soon moved out, but his relationship with his brother held, and they remained close until Beethoven's death.

In these final years of great musical productivity and ongoing family problems, Beethoven suffered a significant decline in his health. He had a variety of ailments and spent many weeks in bed. During his final six months, Beethoven became even more severely ill.

In September of 1826 he and Karl journeyed to Nicholas Johann's estate at Gneixendorf, and all three of the remaining Beethoven men spent several months together. While Karl's strength returned from his suicide attempt, Beethoven lost his appetite, and his stomach and feet began to swell. He continued work on his final string quartet, but his strength was leaving him.

At the beginning of December, Beethoven and Karl headed back for Vienna in a storm. They spent a night in a cold and drafty inn, and by the time they reached the capital, Beethoven was seriously ill. When a doctor was called in three days later, he was diagnosed as having pneumonia. Soon thereafter he developed liver and stomach pains. He became jaundiced, and the swelling grew in his abdomen and feet. Doctors performed several operations to drain the abdominal fluids.

Beethoven remained conscious a good deal of the time and was able to carry on brief conversations with the many people who came to visit and pay their respects. He was touched by special presents, such as his favorite Rhine wine and a special edition of Handel's *Messiah*. He particularly liked a lithograph of Haydn's birthplace that was brought to him. He hung it by his bedside. He occasionally talked about future projects, but his mind would wander, and toward the end he became delirious.

Word of his impending death brought a great outpouring of emotions. His friends flocked to see him, and messages and gifts came from as far away as London. (The Philharmonic Society sent £100, having been mistakenly led to believe that he was quite poor.)

By late March 1827, it was clear that the end was near. On March 23 Beethoven signed his final will, leaving his estate to Karl. The following day he received last rites and made his famous remark to his friends Schindler and von Breuning:

> Plaudite, amici, comoedia finita est. (Applaud, friends, the comedy has ended.)

He fell into a coma. On March 26th there was a snowfall and thunderstorm. Shortly after 5 P.M. there was a flash of lightning and a loud clap of thunder. Beethoven awoke momentarily, raised his right hand and clenched his fist in a last defiant gesture. When his arm fell back, he was dead.

Only two people were with him when he died. One was a friend, Ansel Huttenbrenner. The other was, surprisingly, and perhaps fatefully, Johanna, his once-despised enemy and sister-in-law, the mother of Karl.

Three days later, on March 29, 1827, well over ten thousand people gathered to bid farewell to the great composer. The prominent poet Grillparzer wrote a special oration that was read by a popular actor. A choir sang to the accompaniment of trumpets. There was a great procession featuring many of Beethoven's friends and leading Viennese musicians.

He was buried in the suburb of Währing. Some sixty years later his remains were moved to the Central Cemetery in Vienna, and he rests there today along side the body of Franz Schubert.

Beethoven's Personal Characteristics

In the previous section I outlined the chronology and some of the major events in Beethoven's life, putting special emphasis on his difficult family situation and his disappointing attempts in establishing a close relationship with a woman. Let us now take a more detailed look at some of the other important characteristics of Beethoven that will give us further insight about him and his works.

Appearance

Beethoven was a man of about five feet four inches with a rather large head and a broad forehead. His thick, bushy hair turned from black to gray as he aged; as one contemporary stated, "Neither comb nor scissors seems to have visited it for years." A childhood bout with smallpox left him with a somewhat pockmarked and ruddy complexion. His eyes were the one feature that seemed to have left the strongest impression on people. They are described by various acquaintances as "being full of rude energy," "small and shining," "fiery," "unbelievably full of life," and "lively."

Up until his mid-thirties, Beethoven was quite lean. He filled out in his later years, however, and became stocky, with a strong body. He had broad shoulders and powerful hands with thick, short fingers. These physical characteristics resulted in a man whom no one ever described as handsome and some called ugly. But somehow he came across as unusual and memorable. The strength of his eyes and the force of his personality strongly affected people.

He was something of a klutz physically. An account by his friend Ferdinand Ries sums up this aspect of him:

> Beethoven was most awkward and bungling in his behavior; his clumsy movements lacked all grace. He rarely picked up anything without dropping or breaking it —Everything was knocked over, soiled, or destroyed. How he ever managed to shave himself at all remains difficult to understand, even considering the frequent cuts on his cheeks—He never learned to dance in time with the music.

Beethoven was inconsistent in his outer dress. In his early years in Vienna, he was generally neatly outfitted and even occasionally appeared fashionable and elegant. As he grew older, however, he took less interest in how he looked. There are many descriptions of his disheveled, sloppy and out-of-style appearance. Occasionally, in his latter years, he would dress stylishly (often in clothes bought for him by friends), but mostly he would wander about in old, and often dirty, apparel, with no concern for his appearance.

Habits and Lifestyle

Beethoven's generally impatient nature, his erratic personality and possibly his desire for a family clearly expressed themselves in his continuing search for more satisfying living quarters. He never stayed in one place for long, and it is estimated that he moved over seventy times during his nearly forty years in Vienna. Excluding his summer residences outside of the city, he lived at about thirty different addresses in Vienna (coming back to some of them several times). He was always finding fault with his living situation and regularly had disputes with his landlord or neighboring tenants. The constant moving was surely time-consuming and financially draining. Often he'd have several apartments at once.

While settled in a dwelling, he lived in a state of chaos and messiness. Several comments from visitors to Beethoven's quarters give a good picture of his typical living conditions.

From the memoirs of a visitor from Frankfurt in 1808:

> His apartment, I think, consisted only of two rooms. The first contained an enclosed alcove, in which his bed stood, so small and dark that he had to perform his toilet in the next room or in the drawing room. Imagine all that is most filthy and untidy: puddles on the floor, a rather old grand piano covered in dust and laden with piles of music, in manuscript or engraved. Beneath it (I do not exaggerate) an unemptied chamber pot. The little walnut table next to it was evidently accustomed to having the contents of the inkwell spilled over it. A mass of pens encrusted with ink—and more musical scores. The chairs, most of them straw chairs, were covered with plates full of the remains of the previous evening's meal and with clothes, etc.—

A description of a visit to Beethoven's quarters in the 1820s:

> The three men were moved when they entered the dreary, almost sordid room inhabited by the great Ludwig. The room was in the greatest disorder: music, money, clothes lay on the floor, linen on a heap on the unclean bed, the open grand piano was covered in thick dust and broken coffee cups lay on the table.

The locations that were probably the most meaningful to Beethoven were the small, rural villages outside of Vienna where he spent many summers. These getaways were important to his health and his creative output. He truly loved nature and the out-of-doors and would spend hours walking in the countryside, gaining strength and musical inspiration.

Finances

Over the course of his life, Beethoven earned quite a bit of money—certainly enough to overcome any impression (often his own) that he had severe economic problems. He spent his money freely but did not live lavishly. His friend Ries wrote:

> Beethoven needed a good deal of money even though he enjoyed very little benefit from it, for he lived moderately.

For many periods of his life, he believed he was in financial trouble but in fact was not. During his early years in Vienna he earned a decent living from a combination of performing, teaching and some publishing of his works. By 1796 he could afford a servant. The annuities from patrons began about 1800, and he soon was making a profit from benefit concerts as well.

He started receiving the large annuity from three of his major patrons in 1809. Subsequent devaluation of currency and the debt of one of the patrons did cause some financial hardships for him in the years 1811–1814. But the situation improved around the time of the Congress of Vienna, and Beethoven was paid handsomely for his work during this period.

After that, his expenses rose faster than his income. By 1816 he was complaining to friends about his financial woes. His obligations at this time were considerable, and they included funeral expenses for his recently deceased brother Carl, the cost of his servants, his high rent, and the support of his nephew Karl. During the following years, his income dropped and expenses continued to rise, mainly because of the legal expenses in the battle for Karl. During this time, Beethoven went into debt.

For some years he was desperately concerned about his financial position. The desperation, no doubt, caused him in 1820 to enter into rather shady dealings regarding the publishing and selling of the *Missa Solemnis* manuscripts. Nevertheless, through all these difficult times, and in spite of his debts, Beethoven maintained a decent standard of living, employed servants, summered in nearby Baden and continued to hold the bank shares (investments) he had purchased in 1819. One of these shares had to be sold in 1823.

Beethoven's correspondence during his final three to four years of life is full of references to money and his financial concerns. It is ironic that during his last years, when his creative efforts were at their peak, he was not getting the immediate financial rewards he felt he needed and deserved.

Beethoven died thinking he was poor. He was wrong. Even though his liquidity was down when he died, his estate, made up of the bank shares, his effects and uncollected subsidies, was quite substantial.

While Beethoven worried about his own money situation, he was quite generous when it came to assisting others. Early on he provided for both brothers financially, and he gave considerable aid to his brother Carl's family before he died. He also enjoyed looking after friends. At one point he wrote to Ries, "Not one of my friends is to be short of money as long as I have some." Often the proceeds from his concerts would go to charitable organizations. His desire to help others is perhaps best demonstrated by his offer to assist his often-estranged sister-in-law, Johanna, in 1823 at a time when he was least able to do so.

In understanding Beethoven's financial situation, it's important to keep in mind that he earned his living in a different way than the great composers that preceded him. The variety of his sources of income—teaching, performing, annuities, special commissions, benefit concerts, publishing and, on occasion, special works—gave him a greater degree of artistic freedom. He was generally able to pursue his artistic goals quite freely, composing in the musical form he preferred with complete control over content. Unlike Bach and Haydn, who worked mainly for specific patrons, Beethoven had enough different types of musical businesses going that he was never indebted to, and never had to work for, any one person or organization. (Mozart had tried to make it as a free-lancer, but had failed.)

Certainly, Beethoven wrote individual pieces for specific patrons and sonatas for specific musicians, and he composed for specific dramatic or musical productions. But to a greater extent than previous composers, he was able to achieve a financial independence that allowed him considerable artistic freedom.

Personality

Beethoven was a complex, contradictory and driven human being. The many accounts of Beethoven's behavior by contemporaries, plus his own writings, give us a fairly complete picture of a man who seemed to struggle constantly with himself and those around him.

Even as a young man, Beethoven stood out because of his moodiness, bluntness, lack of etiquette and often violent temper. As he grew older, these characteristics stayed with him and were probably accentuated by the stress and shame of his deafness.

Still, like many people with strong personalities, he attracted others and throughout his life had many friends and followers. He seems to have had a magnetic personality that bound people to him even though his behavior was often not worthy of their loyalty. His friendships almost always had their ups and downs. Quarrels or even physical violence was often followed by expressions of remorse and reconciliation. Letters written to his friend, the composer and pianist Johann Hummel, within a few days of each other illustrate this:

> Don't come to me anymore. You are a false dog and may the hangman do away with all false dogs.

This is followed by:

> Dear little Ignaz of my heart! You are an honest fellow and I now realize that you are right—kisses from your Beethoven, also called Dumpling.

Over his lifetime, Beethoven had perhaps half a dozen close friends with whom he could share things of importance. But he would even fight with some of these men, causing long breaks in their relationships. Interestingly, two of these close friendships (with Wegeler and Amenda) were carried on primarily by letter after the friends moved from Vienna in the early 1800s.

Beethoven also had a larger group of friends who were not as close to him. He would occasionally openly express that he valued them "mainly for what they can do for me."

Among his patrons, Beethoven was closest to Prince Lichnowsky and the Archduke Rudolph. However, even with Lichnowsky he had periods of estrangement. It seems, though, that his relationship with Prince Rudolph was quite steady and warm throughout his years in Vienna.

While Beethoven possessed a wild and often violent temper and was frequently at odds with his friends, he also had a gentle and kind side that was quite endearing. Intimate friends were also treated to his witty, but sometimes sarcastic and crude, sense of humor. A man who met Beethoven in 1811 wrote:

> I made the acquaintance of Beethoven and found this reputedly savage and unsociable man to be the most magnificent artist with a heart of gold, a glorious spirit and a friendly disposition.

Those who knew him over long periods of time could see the contrasting aspects of Beethoven and noted his kindness and concern for others as well as his temper and his moods.

Beethoven also displayed a bit of a paranoid streak. His crude manners and temper no doubt created real enemies. But his basic insecurities and his jealousies of potential competitors fueled his belief that he had a great number of adversaries. He would often refer to "them" in a generalized way, but at times he would single out specific pianists, theater managers, musical personalities and, on one occasion, his tailor. His delusions about his "enemies" and those he thought were working against him became especially strong during his struggles over the guardianship of his nephew. In his later years he imagined that he was being deceived and cheated by a variety of people.

Beethoven developed an elitist outlook early in life. He felt he was special and noble, and he had a basic distaste for common people. He believed in two-thirds of the slogan of the French Revolution—liberty and fraternity—but not equality. He felt his work and his genius had elevated him to noble status, and he thought of himself as the equal of the upper class. It is said that after a quarrel with Prince Lichnowsky in 1806 he wrote:

> Prince, what you are you are by accident of birth; what I am, I am through my own efforts. There have been thousands of princes and will be thousands more; but there is only one Beethoven.

In spite of Beethoven's elevated feelings about himself and his artistic stature, he had the normal need for praise and recognition. He took great pleasure and pride in receiving acknowledgment of his accomplishments, be they medals, awards, reviews or money. Even in his last years, when his fame was assured, his desire for recognition drove him to request that several newspaper editors spread the news that he had been elected to the Royal Swedish Academy of Music:

> I should consider it an honor if you would be kind enough to mention in your so generally esteemed paper my election as foreign member of the Royal Swedish Academy of Music.

Overriding all of Beethoven's personal and emotional problems was his deep sense of mission and commitment to his art. He was convinced that his work had great significance and a noble and high purpose. He believed in sacrifice and was willing to devote his life to his art.

Most of our knowledge about Beethoven's character and personality comes from the comments and observations of others. However, the remarks made by Beethoven about himself give us further insight into the inner nature of the man and the perceptive intellect he possessed. He saw himself as having good intentions and noble aspirations but was aware of his faults and the difficulties he caused others. Early on he was able to write about his temper:

> I am not bad; hot blood is my wickedness, my crime is youthfulness. I am not bad, really not bad; even though wild surges often accuse my heart, it is still good.

In 1804 he reported to Ries about his quarrel with Stephen von Breuning:

> I have the gift to conceal my sensitiveness touching a multitude of things; but when I am provoked at a moment when I am more sensitive than usual to anger, I burst out more violently than anybody else.

He also recognized the sloppiness of his personal habits. In 1801 he wrote to an acquaintance:

> Perhaps the only thing that looks like genius about me is that my affairs are not always in the best of order, and that in this respect nobody can be of help but myself.

Beethoven's unusual character can best be summed up by listing some of the adjectives that have been used to describe him: self-centered, eccentric, ill-mannered, obsessive, rude, caring, warm, deranged, difficult, reserved, haughty, arrogant, comical, mischievous, disciplined, powerful and "an unlicked bear."

Philosophy and Religion

Beethoven's lack of a formal education did not prevent him from developing deep philosophical convictions. These were based on the principles of the Enlightenment and the French Revolution, as well as on Beethoven's readings of a wide array of poets and philosophers. Throughout his life he would regularly set aside time to read the Greek and Roman classics (i.e., Socrates, Homer, Virgil and Plutarch), the drama and poetry of Goethe and Schiller and the plays of Shakespeare. He had a lively, inquisitive mind, and his letters and diaries are filled with references to morality, politics, war and philosophy (as well as music and personal issues).

He believed strongly in the main values of the Enlightenment—reason, freedom, virtue, progress and the brotherhood of humanity. He spoke often of ethical actions, acting nobly and doing good. To him the search for truth, and sacrifice in the causes of humanity and art, were the highest callings. In his diaries (*Tagebuch*) he wrote in 1816:

> The chief characteristic of a distinguished man: endurance in adverse and harsh conditions.

And to Goethe he wrote:

> I love truth more than anything.

Probably the clearest expression of his belief in personal sacrifice and will power came in his letter to Wegeler in 1801:

> I will seize Fate by the throat; it shall certainly not bend and crush me completely.

In spite of his elitist outlook and his contempt for the lowly, he believed it was his noble duty to serve humanity (in the universal sense) and to help those in need. He would often assist friends who were in trouble, and wrote:

> I count myself exceedingly fortunate when my art is turned to account for charitable purposes.

Beethoven believed in a personal God—one he could and did turn to in times of personal crisis. Yet he had very little time for the Catholic Church or formal religion in general. He showed little respect for the Church hierarchy and traditions and rarely attended services. In his final days he had to be talked into receiving the last rites.

The religious beliefs Beethoven did have were based not just on traditional Christianity but on his broad readings of the classics and Oriental religions. There was also surely a spiritual aspect to his love of nature and the countryside.

In the early years of his deafness, and during periods of despair throughout his life, Beethoven would cry out to God in both his prayers and his writings, lamenting his problems and asking for strength and comfort. Several entries in his *Tagebuch* show the intensity of his relationship with his God:

> Oh God, give me strength to conquer myself, nothing else must fetter me to life.

> Oh God, God, look down upon the unhappy B, do not let it continue like this any longer.

> God, God, my refuge, my rock, O my all, Thou seest my innermost hurt and knowest how it pains me to have to make somebody suffer through my good works for my dear Karl!! O hear ever ineffable One, hear me, your unhappy, most unhappy of all mortals.

His religious intensity was not consistent, however, and there were periods when he provided little evidence of any interest in the subject. After about 1815, though, when Vienna was undergoing something of a religious revival, Beethoven took greater interest in religion. He explored Eastern and Egyptian religions and mystical writings, and increasingly spoke about composing religious music. In addition, the adoption of his nephew Karl probably caused him to refocus on religious issues. (He even stated in the court proceedings that he and Karl prayed together regularly.) Also, there can be little doubt that in his final years, as death approached, his thoughts turned to the next world and his relationship to his God.

The basics of Beethoven's beliefs were a personal omnipotent God, freedom, love of nature, service to humanity, personal integrity and creative struggle. With some notable exceptions, he was generally consistent in conducting his life around these themes.

Health

Beethoven was plagued by ill health throughout much of his life. He had smallpox as a child and a serious bout of high fever and asthma when a teenager. Even though he generally appeared robust and fairly healthy, he suffered regularly from, among other things, colds, headaches, bronchitis and pneumonia.

As he moved through his forties, we see more evidence of sickness, and in 1815 his health started to decline steadily. In 1821 he spent six weeks in bed with rheumatic fever. Later that year he developed jaundice, an ailment that was to continue to plague him for the next six years and would contribute to his final illness. In the years from 1822 to his death in 1827, he had a series of health problems including gout, inflammation of the eyes, abdominal pains, severe diarrhea, nosebleeds and coughing up blood. He was often unable to work, and in 1825 was put on a strict diet of bland foods and a severely reduced alcoholic intake. This was difficult for Beethoven, since he very much enjoyed his wine. His adherence to these dietary restrictions was spotty at best.

Beethoven consulted with many doctors over the years. Predictably, he was a difficult patient. He tried a variety of cures for his problems and would not hesitate to condemn one doctor and demand something better.

It was Beethoven's deafness, though, that was his most significant health problem. His hearing began to fail at about age twenty-seven and he was almost completely deaf for the last ten years of his life, from about 1817 onward. This loss of hearing had a most profound effect on Beethoven—emotionally, socially and artistically. He sought help to alleviate the problem and tried many cures. But nothing stopped the progressive deterioration of his hearing, and in 1822 he finally concluded that nothing could be done about it.

Beethoven's deafness was a most depressing and shocking condition for a man who believed so strongly in his musical destiny. He felt cut off from part of the normal human experience and socially became more withdrawn and solitary. His tendency toward moodiness and depression was surely exaggerated by his deteriorating hearing.

Artistically, his deafness had significant consequences. Beethoven's careers as a popular piano virtuoso and a conductor were drastically reduced because of his hearing problems. Partially as a consequence of this, he focused earlier and more intensively on composing. After the emotional crisis of the early 1800s, when he faced up to the fact of the permanence of his disability, he intensely concentrated his efforts almost completely on composing and fulfilling what he felt to be his artistic destiny.

It is important to note that in the last six or seven years of his life, when he was almost totally deaf and suffered from a continuing series of severe illnesses, he completed some of his most profound, innovative and uplifting masterpieces.

Inner Conflicts

Beethoven's life was filled with contrasting forces and much conflict between opposing influences and desires. He never really seemed at peace with himself. He would profess a desire for one thing while acting in a way that prevented him from achieving his goals. Whether it was having an intimate and lasting commitment with a woman, building a close family with his brothers or his nephew, or developing more meaningful friendships, Beethoven's behavior and temperament seemed to prevent him from establishing the kind of relationships he wanted.

Concurrent with his relationship problems, he struggled with other issues. He worried about his financial situation to an extent far beyond what was merited. Also, he never did accept the reality of his common birth and was constantly having to remind people of his innate nobility.

The ending of the Age of Enlightenment and the failure of Napoleon to live up to the ideals of the French Revolution also added to his philosophical conflicts. After 1815 Europe was focused politically on restoring regimes that did not practice the values that Beethoven professed to cherish. In fact, for most of his life he lived in a dictatorial police state that reflected very few of the values of the Enlightenment.

However, the central theme of Beethoven's life was the conflict between his desire for strong and normal relationships and his almost obsessive commitment to his art. Over the years all else became subordinated to his artistic efforts. In 1812, in the first entry in his *Tagebuch,* he wrote:

> for you there is no longer any happiness except within yourself, in your art...

Later in the *Tagebuch* he expressed the same thought again:

> Everything that is called life should be sacrificed to the sublime and be a sanctuary of art.

And again he wrote:

> Live only in your art, for you are so limited by your senses. This is, nevertheless, the only existence for you.

Beethoven was a man of strong will and firm beliefs. He knew what he needed to do and he let very little get in his way. When he was in his mid-forties, he wrote in his *Tagebuch*:

> Follow the advice of others only in the rarest cases; in a matter which has already been thought through, who knows all the present circumstances as well as oneself?!

Beethoven's Works

Beethoven today is widely acknowledged as one of the preeminent composers in all history, and certainly one of the most influential on the course of Western music. His mastery of a wide range of musical forms, the unique structuring of his compositions, his evolution and growth as an artist, and finally the glorious, beautiful and moving music that he composed give him and his works an unparalleled place in the cultural life of the world.

Let us now examine how Beethoven worked, what influenced him, what he thought of his compositions, how they influenced others, and the works themselves.

Stylistic Periods

Beethoven's works have been somewhat arbitrarily divided into stylistic periods. These are blocks of time that roughly represent reasonable groupings of his musical output by common stylistic elements. There has been much debate over this type of analysis. A number of variations (i.e., three, four, five or even six periods) have emerged—three being the most popular and broadly accepted. While there are certainly overlap and some inconsistencies in this approach, it can be helpful in tracing Beethoven's evolution throughout his career.

For our purposes, I will use the following rough scheme in looking at Beethoven's work:

Early period, ending about 1802. Includes works of young Beethoven in Bonn, plus early works in Vienna, when much of his time was absorbed as a performing pianist. Compositions during this period are generally close to the traditional Classical style.

Middle period, ending about 1812. A very productive time for Beethoven. This period starts roughly with the Heiligenstadt crisis and ends with the emotional trauma of the "Immortal Beloved" letter. He established his reputation and became famous during this time. What we know now as Beethoven's "heroic" music was written during this period.

Late period, from 1814 until his death in 1827. There are really two sub-periods here. During the years 1815–1818/1819 his output was low, as he was severely stressed by personal problems. But the final years, from about 1819 through 1826, gave us some of his most important and innovative works.

These rough stylistic periods (and sub-periods) of time interestingly correspond roughly to some major changes in Beethoven's personal life. There are also rough parallels to his economic and patronage activities, and to his composing methods.

Influences on His Work

Starting as a young boy, Beethoven would talk about his inspiration to write music. He also talked about his sense of mission and his desire to achieve greatness through his music. He was committed to a musical career at a very early age and never seems to have contemplated doing anything else. While Beethoven did eventually establish himself as a free-lance musician, and thus had more artistic freedom than his predecessors, his working life was still strongly influenced by a variety of external forces. Money was, of course, one of these forces.

The nature of Beethoven's potential income, and thus what he decided to write, changed over the years. In the early period in Vienna when he was getting established, Beethoven wrote mainly piano and chamber music for his expanding group of patrons. They wanted these smaller pieces for performance in their homes. Later he would write concertos that he could perform in public (for a fee) or symphonies that could be presented in grand concerts where there was an opportunity to make money.

He also wrote for the theater, as exemplified by his score for the ballet *The Creatures of Prometheus* (1801) and the overture and incidental music to Goethe's play *Egmont.* Writing specifically for publishers and doing special commission work for a variety of people were other major sources of income. In fact, several of his symphonies (nos. 4 and 5) and two groups of string quartets, including the final ones, were written as specific commissions. And, of course, his opera *Leonore/Fidelio* was motivated by the popularity of that genre in Vienna at the time.

There were, though, occasions when it appears that Beethoven wrote for himself, with no other motivation than to express his feelings. For instance, after his Heiligenstadt crisis in 1802, he poured out his feelings of suffering in the emotional oratorio *Christ on the Mount of Olives.* Similarly, he wrote a song cycle in 1816 that seems to have been an expression of his feelings for Antonie Brentano, the object of his emotional "Immortal Beloved" letter.

Although Beethoven often had to compose what others wanted or what would sell in order to make a living, it is quite clear from correspondence, and from the works themselves, that this influence was only on the musical forms Beethoven would employ, not on any work's contents or style. In these areas Beethoven retained complete control. Behind all of Beethoven's motivation was his strong and basic commitment to the composing of great music.

Work Routine

For all of Beethoven's messy living habits and otherwise disorderly lifestyle, his approach to his work was generally controlled and quite thorough. Though his composing routine changed somewhat over the years, depending on his health and other specific circumstances, there was a certain disciplined sameness to it. His general routine was probably best summed up by one of his biographers, Schindler:

> Beethoven rose every morning the year round at dawn and went directly to his desk. There he would work until two or three o'clock, his habitual dinner hour. In the course of the morning he would usually go out-of-doors once or even twice, but would continue to work as he walked —His afternoons were regularly spent in long walks. Late in the afternoon he would go to a favorite tavern to read the papers—Beethoven always spent his winter evenings at home reading serious works of literature. Only very rarely did he work with musical scores during the evening, for the strain on his eyes was too great—He would go to bed at ten o'clock at the latest.

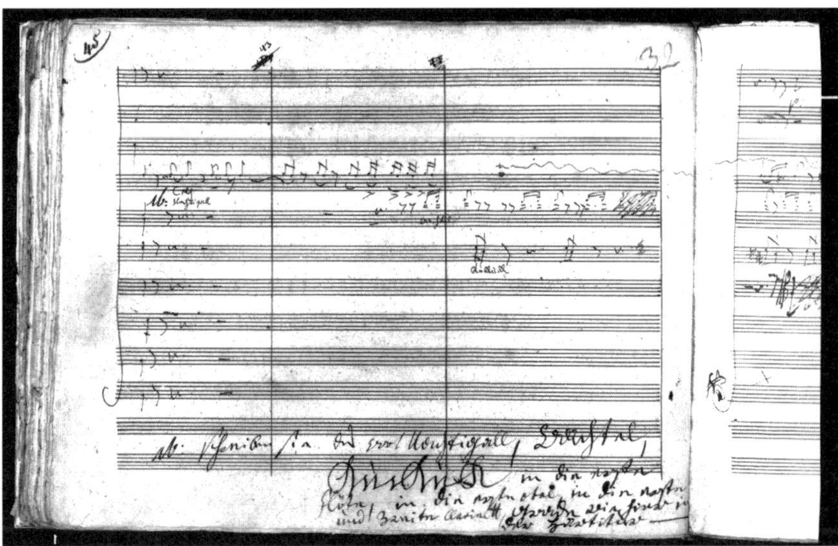

Autograph score of second movement of the Pastoral *Symphony. At the bottom is Beethoven's instruction to a copyist: "NB: write the word nightingale, quail, cuckoo, in the first flute, in the first oboe, in the first and second clarinets, exactly as here in the score."*

By permission of the Beethoven-Haus Bonn

While he was out on his walks Beethoven did much of his thinking. He generally had sketch paper or a little notebook with him and would regularly stop and jot down his musical thoughts as they came to him. These would then be developed when he had returned to his lodgings.

During the summer months Beethoven would move to the country, generally the villages in the wooded hills and valleys surrounding Vienna. (One can still visit some of the houses where Beethoven stayed in these small towns, which are now suburbs or sections of Vienna.) This time in the country was especially important to Beethoven. In 1810 he wrote to a friend:

> No one can love the country as much as I do.

He would spend hours walking in the hills or by a stream. He always had his paper and pencil along to write down his ideas. He was often inspired by nature, and several of his works directly reflect this. His sixth symphony (*Pastoral*) portrays a different rural scene in each movement.

Beethoven's daily routine changed if he had to deal with publishers or work on other matters. And there were, of course, a number of periods when he was distracted by family issues. But the discipline of a regular work routine dominated a large part of Beethoven's adult years.

Composing

Understanding how Beethoven actually worked at composing his music has been improved by a recent study of nearly eight thousand surviving sketches. We now have a fairly accurate picture of how this artist created many of his greatest works of art.

Beethoven began writing down his musical thoughts at an early age. Originally this was done on loose scraps of paper, which were used as the basis for his early compositions and in some cases were saved for possible later use. When Beethoven arrived in Vienna in 1792, he brought with him a sizeable portfolio of these sketches.

As he walked in his younger years, he would continue to use scraps of paper to jot down his thoughts as they came to him. But as his works grew more complex, he began using pocket-sized books on his walks. Thus he could capture, in a more complete way, the complexity of his ideas. He would then write them out more fully in larger sketchbooks at home. This method was well suited to the difficult and intricate pieces he wrote in his later years.

Beethoven would generally start out with a simple musical concept—a theme, structure or basic melody (often he noted the key). This would be written down as very rough notes. In subsequent sketches he would elaborate and refine his ideas, expanding them into the musical form he had in mind. The sketches tend to show much revision and experimentation, but always progress toward the final form. As he developed as a composer, his sketches became more thorough and more detailed, reflecting both his maturity and the complexity of the works.

In a given time period he would often be working on several compositions, but once into the detailed sketching phase he would generally focus on one work and proceed through it in sequence, movement by movement. Working through a series of increasingly detailed and refined drafts on a specific piece, Beethoven would end up with something close to a final version. Then a full score would be written out, with further details added and revisions made.

This detailed sketching process, sometimes involving twenty or more sketches for a particular section, reflected Beethoven's intensity and drive for perfection. He was able to integrate many complicated ideas into a single entity, tying the various pieces together in a logical and beautiful manner. His sketches show that he paid particular attention to the little sections that bind the main elements together. These short connecting sections are rarely noticed by the normal listener, but they play a big part in his music's sense of movement.

It's important to understand that this intense sketching process, with its many revisions and attention to detail, doesn't indicate that Beethoven's creativity only surfaced after long, laborious hours scribbling on countless pieces of paper. His mind was full of musical ideas and he could, and did, bring them forth in near final form on many occasions. His improvisations at the piano show an astonishing degree of instant creativity. He was famous for taking a simple theme (his own or another's) and devising unique and lovely variations, often for long periods of time, in full view of an audience.

What Beethoven's sketches show is that he was constantly inventing, devising musical surprises, and doing things in new ways. He would shift keys, invent novel rhythmic patterns and create new forms. The image of Beethoven struggling with his work is more a reflection of the uniqueness and intricacy of his compositions (see below) than it is of any lack of instant creative inspiration. He had plenty of inspiration. His task, as he saw it, was to take that inspiration and mold it into works that went beyond what others had done.

A very important part of Beethoven's personal mission was his quest for perfection. In his own eyes he never achieved it. He was constantly revising his works up to the last minute—and occasionally after they had been performed. In his later years he expressed dissatisfaction with many of his earlier pieces. He often talked about reissuing them after some revisions, but he never got around to it.

Beethoven, like most composers, was not above reusing the same musical ideas many times. He would often adapt themes from an earlier work for a later piece. And while Beethoven was able to write extremely beautiful melodies, his primary preeminence and uniqueness was in his ability to take simple musical themes and rhythms and develop and vary them in a wide variety of forms, weaving them into a complex but very comprehensive whole. His fifth symphony provides a good example of this as the distinctive four opening notes are modified and used in many variations throughout the entire piece. Although there was a definite growth and progression to his work over the years, many of his musical ideas and devices occur across all periods.

Beethoven's work on some compositions spanned a number of years. Others, sometimes because of deadlines, were completed rather quickly. And, as we have seen, there were periods of relative creative dryness when he wrote little. But throughout most of his years Beethoven's life revolved around composing music. There was a great intensity to his work. His composing efforts were distinctive and different from others mainly in the amount and detailed nature of his sketching but also because they resulted from his abundant thinking and working out-of-doors.

His Output

Beethoven wrote literally hundreds of extremely high quality pieces of music. It's a truly astounding array of masterpieces in all of the major musical forms. Below I'll briefly summarize his output in each form.

Symphonies. Beethoven wrote nine of them. They are "bigger" compositions than those of Haydn or Mozart, and they clearly demonstrate the movement from the Classical to the Romantic era. They are all complex, intricately structured pieces. Each is in four movements (except no. six, which is in five).

Numbers one and two are similar to Haydn's work, but already signs of innovation are apparent. The third (*Eroica*) was truly revolutionary in scale and content and marked a clear move into Beethoven's middle stylistic period. The middle symphonies (four through eight) show a combination of innovation, expansion and integration. The ninth symphony, of course, is one of Beethoven's supreme masterpieces. The choral treatment of Schiller's "Ode to Joy" in the last movement expresses Beethoven's optimistic view of humanity and is one of the most uplifting and glorious pieces of music ever written. The novelty of combining chorus with orchestra in a symphonic format, as well as the power of the piece as a whole, has had a tremendous impact on succeeding composers. The work represents a clear position in the Romantic style that was then emerging. A tenth symphony was in the early sketch stage when Beethoven died.

Concertos. Beethoven wrote seven in all—five for piano, one for violin, and one for a trio of violin, piano and cello. The first two piano concertos reflect the Classical style of Mozart. The latter works are more integrated and symphonic in nature, with less emphasis on the soloist. They are rich in melodic content and orchestration and contain some of Beethoven's most beautiful music. All but the first two piano concertos were written in Beethoven's middle period. After completing the fifth piano concerto in 1809, he never produced another work in this format. He did do some preliminary work on a sixth piano concerto up until 1815, but he never finished it.

He also wrote several concerto-like romances. These were short pieces for orchestra and solo instruments—two for violin and orchestra and one for orchestra and flute, bassoon and piano.

Opera. Beethoven wrote only one, *Fidelio*, and it went through many revisions. It was started in 1805 and finalized in 1814. It's an expression of Beethoven's basic beliefs of heroism and righteousness triumphing over evil. Leonore, its heroine, represents the ideal faithful woman Beethoven never had. The work contains some very moving orchestral and vocal parts. Over the course of its revisions, a total of four overtures were written: *Leonore I, II* and *III*, and *Fidelio*.

Beethoven was interested in writing other operas, but only if he could deal with important subjects. He had no interest in the light or comic operas that were popular in Vienna in the early 1800s. He never did find another libretto that was to his liking.

Choral Works. Beethoven wrote three major choral works that are still quite popular today. His only oratorio, *Christ on the Mount of Olives*, was completed in 1803–1804. It's a highly emotional piece that reflects in Christ's sufferings some of the inner despair Beethoven was feeling.

In 1807 he wrote a Mass in C Major for Prince Nikolaus Esterházy, the patron of Haydn. Expecting it to be compared to Haydn's many religious works, Beethoven composed a very original piece of music. The prince didn't care much for the results, but Beethoven liked it and said it was especially dear to his heart.

By far the most significant choral work Beethoven composed was his Mass in D Major, the *Missa Solemnis*. It was a major undertaking that took him almost four years to complete. It is monumental in its scope, originality and complexity. Beethoven later wrote:

> My chief aim when I was composing this grand Mass was to awaken and permanently instill religious feelings not only into the singers, but also into the listeners.

A number of other smaller choral works deserve mention. Probably the best-known of these is thc *Choral Fantasy*. This was composed very quickly in 1808 for one of Beethoven's public concerts. It is unique in that it begins with solo piano, then chorus is added, and finally orchestra and chorus join in a rather uplifting and rich-sounding finish. The *Choral Fantasy* clearly previews the last movement of his ninth symphony, as it contains very similar elements.

Several cantatas are also part of Beethoven's choral repertoire. In 1790 (at age twenty) he wrote one commemorating the death of Emperor Joseph and another on the occasion of Leopold II's ascension to the throne. Years later, in 1814, he wrote a sizeable piece (*The Glorious Moment*) for the Congress of Vienna to celebrate the defeat of Napoleon.

Additional choral works include renditions of two Goethe poems in "Calm Sea and Prosperous Voyage," and the "Elegiac Song" for four voices and orchestra. Several more choral works are rarely performed.

Songs and Smaller Vocal Works. Here we can see further evidence of Beethoven's great versatility as well as impressive productivity. He wrote seven works for solo voice with orchestra, the most famous being "Ah perfido!" of 1796. He also wrote some fifty canons, mostly after about 1813. These were short little pieces for two or more singers where the voices overlap and imitate each other. Beethoven had dashed these off as gifts for friends. Many of them are quite witty and full of puns, while others are more philosophical and serious in nature.

Beethoven is now generally acknowledged as the creator of Romantic German Lied, and his work in that genre had a strong influence on succeeding generations of composers. These songs, usually accompanied by piano, have text derived from poetry, and in some cases Beethoven's own words as well. Many of them are quite complex and full of subtleties. He wrote over sixty of these, and many are excitingly beautiful in their melodic flow and emotional outpourings.

A little-known part of Beethoven's output is his arrangements of folk songs of various countries. He would take the basic folk melody, then embellish and arrange it, adding harmonies. Then he would score it for accompaniment with piano, and often cello and violin. He started doing arrangements for the Scottish publisher George Thompson in 1809 and worked on them sporadically for about ten years. He wrote somewhere over one hundred fifty of these and was paid a small amount for each. The majority (well over one hundred) are settings for Scottish, Irish and Welsh songs.

Other Orchestral—Stage and Special Occasion Works. Periodically throughout his career, Beethoven was asked to write orchestral pieces for a variety of special occasions and to accompany ballet or stage works. Though most of these are infrequently performed, several contain some of Beethoven's most lively, pleasant and uplifting music.

Probably the most significant of these in Beethoven's career is his ballet music, *The Creatures of Prometheus.* Written around 1800, this can be considered a transitional piece between Beethoven's early and middle periods. It has a heroic theme that appealed to Beethoven and contains an overture and sixteen pieces of music.

Later in his so-called middle period, Beethoven wrote several more works to accompany heroic dramas. The *Coriolan* Overture, written in 1807, depicts the heroic tale of the ancient Roman Coriolanus. The *Egmont* Overture and incidental music were composed in 1810 and written for Goethe's drama that portrays a theme of national liberation. Other stage works include *King Stephen* and *The Ruins of Athens,* both written in 1811 to accompany dramas celebrating the opening of a new theater in Pest. In 1822, well into his late period, Beethoven wrote the rousing overture *Consecration of the House* in honor of the opening of a theater in Vienna.

Of less importance are several works written for specific nondramatic occasions. The *Namesday* Overture was turned out for the Kaiser in 1814. Also about that same time, when Beethoven was entering a period of diminished creative output, he completed his unusual *Wellington Sieg* (*Battle* Symphony). Originally composed as a piece for a new musical invention, the panharmonium, it was soon scored for full orchestra, military instruments, live cannon and muskets. It's bombastic and very much a program piece depicting Wellington's victory at Vittoria. It is not one of Beethoven's best, but the victorious and nationalistic mood around the Congress of Vienna made it very popular. As a result, it was one of Beethoven's most successful efforts from a financial standpoint.

Marches and Dances. Beginning in 1795, and periodically over the next ten years, Beethoven was asked to compose dances and minuets for social events. The result was a series of short pieces (one to three minutes each) for orchestra or smaller groups. Some of these have been lost; the authorship of others is unclear. But over fifty are in existence today.

The marches were composed toward the end of Beethoven's middle period. They are short, single-movement works composed for special occasions. Scored for winds and percussions, some of them are quite lively. In a letter to his friend and patron Archduke Rudolph, Beethoven apparently refers to one of these energetic marches:

> I see that your Royal Imperial Highness wants to have the effects of my music tried on horses as well. All right. But I must see whether the riders will thereby be enabled to make a few skillful somersaults.

Chamber Music. Beethoven produced a tremendous body of work that falls under this general title. His string quartets make up the most substantial, and by far the most important, part of his chamber music. This was a genre that did not come easily to Beethoven, but the evolution of his string quartets beautifully reflects his growth as a composer. The major quartets nicely fit into groups in each of his main stylistic periods. The first six were written in 1798–1800 and are close to the Classical model of Haydn. They do, however, show signs of innovation and experimentation. The five string quartets from Beethoven's middle period are dominated by the three named after Count Razumovsky that were written in 1806. These are larger works, more symphonic in nature, and contain the heroic feeling characteristic of this period. These were followed by two more in the years 1809 and 1810.

It was not until 1823 that Beethoven again worked in this important and challenging form. In November of 1822 he received a commission from Russian Prince Niklaus Galitzin. This resulted in three quartets (opp. 127, 132 and 130). Before he died he wrote two more, opp. 131 and 135, plus a Grosse Fugue (Op. 133), which had originally been the too-long final movements of Op. 130. These last works are considered to be among the finest pieces in all of Beethoven's oeuvre. They are highly complex, and their subtleties and intricate structures go far beyond anything that had been done before. They were extremely difficult to play, and it took some time for audiences to appreciate their unique character. Some of the quartets have the traditional four movements, while others have up to seven.

Today they are acknowledged as Beethoven's most innovative and influential compositions.

Early in his career, Beethoven wrote a number of chamber works for wind instruments. These were influenced by Mozart's serenades and *divertimentos* and were generally light and lively in mood. Most of these pieces were composed during Beethoven's first years in Vienna. By around 1800, however, he had moved on to more serious undertakings. In all, he wrote about twenty of these pieces.

Beethoven also produced a number of works composed for piano and strings. These consisted mainly of violin sonatas, cello sonatas and piano trios. The most famous of these are two violin sonatas, *Spring* and *Kreutzer* (Money), written in the period 1801–1803. The *Archduke* Piano Trio (for piano, violin and cello), written in 1810–1811, also remains very popular.

Piano Music. Beethoven's solo piano work is composed of sonatas, several groups of variations on a theme and a variety of assorted short pieces. In these we can trace Beethoven's development as a composer. What he composed for the piano, and the amount he composed, were both clearly influenced by his own skills as a performer. The evolution and improvement of the instrument itself over his lifetime also influenced his compositions. For instance, his powerful *Hammerklavier* Sonata, written in 1818, would not have been playable on the smaller and weaker pianos of the late 1790s.

The heart of Beethoven's piano works are his thirty-two piano sonatas. He began writing them early (in 1793, at age twenty-three) and composed his last in 1822 at age fifty-two. Composing them was difficult work. Most of them are complicated, finely structured compositions with two, three or sometimes four movements. They run between ten and forty minutes in length and represent some of his most imaginative compositions.

Some of Beethoven's most notable and beautiful sonatas were written during his early stylistic period. Among these, the *Pathetique* no. 8 (written in 1797–1798) and the *Moonlight* no. 14 (1801) are the most popular. The *Waldstein* Sonata no. 21 (1804) is a piece more typical of Beethoven's heroic mode and is symbolic of the early years of his middle period. The *Farewell/Les Adieux* Sonata no. 26 (written in 1809) is a very personal and emotional work

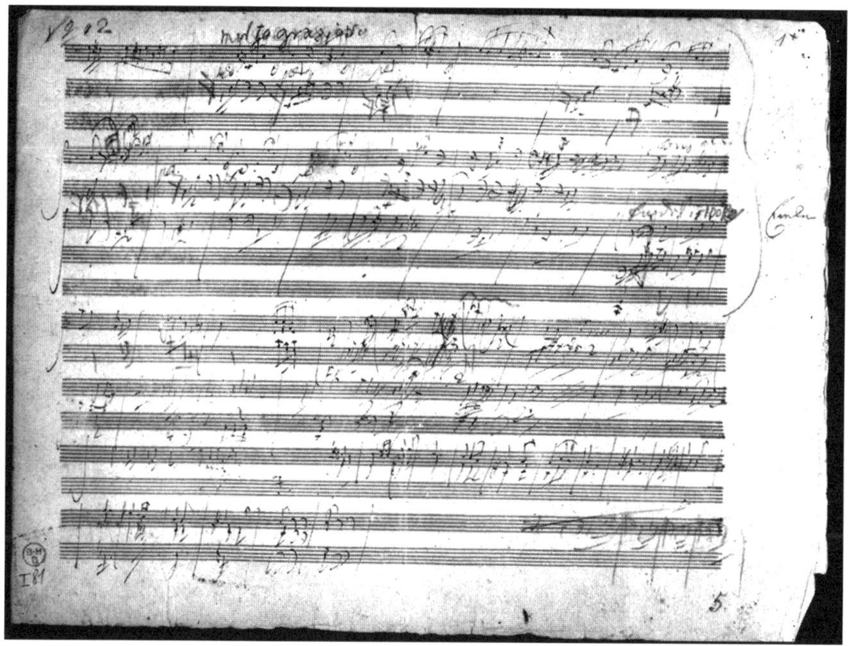

Draft for "Für Elise," 1808–10. The messy annotations of 1822 are typical of Beethoven's later years.

By permission of the Beethoven-Haus Bonn

expressing Beethoven's feelings regarding Archduke Rudolph's evacuation from Vienna because of the French invasion.

Beethoven's most striking work in this genre is the *Hammerklavier* Sonata no. 29 (1818). It's a big and very powerful piece running nearly forty-five minutes. It was written toward the end of a period in Beethoven's life that was full of family problems rather than the production of great works. This sonata marked the beginning of his extraordinary productive final years.

All thirty-two of these sonatas are considered masterpieces and are part of the basic repertoire of the great pianists today, nearly two hundred years later.

The most famous of Beethoven's variations is the set written for the publisher Anton Diabelli between 1819–1823. There are thirty-three variations of a simple theme. The work runs over fifty minutes in length and is full of innovation, cleverness, beauty and a wide variety of moods and harmonies.

Earlier Beethoven had written a number of other variations for many different occasions. Some of them reworked the themes of other composers; some drew from his own themes; and some were based on nationalistic themes, i.e., "God Save the King." The most memorable of all of these is his fifty variations on a theme used in his Eroica Symphony. All in all, there about twenty of these sets of variations.

Other piano works written over the years include many sets of *bagatelles* (French for "little pieces"), some marches, a few lively rondos and a variety of small incidental pieces. His brief but enduring "Für Elise" (1808 or 1810) was written for one of his periodic lady friends, Therese von Malfatti. It remains a staple of all those who have ever taken piano lessons.

His Legacy

Beethoven's early works generally grew out of the formal Classical tradition that he inherited and then mastered. But it was his ability to move beyond these Classical forms that really sets Beethoven apart. He was not constrained by tradition. He freely changed preexisting structures to suit his own expressive needs. His innovation, plus his sublime ability to communicate emotion, led the musical world into the Romantic period, where composers focused even more strongly on expressing both personal emotions and grander sentiments, such as love of one's country. Musically there was very little he could not or did not do.

Beethoven exerted significant influence over most of the great composers who followed him, particularly Romantic masters like Berlioz, Liszt, Schumann, Brahms and Mahler. His musical departures and the sheer quality of his work set a standard that made the task of his successors more difficult. The awe and admiration that subsequent composers felt for Beethoven can be seen in some of their comments.

Franz Schubert once complained to a friend:

> Secretly, in my heart of hearts, I hope to make something out of myself, but who can do anything after Beethoven?

Hector Berlioz upon hearing Beethoven:

> ...I saw the giant form of Beethoven rear up. The shock was almost as great as that of Shakespeare had been. Beethoven opened before me a new world of music, as Shakespeare had revealed a new universe of poetry.

When Giuseppe Verdi was asked to allow his name to be added to the honors' list of the Beethoven birthplace in Bonn, he answered:

> I cannot refuse the honor that is offered to me. We are talking about Beethoven! Before such a name, we all prostrate ourselves reverently.

Johannes Brahms had something of a block trying to write his first symphony. Some four decades after Beethoven's death, he exclaimed to a friend:

> I will never write a symphony! You have no idea what it feels like for someone like me always to hear a giant like that Beethoven marching along behind me.

Beethoven's appeal is both long lasting and universal. Today, some one hundred seventy years after his death, his reputation continues to grow. In the mid-1990s, Beethoven was by far the most frequently performed composer among the one hundred largest U.S. orchestras, with five of his compositions among the ten most frequently conducted works. Interestingly, he is nearly as popular in Japan as he is in Europe and the rest of the Western world.

It is difficult to define clearly what it is that makes Beethoven's music so special. Over the years music scholars have written extensively on this subject. Opinions differ, and much of the theorizing is no doubt very subjective, being in the ears of the beholder. But even for the nonexpert, several general themes appear.

First of all, Beethoven's music seems to have a certain wholeness and completeness about it. He was a master at making the various parts of a piece work together. Common themes and keys are used in different movements. Within movements, Beethoven could masterfully tie the pieces into an integrated experience for the listener. He paid particular attention to the brief transition phrases that link sections of music together. This is one of the methods Beethoven used to give his music its driving, forward-moving feeling.

Much of Beethoven's music is truly grand in structure, scope and feeling. Beginning with the almost hour-long Symphony no. 3, *Eroica* (1803), he opened the way for bigger concertos and larger works for chamber ensembles and solo piano. He increased the sphere and breadth of many forms.

There is also a certain richness in his music that had not existed previously. When one listens closely to the orchestral works, there is an incredible amount of nuance and complexity. Beethoven's attention to detail enabled him to write music with more depth than his predecessors.

Another characteristic of Beethoven's music that one hears, or more accurately *feels*, is the logical nature or rightness of it. The music seems to proceed along the right route toward its natural conclusion. Though it is often full of musical surprises and inventions, the music leads the listener on an auditory and emotional path that feels almost predestined. At the end of the piece there is no question that it took the right path to the final destination.

And finally, Beethoven's melodies, rhythms, and orchestration have a way of communicating and touching deep emotions in all of us. He was uniquely skilled in his ability to express and elicit a wide array of feelings, from the quiet, reflective longing in the *Moonlight* piano sonata to the glorious exhilaration of the final movements of the fifth and the ninth symphonies. Much of his music is marked by great contrasts, as he could quickly shift from violent explosive sounds to a gentle and sensitive mood. His music, in its totality, but not necessarily specifically programmatically, expresses his deepest feelings, his beliefs, his highs and lows, his triumphs and his tragedies. It's truly a reflection of the man, his struggles and the times he lived.

Some of the lines from Beethoven's funeral oration by the Viennese poet Franz Grillparzer (March 29, 1827) beautifully sum up Beethoven's greatness, as seen by his contemporaries:

> ...the last master of resounding song, the gracious mouth by which music spoke, the man who inherited and increased the immortal fame of Handel and Bach, of Haydn and Mozart, has ceased to be; and we stand weeping over the broken strings of an instrument now stilled.
>
> For he was an artist, and what he was, he was only through art.

He was an artist, and who shall stand beside him? As the behemoth sweeps through the seas, he swept across the boundaries of his art.

He was an artist, but also a man, a man in every sense, in the highest sense.

He whom you mourn is now among the greatest men of all time, unassailable for ever. Return to your homes, then, distressed but composed. And whenever, during your lives, the power of his works overwhelms you like a coming storm; when your rapture pours out in the midst of a generation yet unborn; then remember this hour and think: we were there when they buried him, and when he died we wept!

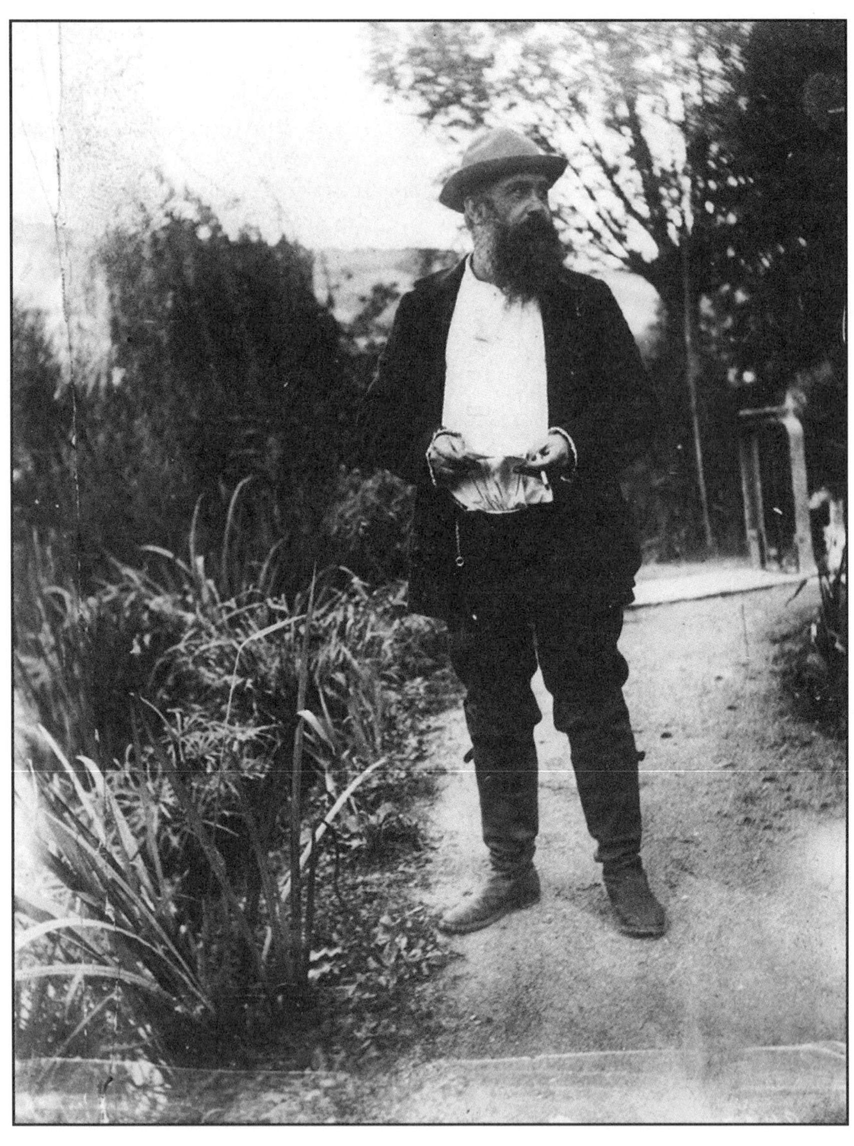

A robust, fifty-five-year-old Monet in his garden at Giverny. Photo by Margaret Perry, the daughter of American painter Lilla Cabot Perry, taken on September 28, 1895.

Photographed by Margaret Perry, Lilla Cabot Perry Photographs, Archives of American Art, Smithsonian Institution

Claude Monet (1840–1926)

During his eighty-six years, Claude Monet lived through times of enormous technical invention, economic growth, social change and artistic innovation. The period also saw the rise of nationalism and the consolidation and realignment of Europe.

The Industrial Revolution, with its accompanying mechanical inventions and economic and social reordering, was the basic driving force behind most of the progress and turmoil. Technical progress in such areas as railroads, telephones, photography and automobiles changed people's lives forever. As economic opportunities developed and the workplace changed, millions of people found themselves in new circumstances—occasionally better off, but often further down the socio-economic ladder. As a result, the last half of the nineteenth century was a time of much social unrest.

Beginning with the revolutions of 1848, there was a persistent but somewhat irregular movement to rearrange society, and to redistribute economic power and resources away from the upper classes and toward the emerging middle classes—and in some extreme cases, the lower working classes. These political and economic forces resulted in great instability in many governments, especially France. This increased economic activity did, however, provide the resources for building the cities and infrastructures in the leading countries of Europe.

During this period there emerged a larger, stronger, materialistic middle class, or bourgeoisie. It was this group that provided much of the economic activity, the social mores, and the artistic patronage that characterized this extremely vital period in French and European cultural history.

Monet, being an acute observer, was certainly aware of the changes and turmoil that surrounded him through much of his life. He was not, however, an active and passionate participant in the major political or philosophical issues of the day. Even though he counted among his friends a number of leading writers and intellectuals, his interests were mainly in art, his family and, when he could afford it, a comfortable life.

Monet came from the middle class. His father was a merchant. He spent most of his life associating with people of the same general economic and social background. Although he had periods of significant economic problems, his later years were spent in relative comfort as he led the life of the well-to-do bourgeoisie. He lived and worked for almost all of his life in a small area consisting of Paris, some of the small towns along the Seine, and the Normandy coast.

The fertile intellectual, social and artistic life of nineteenth-century Paris provided an excellent environment for the emergence of an innovative group of artists that became known as the Impressionists. They grew out of a rich tradition of French painting that had recently gone through periods of Neoclassicism, Romanticism and Realism. Much of the art of these earlier periods dealt with classical and biblical subjects or with nationalistic glories. Throughout most of the 1800s, the Parisian art world revolved around the official Salon and the government-run École des Beaux-Arts. It was through this system that the typical artist hoped to gain patronage, income and some degree of fame. Most of the Impressionists, including Monet, flirted with this system, sometimes participating, sometimes not, but they were never fully a part of it. They were able to exist on the outside only through persistence, strong artistic vision and the help of a number of bourgeoisie patrons and supporters.

As France was working its way through a series of economic crises and considerable social unrest, Monet followed his personal path toward his very own self-driven artistic destiny. He was influenced mainly by his inner need to grow and explore his art, by his fellow artists, and by his personal economic circumstances. Monet was a painter first, foremost and last. He was concerned with issues such as light and color as well as capturing the mood of a particular scene at a specific time. He was deeply absorbed in his work and spent much of his nonpainting time discussing the subject and trying to figure out how to make a living at it.

His work reflected contemporary life but rarely dealt with the issues or problems of the times. However, it is important that we briefly survey the major historical movements and events that took place during Monet's life, as it will help us understand both the nature of his work and the economic and artistic environment that influenced him.

Surprisingly, little in-depth biographical material has been published on Monet, though there are some excellent books and articles that explore his work and trace his artistic growth and changing styles. The most definitive source is a 1974 work published in French by Daniel Wildenstein. It includes Monet's three thousand letters, plus accounts of the artist's life from family and friends. Out of Wildenstein's work has come most of the books that are available today.

In studying Monet, one must be aware of the artist's desire to create an image of himself that differs somewhat from reality. He was often a bit misleading in telling people how he worked and what struggles he had gone through. Frequently we find that his recollections of his early years, made late in his life, are hazy at best.

Monet's Times

France and Europe—Mid-Nineteenth Century

France in the mid-nineteenth century was still trying to resolve many of the basic issues raised by the French Revolution. The Bourbon monarchy had been restored after the fall of Napoleon in 1815. It ruled until 1830, when it was replaced by another branch of royalty—the Orleans monarchy, under Louis Philippe. His reign (1830–1848) was one of internal prosperity, lack of foreign adventures and general conservatism.

However, toward the end of his rule, the issues of human rights, freedom and broader political power became popular, and in response Louis Philippe became increasingly repressive. His opponents began to organize "banquets" where talk of revolution was a favorite topic. The king's attempts to bar these gatherings provoked open revolt, and in February 1848 another French Revolution began. Riots ensued, barricades went up in the streets, government troops responded and fighting broke out. Louis Philippe did the noble thing and abdicated, then fled to England. A group of the opposition elements got together and proclaimed the Second Republic.

The revolutionary spark from France quickly spread to other countries. The rulers of Europe, afraid of broad-scale upheavals, moved toward accommodation and started dealing with their liberal opponents and their demands for constitutional governments and greater civil rights. These trends, combined with the potent forces of nationalism, caused great unrest and violence across Europe, particularly in Germany and Italy. When things settled down, there was neither a great reordering of the map of Europe nor a great turnover in the class of rulers who were in control. However, there had been significant change in other ways, and a basis for a new era in Europe was formed. For the first time the working class emerged as a legitimate force, and more liberal constitutions were adopted in a number of European countries.

France—Second Republic/Second Empire, 1848–1870

During much of 1848, the basically conservative interim government of the Second Republic dealt with pressures from the more liberal elements for major changes in the government's policy, and for a revision of the whole economic structure of the country. There was much unrest, and threats of further revolution. By the end of 1848, the forces of the right and center were firmly in control, and much of the country had had enough agitation and uncertainty. People wanted a strong government that could keep things under order. In December 1848 Louis Napoleon was elected head of the Second Republic.

Charles Louis Napoleon Bonaparte (1808–1873) was the third son of Louis Bonaparte, former King of Holland and brother of Napoleon I. Thus, Louis Napoleon III was a nephew of the original Napoleon and the recognized head of the family. His election began a rule of over twenty years, first as president, then as Emperor. His reign encompassed a period of growth, glory and political activity that enabled France, and Paris in particular, to emerge as the cultural, commercial and artistic center of Europe. It was during his rule that much of the Paris that we know today was built. Also during his reign, the group of painters that we know as the Impressionists first came to Paris.

Any hopes that Louis Napoleon would usher in a new age of liberal republicanism were quickly dashed. Within a few years, he was positioning himself for the long term through arbitrary changes in the electoral laws and widespread bribery of his political supporters. He assumed dictatorial powers in 1851 and in December 1852 proclaimed himself Emperor Napoleon III. Thus the short-lived Second Republic became the Second Napoleonic Empire.

Napoleon III was not an outwardly impressive man. He was, though, a master manipulator of people and of the levers of power. His goal was to bring glory to France and his family. The first years of his regime were quite repressive as he tried to censor the press, control the educational system and exile his opponents—among them Victor Hugo. He built his power base by promising glory and prestige to the army, giving higher salaries to bureaucrats, and acting in ways to enhance the national stature and glory of France.

During the 1850s France did well. There was an economic boom, and credit was widely available through a new system of banks and credit organizations. The railroad and telegraph systems were greatly expanded. A series of international exhibitions and festivals brought thousands of people to Paris, which added to France's prestige and built its international trade.

There were problems, though, particularly on the international front. Napoleon III had an aggressive foreign policy, engaging France in a series of costly wars. His armies fought in Russia, Africa, the Middle East, Italy (against Austria) and Mexico. The expedition to Mexico, taken during the American Civil War, was particularly destructive, and it resulted in the execution of his puppet emperor, Maximilian. He also invested huge sums in the construction of the Suez Canal. All this adventuring was extremely expensive and left France with a huge debt, many enemies and disgruntled neighbors.

The demise of the Second Empire occurred with France's defeat in the Franco-Prussian War of 1870. Napoleon III had gotten himself into a very serious conflict with Prussia over the succession to the Spanish throne. After a series of demands, intrigues, insults and nationalistic speeches, France declared war on Prussia in July 1870. The Prussian Chancellor, Otto von Bismarck, was generally pleased with the course of events. He had egged the French on, as he felt that such a war would be the best way to bring all of the German lands together into a united Germany. This in fact happened.

A sickly Napoleon led his troops into battle in early August of 1870. The overconfident French were quickly pushed back and forced into retreat. Napoleon and thousands of his troops were surrounded in the town of Sedan. They surrendered almost immediately and the Emperor and his men were taken prisoner. Napoleon was deposed and the Second Empire came to an end. The French people had suffered a major humiliation. The Prussian armies continued on to Paris.

The Third Republic

The Third Republic was proclaimed in Paris soon after the news of the fall of Sedan reached the capital. Its early years were marked by extreme unrest and violence. These events, plus the stunning, unexpected and swift defeat in the Franco-Prussian War, left deep marks on the French psyche. The underlying emotions and the divisions in society that arose were the base of many problems that confronted the French throughout the entire period of the Third Republic (1870–1945).

The seven to eight months after the surrender at Sedan featured high drama and severe tragedy for the French. The Prussian/German armies continued to Paris, which they proceeded to surround with the goal of starving it into surrender. In early January 1871 the city was nearly out of food. People were eating their dogs, cats and even the rats. The Prussians and Germans started a bombardment, and Paris surrendered on January 28. The peace terms were harsh, including the secession of Alsace and Lorraine, plus an indemnity payment of five billion francs.

As the war was winding down, revolutionary elements—the working-class Proletariat—began to organize in Paris. After peace was declared, the new provisional government tried to disarm the workers, who had been issued guns during the siege. Violence ensued and the government fled to Versailles. The radicals now in charge of Paris set up a Commune, which issued socialist manifestos and set up a socialist program. Lacking any support in the country, the idealistic, extremist Commune was isolated and weak. The army rallied to the side of the temporary provisional government and marched on the city. By April 1871 Paris was once again under siege—this time by the French army. Within a week, government soldiers had broken into the city and had the rebels cornered in the northeast section. There was a horrible massacre. Both sides committed terrible atrocities. In all, some twenty thousand people died. A legacy of bitter anger and hatred grew out of this unfortunate episode and influenced class relationships in France for many years.

Following the fall of the Commune, there was a period of great instability while the temporary government struggled to draft a constitution and install a permanent government. There was much intrigue as various forces tried to push forward their favorite candidates to head up a restored monarchy, while others maneuvered for power within a republican government. Finally, in 1875, a regular government was established and some constitutional laws were passed. It then took several more years and further crises before the Third Republic became a legitimate player on the European scene.

In spite of political instability, the interim government did make progress, especially on the economic front. The currency stabilized and the economy improved. Remarkably, the German war debt of five billion francs was paid by September 1873, two years ahead of schedule, and soon all German troops left French soil. In addition, the army was rebuilt with modern weapons, and by 1875 it was almost as large as Germany's. In the end, democracy, albeit in a wobbly form, did triumph over attempts to return to the past. After its shaky start, the Third Republic was to survive for over seventy years.

This period of the early 1870s was one of huge difficulty for Monet and his fellow Impressionists. The war and its immediate aftermath caused great disruptions in their lives. Some joined the army and were killed. Others fled the country, while still others stayed in Paris and endured the extreme hardships of the early months of the Third Republic. Many of their paintings were lost in the violence and confusion. Soon thereafter, however, they were all back in the Paris area, continuing their efforts to achieve some recognition and compensation within a still shaky economic and social environment.

The Last Decades of the Nineteenth Century

For France, like much of Europe, the last twenty-five years of the nineteenth century formed a period of fairly regular political crises, economic and technological growth, and relative peace and stability on the international scene. France, with its republican form of government, was unique among the leading countries of Europe; the other major players hung on to their weakening monarchies. (It would not be until the early twentieth century that many of these would fall.) While the Third Republic faced a number of threats from both the right and the left, France survived and evolved into a politically and socially conservative country.

The economy grew, enduring a number of recessions that affected most of Europe. Economic power moved toward the financial institutions, and with the help of a pro-business government policy a wealthy merchant class thrived. The expansion of railroads continued.

In external affairs, France's activities were limited. The power of its neighbors, England and Germany, hemmed in the country. The French government did conduct some forays into north and central Africa, including the conquest of Tunisia—which, along with Algeria, gave France a major presence along the southern Mediterranean. France also expanded colonization activities in Indochina. Underlying much of its foreign policy was a continuing fear and hatred of the Germans and a desire for revenge for the humiliating defeat of 1870.

Overall, in the middle and upper strata of French society there was a feeling of satisfaction. The now-influential and growing bourgeoisie became complacent and essentially conservative in its outlook. Its priorities were basically materialistic—to enjoy their wealth and protect the status quo.

During the 1880s and 1890s, however, there were some disturbing and unsettling aspects of French, and particularly Parisian, society. In the middle of material progress and a satisfying lifestyle, many people had doubts about the moral health of the country. The unending series of government scandals and incidents of improper behavior also added to the spiritual unrest.

Out of all this ferment, materialistic wealth, and political and social unrest, there emerged in Paris a society that was conducive to a high level of artistic and literary activity. Those in the arts pushed their art forms in new directions and formed the core of movements that were to be significant for many years.

Toward the end of the nineteenth century, two long-existing and ominous aspects of French society became more prominent: nationalism and anti-Semitism. Nationalism had, of course, always been a potent force in French internal and external affairs, but it took on an even stronger tone after the Franco-Prussian War. There was also an increasingly intense feeling of anti-Semitism in much of French society, partially caused by the perception that Jews controlled the increasingly powerful financial institutions which dominated French commerce. These two trends came together in the notorious Dreyfus Affair, which savagely divided the country and nearly shattered several of the major institutions of the Third Republic.

Dreyfus Affair

The Dreyfus Affair lasted for nearly twelve years (1894–1906) and is a complicated, tragic and embarrassing chapter in French history. In the course of the affair, the French army was shamed, friends and families split apart, and for periods of time people and their government spoke of little else. Even the usually uninvolved Monet took a stand. And the activist author and critic Émile Zola, who played a major role in promoting the Impressionists, became a key player in the Dreyfus Affair with his anti-government articles.

We do not need to go into the details of this fascinating episode, but understanding its basic elements will be helpful for us.

In 1894 a Jewish army captain from Alsace, Alfred Dreyfus, was accused (falsely) of passing military secrets to the hated Germans. He was convicted by the conservative monarchist army and sentenced to dishonorable discharge, military degradation and life imprisonment on Devil's Island. A wave of violent anti-Semitism followed. Through 1896–1897, Dreyfus's family and a few others struggled to reopen the case. They had no success.

In 1898 Émile Zola, who had previously written critically about the verdict, published an open letter to the President of the Republic—the famous "J'accuse"—accusing the war office of crimes. Zola was subsequently tried and found guilty. He fled to England.

The case now aroused public interest, and passions mounted. A campaign for a new trial was launched. The various groups in society took sides. Those favoring the pursuit of justice at all costs became known as the Dreyfussards, and those interested in protecting the institutions of society, particularly the government and the army, were the Anti-Dreyfussards. The more conservative Impressionists (Renoir, Cézanne and especially Degas) sided with the anti-Dreyfussards. They came into conflict with Dreyfussards such as Mary Cassatt and Pissarro, who was Jewish.

In 1899 Dreyfus was brought back from Devil's Island for a new trial. He was a broken man. It soon became clear that the army had lied and fabricated the evidence in the first trial. It lied again, supposedly to save its honor. Dreyfus was unjustly convicted again, but this time with extenuating circumstances. His sentence was reduced to ten years' detention. A presidential pardon followed.

The argument raged on for six more years. Finally, in 1906, an appeals court quashed the earlier verdict and concluded that Dreyfus had been convicted by "error and wrongfulness." It forbade any further trial. Dreyfus was promoted to a major.

France—Early Twentieth Century

Today we look back on the period in France before the First World War as the Belle Époque—the good old days. Things did in fact go quite well in France during this period. The progressive forces in the government, and in society in general, were strengthened. Incomes rose. Foreign trade increased, the French colonial empire expanded, and the country became a major producer of iron and steel. By 1913, France was the leading producer of automobiles and had the best road system in Europe. This was in addition to its ever-expanding railway system. In spite of many changes in the government and periodic threats from both the left and the right, the Third Republic survived and continued to surprise its many internal critics with its resilience.

The artistic environment in Paris was extremely lively and creative during these years. The Impressionists who were still alive had moved on and no longer constituted a group. But other artists flocked to France to learn about the efforts of earlier generations and then to move in new directions. This was the time when Picasso was establishing himself and creating a stir with Cubism and his very different creations. It was also during these early decades of the twentieth century that Sergei Diaghilev and his Ballet Russe, along with Igor Stravinsky, introduced some of the most controversial, creative and dramatic works in the history of music. (While all this was going on, Monet was comfortably settled in his home in Giverny, west of Paris, enjoying his fame and his increasing fortune. He had little involvement in outside issues and focused almost exclusively on his work in his immediate surroundings.)

The Belle Époque, of course, came to a crashing end with the start of World War I. The tragic march of events that led to the war, and eventually to Allied victory, are beyond our interest here. However, one of the heroes of the war was Georges Clemenceau. He had been in and out of the government for many years, but toward the end of the war he became Prime Minister. He ruled dictatorially, restored confidence, helped bring ultimate victory and then played a major role in peace negotiations. Clemenceau and Monet became close friends in their later years, and he was with Monet when the artist died in 1926.

Paris—The City

The Paris of Monet's youth was still a basically medieval city. Incredible filth and squalor filled its many narrow, winding, unpaved streets. It had very little drainage or sanitation and practically no street lighting. The place de la Concorde turned to mud after each rain, and areas not far from the Seine were essentially semi-rural settlements complete with farm animals and windmills.

By the 1860s, though, when the Impressionists started to come together, all this had begun to change. In a period of some twenty years, Paris was transformed into the beautiful and glorious "City of Lights" that we know today. The impetus for this transformation came from Napoleon III, but the man who made it happen was one Baron Haussmann (1809–1891). He served as the Prefect of the Department of the Seine and was instructed by Napoleon to rebuild Paris and make it the showplace of Europe.

This he did efficiently and ruthlessly. He built the wide, straight boulevards and round plazas we see today. Along the avenues that radiated from the plazas, he constructed great stone buildings for elegant apartments and places of commerce. The thirty-one miles of grand boulevards and avenues he created provided stunning vistas and gave Paris a unique grandeur. These broad streets also had a more practical purpose for the Emperor: their width made the erection of barricades more difficult and facilitated the rapid movement of troops in case of insurrection. As one observer put it, "The new broad streets were beautifully accessible to light, air—and infantry."

In addition to the new street plan, large areas were set aside for parks, and the city was divided into the present twenty *arrondissements.* Churches and train stations were built, construction of a new opera house began, and the area around the Louvre was cleaned of the trash piles, flea markets and animals that had been there for years. Systems were built for supplying public water, for providing gas illumination and for underground removal of sewage.

All this took place at great cost and sacrifice to the workers and the lower classes of Paris. Baron Haussmann operated ruthlessly, with no regard for the people who had to be moved. Over 350,000 people were displaced. The evicted workers, many already impoverished, moved to the outskirts of the city. There was great unrest, but no open revolt. In spite of the pain it caused, the rebuilding of Paris was a monumental accomplishment. The project did provide many jobs and, in the end, the living conditions of many Parisians improved. The final results of all the work left a city of breathtaking beauty and splendor.

Center of the Arts

It was this new Paris that so attracted Monet and his fellow Impressionists. The glorious vistas, the broad avenues, the grand buildings and the beautiful parks became the subjects of hundreds of their paintings. The city's active and vibrant artistic life also brought the Impressionists to Paris. The Third Republic produced painters, writers and musicians in such great quality and quantity that the period is now viewed as the greatest artistic period in French history. Important activities were spread across nearly all of the art forms, but it was the rich array of activity in the visual arts that made Paris so attractive to the painters. The Louvre, which had continued to build its great collections since the early 1800s, was a haven for many of the Impressionists. It was common practice for young painters to spend hours there, studying and copying the masters. The collection at the Palais du Luxembourg became a gallery of living French art and made its acquisitions primarily from the official Salons. There were also a number of other excellent public museums and galleries that opened in the last half of the century.

The annual official Salon occurred each spring and was usually the focal point for many of the painters living in and around Paris. Associated with the official Académie, it reflected the generally conservative views of the government and the establishment. It wielded great power and had a strong bias toward conventional works and historic, religious or mythological subjects. Artistic innovation or portrayal of modern life was not rewarded. Each year the Salon showed some four to five thousand paintings by over two thousand artists. To be accepted for the show was a major accomplishment and often the difference between an artist selling or not selling his paintings. The issues of what was accepted, what was not, where the pictures were hung, and the politics involved provided hours of debate and gossip among the artistic community.

There was also a thriving commercial art industry that catered to the increasing number of collectors among the growing middle and upper classes.

In the early 1860s, for example, there were over one hundred commercial galleries, each mounting an average of eight exhibitions per year.

Added to all the fine museums and the regular series of exhibitions and Salons was a cycle of international exhibitions. Paris hosted five of these huge events in the last half of the nineteenth century. (The Eiffel Tower was built for the one in 1889.) They attracted thousands of foreign tourists, and each one had a large section devoted to art. Visitors could not only see what was happening in French art, but also view works reflecting the cultures of France's far-flung colonial empire. The international exhibitions enhanced the reputation of the art of France and served as a vehicle for foreigners to add French works to their collections.

Cafés and Social Life

One of the distinctive and lasting institutions that evolved during Monet's lifetime was the Parisian café. These gathering places played a special role in all levels of society. They served as social centers and as places for relaxation, reading, general social interchange, eating and often active discussion on issues of the time. Their growth was stimulated when Baron Hausmann created the wide avenues on the right bank of the Seine. This space allowed for the creation of the *terrasse,* which gave the cafés an open, inviting feeling.

Cafés sprung up all over Paris, and by late in the century there were thousands of them, each with its own character and distinctiveness. Some took on a regional flavor and served as a meeting place for people who had migrated to Paris from a particular area of France. Others drew people who shared certain political beliefs or worked in the same profession. These cafés played an extremely important role in the intellectual and artistic life of Paris. It was here that discussions took place regarding novel concepts, new techniques and controversies surrounding particular artists or artistic theories.

The Impressionist movement was essentially conceived and developed in cafés. Regular gatherings took place between those artists whom we've come to know as the Impressionists. They discussed their works, hopes and problems, and laid plans for their series of exhibitions. Two cafés were particularly significant to the Impressionists:

Café Guerbois. This café became popular with the Impressionists and a group of intellectuals and writers in the mid-1860s. It was located at 11, rue de Batignolles, in an area that is now the avenue de Clichy. Manet first started frequenting the café and was followed by his friends Zola, Gaspar Nadar (a photographer) and others, including Monet. Many of the painters had their studios nearby. (At one point, the group that later became known as the Impressionists was called the Batignolles Group.) Gatherings usually took place on Thursday evenings and were full of lively debate. Monet would later note:

> Nothing could have been more stimulating than the regular discussion which we used to have there with their constant clashes of opinion. They kept our wits sharpened and supplied us with a stock of enthusiasm which lasted us for weeks and kept us going until the final realization of an ideal was accomplished. From them we emerged with a stronger determination and with our thoughts clearer and more sharply defined.

Nouvelle-Athènes. Around 1875 the action shifted from the Café Guerbois to the Café de la Nouvelle-Athènes in the Place Pigalle in Montmartre. Here the discussion of ideas, arguing and planning continued. The café attracted political dissidents, such as Georges Clemenceau, as well as artists. Several of the Impressionists used the café as the setting of some of their best paintings.

As the Impressionists aged and moved out of Paris, their visits to these two cafés decreased. But when they did come back to the city, they would still gather at particular cafés or restaurants to discuss their work.

In the late nineteenth century, Paris was looked upon as the glorious artistic and cultural center of France, if not of all of Europe. It stood as one of the largest cities on the continent, with over two million inhabitants by 1880. People from the provinces were in awe of the glamour, elegance, and activity of the capital. One observed that it "throned royally" over the rest of France.

Technology

Significant new technology came into the lives of the French during the early years of the Third Republic. We will look at two of the innovations that had particular relevance to the Impressionists.

Railroads. The first steam-powered train began operating in France in the early 1830s. By the last half of the nineteenth century, major railroad building was going on all across Europe, with the activity particularly strong in France during the reign of Napoleon III. The railways provided an active stimulus to the Industrial Revolution. Demand for great amounts of iron, coal, concrete and other materials created new industries and provided an outlet for entrepreneurial skills and investment capital. The railroads also helped build the big urban centers, as they could effectively move large quantities of goods in and out of factories to distribute them across Europe.

The availability of railroad transportation also made the towns of rural France more accessible. This was particularly true of the towns in Normandy, along the Channel coast. These beautiful villages were turned into resorts and summer residences for well-to-do Parisians. In Paris, six imposing train stations (*gare*) were built throughout the city.

Trains fascinated the Impressionists and appealed to them as a sign of progress and modern life. They often depicted railroad bridges, the stations and the trains themselves in their paintings. The most famous of these is Monet's series of the Gare St.-Lazare. Trains also provided the opportunity for the Impressionists to get out into the country quickly to paint at the seascapes and landscapes. They also made it more convenient for some of the Impressionists, including Monet, to move out of Paris to cheaper lodgings in villages along the Seine, yet still be able to travel in and out of Paris.

Photography. Details of the workings of the photographic process were first published in 1839. There was debate on the effect this new technology might have on the art of painting. Artists were torn between the visual potential of this new device and the fear that it could replace some of the portrait painting they often depended on for their livelihoods.

By the time of the Impressionists, the snapshot camera had been developed. Its unposed photos were in some ways similar to what these inventive painters were trying to capture on canvas. The different croppings, unusual juxtapositions of figures, and blurring effect that was possible with a camera were particularly appealing to the Impressionists. Degas was particularly fascinated by cameras, and in the 1880s Monet owned four of them. It is ironic, and possibly symbolic, that the first Impressionist exhibition in 1874 was held in the studio of Gaspar Nadar, one of the most innovative and famous photographers of the day.

Philosophical and Intellectual Trends

Underlying the many developments of the last half of the nineteenth century were a number of ideas and theories that influenced whole countries, their governments and individuals alike. These doubtless influenced the lives and work of Monet and his fellow painters.

Faith in Science, Realism. Faith that science could answer the most difficult questions, explain natural phenomena and lead to a higher level of civilization became widespread. The progress of science, and the resulting inventions and industrialization, were a part of everyone's life. People constantly read or heard about discoveries and new theories on how things worked. This scientific approach served the Impressionists well in their quest to understand the phenomena of light and color.

Concurrent with, and tied to, this scientific thinking was a strong sense of realism among a large part of society, especially the educated middle and upper classes. People turned away from the abstract and ideal and toward facts and evidence. They felt they should endeavor to view the world as it actually was—to face the facts. Underlying much of this realistic and scientific thinking was the work of the English naturalist Charles Darwin (1809–1882), whose influential research, published in 1859, gave a scientific explanation for the development of humanity.

Liberalism. Classic liberalism gained great influence after the revolutions of 1848. This liberalism was based on faith in human nature and a belief that human beings, using reason and the scientific approach, could understand the natural order of things and make progress. It grew out of the tradition of the Rights of Man of the French Revolution. Its underlying principle was individual freedom. A central belief of liberalism was that there should be very little infringement on this freedom from outside forces such as governments, churches or workers' organizations. Liberals believed in free enterprise and the protection of private property.

These classic liberal beliefs were strongest in the middle class—those who had rights and property to protect. There was a continual conflict between liberalism and those on the extreme right, who wanted stronger governmental controls and either the restoration of the monarchy or a dictatorial leader.

Another threat to classic liberalism came from the other direction, the socialists of the left. This group believed in more regulation and less individual freedom. It felt individual rights might have to be sacrificed for the good of the larger society. Socialists saw the free enterprise system as unjust and believed the government should have some control over the means of production so that workers could get a larger share of economic rewards.

Socialist thinking had strong appeal in a society going through industrialization, where the number of low-paying factory jobs was growing and many people were living in poverty and poor health. The publication of *Das Kapital* by Karl Marx (1818–1883) in 1867 provided, for some, a clear explanation of the economic forces of an industrialized world. The work laid out a path for social revolution that would ostensibly lead to an ideal world of equality based on economic laws.

Socialist forces remained active in France through the entire Third Republic. Believers in socialism played a leading role in the Commune of 1871, and throughout the later years of the nineteenth century they were active in pressing for workers' rights. However, they were a splintered group, and a united socialist movement only came into being in the early twentieth century.

The ideals of the socialists were particularly appealing to some intellectuals and rebels of the middle and upper classes. Several of the Impressionists were attracted to socialism, particularly Monet's friend Camille Pissarro.

Nationalism. Of all the ideological forces influencing nineteenth-century Europe, nationalism was the most powerful. Out of this strong movement came the unification of Germany as well as the consolidation of Italy. It also played a big role in shaping the policies and character of France.

Nationalism was based on the belief that people who had a common language, heritage and attitude toward life should be united in a single country.

Nationalists believed that the goals and destiny of the father/motherland should be the supreme values to which all individuals should pledge their loyalty. These thoughts had great appeal to many of the citizens of Europe, whose countries were continually arguing over borders, colonial expansion, trade laws and diplomatic issues. To build national will and justify government practices, countries emphasized their national origins, past glories and prior tragedies. In addition, they built upon the myths and folklore of their histories. Love of one's country and the glorification of its history, art and music became widespread. The nationalistic music of Wagner, Dvořák and Smetana was especially popular at this time.

Naturally, a feeling of superiority followed in the wake of nationalist sentiment. This often gave way to bigotry. Relations among nations took on a more emotional tone. The humiliation of France by Germany in the Franco-Prussian War led to calls for revenge and the reestablishment of France as the foremost culture and society in Europe.

This pride in country, in a general sense, was part of the French Impressionists' thinking, as they found new ways to reflect the beauty and life of their country. Though several of the Impressionists had non-French backgrounds, most were French by birth, most came from the French tradition, and most were part of a French/Parisian society which felt itself to be unmatched in its sophistication.

Artistic Environment and History

The art of painting changed rapidly during the nineteenth century. Earlier artistic eras such as the Renaissance or Baroque had each lasted for many years. However, the 1800s had a series of movements that relatively quickly were succeeded by new styles, each one representing either further evolution or a countermovement. The major movements were Neoclassicism, Romanticism and Realism. These artistic periods are often viewed with a degree of separateness and clarity that did not, in fact, exist at the time. They overlapped and often existed side by side in competition. Still, they represent real differences in approach.

Concurrently, the status and role of painters changed during the nineteenth century. They less frequently had commissions for specific institutions or clients, and over the years they began to work more for themselves, creating works that expressed their own emotions or views. It was out of these changes that Impressionism emerged during the 1860s. It did not just appear, but grew out of the tremendous artistic activity—and the evolving styles—that preceded it.

Neoclassicism

Neoclassical art emerged in the late 1700s and was a dominant style in official circles in the early part of the nineteenth century. It arose in reaction to the ornate, delicate, highly stylized superficiality of the Baroque and Rococo eras. Neoclassical art reached back to the glories of ancient Greece and Rome for its inspiration and its subject matter. It was rational in tone, reflecting the ideals of the Enlightenment. Meant to be inspirational and uplifting, it often portrayed its ancient subjects in an idealized manner. Neoclassical art emphasized clarity of line and the importance of draftsmanship. Color was a secondary element. Neoclassical paintings have a very finished appearance, with no trace of brush strokes.

The leading painter in this style was Jacques Louis David (1748–1825). His works dealt not only with ancient Greece but with idealized scenes of the

French Revolution and the glories of Napoleon. He painted with precision, and his works have a smooth, almost glossy finish. His tightly arranged and perfectly executed compositions served as the official model for French art for over a quarter of a century.

One of his pupils, Jean Auguste Dominique Ingres (1780–1867), became Neoclassicism's major proponent as it came into conflict with other styles during the mid-1800s. Ingres was a superb draftsman who combined accuracy and elegance. His works, especially his portraits, demonstrate a clarity of line, balanced composition and a clear, precise and idealized representation of subject matter. Ingres paid particular attention to details in the clothing, hair and skin of his subjects. He was able to capture the actual appearance of a scene with photolike accuracy while also conveying a sense of the ideal.

He was a popular painter, a rather formal and egotistical man, and one of the most influential artists in France for thirty years. His most direct link to Impressionism was with Edgar Degas, who was strongly affected by Ingres' advice to him:

> Draw lines, young man, and even more lines. From life and from memory. This is the only way you will become a good artist.

During much of his later years, Ingres served as the spokesman for the conservative element in French art. His emphasis on technical skill, drawing, rationality and faithfulness to the standards of classical art put him in conflict with Romanticism.

Romanticism

The essence of Romanticism is emotion, intuition, subjectivity and passion. The Romantic era (approximately 1800 through 1850) and the feelings of spontaneity and heroism underpinning it produced great artists in many fields. The writers Keats, Byron and Shelley and the composers Berlioz and Liszt were clearly part of this movement.

In painting, the reaction to the rationality, objectivity and formality of Neoclassicism took the form of Romantic works that were more imaginative, more exotic and generally more innovative. Romantic artists tended to use quicker, less-finished brush strokes, and their paintings were less formal and refined. Color became more important and paintings had deeper, richer shades. Subjects were chosen that inspired the individual artist and reflected his beliefs and passions. Nature and landscape took on much more important roles.

The leading painter of the Romantic movement was Eugène Delacroix (1799–1863), a man of great passion and a rival of the Neoclassicist Ingres. Delacroix chose his subjects from medieval myths, the works of Dante and Shakespeare, and recent topical events and portrayed them with high physical and emotional energy. His work was in clear contrast to the more conservative, restrained and less sentimental work that surrounded him. His brush strokes were broad, and his works had a rougher look to them than those of Ingres. He emphasized color over line, and his use of pure vibrant colors and vivid light/dark contrasts was perhaps his greatest skill.

Delacroix struggled in his early years, and official recognition was slow in coming. He was a hyperactive worker, attacking the whole canvas at once.

His influence on the Impressionists was significant in several ways. One was his free, more open style with less finished surfaces, which served as examples for many of his successors. But probably more significant was his use of color as a way to model forms. He moved painting away from the age-old concept of using color as a mere tint over forms defined by a line drawing. Delacroix used color and adjacent tones as major elements in *defining* forms. This approach had a great effect on the Impressionists, particularly Renoir and Degas, as well as Post-Impressionists such as Cézanne and van Gogh.

Delacroix was a painter who defied tradition and painted as he pleased. He played a major role in liberating painting from its more formal past, and he helped create the environment that would eventually lead to Impressionism.

Realism

By the mid-1800s a new force was beginning to be felt in French art: Realism. This movement would play a dominant role throughout the remaining years of the nineteenth century. Realism emerged partly in reaction to both the tradition-bound, highly finished style of the Neoclassicists and the subjective, highly emotional, often escapist work of the Romantics.

Realism in painting also reflected broader trends in society. It was, in many ways, an expression of the growing importance of the bourgeoisie and the liberalizing of the political and social system. The trend moved away from the conservative monarchists toward a more open and democratic society, with the life of common people gaining greater recognition. The Realist movement had a radical left-wing aspect to it that was thrilling for a number of young artists but threatening to many in the Establishment.

The Realist painters' aim was to paint what they saw—without idealizing it and without alterations. They wanted to portray the facts of the modern world—what they could see or touch. For subject matter they dealt with the everyday existence of ordinary peasants and working-class people. They painted landscapes that they knew, or personal friends, or scenes reflecting social conditions. Their works often expressed ethical values. Gods, heroes from antiquity, and historical episodes were not of interest to them.

Visually, the works of the Realists depict their contemporary subjects in a clear, straightforward, unposed, nonidealized way. Colors were also used in a realistic manner and were generally less bold and dramatic than in Romantic works.

This powerful, honest attitude about painting made a strong imprint on French art throughout the last half of the nineteenth century and provided a foundation for Impressionism. The quest for objective truth, the choice of ordinary life as subject matter, the snapshot-like natural scenes, and the overall role of the independent artist working outside the official system were key elements of Realism that were also strongly embraced by the Impressionists.

The Barbizon School. Beginning in the late 1830s and continuing for thirty years or so, there existed a group of Realist painters who had a special interest in landscape painting. They wanted relief from the turmoil of Paris and a place where they could paint actual rural scenes, not imagined ones. They are known as the Barbizon School, as they worked out of the village of Barbizon, south of Paris near the forest of Fontainebleau. They would go there regularly and work out-of-doors. The landscape and rural scenes they painted reflect their close observation of nature and their commitment to a realistic, unromanticized view of it.

The leading painters of the Barbizon School were Jean François Millet, Théodore Rousseau and Constant Troyon. Camille Corot (discussed later) was also associated with this group.

During the 1860s, as the Impressionist movement was just forming, a number of Impressionist artists went to Barbizon to paint with the older artists working there. Some of the early works of Monet and Renoir were done in this area.

Gustave Courbet (1819–1877). The most influential proponent of Realism was Courbet, a man with a strong artistic commitment and a driving personality who had a very significant effect on many of the Impressionists.

Courbet was born into a well-to-do family in the small French town of Ornans, near the Swiss border. He studied art locally and then went to Paris, where he spent a great deal of his time studying and drawing the works of the masters in the Louvre. He threw off the initial appeal of Romanticism and soon became the acknowledged leader of the Realist group. Courbet strongly believed that painters should paint only what they could experience themselves. As a realist and a pragmatist, he had no time for poetic or historical subjects. In describing his views of painting, he wrote:

> Painting is an art of sight and should, therefore, concern itself with things seen; it should eschew both historical scenes of the classical school, and poetic subjects chosen from Goethe, and Shakespeare of the kind chosen by the romantics.

When asked to paint an angel, he is said to have replied, "I have never seen an angel. Show me an angel and I will paint one."

He gained some acceptance in official circles and had works at the Salons of 1849 and 1850. His works were of the life he knew, such as *Afternoon at Ornans.* He used broad brush strokes to apply a heavy impasto (thickly applied pigments with uneven surfaces), which added a vibrant texture to his forms. His compositions were bold and well balanced, with considerable detail appearing in all of the major elements of each picture.

In 1855 the jury of the International Exhibition turned down two of Courbet's works that he felt were very important. The artist was furious, and he set up his own exhibit in a building he called the Pavilion of Realism. It was the first one-man show ever.

Courbet had deeply held socialist convictions, and he became a rebellious symbol against both the artistic and the political establishments. After the fall of the Second Empire in 1870 he became involved with the Commune and was named its Minister of Fine Arts. When the government regained control in 1871, he was held responsible for the destruction of the Vendôme Column and was put in prison. Monet, among others, visited him there. He was eventually required to pay for the column's restoration. He soon fled to Switzerland, where he died in 1877.

Courbet exerted a personal, symbolic and stylistic influence on the Impressionists. His fierce independence, his separate exhibits and his general willingness to come into conflict with the system provided them with a role model. More specifically, his choice of everyday subjects, the realistic, nonemotional way he portrayed them, and the rough vibrancy of his surfaces made him a major precursor of (and a major influence on) the Impressionists.

Monet's work in particular was strongly influenced by Courbet, at least up until 1869, and the two artists were in close contact for a number of years.

Corot

There was one artist who does not fit cleanly into any movement but who had extraordinary influence on the Impressionists: Camille Corot (1796–1875).

Corot was the son of a textile merchant in Normandy. After an initial stint in the family business, he turned to painting full time and received Neoclassical training. Soon he moved on to landscape painting, and that became his passion for the rest of his life. He was something of a nomad, spending considerable time on the Normandy coast, in the forest of Fontainebleau (associated with the Barbizon painters), and traveling throughout most of the provinces of France. He also made several trips to Italy, which inspired him.

He was innovative in his techniques, especially in his use of tonal contrast to create a sense of space. His paintings have a muted, often rather grey and silvery tone, in contrast to the brighter colors being used by many of his contemporaries. He had a natural objective style that could capture the essence of a particular place. His works have a feeling of spontaneity and freshness to them. In 1856 he told a student to always submit to a first impression—"Never abandon it."

Corot became quite popular, and his works were regularly shown at the Salon. He was somehow able to walk the fine line between producing works that were popular with the official art world and being an innovator who influenced the younger generation of painters. Many of his paintings that were not submitted to the Salon are, in fact, quite similar to the Impressionists' work of the 1870s.

During the last twenty-five years of his life, Corot became an inspirational figure to many artists, encouraging experimentation by younger painters. He worked closely with Pissarro, and his direct influence can be seen in Pissarro's early works. He also advised Berthe Morisot.

Other Influences

Before we move on to Impressionism and the artists directly involved in it, we need to briefly examine three technical and stylistic developments that had a strong influence on how the Impressionists painted.

Color. The research on color done by the French chemist Eugéne Chevreul, published in 1839, provided a base for much of the Impressionists' innovation. Chevreul showed that neighboring colors modify each other and that unique optical effects resulted from placing certain colors next to each other. He also discovered that if two patches of the same color (but of different shades) are placed next to each other, the part of the lighter patch near the dark patch will appear lighter than it actually is, and vice versa. It was from Chevreul's work that the Impressionists developed the important technique of placing pure colors next to each other and having them blend in the viewer's eye. The result was a unique effect that was stronger and more dramatic than if the colors had been mixed on the palette. This is called optical mixing or blending.

Chevreul's scientific theories on optical combinations and divisions of colors had a significant influence on the Romanticist Delacroix and others throughout the mid-nineteenth century. However, it was the Impressionists who took this knowledge and used it in dramatic and revolutionary ways.

Monet was a great colorist and was deeply influenced by Chevreul's theories. He produced unusual colors of great technical complexity. He was a master of matching colors side by side, as well as producing contrasts that give his works a unique and vibrant appearance.

Paint Technology. Concurrent with the development of color theory, and the use of color as a multifunctional element in painting, was an improvement in the quality and versatility of paint.

For centuries artists had been trained to grind their own paint by hand. They used earth pigments and mixed them with linseed oil to make oil paint. Only a very narrow range of colors, which came from the earth, was available.

In the nineteenth century there were significant advances in paint technology. Using machines, professional tradesmen started manufacturing paint. A wider variety of colors was produced and often sold by special color merchants. Manufacturers switched to poppy seed oil, and as a result the paint retained brush marks to a greater degree. This allowed some of the Realists and most of the Impressionists to use their rough brush strokes as an integral element in their works.

Paint was originally sold in jars or small pouches and would harden quickly after exposure to air. In 1840 a seemingly insignificant event occurred—the invention of collapsible paint tubes. This was to have a great effect on the Impressionists. These tubes gave the artist more mobility. In effect, the studio became portable. It is from this point on that we see artists outside of their studios, not only sketching, but actually painting and even finishing works on site. The whole *plein-air* (open air) approach was made possible by these small tubes.

Monet was a major proponent of *plein-air* and regularly worked outside in all conditions. For several years he even painted from a boat on the Seine.

Japanese Art. By the late 1850s, Japanese woodblock prints had become quite popular in France. Called *Ukiyo*—images of "the floating world"—they depicted informal scenes from contemporary life in Japan. It was the first non-western art to have a major influence in Europe.

These prints were both an inspiration to the Impressionists and a confirmation of many of the innovations they were already working on. Some of the elements in the prints that particularly interested the Impressionists were off-center compositions, lack of a single perspective point, depiction of urban life, a rather flat surface with depth implied by objects placed in overlapping planes, and figures cut off by the edge of the picture (as in a snapshot). Many of these techniques show up in Impressionist works.

Most of the Impressionists had a strong interest in these prints. In the early years of the Batignolles Group (the late 1860s), the artists were even, for a time, labeled the "Japanese of painting." Pissarro talked about how Impressionistic some of these prints were.

Monet had a large collection of Japanese prints that he studied. They can still be seen in his home in Giverny. He expressed the sentiment of the Impressionists when he wrote in 1874:

> Their refinement of taste has always pleased me, and I approve of their aesthetic doctrine which evokes the presence of something by a shadow; and the whole by means of a fragment.

Impressionism

A review of the Impressionist movement will provide the remaining essential background for understanding Monet.

General Background

Considering its significance and far-reaching revolutionary effects, the Impressionist period lasted for a relatively short time—about twenty-five years. The group of painters we now call Impressionists started together in Paris in the early 1860s, and by the late 1880s their group exhibitions were over, and many of them had moved on to other styles or approaches to painting.

Monet was at the center of the Impressionists from the earliest days, and it was he who most closely followed the Impressionist approach, even as his work continued to grow and evolve until his death in 1926.

The Impressionists decisively moved away from some of the principles and practices (i.e. perspective and idealized figures) that had dominated painting since the Renaissance. They also departed from both the subjectivity and emotionalism of the Romantics and the photographic accuracy and social/ethical content of the Realists. The Impressionists were more interested in portraying their individual perception of the contemporary world as they saw it. without any social or moral comment. The techniques they used to do this were innovative and original, but they, too, evolved from the work of earlier artists such as Delacroix, Courbet and Corot.

The Impressionists were never a close-knit school of painting with clear rules or procedural techniques. They produced no manifesto and never did clearly outline what Impressionism was. It has been said that there was no Impressionism, there were only Impressionists. And, in fact, many of them differed significantly from one another in their painting. However, the Impressionists shared many beliefs about the nature of painting and felt very strongly about some of the approaches they used to convey their visions on canvas. These beliefs and approaches make up the core of the Impressionist movement and give it its significant position in the history of Western art.

Characteristics of Impressionism

These general beliefs and approaches (with numerous exceptions) were common among Impressionist painters:

• The primary goal was to record an "impression"—the initial sensory perception seen by the artist. Impressionists rejected the idealizing or rearrangement of subject matter for compositional or content purposes.

• They depicted modern life as they saw it, not history or mythology. Their work was un-idealized and without social or moral judgment. They painted contemporary Paris or scenes from the country often showing the ordinary (people sitting in a park) or the modern (trains).

• They tended toward landscape painting. Generally, people played a less central role in their works. (Degas is an exception here.) A relatively small percentage of their paintings are portraits.

• They painted out-of-doors to a much greater extent than their predecessors. They didn't just make their sketches and do the preliminary work outside but often completed entire works *en plein air*.

• Of major importance was the effect of constantly changing light on objects. Trying to capture these changing perceptions was critical to their work.

• Color was also a central element. The Impressionists tended to use bright, bold colors, but in a unique and complementary manner. They went beyond the use of color as merely a descriptive element of a form and used it for a variety of purposes, such as conveying shape and distance. To them color became a strong independent element in a painting that could be used to express emotion and capture the immediate impression of a scene. Through their study of the basic science of color, they were able to achieve unique effects by placing pure colors in such a way that the human eye actually did the mixing and blending. They believed that color was not a permanent characteristic of an object but that the color of that object depended on the effects of light and atmosphere surrounding it. Even shadows and the "noncolor" black were dealt with in terms of color. The Impressionists often depicted shadows as including the complementary colors of the object creating the shadow.

• Color and light thus became the core unifying elements in a painting. They took on a greater importance than the traditional compositional techniques such as perspective, sharp contrast of white and shade, and balance.

Impressionist works often seem flat and not perfectly composed, but the viewer reacts to the spontaneity of the scene and the brightness and richness of the colors.

• Most of the Impressionists used short, choppy brush strokes to capture the changing qualities of light. The small daubs of individual pure color could also build up brilliant mosaics of rich, full colors. This technique of small, quick strokes allowed them to capture reflections and the shimmering of water that is so characteristic of many of their works. When viewed up close these strokes of color appear confusing and random, but when viewed from a distance the eye fuses them into luxuriant and complex colors and forms.

• The specific subject of a painting was relatively unimportant to the Impressionists. What mattered was the artist's capturing the reality of a subject (almost any subject) at a given moment. Thus, many Impressionist paintings are of remarkably ordinary scenes. Some of the Impressionists, particularly Monet, would even paint the same subject or scene over and over. The essential goal was to capture the changing nature of the scene according to the varying light and atmosphere.

Camille Pissarro captured the essence of Impressionism, describing it as:

> A highly conscientious art based upon observation and derived from a completely new feeling; it is poetry through the harmony of true colors.

Chronology of the Movement

By the mid-1850s, many of the Impressionist painters, with their wide variety of backgrounds and training, were coming to Paris. A few became acquainted with one another as they studied in the Louvre, enrolled in various studios, or gathered in cafés. The art world was still dominated by the Salon, but these artists were starting to experiment with novel techniques, and they had new attitudes about painting.

The first stirrings of Impressionism occurred in Paris around 1862. It was at this time that Monet, Renoir, Bazille and Sisley became students at the studio of Charles Gleyre. Monet had earlier met Pissarro at another studio, Academie Suisse, in 1859. The four students showed an interest in outdoor painting, and they soon became close and started traveling out of Paris to paint with the artists in Barbizon.

During the 1860s most of these young painters submitted work to the Salon. They were often rejected. It was a frustrating time, and many of them were quite poor. They developed and discussed their new techniques but found very little acceptance among the art establishment or the public. In 1863, after an unusually high number of entries had been turned down by the Salon, an additional show was mounted for the rejected works. The Salon des Refusés was not really a success, but it did cause a public outcry. It also gave some exposure to a number of younger artists, and it started clarifying the differences between them and the official art establishment. Manet, Pissarro and Cézanne all exhibited in this show.

During this period, Manet was gaining some respect and a lot of notoriety. His *Le Dejeuner sur l'herbe* (Salon des Refusés, 1863) and *Olympia* (Salon, 1865) caused great scandals, and the artist was violently attacked by the press. Out of this turmoil Manet emerged as the leader of the anti-establishment movement—a position he never sought nor claimed.

Starting in the mid-1860s, the Impressionist group (still not yet known by that name) gathered regularly at the Café Guerbois along with writers, intellectuals and journalists. Here they developed their theories, exchanged ideas, built friendships, fought with each other and planned their painting excursions in the country.

In 1869 Monet and Renoir painted together for a period of time at La Grenouillère, a small restaurant and meeting place on the Seine, near Bougival. This was a decisive point in the development of Impressionism. They were both poor and going through difficult times. It was here, working side by side in very similar styles, that they developed many of the techniques that were to be the core of Impressionism. Their works catch the sparkling atmosphere of the light and water; and the use of pure unmixed colors and free, quick brush strokes make their paintings from Bougival some of the most purely Impressionistic works.

The year 1870 saw the start of the Franco-Prussian War. The Impressionists scattered. Monet and Pissarro went to England; Renoir became a cavalry orderly in a barracks away from the fighting; and Cézanne avoided the draft and lived in the south of France. Manet and Degas stayed in Paris and joined the military, but neither saw action. Only Bazille got into the fighting. He was tragically killed in November 1870.

During their stay in London, Monet and Pissarro met the art dealer Paul Durand-Ruel who was to become a major factor in many of the Impressionists' economic lives. Throughout the 1870s and 1880s he helped a number of them, buying and exhibiting their works.

In 1874 the frustrated and generally outcast Impressionists organized the first of their eight exhibits. The first one got under way after much arguing over location, name, timing and so on. As in all their other exhibits, there were strong and conflicting opinions regarding who should be included. Some felt they should show only artists who were true to their ideals. Others wanted to open up the exhibit in order to attract more customers or include friends or other artists they liked. These battles often resulted in one or two of the artists pulling out in protest. Degas and Pissarro were often in the middle of these battles.

A comment by Pissarro, later in life, gives some feeling for the excitement and newness surrounding their earlier efforts and the first exhibit:

> I remember that, though I was full of ardor, I did not have the slightest idea, even at the age of forty, of the profound aspect of the movement which we pursued instinctively, it was in the air.

The public and critical reaction to the first shows was quite negative but became considerably better for the later ones, when the Impressionists had become more popular (or less unpopular). Most of the exhibits were financial failures, and often turned out to be disheartening and difficult emotional experiences for the participants. They were, though, of great importance to the Impressionist movement, as the painters received broad exposure and publicity—although often that publicity was negative. The exhibits continued over a period of twelve years in spite of external criticism and internal conflict. They are a testimony to the perseverance and commitment of these strong-willed artists.

During the eight exhibits, a total of fifty-five artists participated. There were thirty in the first one. Many of these artists have properly sunk into historical oblivion. However, all the major Impressionists except Manet took part in at least three or four. Pissarro was in all eight, Degas in seven, Renoir in four, Morisot in seven, Sisley in four and Monet in five.

The first show in April/May 1874 was called, after much debate, "Société Anonyme des Artistes, Peintres, Sculpteurs, Graveurs, etc." One of Monet's works in the exhibit, *Impression: Sunrise,* gave the group its name. The term *Impressionists* came out of a rather scathing review of the show in which the reviewer used the word in a derogatory manner. Eventually the name stuck, though it was never strongly endorsed by the group. None of the eight exhibits used the word Impressionism in its title.

During the late 1870s and early 1880s the Impressionists moved in and out of Paris, painting rural scenes in a variety of locations. Over the years they focused their painting activity in five general areas:

1. Paris, which was their headquarters until the 1880s.
2. Along the Seine, in the villages and countryside to the north and west of Paris.
3. Barbizon and the forest of Fontainebleau, south of Paris.
4. The Normandy coast.
5. The south of France, both on the coast and inland.

Some of them also painted outside of France, with occasional trips to Italy, North Africa or Holland.

The final Impressionist exhibit was held in 1886. Interestingly, the major work at the show was by the young Georges Seurat, who was not even considered a part of the group. His huge painting, *A Sunday Afternoon on the Island of La Grande Jatte,* was a revolutionary work which employed pointillism, a new "scientific" method of juxtaposing hundreds of tiny dots of paint. This technique challenged some of the basic premises of Impressionism and became the new avant-garde.

By the end of the last exhibit, the Impressionist movement was no longer considered radical and was starting to break up. The older revolutionary painters were now more accepted, and their works were being shown in several cities in Europe and in New York as well as in galleries in Paris. While a number of these artists remained close friends, they generally grew apart from each other. Several explored new approaches to paintings. Things improved financially for most of them after years of struggle and hardship.

Manet died in 1883. Most of the rest continued working and growing artistically. By 1890 the common commitment and camaraderie of the 1860s and 1870s were clearly over. Impressionism had made its mark and would serve as a basis for further innovation and the "modern" era of the twentieth century.

The Impressionist Painters

The Impressionists were a loosely associated group of painters with some principles and goals in common; nevertheless they were in many ways very different from one another. They came from different backgrounds, had a wide range of personalities and enjoyed a variety of lifestyles. What brought them together was a shared commitment toward painting and the role of the artist in society.

A central unifying element was their rejection by (and their opposition to) the French art establishment. They wanted to express themselves outside of the conservative rules and traditions of the official system. Even though they often tried, and occasionally succeeded, in exhibiting at the official Salon, they generally painted in ways that were different from the majority of artists. Because of this rebellious element, the Impressionists were often suspected of having political motives, or even an intention of undermining the government. These charges were, of course, untrue. The revolutionary aspect of the Impressionists had more to do with their beliefs about the artist's independence and their rejection of the establishment than it did with any political or social doctrine. Indeed, the Impressionists were all very independent individuals who held a wide variety of opinions on the political and social issues of the day.

In total, about fifteen to twenty painters were the main participants in the Impressionist movement. In addition to Monet, four of them stand out:

Edouard Manet (1832–1883). Manet is a transitional figure who is difficult to classify. He was a bit older than most of the Impressionists and had a somewhat different outlook on painting. He was born in Paris into an upper-middle-class family. He received classical training and studied the old masters in the Louvre. Being of a higher social standing, he was motivated to have his paintings accepted by the official Salon and to gain recognition and fortune by the traditional route. However, he had an independent spirit and a desire to experiment and try new techniques. He eventually became a hero to the younger generation of painters and a leader of the Impressionist group, even though he never exhibited with them. What made him so popular with the younger artists, and often caused scandal among the establishment, was his ability to portray life so candidly and to strip away any idealization.

Manet also developed revolutionary techniques in his use of color. He used broad patches of color and sharply contrasting tones to suggest form, as opposed to the more traditional use of line or subtle gradation of color. His brush work was sketchy and his subjects sometimes come off as flat and severe.

He often used traditional themes but updated them. Two works containing such updated subject matter caused great scandals in the 1860s. These incidents further alienated Manet from the critics and the public but also built his stature among the young rebels. *Le Déjeuner sur l'herbe (Luncheon on the Grass)* was exhibited in 1863, and *Olympia* was displayed in 1865. Both paintings were based on classic Renaissance works, but each one featured a non-idealized and rather hard-looking contemporary nude woman. Both works offended the public on moral and artistic grounds. Today they are recognized as masterpieces.

Manet was a bit of a dandy. He was always well dressed, he was opinionated, and he possessed a sharp wit. He was independently wealthy and as such was able to operate without depending on the Salon or independent art dealers for his livelihood. Still, he was motivated by ego and a desire for official recognition, and this meant exhibiting at the Salon. Thus his artistic life was full of conflict between his desire for status and his revolutionary approach to painting. He did, in fact, exhibit at the Salon a number of times, but it was only late in his life that he received the recognition he felt he deserved.

By the late 1860s Manet was holding court as the leading personality at the Café Guerbois. All the Impressionists were part of the crowd, and Manet's influence on them was significant. By the 1870s, he had grown close to Monet and Renoir and painted with them along the Seine River.

His work became looser, taking on more of an Impressionistic feel. His late masterpiece, *The Bar at the Folies-Bergère* (1882) is clearly an Impressionistic work, featuring daubs of light and color and capturing a normal moment in a very contemporary scene.

Manet is now acknowledged as one of the most significant artists of the nineteenth century and a key figure in breaking away from the old tradition. He was in many ways the inspirational leader of the Impressionists, but he played this role reluctantly. He was not really one of them. He was a generation older, was more secure in his place in society, and was more inclined to follow the established path through the Salon. In a sense, however, he absorbed the initial shock from the art establishment and the public. His strong sense of independence, his rare ability to capture contemporary life in his paintings, and his revolutionary use of color, form and contrast do put him squarely in the world of the Impressionists.

Pierre Auguste Renoir (1841–1919). Renoir moved to Paris at age four. His father was a tailor of modest means. In 1854 he was apprenticed to a porcelain painter, and several years later he took a job painting fans. He also received drawing lessons in these early years.

At age twenty he enrolled in the studio of Gleyre where he met and soon became close friends with Monet, Sisley and Bazille. During the late 1860s, he achieved modest success and exhibited at the Salon on a fairly regular basis. However, like many of the Impressionists during these years, he experienced periods of extreme poverty. He was part of the Impressionist group at the Café Guerbois and became quite close to Monet.

Renoir's canvases express pleasure and joy. He depicted people having fun and exhibiting a sense of relaxation and optimism. Beautiful women, children and flowers were his favorite subjects. He claimed:

> A picture must be an amiable thing, joyous and pretty—yes pretty! There are enough troublesome things in life without inventing others.

His pictures featured rich reds and primary colors. He painted with quick, free brush strokes, and his works often contain blurred figures and have a somewhat hazy feel to them. He specialized in portraying sensuous, full-bodied nude women and paid particular attention to showing healthy flesh coloring. He took great pride in these works, as expressed in his statement:

> I consider my nude finished when I feel like smacking her bottom.

In 1869 he and Monet painted together at Le Grenouillere, near Bougival along the Seine. At that time their two styles were very similar: both captured, in their unique ways, the sparkling atmosphere of the light on the water.

During the early 1870s Renoir's paintings sold fairly well. He continued to work alongside Monet and for a while stayed with him at Argenteuil. Renoir also participated in the first four Impressionist exhibits. However, he was not as passionately involved as many of the other artists, as he had started to build up a group of wealthy patrons. He also continued to exhibit at the Salon.

By about 1881 Renoir felt he had to move beyond Impressionism. After traveling to Italy to see the masters, he started painting in a more structured style, with more classical techniques. The works of Raphael particularly impressed him. He moved away from painting contemporary scenes and worked on more traditional subjects, especially more solid nudes in classical poses. His colors also lost some of their vibrancy during this period.

In his later years he moved to the south of France. He suffered from arthritis but continued his painting. Some of his old bright colors returned, his painting loosened up, and his works again had an Impressionistic feeling to them.

Camille Pissarro (1830–1903). Pissarro was the steady backbone of Impressionism and, after Monet, was the most influential of the Impressionists. Born in St. Thomas, in the West Indies, to a fairly prosperous merchant family of Jewish descent, he showed an interest in drawing at an early age. After traveling a bit and taking a turn in the family business, he came to Paris in 1855 to study painting at the Académie Suisse. There he met Monet, and they were to become lifelong compatriots.

Pissarro was strongly affected by the work of first Delacroix, then Corot, and eventually Courbet. In the mid-1860s he met regularly with Manet,

Renoir, Cézanne, Monet and others at the Café Guerbois. His serious commitment to his work and to the emerging new style of painting made him an influential member of the group.

His work offered an innovative treatment of light and color. He mainly painted landscapes and broad town or urban vistas. His paintings had a light touch, with patchy brush strokes, and they conveyed a peaceful atmosphere. He had works accepted in the Salon in the late 1860s, but, unfortunately, this did not help financially, and he struggled throughout most of his life to support his family.

Pissarro spent much of 1870–1871 in England, after fleeing France during the Franco-Prussian War. There he spent time with Monet and painted landscapes in and around London. Returning to France, he found that all but a few of the fifteen hundred paintings he had left behind had been destroyed by the Germans. Settling in the village of Pontoise, northwest of Paris, he became even more determined to paint in the open air.

Over the years Pissarro maintained contact with, and had a strong influence over, a number of artists, including Cézanne. His calm fatherly manner and his intense commitment to his art seemed to draw people to him. Later in life he had a profound effect on the Post-Impressionist Paul Gauguin.

Pissarro was deeply involved in the discussions and planning of the first Impressionist exhibition in 1874. Over the next twelve years he continued to play a leadership role in the group and was the only one of the leading Impressionists to participate in all eight of the shows.

In the late 1880s he started to paint with a new technique called pointillism or divisionism, the careful arrangement of very small dots of pure color to convey form. This had been developed by Seurat and Signac, whom Pissarro had come to know. (He even helped them become a part of the final Impressionist show in 1886.) Soon, though, Pissarro moved away from this new technique and was painting in a manner closer to his earlier Impressionistic style. Many of his later works are truly beautiful, innovative city scenes from Paris and Rouen. After several successful exhibits, his finances improved, giving him some degree of security for the first time.

Throughout his life, Pissarro was something of an enigma from a political and social standpoint. The most politically involved of the Impressionists, he was an ardent and often vocal champion of his strongly held socialist and anarchist beliefs. However, he was also a patient, calm and gentle person who consistently demonstrated concern for others.

Pissarro was a truly important participant in the Impressionist movement. He pushed the group to move ahead, to continue to exhibit and to be true to its principles. He was also a teacher and an influential force on many of the great Impressionist and Post-Impressionist painters. Without Camille Pissarro, the Impressionist movement as we know it today would not have taken place.

Edgar Degas (1834–1917). Degas was a very contradictory, complex and often difficult person. In many ways, he doesn't fit with the Impressionists, and personally didn't want to be classified as part of the group. Still, much of his work and his general approach to painting clearly associate him with the Impressionists. He was in fact involved in their discussions and participated in all but one of their exhibitions.

Born into a wealthy banking family in Paris, Degas held himself socially above his more middle- and lower-class artistic associates. As a youth he copied the masters in the Louvre and then entered the official École des Beaux-Arts in 1855. He traveled and lived in Italy in the late 1850s and was strongly influenced by the great classical artists he studied. Degas also was in contact with the French Neoclassicist Ingres, who advised to him to "draw lines." This he did, and his works from this period are mainly historical paintings, copies of the old masters, and a few portraits of family and friends. The works have a clarity and linear aspect to them that remained characteristic of his work throughout his career.

In 1862, Degas met Manet, and he was introduced to the crowd at the Café Guerbois. Soon Degas had left "history painting" behind and began to depict contemporary Parisian subjects. Initially, he painted racehorses and then moved on to ballet dancers, working girls, theater scenes, brothels or ordinary people in normal circumstances. His portrayals of the underside and little-noticed aspects of life give his works a fundamental realism.

In many ways Degas was quite different from his associates. He had very little interest in landscape painting, and his works deal mostly with individuals. He emphasized line, draftsmanship, clear contours on his figures, and three-dimensional depth, with no concern for the outdoor phenomenon of the effects of changing light on a subject. In fact, he preferred to work indoors and use artificial light. His paintings have a more finished look to them than the work of most of the Impressionists, who used quicker, shorter brush strokes. But he was an integral part of the movement. His strong opposition to official academic painting and his commitment to realistically reflecting contemporary subject matter made him an important, if often controversial, member of the group.

Many of Degas' works have an unusual unbalanced composition, with the figures viewed from an odd angle. Pictures appear to be cut off at the edge. Often his figures look as if they were caught completely off guard in rather private moments. Much of this uniqueness can be related to his interest in photography and Japanese prints.

Degas regularly exhibited at the Salon in the late 1860s. After 1874 he was an active and driving force behind the Impressionist exhibitions, often fighting with the others on which artists should or should not be included.

In the early 1870s, as his eyesight started to fail, he switched from oil painting to pastels and soon set a new standard for this medium. A number of these works are among his best, and he included them in some of the later Impressionist exhibits. In his later pastels, after about 1890, he brightened his colors, loosened his stroke and worked in a less controlled manner. These are the most Impressionistic of his works. Also, as his eyesight weakened, he turned to sculpture what he called "blind man's art." He did a series of wax figures of dancers and horses. They were cast in bronze after his death.

Degas was often aloof and quarrelsome with his fellow artists. Devoted to his work, he had few deep friendships and evidently no romantic interest in women (he only wanted to depict them in a very un-idealized way). Conservative and against social reform, he often came into conflict with the socialist Pissarro. As an anti-Semite he became an anti-Dreyfussard in the late 1890s and broke with several of the Impressionists over this issue.

He continued his work as his health declined. After about 1908 he became a bitter recluse. Toward the end he said, "When I die they will see how hard I worked."

A number of other artists in the Impressionist group played less important roles yet clearly participated in the movement and made significant contributions. Briefly, these are:

Alfred Sisley (1840–1899). Sisley studied in Paris at Gleyre's studio, where he met Monet, Bazille and Renoir. He accompanied his friends on painting exhibitions to the Barbizon area and was strongly influenced by Corot. He worked with Monet for many years and participated in four of the Impressionist exhibitions. He specialized in landscape painting, and his works bear a close resemblance to Monet's work of the 1870s and 1880s. He was particularly good at depicting subjects in specific atmospheric conditions, especially snow scenes.

Berthe Morisot (1841–1895). Morisot received drawing lessons at an early age and demonstrated considerable talent. She was strongly influenced by Corot, who advised her to work outdoors with the landscape painters. By 1864 she was exhibiting at the Salon. In 1868 she met Manet, and the close friendship that developed was mutually beneficial. She pushed Manet toward outdoors painting; he affected her style and introduced her to the other Impressionists. She eventually married Manet's brother.

Morisot became a mainstay of the group and participated in all but one of the exhibits. On occasion, she also provided a social center for the group by entertaining them in her home. But because of her sex she was unable to participate in the gatherings at the Café Guerbois or work in the studios with the male artists.

She painted mainly domestic scenes of women and children. Her works give a soft and pleasant rendering of the moment and have a minimum of small detail in them. Her brush strokes were quick, using color to indicate form and volume.

Frédéric Bazille (1841–1870). Bazille was one of the dominant participants in the formative years of the Impressionist movement. He possessed tremendous abilities and would surely have been one of the most important painters of the second half of the nineteenth century had he not been killed in the Franco-Prussian War in 1870.

After studying medicine for a while, he began his art studies at Gleyre's studio. There he met Monet, Renoir and Sisley. Over the next years, through the late 1860s, he painted with Monet near Barbizon and on the Normandy coast at Honfleur.

Bazille was well off financially, and at times he shared his Parisian studio with Renoir and Monet. In an 1867 letter he wrote to his parents, we have one of the first known records of a movement among his fellow artists. He wrote of renting a large studio:

> ...where we'll exhibit as many of our works as we wish—Courbet, Corot, Diaz, Daubigny and others have promised to send us pictures and very much approve of our idea. With these people and Monet, who is stronger than all of them, we are sure to succeed.

Because of his early death he did not participate in many of the discoveries and technical innovations of the Impressionists. The few works that survive have a somewhat traditional tone to them. Yet at the time of his death he was a full-fledged and highly talented participant in the emerging Impressionist movement.

Mary Cassatt (1844–1926). An American who studied art in Philadelphia, Cassatt traveled extensively in Europe, and finally settled in Paris in 1874. She soon had a painting in the Salon, and in 1877 she met Degas. They became lifelong friends, and he had considerable influence on her. She was also a close friend of Berthe Morisot. Degas introduced Cassatt to the Impressionist group, and she participated in four of the last five exhibitions. She also gave great support to the movement, both financially and by promoting Impressionists' paintings in the U.S.

Her early work shows an influence from the seventeenth century. After she began her association with the Impressionists, however, she started using softer, brief brush strokes and a lighter, livelier palette. Her works were dominated by a mother/child theme, often catching a wonderful closeness between the figures. Later, in the 1890s, her canvases reflect her interest in Japanese prints. Her draftsmanship became more dominant (a result of her association with Degas), and her figures and colors more clearly defined.

Paul Cézanne (1839–1906). Cézanne was a truly significant artist who interacted and exhibited with the Impressionists for a while but was never really in the middle of the movement. He moved beyond Impressionism quite early, and was a pioneer in breaking down reality into its underlying elements of basic geometry. This had an enduring effect on the subsequent modern developments in painting. Picasso and Braque openly acknowledged Cézanne's great importance.

He was from Aix-en-Provence and returned there often to work. One of his childhood friends was the popular and controversial writer and critic Émile Zola.

Cézanne came to Paris in 1861 and soon became a friend of Pissarro, who was to have a notable influence on him over the years. Pissarro's mild manner was a sharp contrast to Cézanne's wild and eccentric personality. The 1860s and 1870s saw his works regularly rejected by the Salon. He wasn't accepted until 1882.

He did spend some time at the Guerbois and remained close to Pissarro and Renoir. In 1874 he participated in the first Impressionist exhibit, where his work was the object of much ridicule. He was also part of the third show in 1877. After that, he moved in new directions and did not participate again. He did, however, keep up his contacts with Pissarro, Monet and Renoir for a number of years.

Monet's Life

Youth—Paris and Le Havre, 1840–1856

A second son was born to Claude Adolphe (age forty) and Louise Justine Monet (age thirty-five) on November 14, 1840, near the Montmartre section of Paris. They christened him Oscar-Claude, and in his early years he was called Oscar. His brother, Léon, was four years older. The Monets were of the middle class and lived in a fifth-floor walkup in a relatively affluent neighborhood. Claude Adolphe was Louise Justine's second husband, and was evidently not particularly successful in his career as a merchant.

Before young Oscar-Claude was five, the family left Paris and moved to the port city of Le Havre, on the Channel coast. Here Claude Adolph joined the wholesale grocery and ship supply business of his half-sister's husband, Jacques Lecadre. For the Monets the move was a step up, as they settled in a sizable house just north of the city. They also had access to the Lecadres' summer house in the nearby resort town of Sainte-Adresse.

It was in the prosperous trading town of Le Havre and the surrounding coastal areas that young Oscar-Claude spent his apparently normal childhood. He would later recall the many days spent playing on the hills and beaches along the Normandy coast—scenes that he would eventually paint.

At age ten, Monet entered a primary school in Le Havre. The curriculum was typical for the time—grammar, history, Latin, Greek, mathematics, etc. There were also classes in drawing. Monet's first teacher was Jacques-François Ochard, an artist of some local standing and a former student of the great Neoclassicist painter Jacques Louis David. School records report Monet as "a very good-natured boy, who gets on well with his fellow pupils." However, in later years, Monet would recall:

> I was born unruly. I could never bend to any rule, even as a small child...The school always seemed to me like a prison, and I could never resign myself to living there even for the space of four hours a day.

He would often skip classes and spent considerable time roaming the beaches and cliffs along the beautiful coast.

He showed an early interest in drawing, and as his skills developed, his work took on a somewhat sarcastic and impudent character. He spent hours drawing irreverent caricatures of local celebrities, his teachers and fellow students. These drawings soon became popular, and by age fifteen the enterprising young Monet was making some money exhibiting and selling his works in the shop window of a local picture framer.

His drawing activity went beyond these popular caricatures; sketchbooks from his mid-teen years show considerable skill in depicting landscapes, sailing vessels, seascapes and trees, as well as the people of the area. He signed his drawings "O. Monet" or "Oscar."

Monet's mother was generally supportive of her son's artistic interest. His father was less so, as he hoped the boy would follow him into the family business. Monet's mother died in January of 1857, when Monet was just sixteen, and the two Monet boys and their father moved in with the Lecadres. Young Oscar-Claude became close to his aunt (Marie-Jeanne, known as Sophie), who now looked after him. She was an amateur painter who had contacts in the Parisian art world. Aunt Sophie encouraged Monet's interest in drawing, often to the dismay of the boy's father.

Early Development as a Painter, 1856–1862

In 1856, Monet met the local painter Eugène Boudin (1825–1898). This was an important turning point for the young man, just sixteen, who spent most of his free time drawing. Boudin possessed considerable skill and had studied in Paris. At the time, however, he was an unsuccessful local painter of beach and rural scenes. He was considered a bit eccentric because of his practice of painting out-of-doors. He had been a partner in the art supply and picture framing store in Le Havre where the young Monet showed his caricatures. Initially, Monet was not impressed with Boudin's work and expressed no interest in meeting this painter who was fifteen years his senior. Eventually they did meet, though, and the effect on Monet was significant. Boudin convinced

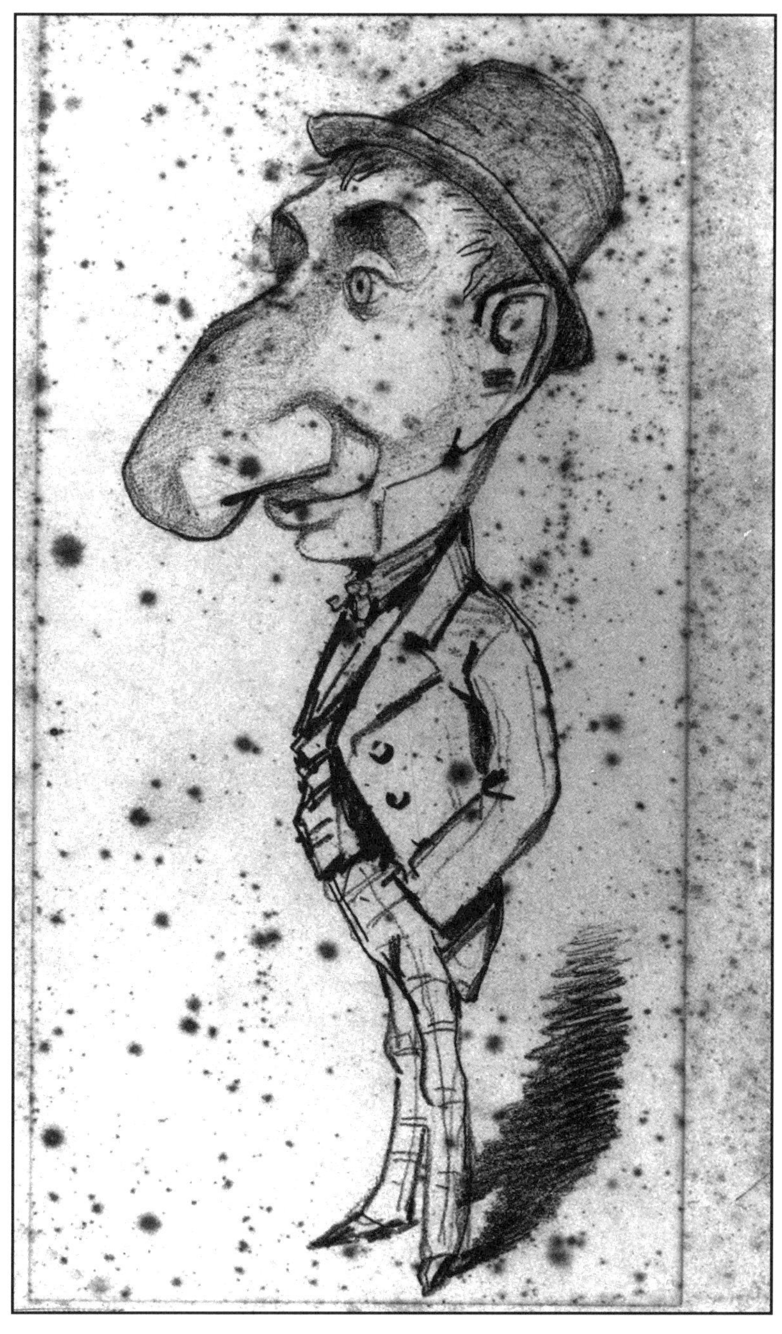

Drawing from around 1857–58. Monet did caricatures as a youth to earn money.

Claude Monet, French, 1840–1926. Caricature of a Man with a Large Nose, graphite on tan wove paper, c. 1855/56, 24.9 x 15.2 cm, Gift of Carter H. Harrison, 1933.895

him to go out in the country and paint with him. It was a major conversion. Monet said:

> For me, it was like the rending of a veil; I understood, I grasped what painting could be; my destiny as a painter opened up before me.

As an old man, Monet would write to a friend:

> One day, Boudin said to me: "You've got talent. You should give up this sort of work; you'll get fed up with it sooner or later. Your sketches are excellent, but you shouldn't stop there. Do as I do: learn to draw properly and value the sea, the light, the blue sky." I took his advice, and we used to go on long expeditions together, when I could paint things directly from nature. That way, I came to understand nature and love it passionately. I also became more and more appreciative of Boudin's light-filled paintings. I can only repeat that I owe all I have done to Boudin, and all the success I have achieved.

With Boudin's encouragement, Monet completed his first oil painting, and it was shown in an 1858 Le Havre exhibition. Even though he continued to do his popular and often biting caricatures, Monet seems to have made a firm commitment to becoming a full-time painter at about this time.

He realized he needed some academic training and started to work on a plan to go to Paris. He twice applied, and was turned down, for a scholarship from the municipality of Le Havre. Unfazed and determined to get to the capital, Monet used money he had earned from his drawings, plus some support from his aunt, and set out for Paris in May of 1859.

With letters of introduction from his aunt and Boudin, Monet met with several established painters, including Constant Troyon, a successful painter of the Barbizon school. Monet wrote to Boudin describing the meetings:

> I showed him my two still lifes. His comment was "My dear fellow, your color is fine: the effect really works. But you must apply yourself to some serious study. All this is excellent as far as it goes, but it comes very easily to you: it is something you will always have, come what may. If you take my advice and are serious about art, you will start by enrolling in a studio that concentrates on figure painting. Learn to draw; that is where most of you youngsters fall short today. Pay attention and you'll see that I'm right. Draw for all you are worth; you can never learn too much. But don't neglect painting. Go into the country every so

often to sketch, and whatever you do be sure to work the sketches through. Copy pictures at the Louvre. Don't be a stranger; come and see me and show me what you are doing. With courage you will get there."

During his first month in Paris, Monet attended the Salon. In his letters back to Boudin, he showed a mature, critical and discriminating eye for the works he viewed. The eighteen-year-old Monet was particularly impressed by the works of Corot ("unadorned marvels"), those of Rousseau ("very beautiful") and some of the Troyons. His sophisticated eye also found fault with some of the masters, as he pointed out mistakes in coloring, light and overall composition. These remarks revealed not only an accurate and discerning sensibility, but a high degree of self-confidence and competitiveness.

Within a few months, Monet enrolled himself in the Académie Suisse, a loosely structured studio on the Ile de la Cité. He had ignored Troyon's advice to study with the more established and traditional painter Thomas Couture. The Académie Suisse attracted the younger emerging artists with its low cost, live models and flexible schedule, with no examinations and few formal critiques. It was perfect for the young, headstrong Monet. It was here that he met the then-twenty-nine-year-old Camille Pissarro, and their long, sometimes warm and sometimes strained, friendship began.

Monet spent the next year or so trying to make a living doing caricatures and small paintings, while developing his skills by visiting numerous museums and receiving occasional instruction at the Académie Suisse. He also spent considerable time hanging out at the Brasserie des Martyrs, a cafe frequented by various artists, writers and political personalities. It served as the center of the Realist movement in painting. It was here that Monet met the great and colorful Gustave Courbet, who was to become a supporter of the young painters who evolved into the Impressionists. Courbet became particularly close to Monet.

As Monet worked to establish himself as a painter, he did not seem very different from many of the other struggling young artists. However, even in these early years, Monet showed a high degree of confidence and independence. These qualities would set him apart as a leader, a man who would do things his own way, regardless of what others thought.

By this time, Monet's family situation had changed. In late 1858 Jacques Lecadre, husband of Aunt Sophie and owner of the family business, died. As a result, the now-widowed Sophie could focus more attention on her nephew and encourage him in his artistic interests. Over the next dozen years, she would help Monet by introducing him to her artist friends in Paris, occasionally giving him financial support and, in late 1862, buying him out of the army. Also as a result of Jacques Lecadre's death, Monet's father took over the business. This gave him a greater degree of financial security and at least the potential to support his somewhat rebellious artistic son. This situation was clouded, though, when in January 1860 Monet's father's companion and former domestic servant gave birth to a daughter, thus creating competition for the family's financial resources.

Monet's bohemian life in Paris was rather dramatically altered when, in March of 1861, he was notified that he was about to be drafted into the military. He was thus obligated to serve seven years. There were discussions with his family of buying him out. A conflict arose. Monet was unwilling to accept his father's terms: that he give up painting, return to Le Havre and pursue a traditional job. Thus Monet, exerting his independence and excited by the potential for adventure, shipped off to Algeria in June 1861 as a member of the African Cavalry.

The months he spent there were not a complete waste, as he traveled some and did a number of drawings and watercolors. Later he would recall:

> How much my vision benefited by this. The impression of light and colors I received there only fell into place afterward; but the germ of my future interests emerged in Algeria.

After just a year, he came down with typhoid and was sent home to Le Havre to convalesce over the summer of 1862. When it came time for him to return, Monet's aunt intervened and paid the buy-out fee, over three thousand francs, to release him from further service. He was honorably discharged in November and was once again free to pursue his painting career.

The fall of 1862 also marked another critical point in Monet's artistic development. Soon after returning to Le Havre, Monet met the Dutch painter Johann Barthold Jongkind (1819–1891). A superb landscape painter with a light brush stroke and a loose style, Jongkind was a precursor to the Impressionists. He had exhibited in the Salon in the late 1840s and early 1850s. Because of poor health and drinking problems, he had fallen on tough times, and in 1862 was painting on the Normandy coast. The two men worked together, and Monet was greatly influenced by both Jongkind's style and his method of painting out-of-doors. Years later Monet would recall:

> From that time on, Jongkind was my true master. I owe to him the final development of my painter's eye.

Years of Growth and Struggle—The 1860s

In late 1862 Monet returned to Paris. As a condition of his receiving an ongoing allowance from his family, Monet had agreed to study at a legitimate studio as he pursued his career. He chose the studio of Charles Gleyre (1808–1874), a rather traditional and uninspiring Swiss history painter who had exhibited at the Salon and had a good relationship with the official art establishment. The routine there was loose. Gleyre encouraged independence among his students, and they were able to come and go as they pleased and received only occasional critiques and comments.

The most significant result of Monet's year or so at Gleyre's was the friendships that developed among four young artists who were to be at the core of the Impressionist movement. Soon after arriving, Monet met Bazille, Renoir and Sisley. The four were quite different in background and temperament, but they had generally similar views on painting. They spent hours together in the studio or on landscape-painting excursions in addition to much socializing in the cafés, discussing their artistic ideas.

Monet's attendance at Gleyre's was spotty, and he had occasional conflicts with the teacher over Gleyre's desire to idealize a painting's subject matter. Monet gave an account of one such incident:

> While we were drawing from a superb model, Gleyre came and criticized my work. "It's too bad," he said, "but the breast is heavy, the shoulder too powerful, and the foot out of proportion." I can only draw what I see, I answered, timidly. "Praxiteles took the best elements from one hundred imperfect models to create a masterpiece." Gleyre answered dryly. "When you are doing something, you

> must always think of the antique." That same evening, I took Sisley, Renoir, and Bazille aside. Let's get out of here, I said, the place is unhealthy. They are lacking in sincerity.

The school eventually closed in mid-1864.

Monet became especially close to Bazille. Over the next several years, the two of them traveled to the Barbizon area to paint landscapes and spent considerable time together working on the Normandy coast. Economically, times were sparse but not desperate. Monet survived initially on the continuing small allowance from his father, plus an occasional sale of a small painting or drawing. In late 1864, however, he had a falling out with his family, and their financial support stopped. After that he fairly regularly begged and borrowed from friends. Luckily, at that time Monet acquired his first patron, a Le Havre collector named Louis-Joachim Gaudibert, who commissioned him to paint two works.

The inconsistency between Monet's actual financial situation, his outward expression of it, and his lifestyle started to show during these years. Renoir would later recall:

> Back then Monet amazed everyone, not only with his virtuosity, but also with his ways. Jealous of his superb appearance when he arrived in the studio, the students nicknamed him the "dandy" because although he did not have a penny, he wore shirts with lace cuffs, affected an aristocratic arrogance of manner, and had the best tailor in town, whose bills he never paid, dismissing demands with a loud "Sir, if you insist I will withdraw my custom."

Even in his early twenties we see this desire for the good life and a belief that one way or another, things would work out. As we will see, throughout the 1860s, 1870s and 1880s, the self-confident and often arrogant Monet was not afraid to ask others for money in order to continue to live a comfortable lifestyle.

In January 1865 Monet, with some renewed financial help from his father, rented a combination apartment and studio. He shared the space with Bazille. Here, over the winter, he completed two paintings from studies made on the Normandy coast in 1864. They were accepted at the Salon, which opened in May 1865. These two large marine paintings (*Headland of the Héve River at Low Tide* and *The Mouth of the Seine at Honfleur*) were of the style both familiar and popular with Salon attendees of the times. They are not revolutionary in technique or coloring, but are very strong in their composition and in their depiction of the water and sky. They proved to be quite popular with the critics. The art critic Paul Mantz wrote in the *Gazette des Beaux-Arts*:

> A new name must be recorded here. We were not previously acquainted with Monsieur Claude Monet; a taste for harmonious coloring...a bold way of seeing things and of capturing the observer's attention, these qualities Monsieur Monet already possesses to a high degree. We shall not forget him.

This was the first big success for the now-twenty-four-year-old Claude Monet (the Oscar was dropped in 1862). Things were going well. He'd had his work praised in the official Salon, he had proven to his family that he did have a future as an artist and he was emerging as a leader among a group of talented young painters. His particular skill was in landscapes and seascapes. The next step seemed quite clear paint more of these outdoor scenes and earn a living doing works that were likely to sell.

But Monet chose a different path, moving to expand his repertoire and to make a bold artistic statement. Immediately after his paintings appeared in the 1865 Salon, Monet went to the town of Chailly, near Barbizon, to begin oil studies and sketches for a huge work to be called *Luncheon on the Grass,* or *The Picnic.* It was unlike anything he had ever done before in both size (13 by 20 feet) and composition (twelve life-size figures enjoying a picnic in the forest). Probably inspired by Manet's 1863 controversial work of the same title, it was to be the obsessive focus of Monet's life for nearly a year. He wrote to Bazille:

> I think of nothing but my picture, and if I knew I was failing with it, I think I would go mad.

Bazille served as a model for several of the figures. Courbet, who came to Chailly to comment on the works in progress, also was used as a model. Monet worked feverishly on the painting in studios in Paris during the fall of 1865 and the winter of 1866. His goal was to exhibit it in the 1866 Salon. By midwinter it was clear that it couldn't be completed in time, and he abandoned the work. It was put aside and years later used as collateral on a debt with a landlord. Only several pieces of it exist today.

Still determined to exhibit at the 1866 Salon, Monet quickly turned to painting a life-size picture of a woman in a long flowing green dress. The model was Camille Doncieux (1847–1879), an eighteen year old from Lyon whose family lived in the neighborhood of Monet's studio. She had also served as a model for several women in *The Picnic.* Camille soon became Monet's mistress.

The painting of her, known as *Camille in a Green Dress,* was completed very quickly—legend says in just four days. It was an amazing accomplishment. The work masterfully depicts the beauty and character of the model as well as the intricate color nuances and folds of the long striped green dress.

The canvas, along with a large landscape painted in 1864, was accepted and shown at the 1866 Salon. Monet was delighted by this significant recognition of his work, while he was still only twenty-five years old. Adding to his pleasure were the comments of several critics. Among the most positive reviews was one by Émile Zola, who would eventually become a friend of the artist:

> Just consider that dress. It is both supple and firm. Softly it drags, it is alive, it tells us quite clearly something about this woman—Truly, this is a temperament, this is a real man in this pack of eunuchs.

Monet was also compared to the better-known Manet. One critic wrote:

> Monet or Manet? Monet. But we have Manet to thank for Monet. Bravo Monet! Thank you Manet!

That spring Manet and Monet actually met, and they developed a strong friendship that lasted until Manet's death in 1883. The innovative Manet, who was very supportive of the younger emerging artists, was particularly helpful to Monet.

Along with Monet's success at the Salon came some financial rewards. He sold several pictures, and his family (mainly his aunt), impressed with his success, resumed sending him a small allowance. Feeling more secure, Monet was able to rent a small house in Sèvres, just outside of Paris, and he moved there with Camille in the late spring.

He immediately began working on another very big painting of four large figures, *Women in the Garden.* He was committed to painting the work out-of-doors and not repeating the problems he'd encountered with *The Picnic,* where he had to transfer the large sketches made out-of-doors to the large canvas in the studio. In order to deal with the size of the canvas (over eight feet tall), Monet dug a trench and built a pulley system so that the painting could be raised or lowered as required. It was a huge undertaking, and Monet's unique approach drew good-natured barbs from Courbet when he stopped by to observe and comment on the work. Again, Camille served as model for at least three of the four women.

In late summer, Monet and Camille traveled to Normandy, where he completed the painting in a studio near Honfleur at the rural Hôtel Ferme Saint-Siméon, where many of the artists from Paris would come and work. During the fall and winter, Monet labored steadily on a number of paintings, including a series of snowscapes. This recollection from a writer of the time describes Monet's commitment to working out-of-doors:

> We glimpsed a little heater, then an easel, then a gentleman swathed in three overcoats, with gloved hands, his face half-frozen. It was M. Monet, studying an aspect of the snow.

Monet's goal was of course to show at the Salon again in 1867. He submitted two works, including *Women in the Garden.* Both were turned down, as were all the submissions of Renoir, Pissarro, Bazille and Sisley. The disappointed artists, along with some of the more established painters like Corot and Courbet, talked about mounting an independent exhibit to take advantage of the many people attending the Universal Exposition that spring. However, nothing came of the talks—except the idea of an independent group exhibit was planted in their minds. (It would be fulfilled some seven years later.)

For Monet the disappointment was partially offset by some favorable comments in the press on his refused works and by the willingness of some Paris art dealers to show his paintings in their shops. Also, to help Monet's increasingly problematic financial situation, Bazille paid twenty-five hundred francs for *Women in the Garden.* (This was as much as an average factory worker earned in a year.) Interestingly, the payments were to come to Monet at the rate of only fifty francs per month.

Monet's personal situation became particularly difficult starting in 1867. During the winter, Camille informed Monet that she was pregnant, with a child due in August. Still not married, and apparently far from ready to make a firm commitment to his mistress, Monet faced a very uncomfortable situation. His father had never felt Camille was up to his son's level socially, and he had regularly expressed his thoughts about the situation, often threatening to withhold financial support. Camille's pregnancy further strained the relationship. When he learned of her pregnancy, Adolphe urged his son to leave her.

It's hard to understand Monet's actions over the following months. He left Camille in Paris with virtually no money and only several friends to look after her. He spent the summer at his aunt's house in Sainte-Adresse on the coast. There he lived the bourgeois life, hoping to secure the continuing support of his family. Evidently he led his father and aunt to believe that he had left Camille. That summer he worked on over twenty paintings of gardens, seascapes and life on the coast. Meanwhile, the twenty-year-old Camille was back in Paris with few resources, preparing for the birth of her child. Monet was in a quandary. His conflicting feelings and concerns are expressed in a series of letters to his friend, Bazille. On June 25th he wrote:

> Do you know that before I left Paris I sold a small seascape to Cadart, and one of the Paris views to Latouche. I was so happy and relieved, as it enabled me to help poor Camille. But, my dear friend, what a painful situation it is with her, all the same. She is so kind, a really good girl, and sees things very level-headedly, which makes me even sadder. On this score, I am writing to you to ask you to send anything you can, the more the better. Please send it by the first. At the moment I am getting on well enough with my relations, and they say I can stay here as long as I like. But they warn me that if I need any actual money I shall have to earn it. Don't let me down, will you? I have a special favor to ask of you. Camille's baby is due on July 25, and I'm going to Paris for 10 days or a fortnight, and I'll need money for a lot of things. Do try to send me some extra then, if only 100 or 180 francs. Remember without it I will really be in difficulties.

In another letter, he talks of having no clothes, blankets, crib or toys for the baby.

The baby was born on August 8, and Monet was in Paris for the birth. He and Camille registered the child three days later as Jean-Armand-Claude Monet, the son of Claude Monet.

Monet immediately went back to the coast to resume his work, although throughout the late summer and fall he made occasional visits to see Camille and the baby.

Even though Monet's main focus was his work, the child did touch him emotionally. Four days after the birth, he again wrote to Bazille (who would become the child's godfather):

> A fat and beautiful boy whom in spite of everything I feel I love, I don't know how. It pains me to think that his mother has nothing to eat.

This whole situation tells us something of the emotional make-up of Monet. His letters often express a real feeling and concern for Camille, but very little sense of deep love or lasting commitment. Throughout his life, such divided and contradictory leanings appear in his relationships with family and friends. His strong sense of self and his dominating personality required attention and devotion. And he could, on occasion, return that devotion and feeling, but only to a degree. His passion was his work, and that seems to have used up most of his emotional energies.

The late 1860s were a time of general financial difficulties for Monet. Even though he did occasionally sell some paintings, and at times had a decent income, he was regularly short of funds. His correspondence during these years, especially to Bazille, is filled with pleas for loans and requests for materials so he could continue to paint. As he and Camille left Sèvres in the summer of 1866, their creditors were after them, and in late 1868 four of his works that were on display at a Le Havre exhibition were seized by some of those creditors.

Monet led a hectic life trying to please his father and aunt, attempting to be a reasonably good husband and father, and hustling around Paris and Le Havre, trying to exhibit and sell his works. One painting was accepted in the 1868 Salon, and occasionally he had some works shown in other cities around France. Still, there were periods of real depression and discouragement. In the fall of 1868 he wrote to Bazille:

> My painting isn't working at all. I no longer expect fame...Everything looks black. On top of it all, there is still no money. Disappointments, affronts, hopes, more disappointments—there you have it, my friend.

Still, he painted, and the large number of works from these times reflect very little of the turmoil and frustration in his life.

Occasionally he was even able to express some sense of contentment. Again writing to Bazille in late 1868, from Etretat on the coast, he said:

> Here I am surrounded by everything I love. In the evening, my dear friend, I come back to my little house where there is a good fire and a good little family. If you could only see your godson, how sweet he is at present. My friend, it's quite lovely to watch the little creature grow, and God knows I am happy to have him. I plan to paint him for the Salon.

However, the optimism didn't last long. Monet's spirits fell and his financial situation worsened when, in the spring of 1869, his submissions to the Salon were refused. And even though some of his works were shown around Paris and favorably received, Monet sold very little. From the small town of Saint-Michel in the area of Bougival, where he had moved with Camille and Jean, Monet wrote in June 1869:

> I have plenty of energy for work, but, alas, that fatal rejection has taken the bread from my mouth; despite my low prices, dealers and buyers turn their backs. It's sad how little people are interested in a work of art that has no public recognition.

Throughout the summer, he continued his appeals to Bazille:

> No bread, no fire in the kitchen, no light for the last eight days.

> I can't paint, I haven't a drop of color left.

In 1869 he also accepted food from Renoir, who was living nearby.

Over that summer, Monet and Renoir painted together for several months. The works they produced in this period are today viewed as masterpieces and classic examples of the Impressionist style. The two artists painted side by side, depicting the local bathing resort, La Grenouillère. Each, in his own unique style, brilliantly captured the summer light, sparkling water reflections, and the gaiety of the people enjoying their holiday by the river. Monet submitted one of these La Grenouillère paintings, along with an earlier work, to the Salon of 1870, but they were both refused. This rejection for the second year in a row was made worse by the fact that many of Monet's contemporaries, such as Bazille, Renoir, Sisley and Pissarro, had their works approved. In spite of the fact that two of the older, recognized artists, Corot and Daubigny, resigned from the panel in protest, Monet took the rejection very hard. He did not submit a painting to the Salon for another ten years, and after that he never submitted his work again. The need to find an alternative to the official Salon now became even more important.

Beside this rejection by the Salon jurors, the year 1870 was filled with other significant events for the not-yet-thirty-year-old Monet. On June 28, he married Camille in Paris, with Gustave Courbet as a witness. The couple spent the summer in the Channel resort town of Trouville, just west of Honfleur. Shortly after they arrived, Monet's aunt, the most supportive of his relatives, died. Monet painted through the summer and produced a number of pictures that captured the pleasant life of the vacationers. He also painted several wonderful portraits of Camille on the beach.

While Monet and his small family were enjoying the surroundings and living in relative financial comfort, the country of France was going to war. On July 19 the Franco-Prussian War was declared, and the proud and confident French were quickly defeated. Napoleon III surrendered in early September, and the Prussians advanced on Paris.

All this was, of course, of great concern to Monet. As part of his registration for his recent marriage, he had become part of the reserves. He had no interest in serving, so on September 5 he acquired a passport and four days later was on his way to England, to be joined shortly thereafter by Camille and Jean.

The disruption and tragedy continued for Monet when he learned that his close friend and frequent financial backer, Bazille, had been killed in combat on November 28. He was only twenty-nine.

Exile, 1870–1871

The Monets stayed in London for only about eight months. These were not happy or productive times for the artist. Without much money and speaking no English, Monet found life in London difficult and frustrating. They lived first near Piccadilly, then moved to Kensington. He completed only six works during his time there.

Things were made more difficult when he received news of the death of his father, who had passed away on January 17, 1871. The aging Adolphe had just recently married his ex-employee, Armande-Célestine Vatine and openly conceded that he was the father of their daughter Marie, Monet's half-sister.

Several positive things did come out of the London visit, though. Monet was able to see the city's museums and was exposed to the works of the great English painters John Constable (1776–1837) and J. M. W. Turner (1775–1851). The paintings of Turner particularly impressed him. He spent time with Pissarro, who, like a number of other artists, had fled to England. It was in a cafe frequented by these Frenchmen in exile that Monet came across the painter Charles Francois Daubigny, whom he had known in Paris. This chance meeting turned out to be most important. In late 1870, the older artist introduced Monet to the Parisian art dealer Paul Durand-Ruel, who had also moved out of France during the war. Referring to Monet, Daubigny told the dealer:

> This is a man who will be greater than any of us. Buy his work.

The contact between the two grew into a lifelong relationship. A canvas by Monet was included in Durand-Ruel's exhibit at his new London gallery on New Bond Street. Soon he started buying Monet's paintings, and from then on he was a regular source of income and support for Monet, as well as for many other Impressionists. Because of his strong belief in the Impressionist painters, Durand-Ruel played a major role in the development of the movement, and at crucial times helped its artists through financial and emotional difficulties.

In the spring of 1871, Monet (along with Pissarro) had several works displayed at the International Exhibition at the South Kensington Museum, now the Victoria and Albert Museum. Before leaving London, Monet learned of the horrors and massacres that had recently taken place in Paris in connection with the Commune. Informed, incorrectly, that his friend and supporter Courbet had been killed in the fighting, the disturbed Monet told Pissarro:

> You have undoubtedly heard of the death of poor Courbet, shot without a trial. The vile conduct of Versailles (the official government). It is all too atrocious and sickening. I cannot put my heart into anything. It is all utterly distressing.

This emotional outburst is one of the first indications we have of Monet's beliefs about governmental affairs. It indicates a liberal anti-government bias that surfaced occasionally in his later years.

Not feeling it was yet safe to return home, the Monets left England for Holland in late May and settled in rural, picturesque Zaandam. Monet was fascinated by the beauty and color of the country. During his brief stay, he completed some twenty-four paintings. He also visited the great Rijksmuseum in Amsterdam and the Frans Hals Museum in Haarlem. To help make ends meet, Camille gave French lessons.

The family returned to Paris in November of 1872 and found much of the city in a shambles from the ravages of war. They rented a small hotel room for a month or so, and Monet went about setting up a studio, reconnecting with his friends. During this time he did only one painting.

Argenteuil—The 1870s

In December, Monet decided to move from the city. He rented a house in Argenteuil, a small town of eight thousand people on the Seine, just fifteen kilometers northwest of Paris. The town was connected to the capital by hourly train service to the Gare St.-Lazare. It was only a fifteen-minute ride. Argenteuil had been a peaceful little town until the early 1850s, when the railroad came through. Now it was undergoing a transition to a semi-industrial suburb of Paris. It had many aspects that were attractive to a painter, including very picturesque areas along the river and in the surrounding countryside. In town there was an abundance of modern active scenes to paint, including the bridges over the river—one of which was being repaired after suffering damages in the recent war. Argenteuil was best known as a yachting center, as many

Parisians would come down on weekends to sail their boats on the Seine, which was particularly wide at that point. Monet captured all of these scenes, both rural and modern, as well as his own home and garden, in his singular style during the 1870s.

Monet and his family lived in these peaceful and attractive surroundings for nearly seven years. Except for occasional trips to the Normandy coast and Paris, plus one trip to Holland, he never left. His personal life took on a stability he had not known before, and despite his continuing cries for financial help, he generally lived comfortably off the sale of his paintings and the support of his friends.

Artistically, the period was extremely important. His productivity and artistic development were enormous. The 170 paintings he completed during this period constitute the core of his most Impressionistic works. The paintings he and other artists did in Argenteuil make this period one of the most significant in the history of French art.

Monet's early years in Argenteuil were particularly active. In 1872 alone he painted about sixty pictures. His income in that year from sales amounted to about 12,000 francs, equal to the income of a lawyer in Paris. Records show that the Monets employed a gardener and two servants and bought a lot of wine. He also bought a small boat and equipped it with a cabin, turning it into a floating studio for his work on the river.

During his years in Argenteuil, Monet averaged an income of over 14,000 francs a year, with a high of 24,800 in 1873. However, with his comfortable lifestyle and his expenditures on painting supplies, he was always living on or beyond the edge. He regularly had to beg friends for help, particularly in the late 1870s. Manet and Gustave Caillebotte, a painter and businessman who lived nearby, were particularly generous. Many of Monet's paintings were sold to Durand-Ruel, who by now was an active art dealer in Paris and London.

In his work Monet was often joined by other young painters. Sisley painted alongside him for several periods of time. Renoir painted a number of portraits of Monet's family members. He was also visited by Pissarro.

Most significant from a historical standpoint was a visit by Manet over the summer of 1874. He painted with Monet and Renoir and adopted their looser and more open Impressionistic style in his own painting. Manet made several portraits of Monet painting in his studio boat. The works are somewhat incomplete, however, as Monet evidently was unwilling to pose for long periods of time.

Monet's situation and artistic goals seemed to have been summed up by his old mentor Eugène Boudin when he wrote in 1872:

> We often see Monet and went to his housewarming recently. He is very well established and seems to have a strong desire to carve out a place for himself. I think he is destined to take one of the leading positions in our school.

There had been no Salon in 1871 because of the war. As it prepared to reopen in 1872, the Salon created much speculation as to whether it would be more accepting of new ideas or continue to favor the more conservative, traditional paintings. The hopes of the young Impressionists were dashed as the 1872 jury proved to be utterly uninterested in their type of work. This attitude of the Salon was reflective of the government's general desire to restore order after the unpleasantness of the radical Commune.

It was in reaction to this repressive atmosphere that the idea of an independent exhibition finally took hold after a number of years of general discussion. Monet was to play a leading role in pushing the concept. Plans were developed by several of the artists at meetings held in Argenteuil and Paris during 1873. In several letters to Pissarro, Monet refers to their plan:

> Everyone thinks it is a good thing, only Manet is against it.

> I have not forgotten our society, I am doing what I can.

Official articles of incorporation were drawn up and signed in December 1873 by Monet, Pissarro, Degas, Sisley, Morisot and Renoir. Manet refused to sign. The corporation was set up as a type of joint stock company, with all artists contributing equally. They hoped to build sales and their reputation with a non-juried exhibition during the time of the Salon. The group also hoped to publish a magazine.

Immediately after securing space for the first show, at the photo studio of the famed Gaspar Nadar (35, blvd. des Capucines), Monet went to Paris to paint two views of the street just below the gallery. His desire was to allow the exhibition visitor to be able to contrast the actual scene from the window of the gallery with his own personal depiction of it.

The historic show opened on April 15, 1874, for one month. Thirty artists and 165 works were on display. Monet was represented by five paintings (including *Impression: Sunrise*) and seven pastels. The results were disappointing. Comment by the critics was generally negative, few pictures were sold and the debt-ridden corporation was dissolved before its first anniversary.

The history of the eight Impressionist exhibits over a twelve-year period is a complex story involving many artists, locations, personal conflicts and problems. Monet's interest in and involvement with the exhibits generally decreased over the twelve years, though he did gain some artistic acclaim and a few sales from some of the shows. He displayed his works in five of them and was a strong presence within the group even when he was not participating.

Representing some of the more advanced thinkers, the critic Émile Zola summed up his view of the Impressionists and Monet in the late 1870s:

> Without doubt we are seeing the birth of a new school. Here there is a revolutionary ferment that little by little will prevail over the Academie des Beaux-Arts itself and in twenty years will have transformed the Salon from which these innovators are now excluded.

He wrote specifically of Monet:

> Without a doubt, Claude Monet is the leader of the group. His brush is distinctive for its extraordinary brilliance.

During the mid-1870s, Monet started to sell his paintings to a few collectors who took a particular interest in his work. The Romanian-born Dr. Georges de Bellio and the famous baritone from the Paris opera, Jean-Baptiste Faure, both began to build significant collections at this time. Manet and Caillebotte made purchases, and the textile merchant Ernest Hoschedé was also involved in buying and selling Monet's works. This activity helped offset the decreased buying by Paul Durand-Ruel, who fell on hard times during a recessionary period and had to suspend his activity for a few years.

There were a number of art auctions during this time; these yielded mixed results for Monet and his fellow Impressionists. One, in January 1874 at the

Hôtel Drouot, did quite well, with the Impressionist artists procuring good prices. Another one held just fifteen months later, in March 1875, was both unsuccessful and contentious. Monet sold only half his works, and at very low prices. The paintings were so controversial that they caused a riot, and the auctioneer was forced to call the police to calm things down. The critic Albert Wolff gave the event mixed reviews in *Le Figaro,* saying that the Impressionist painters made him think of:

> a cat walking on a piano keyboard or a monkey who has gotten hold of a box of paints.

The vagaries of the art market, and the still-limited acceptance that his work enjoyed, made things difficult for Monet. His income was decent, but he continued to spend more than he could afford. In October 1874 he moved into a larger, newly built house in Argenteuil, complete with a garden, and his trips to Paris and the coast continued. As a result, he regularly asked friends for money. He appealed to Manet several times in 1875:

> Although I have faith in the future, the present is very hard to bear.

> My color box will stay closed for a long time now, if I can't get out of this mess.

In October of that year, Camille had to sign over the rights to an inheritance to settle Monet's account at an art supply dealer.

Monet continued to paint beautiful and sensitive works portraying his family and scenes of Argenteuil, plus a number of captivating paintings of the Tuileries Gardens and the Parc Monceau in Paris. He did all this outstanding work while he was also striving to sell his paintings, borrowing money and pleading with his friends to help him out. In the midst of this busy schedule, Monet completed his most ambitious, innovative and creative series of paintings to date.

For years, Monet had traveled in and out of the Gare St.-Lazare, the railway station in the northwest section of Paris. Monet was familiar with it because it served the towns to the west, such as Argenteuil, as well as the coastal city of Le Havre. In early 1877, with the financial help of Caillebotte, Monet rented a studio near the Gare St.-Lazare. Over the next four months, in a frenzy of activity, he completed twelve canvases of various scenes in and around the impressive steel structure. The motivation to paint them apparently came from his desire to move away from the tranquil pastoral scenes of Argenteuil to the contemporary life of a now-revitalized Paris.

In order to get just the right lighting effects, Monet felt that certain train departures should be delayed. With his characteristic self-confidence, he set about arranging things to his liking. Renoir later recalled the situation:

> He put on his best clothes, pulled his lace cuffs to rights, and, idly swinging his gold-headed cane, handed the Director of the western railways his card. The official froze, and ushered him in forthwith. The exalted personage asked his visitor to take a seat, and the latter introduced himself simply with the words: "I am the painter Claude Monet." The Director knew nothing of art, but did not dare admit as much. For a moment Monet left him twitching on the line, and then he announced the great news: "I have decided to paint your station. For a long time I was undecided whether to take the Gare du Nord or yours, but I now feel yours has more character." Monet got his way in everything. Trains were stopped, platforms closed off, the locomotives fired full of coal so they belched out steam in that way Monet loved. Tyrannically he set himself up in the station and for days, amidst universal awe, he painted, then left again with a half a dozen pictures done.

The result was a series of twelve paintings of various sizes and palettes that capture the steamy and active environment of a modern part of industrialized France. Although the views are from different angles and depict scenes both inside and outside the station, the focus on a single locale signals an important turning point for Monet. Here we see him evolving toward his later series paintings.

Monet exhibited eight of the twelve Gare St.-Lazare paintings in the third Impressionist exhibit, in April 1877. They were recognized for their uniqueness and received broad but not universal praise. One writer observed that:

> (Monet's) brush has expressed not only the movement, color and activity of the station, but also the clamor; it is unbelievable. Yet the station is full of din grindings, whistles that you make out through the colliding blue and grey clouds of dense smoke. It is a pictorial symphony.

Zola was particularly impressed. He wrote in April 1877:

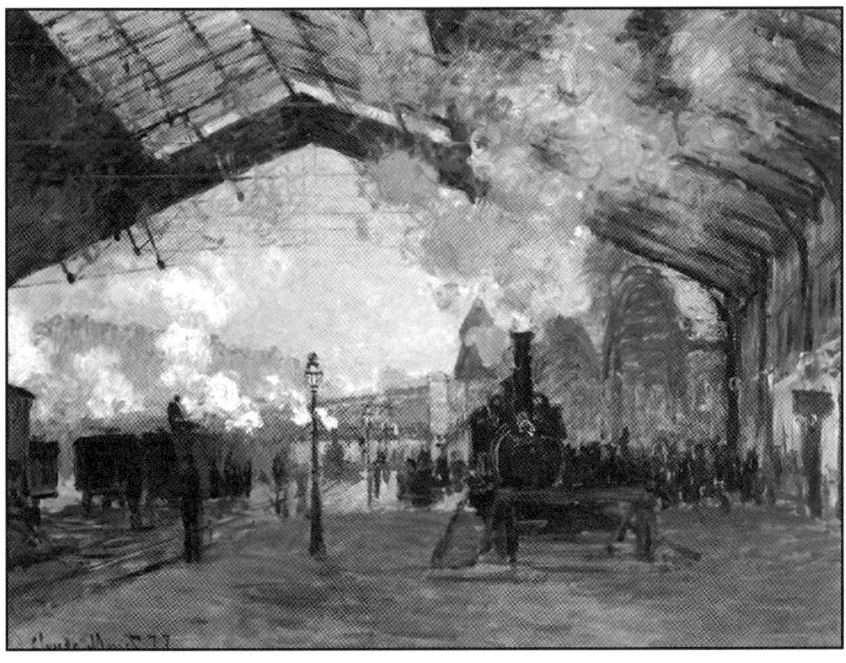

One of a series of twelve paintings of the Gare St.-Lazare done in 1877. The focus on a single locale signals an important turning point for Monet.

Claude Monet, French, 1840–1926. Arrival of the Normandy Train, Gare Saint-Lazare, oil on canvas, 1877, 59.6 x 80.2 cm, Mr. and Mrs. Martin A. Ryerson Collection, 1933.1158

> Monsieur Claude Monet is the most marked personality of the group. This year he has exhibited some superb railway station scenes. In these one can hear the rumbling of the trains and see the smoke rolling and flooding through the huge sheds. Here is the painting of today, in these beautiful, broad, modern canvases. Our artists must look to the poetry of railway stations, as their fathers sought that of forest and rivers.

Personal and Family Problems—The Late 1870s

In September of 1876, Monet was invited by his sometime patron Ernest Hoschedé to come to the Château de Rottenbourg at Montgeron, east of Paris. He'd agreed to paint a series of four large decorative panels for the château's dining room. While working there that autumn, Monet became intimately involved with Hoschedé's wife, Alice. Ernest was often away on business, and it is possible that Monet fathered Alice's child Jean-Piérre, who was born the following August.

To add to the problem, Camille became pregnant over the summer of 1877. It was a difficult pregnancy and she was often quite weak. As a result, Monet had to reduce his painting activity to care for his sick wife. Making matters worse, Ernest Hoschedé's business ventures went sour, and he declared bankruptcy in August. He temporarily fled the country, threatening suicide and leaving his wife and six children alone.

Times were thus exceedingly stressful and desperate for Monet through the end of 1877. He continued to negotiate sales and loans. His goal was to get enough money so he could leave Argenteuil without creditors seizing his household belongings or his paintings. In January his family finally left and moved back to Paris.

In March 1878 the Monets' second son, Michel, was born. Manet was a witness on the birth certificate. Shortly afterward Monet wrote to a collector, outlining his situation:

> My wife has just had another baby, and I find myself penniless and unable to pay for the medical care that both mother and child must have.

His friends once again responded with financial help.

Monet's spirits were further dampened when in June 1878 a forced auction of Ernest Hoschedé's paintings brought very low prices, and the market for Monet's art remained depressed. The disappointing auction did give Monet a new contact, though, that would help in the years ahead. Georges Petit, a Parisian gallery owner, bought several of Monet's paintings, and the two began a long-term relationship. Petit would become an important competitor of Durand-Ruel, thus providing the Impressionists with additional outlets.

By late summer, Monet had had enough of the city, and he decided to move to the country again. The family settled in a small house in the tiny village (six hundred people) of Vétheuil on the Seine, west of Argenteuil. The house was close to the river and had a large garden. The rural setting was just the kind of place Monet had been looking for.

The Monets' living situation changed radically at this time. They were joined in their Vétheuil home by Alice Hoschedé and her six children; since both families were poor, they pooled resources. Also playing a role, no doubt, was the continuing affection between Monet and Madame Hoschedé.

Alice was going through an understandably difficult time herself, as she and her children had been virtually abandoned by her now-bankrupt husband. Unlike Camille, who had come from a poor background, Alice had grown up in a wealthy family and had been exposed to the world of upper-class society. She had brought a considerable dowry to her marriage and had inherited the Château de Rottenbourg. All that was gone now. Moving in her family with the Monets was very unconventional for the times.

The situation was further complicated by the worsening health of Camille. She had not strengthened after the birth of her son Michel, and had developed uterine cancer. Throughout much of 1878 and 1879, Monet was occupied with caring for her. She continued to weaken, and by August she was unable to get out of bed. Struggling economically, Monet constantly expressed his dismay and sadness over his family situation. At the end of December 1878 he wrote to his friend de Bellio:

> I am not a beginner any more, and it is dreadful to be in such a position for my age, forever begging and pestering buyers. As the year ends I am doubly aware of my misfortune, for '79 is beginning as this year has ended, in utter despondency, especially with regard to my dear ones, to whom I have not been able to give even the smallest present.

After months of suffering and being nursed by Monet and Alice, Camille died on September 5, 1879, at the age of thirty-two. Monet wrote that same day to de Bellio:

> My poor wife died this morning…I am filled with dismay to find myself alone with my poor children. I want to request another service of you: to redeem the medallion we pawned at the Mont de Piété, with the enclosed money. It is the only souvenir that Camille had been able to preserve, and I would like to put it around her neck before she leaves us.

Camille had been a beautiful young woman and had gone through many difficult times with Monet. She had served as his model in many paintings, put up with his emotional ups and downs, and, of course, borne him two sons. In late September, after her death, Monet expressed his shaken state of mind in a letter to Pissarro:

> You, more than anyone, will understand my grief. I am overwhelmed; I have no idea which way to turn, nor how I am going to organize my life with my two children. I am much to be pitied.

We see yet another aspect of Monet's grief from a story he told to Clemenceau many years later. Here Monet's words reveal his artistic instincts even in sadness:

> One day, I found myself at daybreak at the bedside of a dead woman who had been and always will be very dear to me. My gaze was fixed on her tragic temples, and I caught myself observing the shades and nuances of color Death brought to her countenance. Blues, yellows, greys, I don't know what. That is the state I was in. The wish came upon me, quite naturally, to record the image of her who was departing from us forever. But before it occurred to me to draw those features I knew and loved so well, I was first and foremost devastated organically, automatically, by the colors. Against my will, my reflexes took possession of me in an unconscious process, as the everyday course of my life took over. Like a draught animal working at a millstone. Pity me, my dear friend.

The result of this very emotional experience is an eerie and touching portrait of the recently dead Camille.

Alice now took over the role of the woman of the house for this unusual blended family. Her husband would come by occasionally but spent most of his time in Paris, trying to recover his lost fortune. The unusual arrangement lasted for the next twelve years. A devout Catholic and with divorce out of the question, Alice would not be free to marry Monet until after the death of Ernest in 1891. Their living situation was often commented upon by acquaintances and may account for the relatively little time Monet spent in Paris during these years.

Vétheuil—An Interlude

In spite of his stressful family situation, Monet's three year's painting around Vétheuil and on the coast were extremely productive. Over this period he completed some three hundred paintings. But these works were different from those he produced in his Argenteuil period during the 1870s. He captured quiet scenes in the backwaters of the Seine and in the countryside. His views of Vétheuil and other villages were often from a distance, and his works contained few people. He had clearly moved away from recording aspects of modern life, such as railroads, bridges and sailboats. His Vétheuil paintings focus on the beauty of the sky and water in rural settings and have a feeling of solitude about them. Of particularly haunting beauty is a series of winter scenes along the river.

Even with such a great artistic output, Monet's economic situation remained difficult. He did sell a number of paintings, but prices were generally low. Once again his friends came through for him especially Caillebotte, who lent him money, bought some of his works and helped him sell others. But the old problem of never having enough continued to plague him. The Monet-Hoschedé household was continually behind in their rent, and several times their servants quit because of unpaid wages. There were also times when Monet was out of art supplies and unable to paint for short periods.

During this time, Monet distanced himself from the Impressionist group in Paris. He had decided not to participate in the fourth group exhibit in 1879. His friend Caillebotte talked him into changing his mind, but the unenthusiastic Monet did not take part in the hanging of his pictures, nor did he attend the show.

His relationship with his fellow Impressionists was further strained when he decided to enter the 1880 Salon and did not exhibit with the Impressionists. Although his decision was surely economically motivated, friends such as Pissarro felt betrayed. A letter from Monet at the time reflects the situation:

> I am suddenly being treated as a deserter by the whole band, but I believe it was in my own interest to make the decision I did, since I am more or less sure to do some business, particularly with Petit, once I have broken into the Salon.

Monet's decision was mockingly and viciously announced in an anonymous letter printed in several publications a couple of months before the opening of the Salon:

> The Impressionist School has the honor of informing you of the grievous loss it has suffered in the person of M. Claude Monet, one of its revered masters. The funeral for M. Claude Monet will take place on 1 May next at ten o'clock in the morning the day after the opening at the church of the Palais de L'Industrie in M. Cabanel's gallery. You are requested not to attend.

The letter also commented on his odd relationship with Alice Hoschedé. Monet was understandably furious. He suspected that some of his old Impressionist comrades were behind the letter. He wrote a rebuttal letter, but it was never published.

One of Monet's submissions was accepted into the Salon, but it was poorly hung. Zola was critical of what he saw. He felt Monet painted too quickly, and implied in a review that the artist painted fast so he could produce and sell more. However, in recognition of Monet's growing reputation, the same article said:

> In ten years, he will be accepted, displayed, and rewarded; he will sell his pictures for huge prices and will stand at the head of the present movement.

This would be Monet's last showing at the Salon. From now on, he would go his own way in trying to sell his paintings.

Monet's popularity and exposure did increase over the next months. In June 1880 Monet held his first one-artist exhibition in the galleries of the magazine *La Vie Moderne.* The month-long show included eighteen works. A number of them sold quickly. In preparation for the catalogue for the show, Monet was extensively interviewed. He seems to have gotten carried away with himself and was a bit misleading in some of his statements. For instance, he claimed that he never had a studio. He waved his arms at the surrounding landscape and claimed, "This is my studio." He also stated that he painted entirely on location in the open air. Neither of these claims was true to the extent Monet indicated. He evidently wanted to portray himself as the rugged anti-establishment rebel who was driven by sudden, on-the-spot inspiration. But those close to him knew of the planning, the intricate calculations and the hard work that went into his paintings. (Monet strove to maintain this somewhat fictional picture of himself until well after he was sixty years old.)

Monet's efforts outside of Vétheuil during this period included a number of trips to the Normandy coast. In September 1880 he spent time with his brother Léon, who had a vacation home in Petites-Dalles, just south of Dieppe. His work there is the beginning of a renewed and more intense interest in capturing the rugged cliffs and churning sea along the Channel. Over the next six years, he would return time and again to this beautiful area that so fascinated him.

In late 1881 Monet and Alice decided to leave Vétheuil and move upriver to the larger town of Poissy. The reason was to get better schooling for their children and probably to get away from their poor credit rating. This decision signaled a clear and final break with Alice's absent husband, Ernest.

Monet was never really inspired by Poissy, and he spent much of his time painting on the coast. He took these trips alone most of the time, but occasionally Alice and their eight children would come along.

The market began to improve for Monet's works, and he pursued a number of sales strategies. He had once again started to work closely with Durand-Ruel, who, in spite of occasional monetary setbacks, continued to display, buy and commission a number of Monet's works. He also provided interim financial assistance, including helping Monet with the cost of moving his household.

Monet exhibited with the other Impressionists for the last time in 1882. He had thirty-five works on display and was generally favorably reviewed. His prices started to increase. In 1883 Monet had a second one-artist exhibit. Held at Durand-Ruel's galleries, it included sixty works. The comments from the press were positive, and the articles now included material about Monet's early life, not just the paintings on display.

The Move to Giverny

Monet grew restless in Poissy. He was now forty-three years old and wanted some stability. He needed a place where he could comfortably settle down in surroundings that provided inspiration and subject matter for his work. After considerable searching, he decided on the town of Giverny, a picturesque little farming village of about three hundred people near the Seine, about eighty kilometers northwest of Paris and some thirty kilometers east of Rouen. He and his family moved there in April of 1883. Their final move was a hectic and complicated event. On arriving at the station, they found that they didn't have enough money for tickets for the whole Monet/Hoschedé entourage. Monet took some of the kids and went ahead, and funds were secured from Durand-Ruel so that Alice and the others could soon follow.

The pink stucco house they rented was one of the largest in the village. It was situated on a slight hill and had an orchard and garden that ran down to a road and the Gisors-Vernon railway line. Beyond was a marsh that was crossed by the tiny Ru River, a small branch of the Epte. The Epte in turn flowed into the nearby Seine.

Monet was to live here for the next forty-three years, until his death. The house provided a large and pleasurable home for his family, served as a base for Monet's many painting excursions and increasingly became the focal point of his art. They rented the place until 1890 and then bought it. Over the years Monet expanded the building and created large studios for his works. It was an ideal place, and to the driven, often solitary Monet, it provided a unique combination of home, working studio and beautiful artistic subject matter. In late 1883 he wrote:

> I am in ecstasy. Giverny is splendid country for me.

If he had not lived here, the art he produced in the last half of his life would have been very different.

The Monet-Hoschedé clans that arrived at Giverny that spring consisted of Monet, his sons Jean, now age sixteen, and Michel, just five; and Alice's four daughters, Marthe (nineteen), Blanche (eighteen), Suzanne (fifteen), Germaine (ten), and two sons, Jacques (fourteen) and Jean-Pierre (almost six). Monet and Alice were still not married, but correspondence between them reflects a feeling of commitment, love and devotion. Their arrangement no doubt caused much gossip among the local farming families around Giverny, but Monet was not one to worry about such things.

Monet's initial excitement about his new home was interrupted by the death of his friend Manet on April 30. Monet immediately went to Paris to serve as a pallbearer at the funeral.

Painting Excursions—The 1880s

During the remainder of the 1880s, Monet spent many months on painting trips to new and different parts of France, plus one trip to Holland. These journeys provided constant artistic challenges for him but were also partially driven by the increasing demand for his paintings, which were now becoming more popular and demanding higher prices.

His excursions, often lasting for months, were mostly taken without Alice and the family. She was thus left to tend to the eight children back at Giverny. Her correspondence with Monet, while mainly tender, occasionally reflects her anger at his being away so much. She even threatened several times to reconcile with her husband, but their commitment to one another survived.

Monet took about a dozen of these intense painting expeditions during the period of 1883–1890. He traveled to some of the most beautiful and inspiring places in France. There were three trips to the Mediterranean coast, one to an island off Brittany (Belle-Ile), several to the beautiful Creuse Valley in central France and, of course, a number of trips to the rugged Normandy coast between Le Havre and Dieppe.

Monet's emotions on these trips often followed a pattern. He was initially delighted by the beauty of the area but would soon be frustrated by not being able to find just the right scene. He would then regularly complain about how difficult it was to capture what he saw and how irritated and discouraged he was. Nevertheless, the large body of work he created on these trips demonstrates his growing mastery in capturing the energies and beauty of nature in a most unique way.

I will not examine all of these excursions, but a sampling of his correspondence and experiences can give us great insight into Monet's emotions and artistic efforts during this period.

• In December 1883 he and Renoir traveled the Mediterranean coast from Marseilles to Genoa. They stopped to visit Cézanne, who was working in L'Estaque in Provence. The scenery fascinated Monet, so he returned with his painting supplies in January and settled just across the Italian border, in the town of Bordighera. This time he came alone, however, and writing to Durand-Ruel, he explained why:

> I must beg you not to mention this trip to anyone, not because it is my deep dark secret, but because I need to do it alone. Though I greatly enjoyed traveling there with Renoir as a tourist, it would be very difficult for me to work there with him. I have always worked best on my own, entirely from my own impressions. So keep my secret until I tell you otherwise. If he knew I was going, Renoir would surely want to go with me, and that would be a disaster for both of us.

Several months later, he wrote:

> One needs a palette of diamonds and jewels here because of the blues and pinks.

He returned to Giverny in mid-April with about forty-five paintings (one for every two days he was there). Many of them were finished in his studio after he got back.

• Between 1883 and 1886, Monet spent many months on the Normandy coast, traveling there at least five times. He worked up and down the Channel, capturing the spectacular cliffs and landscapes. His special focus was the town of Etretat with its fantastic rock formations. To Alice, he wrote:

> You can have no idea of the beauty of the sea...as to the cliffs here, they are like nowhere else.

Monet often worked in terrible weather and on at least one occasion was thrown against the cliff by a large wave, losing his easel, paints and brush.

• During September of 1886, Monet set out alone to visit and work on the island of Belle-Ile, off the coast of Brittany. He lived in a peasant's shack in a tiny village. It was to have been a two-week trip, but he stayed until the end of November. He was fascinated by the savage coastline and the rugged beauty of the island. His fascination with the place is expressed in a letter to Alice:

> I am going to set myself up in a little hamlet of eight or ten houses, near the place called La Me˘r Terrible...It is well named; not a tree for ten kilometers, some rocks and wonderful grottoes, it is sinister, diabolical, but superb.

In another letter:

> The sea is completely beautiful, and as for the rocks they are a tangle of extraordinary coves, spikes and needles.

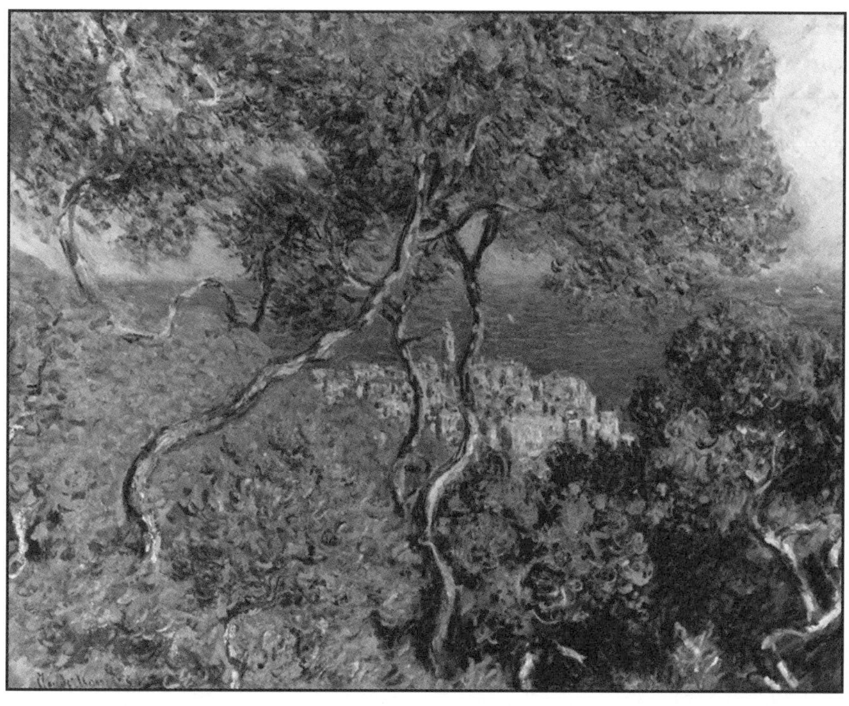

A view of the Italian seaside town of Bordighera painted in February 1884. Monet completed nearly four dozen paintings during his three-month stay on the Mediterranean.

Claude Monet, French, 1840–1926. Bordighera. oil on canvas, 1884, 64.8 x 81.3 cm, Mr. and Mrs. Potter Palmer Collection, 1922.426

The work Monet did on the island has special significance. In the forty pictures he completed, he limited the number of motifs and often painted a single subject from the same or a slightly different viewpoint. While these were not exactly similar to his famous series paintings of the 1890s, they do show him using his extraordinary skills to capture the nuances of changing light and atmosphere on a single subject.

Monet knew he was doing extraordinary work. He wrote to Alice from Belle-Ile:

> One has to do everything, and it is precisely because of that that I congratulate myself for doing what I am doing.

While there, he met Gustave Geffroy, the radical and popular journalist, author and art critic. The two were to become lifelong friends. Geffroy was very supportive of Monet's work and eventually wrote a book about him.

• Monet returned to the sunny and tranquil Mediterranean for four months in early 1888. He worked around the area of Antibes on the Côte d'Azur. Once again, the light and color fascinated him as he painted the colorful trees and landscapes against a background of sparkling water and distant mountains. His letters express his excitement:

> After wild Belle Ile, this will be very soft; there is nothing here but blue, pink and gold.

> What I will bring back from here will be sweetness itself, white, pink, blue, all of it enveloped in this fairy-tale-like air.

He executed over thirty paintings during the trip. These proved to be very popular. The poet Stéphane Mallarmé wrote to Monet after seeing the paintings:

> I have just left the exhibition, delighted by the work you did last winter...For a long time I have ranked what you do above all else, but I believe you are now at the height of your powers.

• Again seeking challenge and contrast from the tropical Mediterranean, Monet's next major effort was in the valley of the Creuse River in central France. He visited the area with some friends in February 1889 and was fascinated by what he called the "awesome wildness of the place." He returned in March for two and a half months, working out of the village of Fresselines, seated high above the confluence of the Creuse and the Petit Creuse Rivers.

He completed twenty-four paintings on the trip. Ten of these are from the same vantage point and differ in color and atmosphere according to the weather and light. They can possibly be considered Monet's first real series of paintings. Work on these paintings was often extremely difficult because of the harsh weather. Monet expressed his feelings in several letters to Berthe Morisot. In February he said that he

> was going to do something astonishing here. Alas, the further I go the more difficult it is to render what I want; and on top of that, miserable weather—rain every day and brutally cold.

And again, later that spring, he wrote to her:

> Here I am again, grappling with the difficulties of a new landscape. It is superb here, with a terrible wildness that reminds me of Belle-Ile. I thought I would do astonishing things, but the further I go, the more trouble I have in conveying it as I would like.

To compound his problems, Monet had to deal with the advent of spring and the resulting change in the foliage. He was particularly upset when one of the trees in his series paintings had started to sprout leaves. He handled the situation in his usual direct manner by paying off the owner of the land, then hiring two locals to carry a ladder down to the river and pick the leaves off the trees. It was a telling incident, as here we see Monet, the worshiper and painter of Nature, pragmatically altering the natural landscape to conform to his artistic desires.

The months in Fresselines were exhausting, but they resulted in some spectacular works. During this time, Monet moved significantly toward his unique series paintings, which would dominate his work in the 1890s. Just before leaving the Creuse Valley he wrote to Alice:

> You will never know what I have suffered during this campaign...I am at the end of my tether.

He returned to Giverny exhausted.

While away on these trips, Monet regularly expressed how much he missed Giverny. Writing to Alice in 1884, he said:

> I am yearning for Giverny. I shall be happy to come back and resume my life in the country. It seems to me I shall derive deep pleasure from painting there.

He did miss his family and had grown quite fond of the Hoschedé children, who were now virtually (if unofficially) his stepchildren.

During his times at Giverny in the mid-1880s, Monet used the Hoschedé girls as models in a number of his works. Of particular significance are a pair of matching pictures of Suzanne Hoschedé, painted in 1886. They portray her in a field with a parasol and are reminiscent of one he did of Camille eleven years before. They are his last large portrait paintings and were done in a very loose Impressionistic style. This was possibly in response to the very tightly constructed pointillistic technique of Georges Seurat, which was then starting to challenge the older Impressionistic style for the leadership of avant-garde art in France.

Recognition and Involvement in Paris, 1889–1890

Much of Monet's nonpainting time during the 1880s was spent in efforts to sell his works. This, of course, required frequent trips to Paris. He worked with both Durand-Ruel and Georges Petit, as well as with a firm managed by Theo van Gogh, the brother of Vincent. He also sold directly to collectors. A series of international exhibitions by Georges Petit was particularly helpful in providing an outlet for the works Monet completed on his various trips. By the end of the decade, he was quite well established as a truly great artist and as a leader of the changes that were taking place in painting.

The most notable of the many exhibits that Monet participated in over these years was a combined exhibition with the great French sculptor Auguste Rodin. It ran June 21 through September 21, 1889, in conjunction with the Universal Exposition of that year. It was a significant event for Monet, and he spent a good deal of effort in the planning and negotiating leading up to it. In early correspondence with Rodin, Monet expressed his excitement:

> I received a note from Petit suggesting a meeting for Saturday morning at 10:00 o'clock, to talk about staging an exhibition—just of you and me [Monet's emphasis]—in his gallery during the Universal Exposition. Are you still interested?...Before doing anything, I need to know if I can count on you...Tell me yes or no by telegram right away, and give me a date for when we can get together.

It was the largest Monet exhibit so far, with 145 paintings. Even though it was referred to as a retrospective, over half the paintings had been done in the previous three years including fourteen recently completed *Creuse Valley* works. Monet also included six of the figure paintings he had recently finished at Giverny. Monet saw the show as an opportunity to really lay claim to being a true leader in the world of art.

There was, as one might expect, tension between the two great artists as they brought their works together. Among other things, Monet didn't like some of the placements of his works. A letter to Petit soon after the opening expressed his pique:

> I saw that my panel at the back is completely lost now that the Rodin group has been set up. The mischief is done; it is very upsetting to me. If Rodin had understood that since we were exhibiting together we should have agreed on the placement of our work...if he had discussed it with me and given a little consideration to my work, it would have been quite easy to work out a fair arrangement without doing each other harm. I only want one thing now, and that is to get back to Giverny and have some peace.

In spite of the bickering and a few criticisms, the show was a success. The critic of *L'Art moderne* wrote:

> In this superb exhibition there is not a lapse nor a hesitation...Nature has never been rendered with more intensity and truth.

Another critic described Monet's work as:

> An exaltation of colors which range bravely above the natural scale.

And the popular critic Octave Mirbeau summed up the general consensus about both artists when he said in *L'Echo de Paris*:

> They are the men who in this century have most gloriously and definitively personified the twin arts of painting and sculpture.

The exhibit attracted many interested buyers, and a number of sales resulted. Americans were among those particularly intrigued, and from that point on, Monet's reputation grew among knowledgeable collectors in the U.S.

Following the show, Monet stopped painting for almost a year. Similar dry periods would occur periodically over the remainder of his life. The exhausting work on the *Creuse River* paintings, plus the stress surrounding the exhibit with Rodin, had evidently taken a toll. Monet needed a rest, or at least a change; but, very quickly, an issue grabbed his attention, and he attacked it with his usual commitment and energy.

Manet's controversial nude, *Olympia,* had been exhibited as part of the 1889 Universal Exhibition. Soon a rumor surfaced regarding an American who wanted to buy the now-famous painting and take it out of France. It was owned by Manet's widow and she needed the money. Monet quickly jumped into the situation and headed up a campaign to raise funds to buy the picture for twenty thousand francs with the intent of donating the work to the French government. The whole effort took some twelve months, and it was a difficult endeavor. He wrote to fellow artists, dealers and acquaintances, trying to raise the money. Persuading the government to accept a work that, when it was shown in 1865, was a scandalous affront to the official art establishment proved to be equally challenging. Such an acceptance would signify official recognition of Monet's style of modern painting. There were still many traditionalists who were not yet prepared for such a step.

By February 1890 Monet had garnered the money, and he officially offered the work to the State in a letter sent to the Minister of Public Institutions. A period of five months of negotiations followed. The frustrated Monet wrote to Berthe Morisot regarding the opposition of the Minister of Fine Arts, Antonin Proust:

> This Proust is a fine ass. I will tell him as much in a letter, and once war has been declared we shall fight to the finish.

The conflict with Proust resulted in Monet's being challenged to a duel. The image-conscious Monet wanted none of that, and a physical conflict was avoided. After lengthy wrangling, an accordance was reached wherein the French government agreed to place the work in the Luxembourg Museum. The stubborn Monet insisted that the State agree not to move the painting out of Paris, as he feared that the conservative forces could, in effect, exile the painting to a small museum in the provinces. (In 1907 the painting was moved to the Louvre.) This venture revealed Monet's considerable political negotiating skills. It also further testified to his leadership role among the modern progressive forces in French art.

It was, of course, important to Monet that Manet's great work not leave France and that his widow receive the financial help she needed. However, it was equally important to Monet that the type of painting he and Manet championed be given official recognition and that he play a major role in obtaining that recognition. Typically, Monet did not attend the official opening ceremony, demonstrating again his distaste for formal functions and the official art establishment.

The Series Paintings of the 1890s

After all the traveling of the 1880s, Monet's focus for the next nine years would be on areas familiar to him. With the exception of one brief trip to Norway, he found new inspiration in subjects closer to home, and he addressed these with both great intensity and a uniqueness of approach.

Monet ended his hiatus from painting in the spring of 1890. He started by working on canvases depicting fields of poppies, hay and oats close to Giverny. After several months, though, things weren't going well, and Monet fell into one of his down moods. He wrote to Morisot in July:

> This devilish painting is making me sweat blood...I might have expected as much, after all that time doing nothing.

His frustrations continued, and later in the month he unloaded his feelings on Geffroy:

> I am in a very bad mood and deeply disgusted with the very idea of painting. It really is a continuous torture. Don't expect to see anything new. I have been able to do very little, and what I have done is destroyed, scraped down, or torn up. You can't imagine what abominable weather we've had unendingly these last two months. When you are trying to evoke the weather, the atmosphere, and the general feeling of things, it is enough to drive you out of your mind with sheer fury. In addition to all this, I've been stupid enough to get a bout of rheumatism. I'm paying for my sessions in rain and snow; it's depressing to think I shall have to give up painting in all weathers and work out-of-doors only when it is fine. Life is really stupid.

Soon his spirits improved, however, and he began a period of intense and innovative work which produced his famous series paintings.

Monet had for years depicted the same or similar subject matter in groups of paintings, e.g., Gare St.-Lazare in 1877. During the 1880s, he further developed his ideas and techniques on painting the same single subject matter under multiple conditions. (A number of his *Creuse Valley* paintings can, in fact, be classified as a coherent series.) But it was with his *Wheatstack* series, started in earnest in late 1890, that he began the daring, single-minded focus on one subject, visually analyzing and capturing it with all the various nuances of color, light and atmosphere. Each series is a complex and intriguing story in itself, with different artistic challenges and solutions. For the sake of this study, I will touch only briefly on the highlights.

• The idea of painting the wheatstacks that were behind his home had been with Monet for several years. In fact, he did several canvases of them in the late 1880s, and these were shown in the 1889 Monet-Rodin show. In September 1890 he returned to the subject with enthusiasm and a commitment to create something quite different from anything he had done before. His letter to Geffroy contains his goals and spirits:

> I am slaving away, working determinedly on a series of effects, but at this time of year, the sun goes down so fast I can't keep up with it. I am becoming so slow in my work it makes me desperate, but the further I get the more clearly I realize how much I have to work in order to capture what I am looking for: "instantaneity" above all, the same enveloping light spread over everything. More than ever simple things arrived at all in one go simply disgust me. Finally, I am more and more enflamed by the need to render exactly what I experience, and I vow to live on productively because it seems to me that I shall continue to progress. You see that I am in a good mood.

Over five or six months, he produced some thirty paintings that superbly capture the effects of the changing light and seasons. Conceived of as a true series of paintings on a single subject, they explore from various angles the wonderful differences in color, shadows and atmosphere that occurred in Monet's perception of the strange, cone-shaped forms. Some pictures have two stacks; some are up close; others reveal hills and poplar trees. But the focus is always on the stacks and the beauty and uniqueness of a particular moment in time.

By spring, fifteen of the works were already on exhibit in Paris. They were a critical and a commercial success. The paintings sold quickly (some before the show even opened) at good prices. Pissarro, among many others, was very positive:

> These paintings seem to me very luminous, undoubtedly the work of a master; the colors are pretty rather than strong, the draftsmanship is fine but drifting, particularly in the backgrounds. Nevertheless, he is a very great artist!...Needless to say, it is a huge success, and is all so attractive that frankly I am not surprised. The pictures breathe contentment.

• Monet next turned to working on a series of poplar trees along the Epte River, close to Giverny. The lovely receding rows of thin trees along the river's edge presented a different challenge from the solid, low wheatstacks. He painted the trees from his floating studio. In the twenty-four canvases he completed during 1891, Monet masterfully contrasted the curving lines of the rows of trees with the verticality of the individual trees. The effect of the bright and changing light on the trees makes these some of Monet's most beautiful and decorative works.

Even though the poplar tree had long been a symbol of France, it was also a commercial crop. Unluckily, soon after Monet had started to paint the trees, the owner decided to auction off the right to harvest them for wood products or firewood. Monet's pleas to delay the sale were unsuccessful. Not to be denied, Monet went to the auction and struck a deal with a wood merchant who planned to bid. He later recalled:

> I asked him how high a price he expected to pay, promising to make up the difference if the bid went over his amount, on the condition that he would buy the trees for me and leave them standing for a few more months.

When the sale was over, Monet and the merchant were co-owners, and the cutting was delayed until Monet was finished.

The paintings went on display in early 1892. They were very popular, and good sales resulted. Monet expressed his pleasure in a letter to Durand-Ruel in March 1892:

> I am very pleased with your news of my exhibition. I have it from several authorities that the effect has been considerable.

• Monet began his monumental series of paintings of the ancient Rouen Cathedral in February 1892. He worked on them during two lengthy stays in Rouen—February through April 1992, and February through April 1993—

and finished them off with considerable work in his studio during 1894 (most are dated 1894). All depict the great facade of the cathedral from close up and from nearly the same angle. He painted from three different locations on the first floor of buildings across the square in front of the cathedral. The works are amazing technical studies of the changing effects of light and atmosphere on the ornate stone front of the church. In some paintings, the cathedral glows in the bright morning sun. In others, it is enveloped in mist, and in still others, the afternoon sun brings forth rare colors. Almost eerie in their individual beauty, each creates an entirely different impression.

The labor of painting this series was difficult, intense and exhausting, and Monet complained regularly. In April 1892 he wrote to Alice:

> Every day I add something and come unawares on some new aspect that I hadn't been able to see previously. How hard it is, yet it is working out…I am broken, I cannot work any more and…I had a night filled with bad dreams: The cathedral was collapsing on me, it seemed to be blue or pink or yellow.

The following March he wrote to Durand-Ruel:

> I am working as hard as I possibly can, and do not even dream of doing anything except the cathedral. It is an immense task.

To catch the changing effect of the light, Monet worked on many canvases almost simultaneously. On one day in 1893, he dealt with a record fourteen.

The paintings required extensive reworking and finishing in his studio in Giverny. He worked on them throughout 1893 and 1894. As a result of his continued reworking, many of the paintings have a very thickly textured surface.

Monet knew these works were original and valuable, and he began negotiating their sale while they were still in progress. Twenty of the thirty *Cathedral* paintings were shown at a major exhibit at Durand-Ruel's in Paris in May 1895 (along with twenty-nine of Monet's earlier works). They were a great success, with the critics very complimentary, as they realized these paintings represented something new and powerful. Even more important, though, were the comments by Monet's fellow painters. Pissarro told his son:

> I am carried away by their extraordinary deftness. Cézanne...is in complete agreement...this is the work of a well-balanced but impulsive artist who pursues the intangible nuances of effects that are realized by no other painter.

Clemenceau published a long article on the series called "The Cathedral's Revolution." Some excerpts:

> Professionals will please excuse me, but I can't resist the desire to establish myself as an art critic for a day. It's Claude Monet's fault. I entered Durand-Ruel's gallery to easily look again at the studies of the cathedral of Rouen, which I had enjoyed seeing at the Giverny studio. And that's how I ended up taking that cathedral with its manifold aspects away with me, without knowing how. I can't get it out of my mind. I am obsessed with it. I've got to talk about it. And, for better or worse, I will talk.
>
> This is, in effect, what the audacious Monet set out to do with his twenty paintings of the cathedral of Rouen, divided into four series that I would call grey series, white series, rainbow series, blue series. With twenty paintings of differing effects, precisely chosen, the painter has given us the feeling that he should have made fifty, one hundred, one thousand paintings, as many as he had seconds in his life, if his life lasted as long as the stone monument and he could fix on a canvas as many different moments as he had heartbeats....

Clemenceau ends by encouraging the President of France, Félix Faure, to buy the paintings for the State:

> Go in, look at the work of one of your countrymen on whose account France will be celebrated throughout the world long after your name has fallen into oblivion...Remembering that you represent France, perhaps you might consider endowing her with these twenty paintings that together represent a moment for art, a moment for mankind, a revolution without a gunshot.

Unfortunately, the government was not yet willing to give that kind of recognition to the old rebel and anti-establishmentarian Monet. The pictures were quickly sold, at prices two to three times those of the *Wheatstacks* and *Poplars* series, and dispersed throughout the world.

• Monet spent two months in Norway in early 1895. He went there to visit his stepson Jacques Hoschedé, who had married a Norwegian woman. He was at first frustrated and disappointed by the differentness of the country. Soon, though, he was hard at work capturing the beauty of the mountains and the scenery outside Oslo. He returned to Giverny with twenty-six canvases. Half of these were a series of Mount Kolsaas painted from exactly the same spot near the town of Sandvika, some fifteen kilometers outside of Oslo. It was the first time Monet had painted a mountain, and he captured it at different times of day with a variety of light effects—clear, foggy and stormy. Seven works from this series were shown in the big May 1895 Monet show, along with twenty *Cathedral* paintings. The *Mount Kolsaas* pictures were moderately well received, but were overshadowed by the *Cathedral* series. None of them were sold, and they remained in Monet's studio until he died.

• After a break of some ten months following his 1895 exhibition, Monet once again traveled to the Normandy coast. He painted there during the winters of 1896 and 1897, working out of the towns of Pourville, Varengeville and Dieppe. He completed a total of nearly fifty paintings, which were numerous studies of a few specific motifs. For example, he did ten paintings of a little customhouse on a cliff at Varengeville, showing it at different times of day.

• During the same period (1896–1897), Monet did twenty-one soft, lush and subtle works known as *Mornings on the Seine.* These are beautiful poetic studies of the progress of the changing light of dawn. Monet arose at three or four in the morning in order to capture the eerie effects of the morning light on the misty river. The paintings were reminiscent of the masterful works of the revered Camille Corot.

Paintings from both the *Normandy* series and *Mornings on the Seine* were shown at an exhibit of Monet's work in June of 1898 at the Georges Petit Gallery. Anticipation was high, as it had been three years since Monet's last show, and the art world was anxious to see what the now very popular and respected Monet had been up to. The show was widely praised, and Monet's popularity increased even further. Within weeks he was the exclusive subject of a special supplement to the newspaper *Le Gaulois.* In it, Monet's work of the previous ten years was enthusiastically praised. It included a rather large photo by Nadar of the well-dressed, prosperous-looking artist.

Personal and Family Change—The 1890s

These years of extraordinary productivity and rising popularity were also a time of considerable activity and change in Monet's personal life. He had become increasingly attached to his family since they all moved to Giverny in 1883. As he traveled during the 1880s, his letters often mentioned how much he missed them. During the 1890s, when he was at home for longer periods, he became more involved with the activities of the household.

In March 1891 Ernest Hoschedé died in Paris. Alice was at his side and brought the body back for burial. After a tasteful interim, Alice and Monet legalized their relationship and were wed in a civil ceremony at Giverny on July 16, 1892. Caillebotte and Monet's brother Léon were witnesses.

At the time of the wedding the Monet and Hoschedé children were almost all adults, and as they started having careers and families of their own, Monet took an active interest in their lives. He wanted to keep his clan together and was often overprotective of them. In the early 1890s, for example, he objected to the involvement of Blanche Hoschedé, then in her mid-twenties, with an American painter. The young man was part of a colony of primarily American artists that had settled in Giverny in the late 1880s in order to paint and be close to the master. Monet, who never did take students, was not always pleased by their presence. Evidently Monet's objection to this particular painter was simply because he was an American, and unable to support a wife. He was also especially protective of Blanche, as she was the only one of the children to show any real artistic skill. No marriage took place.

Blanche's younger sister Suzanne was also pursued by an American, Theodore Butler. After initial resistance from Monet, the two were married on July 20, 1892, just four days after her mother's wedding. Her stepfather gave her away.

Monet's concern with family matters was particularly intense during 1895. His winter visit to Norway had been primarily motivated by his need to have a talk with his stepson Jacques. Evidently the twenty six year old's lack of communication with his mother had upset her, and Monet wanted to find out when he was coming back to Giverny.

After returning from Norway, Monet spent much of the summer of 1895 taking care of Alice, Blanche and Suzanne Hoschedé, who had all become ill.

The family was particularly concerned about Suzanne, who had never regained her health after the birth of her second child in late 1894. Monet spent considerable time attending to her and taking her to Paris for special medical help. She never did regain her health and died in 1899 at age thirty.

The Monet/Hoschedé families were further blended in June of 1897 when Monet's son Jean married his stepsister Blanche Hoschedé. Evidently there was some concern about the relationship on Monet's part. The couple moved to Rouen, where Jean went to work for his uncle Léon and Blanche pursued her painting. And sometime later there was another unusual interfamily marriage of sorts when, after just twenty months, the widower Theodore Butler married his deceased wife's older sister, Marthe Hoschedé. This new family, including the two Butler children, stayed close to Giverny. Monet was able to enjoy his grandchildren.

As the importance of his family increased and he spent more time with them, Monet also put his energies into their extraordinary home. In late 1890, with the aid of an advance from Durand-Ruel, Monet was able to purchase the Giverny home for twenty-two thousand francs. Soon afterward he hired gardeners to help him develop his property into a well-planned and densely planted series of gardens. These provided Monet with an enjoyable avocation and the subject matter for hundreds of paintings. He became intensely interested in plants and took an active role in the planning. The house was enlarged and improved, as Monet and Alice evidently expected their now-grown children to be around for quite a while.

In February 1893 Monet made another purchase in the area. This time he bought the irregular plot of land down the hill to the south and across the railroad tracks from his property. He immediately started to turn the marshy land into a water garden, with a large pool and a small Japanese-style footbridge. His plan included some damming and diverting of the river, which was not popular with the locals. They were concerned that Monet's strange decorative plants might poison the water supply. There was official resistance, and Monet had difficulty in getting the required permits. At one point in the process, a frustrated Monet told Alice:

> throw the water plants into the river; they will grow there....Shit on the Giverny natives, the engineers.

After protracted negotiations the permits were finally issued. Monet continued to refine, enlarge and change the pond periodically over the rest of his life as his art became increasingly focused on it.

In 1895 Monet was once more embroiled in a controversy with local officials. This time it seems that the town council of Giverny wanted to sell a piece of land to a chemical company to build a starch factory. Monet was greatly concerned, as he feared this would disturb the tranquil beauty of the area. He wrote letters to the mayor and even used his connections in Paris to put pressure on the local government. All this was to no avail, so he finally offered five thousand francs to the town if it wouldn't sell the land for fifteen years. The offer was turned down. The persistent and now angry Monet raised his offer to 5,500 francs and, after another eight months of argument, it was accepted.

While involved in all these activities, the driven Monet somehow managed to play an active role in the art world of Paris. During the 1890s he regularly traveled to the capital to arrange for his exhibits and to deal with Durand-Ruel and others. He had by then become a very astute marketer of his works. He continued to be involved with some of his old Impressionist friends, visiting with Pissarro and Renoir a number of times and keeping in touch with Cézanne. Of a visit to Giverny in 1894, Cézanne would later recall:

> Monet is a great lord who treats himself to the haystacks that he likes. If he likes a little field, he buys it. With a big flunky and some dogs that keep guard so that no one comes to disturb him. That's what I need.

Monet was especially fond of Cézanne's works and built a fine collection of his paintings, which he proudly showed to visitors.

Monet was also active in helping with issues arising from the death of some of the Impressionists. After Berthe Morisot died in 1895, Monet went to Paris to help install her memorial exhibition at Durand-Ruel's. Monet was especially touched after learning she had requested that he choose one of her paintings from the estate for his own collection.

Monet was also involved with the events that occurred after the death of his friend and supporter Gustave Caillebotte in 1894. Caillebotte had left his large Impressionist collection to the State, and this was not a desirable event for some of the more conservative officials. Resistance and much controversy ensued over how many paintings of each artist could be on display in the Luxembourg Museum, as well as a guarantee that the collection would eventually be transferred to the Louvre. Complex and lengthy negotiations ensued, with typical bureaucratic inefficiencies. But in the end, the works were accepted by the State, and today they form the core of the renowned Impressionist collection at the Musée d'Orsay in Paris.

Monet's activities following the death of Alfred Sisley give us some insight into his more human and considerate side. Just before Sisley died in January of 1899, he poignantly asked to see his old friend Monet. He and Alice along with Pissarro and Renoir were among the few mourners at the funeral. Monet quickly moved to help the Sisley children by arranging an auction of their father's work. Monet donated one of his paintings done in Norway and helped keep the bidding going by buying one of Sisley's works for his own collection.

The End of the Century

By the end of the 1890s, Monet had been painting for over forty years. He was now widely recognized and financially well off. During those years he had painted hundreds of pictures of many of the most beautiful sights in France, uniquely capturing the beauty of his native country. This nationalistic aspect of Monet's work was summed up by the writer Raymond Bouyer in 1899:

> Monet's work above all expresses France, at once subtle and ungainly, refined and rough, nuanced and flashy—[Monet is] our greatest national painter; he knows the beautiful elements of our countryside whether harmonious or contradictory...the contours of the cliffs effaced by fog, the water running under the fresh foliage, the wheatstacks erected on the naked plains; he has expressed everything that forms the soul of our race—an article of faith: for me [Monet] is the most significant painter of the century; yes, of the century.

After about 1898 Monet's subject matter changed. He no longer roamed his country in search of its unusual and beautiful sights. Over the next twenty-eight years of his life, of the over five hundred paintings he completed, only ten or fifteen would be of a truly French scene. He completed about 140 on foreign trips to London and Venice. Almost all of the rest are paintings of his own flowers and water gardens at Giverny.

The reasons for this change are not clear. Certainly his age and his desire to be at home with family were very important. Also, his financial success allowed him to do and paint as he pleased, and much of his pleasure now came from his unique gardens at Giverny. However, another element also seems to have played a role in his change of focus. Monet, like the rest of his fellow countrymen, was deeply affected by the notorious and nationally shattering Dreyfus Affair, which dominated French life for several years. A different aspect of Monet is revealed as we look at his reaction to this drama.

Monet was generally not very active or vocal politically. Other things demanded his thoughts and energies. But the controversy and moral issues involved in the Dreyfus case deeply affected him. His personal connection to the case was his friend Émile Zola who, with his biting articles, became a major player in the drama. After Zola's two articles defending Dreyfus appeared in 1897, Monet wrote to him:

> Bravo and bravo again for the two beautiful articles...You alone have said what must be said and you have done it so well. I am happy to extend to you all of my compliments.

Several months later, just after Zola's explosive article "J'accuse" appeared in Clemenceau's paper, Monet again wrote:

> Bravo once again, and all of my heartfelt sentiments for your valor and your courage.

The usually uninvolved but now engaged Monet signed a *Manifesto of the Intellectuals* demanding that all the truth be exposed. This was later published in January 1898, after Zola's trial; Monet wrote to him again, saying he had been unable to attend the trial because of ill health:

> Sick and surrounded by others who are ill, I could not come to your trial and shake your hand, as had been my desire. That has not stopped me from following all of the reports with passion. I want to tell you how much I admire your courageous and heroic conduct. You are admirable. It is possible that when calm is restored, all sensible and honest people will pay you homage. Courage, my dear Zola, with all my heart.

The whole episode seemed to change Monet's view of his country. He painted very little for almost a year. Then, in September of 1899 Monet, Alice and Germaine Hoschedé left France for a six-week stay in London.

Monet had grown more fond of England since his short and not particularly pleasant self-exile there in 1870–1871. He traveled to Great Britain several times in the 1890s and sent his sons there to study and learn English. The trip in 1899 was the first of three he was to make during an eighteen-month period. While there he stayed at the expensive and fashionable Savoy Hotel, on the north embankment of the Thames. Since the hotel had glassed-in balconies overlooking the river, Monet was able to paint essentially *en plein air* but with the comfort of being indoors.

Monet was fascinated by the city and the unusual foggy scenes along the river. He told a friend some years later:

> I so love London but I love it only in winter. It's nice in summer with its parks, but nothing is like it in winter with the fog, for without the fog London wouldn't be a beautiful city. It's the fog that gives it its magnificent breadth. Those massive, regular blocks become grandiose within that mysterious cloak.

The result of his three trips was nearly one hundred canvases—the largest series of paintings that he ever produced. There are really three sub-series—*The Charing Cross Bridge* (which was upriver to his right), *The Waterloo Bridge* (downriver to his left) and *The Houses of Parliament.* To get the proper angle on the Parliament buildings he moved across the river to paint from St. Thomas' Hospital. The paintings depict the rich and heavy mist and the often grimy atmosphere of the city. He used short brush strokes, and the paintings have a certain eerie softness about them. The mistiness and the diffusion of light give form, but not sharp clarity, to the bridges and the buildings in the pictures. The views of the bridges often capture the energies of the city, with its traffic of cars and trains. The paintings of the Houses of Parliament portray it as a grand, Gothic monument bathed in often brilliantly diffused sunlight.

Monet worked very hard on the paintings and often had many in progress at once. His standard routine had him starting early and painting from the Savoy in the morning and early afternoon. Then he would move across the river to St. Thomas' Hospital to catch the afternoon sun on the Houses of Parliament. Throughout the day he would shift through his many works in

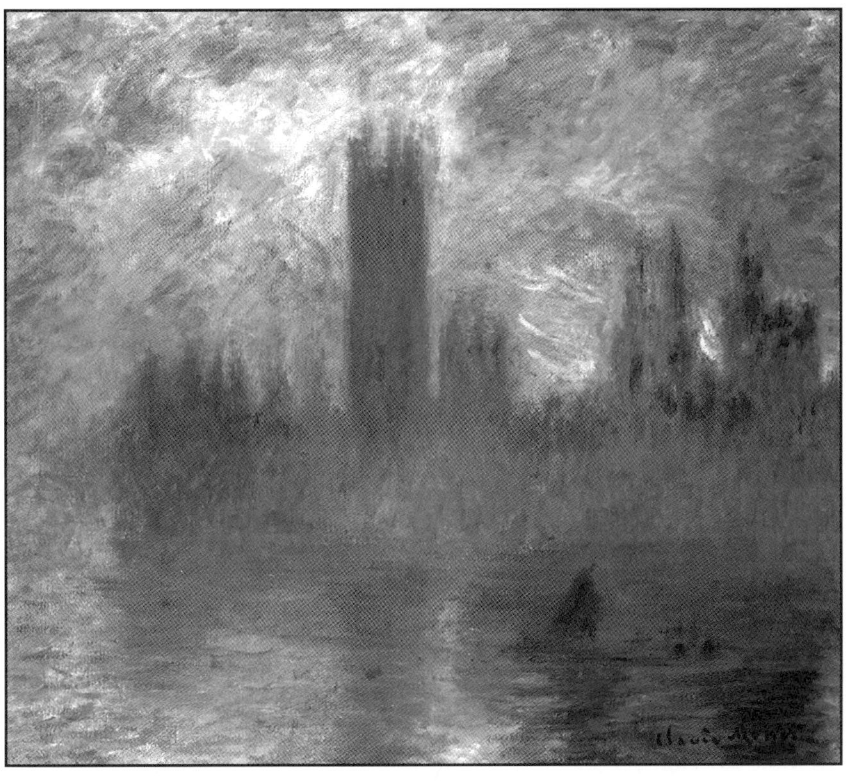

Misty view of the Houses of Parliament painted in 1900–1901 during one of Monet's trips to London. He often had over fifty of these canvases under way at one time.

Claude Monet, French, 1840–1926. Houses of Parliament, London, oil on canvas, 1900/01, 81 x 92 cm, Mr. and Mrs. Martin A. Ryerson Collection, 1933.1164

progress to find just the right one to record the particular effect of light and atmosphere that he wanted. At one point he had sixty-five paintings under way at once.

Very few of the works were completed in London, and Monet was often frustrated by his inability to capture just what he wanted. The canvases were brought back to Giverny, where Monet continued to work on them for several more years. In 1903, nearly two years after returning, he wrote to Durand-Ruel:

> No, I'm not in London except in thought; I'm working steadily on the paintings, which are giving me a lot of trouble. I cannot send you even one London paint-

> ing because, for the kind of work I am doing, it is vital to have them all before me at once, and in truth not one of them is definitely finished. I work on them altogether, or at least a sizable group of them, and I have no idea yet how many I shall be able to show, as what I am doing to them at the moment is very delicate. One day I feel satisfied, the next day everything looks bad again. But at least there have to be several that are good.

The paintings were not ready for exhibition until May 1904, over three years after he brought them to Giverny. Thirty-seven of them were exhibited at Durand-Ruel's. The show was Monet's most successful ever, a critical and financial triumph.

The fact that Monet finished his London paintings in his studio and not on site soon became widely known. Thus the myth that had built up about him painting only from nature and only in front of his subject was now shattered. Monet, who had encouraged the belief, was sensitive on the subject. He commented defensively:

> Whether my cathedral views, or my London views...are painted from life or not is nobody's business, and is of no importance...It's the result that counts.

The London experience was an artistic success, but it was also a physically exhausting experience for Monet, who was in his sixties and not always in the best of health. In addition to his painting in London, he had kept up an active social schedule, dining with many notables of English society. He also spent time with various celebrities, including the American novelist Henry James. He occasionally played tourist as well, visiting the Tower of London and viewing Queen Victoria's funeral procession. All this activity took its toll, and Monet had several bouts of illness, including a case of pleurisy in March of 1901 that kept him from painting for several weeks.

Focusing His Life and Work at Giverny

Monet's life became increasingly focused on Giverny after he purchased it in 1890. In the considerable time he spent there during the 1890s and early 1900s he constantly worked on developing his extensive gardens and the unusual water lily pond. Understandably, he did only a few paintings of the garden, as he was fully occupied with his series paintings and with cashing in on the thriving market for his works.

His first major effort to capture the beauty of his unique gardens was a group of eighteen views of the water lily pond and Japanese bridge done in 1899–1900. They are very focused, contemplative works that show a strong influence of the Japanese art that Monet so admired.

Further development and enlargement of the pond gave Monet even more intriguing subject matter, and after returning from London in 1901 he concentrated even more intensely on the unusual world he had created at Giverny. During approximately 1903–1908 he began over 150 pictures of his gardens. Frustration caused him to destroy many of them. The eighty or so that survive show Monet refining his techniques as he focused more closely on the flowers and the pond itself. The works in 1906–1907 are particularly important, as they concentrate *only on the pond* and exclude the bridge and the banks of the pond. Monet also did a lot of experimenting with various shapes and sizes of canvas during these years.

As with so many of his projects, this group of water lily paintings became an obsession with Monet. In August of 1908 he wrote to Geffroy:

> You should know that I am absorbed by my work. The landscapes of water and reflections have become an obsession. It is beyond my old man's powers, but nevertheless I want to render what I sense. I have destroyed some… and I began some again…and I hope that something will come from so many efforts.

After many delays, forty-eight of the works (called "landscapes of water") were finally shown to the public in May 1909 at Durand-Ruel's Gallery in Paris. Monet presided over the hanging of the show and was present at the opening. It was a major event, as recent works by Monet had not been exhibited since his London works were shown five years earlier. The critics were once again impressed by the astounding and innovative output of the sixty-nine-year-old artist. The Paris correspondent of *Burlington Magazine* wrote:

> One has never seen anything like it…These studies of water lilies and still water in every possible effect of light and at every hour of the day are beautiful to a degree which one can hardly express without seeming to exaggerate…There is no other living artist who could have given us these marvelous effects of light and shadow, this glorious feast of color.

It was the most successful show of Monet's career, and one of the most popular of any artist in the early decades of the twentieth century. The uniqueness and novel nature of these paintings mark the 1909 show as a significant point in the evolution of modern art.

Monet's intense work on his water lily paintings was occasionally interrupted by more relaxed and pleasurable activities. His now-considerable wealth funded a luxurious lifestyle. In addition to his expensive passion for gardening (at times he employed up to six gardeners), he was able to afford ample domestic help and fancy hand-tailored clothes and boots, and to indulge his fondness for good food and wine. His tasteful and energetic eating and drinking habits resulted in both an expanding girth for Monet and a desire by his friends for an invitation to dine with him at Giverny.

Travel and cars also became an outlet for his energies and wealth. He purchased his first car in 1901 and a second in 1904. He loved to ride around at high speeds—always, however, leaving the driving to his chauffeur, who was also his mechanic, wine steward and general assistant. It is recorded that he received a speeding ticket in 1904.

He pursued his interest in travel when he could find the time, and in 1904 he took Alice and his son Michel to Spain. He particularly wanted to see the works of the great seventeenth-century Spanish painter Diego Velázquez.

In 1908 he took Alice to Venice by train. It was to be the last major trip of his life. They stayed for two months, and Monet painted regularly throughout the visit. Monet had a routine where he worked on four different motifs, each for two hours a day. He and Alice were also able to enjoy the tourist sites and the vast collection of art in the city. Monet was particularly impressed by the murals of Tintoretto.

Just before leaving Venice in December 1908 Monet wrote to Geffroy:

> What a shame not to have come to Venice when I was younger and fully daring. But I have spent delicious moments here, practically forgetting how old I am.

A photo from the trip shows the couple, looking rather old and overweight, relaxing and feeding the pigeons in St. Mark's Square.

They returned to Giverny in mid-December of 1908 with thirty-six canvases. Monet hoped to go back to Venice the following year. These paintings, like his London works, were unfinished and required further extensive work in the studio. This did not happen for several years. When twenty-nine of them were finally shown in May 1912, they were subdivided into several groups of motifs (e.g., San Giorgio Maggiore, Grand Canal, various palaces, etc.). The reception was enthusiastic. The artist Paul Signac wrote to Monet:

> These Venice pictures, in which everything unites as the expression of your will, in which no detail runs counter to emotion...I admire them as the highest incarnation of your art.

Monet in His Early Seventies

After the happy trip to Venice, Monet spent a year busying himself with marketing his paintings, arranging exhibits and taking occasional car trips. He did very little painting. Often grouchy, he had periods of poor health and regularly complained about the weather. He was unable to return to Venice. Letters to friends express his concern over headaches and his inability to work.

The year 1910 began badly. There were January floods that submerged his water lily pond and much of the gardens. In February Alice became seriously ill with leukemia. She took radiation therapy but continued to deteriorate. Monet wrote to Geffroy:

> For a month she has had to suffer four crises, several very violent...it's devastating and it diminishes the benefits of the radiotherapy treatment.

Alice died on May 19, 1911, and was buried next to her first husband, Ernest Hoschedé, and her daughter Suzanne. The funeral brought out many of the remaining old Impressionists for the last time. The aging and nearly blind Degas attended. He was able to get around only with the aid of a cane.

Monet was devastated by the loss of his partner of over thirty years. After rereading Alice's letters, he burned them. He was unable to do anything for months. He wrote to a friend in August 1911:

> I am totally worn out....Time passes and I cannot make anything out of my sad existence. I don't have the taste for anything and don't even have the courage to write.

His friends, including Clemenceau, Geffroy and Renoir, came to Giverny to try to console him. Toward the end of 1911, as he contemplated taking up his brush, he told his stepdaughter Blanche that he was

> ...going to give up painting forever. All that I can do these days is completely ruin several Venice pictures which I will have to destroy—sad results. I should have left them just as they were, as souvenirs of such happy days spent with my dear Alice.

Monet characteristically bounced back, however, and by the spring of 1912 he had finished most of the Venice paintings and had them ready for the May exhibition. In spite of the general critical acclaim these works received, Monet remained depressed. He felt that the paintings were not up to his standard and not equal to the *Water Lilies*. To Geffroy he wrote:

> I would like to be as satisfied with them as you appear to be. There are some that are not bad but...I fear that your friendship blinds you.

And to Durand-Ruel he wrote:

> If for so long you have found me profoundly discontented with what I have been doing, that's because that has been how I really think. More than ever, I realize how little all the undeserved success I have had really counts. I always hope to do better, but age and pain have drained my strength. I know perfectly well in advance that you will judge my paintings perfect. I know that, if they are shown, they will have a great success, but I couldn't care less, since I know they are bad; I am sure of it.

He also expressed his morose and bitter mood to Paul Signac, who had praised the works. Monet wrote that even though

> the insidious critics of the first hour (of my career) have left me alone, I remain equally indifferent to the praises of imbeciles, snobs and traffickers.

During 1911–1912, following Alice's death, there was additional family stress. Monet argued with his stepson Jacques Hoschedé over Alice's estate, and also tried to secure a job for his stepdaughter Germaine's husband so she and her family could live close to Giverny. Of most concern, though, was the health of his forty-five-year-old son Jean. He and his wife Blanche (Monet's stepdaughter) had settled up the river not far from Giverny, where he was running a trout farm. In July 1912 Jean suffered a stoke and Monet was, of course, greatly distraught. Jean's condition never really improved, and Monet eventually moved him and Blanche to Giverny. As Jean's condition deteriorated, Monet expressed his anguish to a friend:

> What torture it is for me to witness this decline—there, in front of me, that's what's hard.

Jean died in February 1914. Monet wrote to Durand-Ruel:

> Our consolation is to think that he is no longer suffering, for he was a true martyr.

After Jean's death, Blanche gave up her own painting to run the house and look after Monet. She cared for the aging artist, helped arrange his painting sessions and accompanied him on his occasional trips outside of Giverny. Clemenceau called her the "angel" because of the caring and unselfish service she provided Monet.

To add to the seventy-four-year-old artist's woes, his second son, Michel, also had health problems. Shortly after Jean's funeral, Monet had to take him to Paris for an operation. Concurrently, Monet was also suffering ill health. In addition to severe headaches, he started to have trouble with his eyes. In July 1912, shortly after Jean's stroke, he was diagnosed as having cataracts. His doctors concluded that "the right eye no longer sees anything, the other is also slightly affected," and they suggested that he undergo an operation. Clemenceau, who was also a medical doctor, counseled him to wait. Monet took his advice, but eye problems were a major concern for the rest of his life.

Monet's personal difficulties were but a small reflection of the catastrophe that would descend on France in 1914. In August of that year, the country was once again at war with the hated Germans. Monet, like all Frenchmen, was deeply and directly affected by the conflict. Within days of its start, he sent his stepson Jean-Pierre Hoschedé off to fight. His son Michel was to go the following March. At one point, the front line of the battle was only some forty kilometers from Giverny. The usually uninvolved Monet joined several patriotic committees, donated money to help the soldiers, and participated in a number of sales and exhibits that were staged to fund relief efforts. He even donated most of the produce from his garden to wounded soldiers at a nearby army hospital.

His Art at Giverny

Monet's response to the war and to his personal tragedies was to focus even more strongly on his work. He was determined to carry on doing what he did best—painting. In September of 1914 he expressed his mood to Geffroy:

> As for me, I'm here, and if those savages must kill me, it will be in the midst of my canvases, in front of my life's work.

In December of 1914 he again wrote to Geffroy:

> I am back at work; it is still the best way not to think too much about current woes, even though I should be a bit ashamed to think about little investigations into forms and colors while so many people suffer and die for us.

His work was now entirely focused on his exceptional and lush gardens at Giverny. He started painting much larger pictures, partly to compensate for his continuing eye problems. During the war years he completed around sixty large canvases of the water garden. These are among the most interesting and vibrant works of his career. They depict the unusual flowers and their reflections in a unique, fresh and loose style, and they demonstrate once again Monet's unparalleled ability to use color and forms in new and different ways.

During 1914 Monet also started a project that was to evolve into his most monumental and unique series of paintings. His work on them was to engage his energies right up to the time of his death. These were the *Grand Decorations*—a series of large decorative panels that focused solely on the changing images of the water lily pond. They are also known as the *Water Lilies* or *Nymphéas.*

Monet had been thinking about doing a series of large mural decorations for many years. Back in 1897 he had expressed this concept to the journalist Guillemot:

> Imagine a circular room, the dado below the wall molding, entirely filled with a plane of water scattered with these plants, transparent screens sometimes green, sometimes mauve. The calm, silent, still waters reflecting the scattered flowers,

> the colors evanescent, with delicious nuances of dream-like delicacy.

Now, at last, he was ready to begin in earnest. But as he plunged into the enterprise with his typical enthusiasm, it soon became evident that the works, which are each over six feet high and twenty to fifty-five feet long, would require a much larger studio. In July of 1915 he acquired a permit to build alongside the main house. Using his connections, Monet was able to procure the required building materials, a difficult task in wartime France. By November of 1915 he was working in his new, very large, sky-lit studio. It cost him about forty thousand francs—nearly twice what he paid for the house and property in 1890.

Word of his new project spread, and visitors came to Giverny to see Monet's unique painting. They were impressed. The artist Edouard Vuillard wrote after a visit:

> Monet's large canvases, like the ceiling of the Sistine Chapel, suggest rhythm and color, all works linked by a majestic lyricism.

Monet worked on the huge paintings throughout the war. He planned a total of twelve canvases, and by early 1918 had finished eight.

While his artistic energies were focused on these *Grand Decorations,* he also had a social life that increasingly reflected his stature as a revered figure in French art. Streams of visitors came to Giverny. A day spent with Monet at Giverny was a real honor for the privileged few he would agree to see. Blanche served as the screen and protector of Monet. Increasingly, he preferred to spend his non-working time with a few old friends. He continued to have periods of depression and extreme frustration, as is shown in this letter to one of his dealers:

> Just now I have thrown myself into transformations on my large canvases…and my mood is foul. I lost things that had gone well that I wanted to improve, and I must recover them by whatever means.

At times, he told others that he realized he did not have many years left. In a letter of 1918 he wrote:

> I do not have long to live, and I must dedicate all of my time to painting, with the hope of arriving at something that is good, or that satisfies me, if that is possible.

While Monet's world was centered at Giverny, and most of his contact with the outside world came through the periodic visitors he received, his fame was spreading across the world. Throughout the second decade of the 1900s, there were frequent exhibits of Monet's paintings in America as well as in France. His works attracted the attention of a number of major international collectors, including museums and individuals in Boston, Chicago, New York and Tokyo. Prices were high, and Monet continued to do very well financially.

A special honor was bestowed on Monet in July 1914, when fourteen of his paintings were hung in the Louvre as part of a bequest from a Parisian collector. The occasion was highly significant, as it contradicted the museum's policy of not showing works by a living artist. Monet expressed his consistent distaste for such events and declined to attend the opening, claiming he had to work.

Further diverting Monet from his painting, and adding to his frequent depression, were the deaths of some of his long-time friends and associates. The year 1917 was a particularly sorrowful time for him. In February his friend, the critic and writer Octave Mirbeau died, and Monet was overcome with grief at his funeral. Degas died in September of that year, and the sculptor Rodin in November. The only other remaining impressionist, Renoir, was to hold on until December of 1919. When he died, Monet wrote to a friend:

> With him goes part of my life...it's hard to be alone, though no doubt it's not for long, as I am feeling my age more and more with each day that passes.

Amazingly, in between his extensive work on his *Decorations,* his occasional trips outside of Giverny and his periodic entertaining, Monet was able to complete a number of other paintings of different parts of the garden. Of particular note are a series of ten paintings of a weeping willow tree that grew at one end of his water lily pond. These works, mostly done in 1918, have a certain starkness and anguish to them that probably reflects the growing pessimism of Monet and his countrymen regarding the war. (The Germans appeared to have the upper hand in the fighting at that time.) He also completed a number of other paintings of his garden in these years, including several of the now richly covered Japanese bridge. Some of these are among the most original and nontraditional of all of Monet's works. They indicate that he was possibly being influenced by (or reacting to) some of the more modern schools of painting that were influencing French art in the early twentieth century.

Monet's Final Years

Monet's last years were dominated by increasingly serious eye problems and by his struggle to finish, and determine the eventual fate of, his monumental *Decorations* paintings.

When the war ended in November 1918, Monet, like the rest of the French, felt great relief and pride. Wanting to do his part in the celebration, he wrote to Clemenceau, who had been named Prime Minister in November 1917:

> I am on the verge of finishing two decorative panels that I want to sign on the day of the Victory and am going to ask you to offer them to the State...It's not much, but it is the only way I have of taking part in the victory. I would like these two panels to be placed in the Museum of Decorative Arts and would be happy that they were chosen by you.

He offered a water lily painting and one from the *Weeping Willow* series. The offer was much appreciated, but Clemenceau soon convinced Monet that the gift should not be just the two, but all twelve of the large decorative panels that he had been working on since 1914. The two old friends then set out on a path that would eventually lead to a total of twenty-two panels being installed in the Orangerie in Paris shortly after Monet's death.

It took Monet eight more years to finish the paintings. The negotiations with the state to find and prepare a proper space for the works were especially difficult. Clemenceau, who had long been an avid proponent of Monet's work and was now a close friend, spearheaded the effort. Even after he lost the election for the French presidency in 1920 and resigned as Prime Minister, he continued to use his influence with the State to get the project completed.

The original plan was to build a new structure on the grounds of the Hôtel Biron (Rodin's home and studio), which had been left to the French government when the sculptor died in 1917. The proposal called for a single circular room to house the twelve giant panels. Before arrangements were finalized, though, problems cropped up. There was a debate in Parliament about the appropriateness of the State, still in an economic crisis from the war, spending up to eight hundred thousand francs to house these unusual works, which few people had ever seen. Monet also did not help his standing with the officials in Paris when he turned down an offer to be nominated to the famous Institute of France. He once again showed his distaste for the official establishment in his reply:

> I thank you gentlemen, but I have always been, I am, and always shall be, independent.

After much discussion and examination of alternatives, a revised plan was finally negotiated. On April 12, 1922, Monet signed the Act of Donation. It called for nineteen, not twelve, panels to be installed in two special oval-shaped rooms in the Orangerie in the Tuileries. This obviously meant even more work for the now-eighty-one-year-old Monet, who had already been working on the project for eight years. He not only had to begin the additional panels, but he also had to rethink the whole design, since all the panels had to fit together in two rooms.

One interesting by-product of the protracted negotiations gave Monet special pleasure as well as financial gain. In 1920, as part of his agreement to donate his water lily panels, he persuaded the State to buy his painting *Women in the Garden* for two hundred thousand francs. The irony must have been especially pleasing to Monet as this work, now fifty years old, had been rejected for the Salon of 1867.

Monet's work over the next four years was made very difficult by his eye problems. His eyesight had been declining for over ten years, and he compensated by producing larger pictures, using brighter colors, and often painting in a more abstract and less representational style. He, of course, was determined to carry on nevertheless, and was quoted in a 1921 magazine article:

> Alas, I see less and less...I used to paint out-of-doors facing the sun. Today I need to avoid lateral light, which darkens my colors. Nevertheless, I always paint at the times of day most propitious for me, as long as my paint tubes and brushes are not mixed up...I will paint almost blind as Beethoven composed completely deaf.

In September of 1922 a Paris ophthalmologist told Monet that he was legally blind in his right eye and had only ten percent vision in his left. An operation was recommended. Monet resisted, afraid of the painful and risky procedure, fearing it might leave him permanently blind. He finally agreed, and a series of three operations was performed in 1923. After initial disappointment, they were considered a success, and his vision and color recognition improved. A fourth operation was recommended, but Monet had had enough. He decided instead to use glasses that were specially designed to correct some of the color problems he was still having. He experimented with a number of these special glasses as his eyes continued to deteriorate. His eyesight never did return to anything close to normal, and he had persistent problems with certain colors. However, with a combination of medical and optical technology, plus his own skills and determination, Monet was able to complete some of his most innovative and beautiful paintings in the final years of his life.

The now very moody and often discouraged Monet struggled to finish the panels. He went through periods when he painted very little and felt he couldn't go on. Clemenceau was particularly influential in pushing the old artist to complete his project. In 1924 he negotiated an extension on the contract after Monet missed a deadline. At times when Monet became disheartened and wasn't working, Clemenceau would intervene if he thought the artist was just procrastinating. In October 1924 Clemenceau became particularly angered at Monet's stalling and his seemingly never-ending refinements. He wrote to the artist:

> First you wanted to finish the incomplete parts. That was hardly necessary, but understandable. Then you had the absurd idea to improve the others. Who knows better than yourself that a painter's ideas are constantly changing? If you went back to your Rouen Cathedral paintings, you would change them. You made new works, the majority of which were and still are masterpieces, if you have not ruined them. Then you wanted to make super-masterpieces—and with an impaired visual faculty that you yourself refused to have corrected...At your request a contract was completed between yourself and France. The State has kept its part. You asked for a postponement of your deadline and with my intervention you got it. I acted in good faith and now you make me appear like a conspirator who does a disservice both to art and to France to accommodate a friend's foibles...You must finish this honorably.

Still discouraged in early 1925, Monet told an official of the State that he was backing out of the deal. Again, Clemenceau intervened and angrily wrote to Monet:

> I don't care how old, how exhausted you are and whether you are an artist or not. You have no right to break your word of honor, especially when it was given to France.

Clemenceau also called Monet a spoiled child and told him that their friendship depended on his completing his obligation.

Soon Monet got over his depression and was back at work. By July he would write:

> I warn you in advance that I must be free at 10:00 a.m., being hard at work with an unequal joy, for since your last visit in April, my vision is completely improved. I am working as never before, satisfied with what I am doing, and if the new eyeglasses are still better, then I ask only that I live to be a hundred years old.

He worked diligently through the next months, and in February of 1926 he could tell Clemenceau, their friendship now restored, that the first set of panels was set for shipment as soon as the paint was dry.

In his last years Monet still liked to work out-of-doors if the weather permitted. Blanche was his constant companion and assistant in helping him with his materials. His life became even more centrally focused on his work in Giverny, and he rarely left the grounds. His painting was interrupted only by his health problems and the frequent visitors who came to Giverny to pay homage and often to buy some of the many paintings he had for sale there.

By April of 1926 Monet's health had again seriously deteriorated. In April he wrote a friend:

> I have not been doing very well for the past two months…I'm feeling old and weak.

In that same month, Clemenceau visited Monet to tell him that their friend Geffroy had died. After the visit Clemenceau wrote:

> The human machine is coming apart at the seams. He is stoic and even gay at moments. His panels are finished and will not be touched again. But it is beyond

> his powers to separate them from himself...The poor Monet did not even find the strength to make a tour of his garden and the expense becomes such that he asked if it would not be best to give it up.

In late August Monet was diagnosed with pulmonary sclerosis. During this depressing period, Monet decided to destroy some of his works that didn't satisfy him. He told visitors in July that he had slashed over sixty paintings, but Blanche later said that was an exaggeration.

Monet had one last burst of energy in October. He wrote to a friend in Paris:

> I have regained my courage and despite my weakness am back at work in very small doses.

He also requested that an architect who was working on the Orangerie come to Giverny so they could discuss some details of the *Decorations* project.

Clemenceau visited regularly during Monet's last days, trying to comfort the failing artist. He was there on December 5 when Monet died at 1:00 P.M. Also at his bedside were Blanche and his son Michel.

There was a small, simple ceremony three days later in Giverny. The non-religious Monet had requested no prayers, no eulogies, not even flowers. He was laid to rest in an unmarked grave next to his second wife, Alice, her first husband, Ernest Hoschedé, his first son, Jean, and his two stepdaughters, Suzanne and Marthe. Despite Monet's wishes for a small, low-key event, there was considerable press coverage, and a crowd showed up at Giverny.

Shortly after the funeral, the large panel canvases were shipped to Paris. There were twenty-two of them, not nineteen. They were carefully mounted so that the edges between the panels were obscured and they appeared seamless and continuous.

The opening of Monet's final and most outstanding works took place on May 17, 1927. The reviews were generally, but not unanimously, favorable. As time has passed, though, the works have been universally recognized as truly great. One artist, some years after Monet's death, called the Orangerie "the Sistine Chapel of Impressionism."

Monet's Personal Characteristics

In order to fill out our picture of Monet more completely, let us examine his personal characteristics.

Appearance

By all accounts, Monet was a handsome, well-built man who had a strong physical presence. He was about five feet six inches tall and over the years added considerable weight to his strong frame. As a twenty-one year old about to be shipped off to Africa, he was a handsome, clean-shaven youth. He grew a beard soon after his return to Paris in the mid-1860s, and it dominated his strong face for the rest of his life. In later years, the beard turned a grayish white and was quite long. When he was young, he had thick brown hair that was quite striking. It, too, turned gray as Monet aged. In his middle years, Monet was variously described as "tall with long hair," a "big strapping fellow—pale and hardy," and "a really handsome brunette with a beautiful beard made for the passage of beautiful fingers." Clemenceau's image of Monet at their first meeting in the 1860s was:

> A spirited character, with large fiery eyes, a curved nose that looked slightly Arabic and an unkempt black beard.

As the years passed, Monet's once-lean figure filled out as a result of his rather sedentary lifestyle and his fondness for food and wine. Nevertheless, he remained an impressive figure. From the early 1900s we have several descriptions of him:

> He is now sixty-two years of age, in the prime of his powers, active and dauntless as ever. Each line of his sturdy figure, each flash from his keen, blue eyes, betokens the giant within. He is one of those men who, through dogged perseverance and strength, would succeed in any branch of activity. Dressed in a soft khaki felt hat and jacket, lavender-colored silk shirt opened at the neck, drab trousers tapering to the ankles and there secured by big horn buttons, a short pair of cowhide boots, his appearance is at once practical and quaint, with a decided sense of smartness pervading the whole.

> Notwithstanding his sixty years, Claude Monet is robust and hardy as an oak. His face has been weathered by wind and sun; his dark hair is flecked with white; his shirt collar is open; and his clear, steel gray eyes are sharp and penetrating—they are the kind of eyes that seem to look into the very depths of things.—He has the exquisite and affable manners of a gentleman farmer.

Another description from several years before he died gives us a feeling for the strong, almost regal presence that surrounded this powerful personality:

> The master looks like a leader: full of vigor, simplicity, authority.—He beams like a beautiful portrait. The effect is so satisfying and surprising that some of the details are missed at first—the immaculate beard, the majestic bearing: these are tokens of longevity without its weaknesses. He looks like a poet's vision of old age. When he doffs the carefully dented, little hat he usually wears, his head appears to be without wrinkles: it is quite round and white, with the perfect contour of a snow-covered cupola. His eyes are bright as agates, darting a wild flash.—His habitual stance, his way of throwing back his head and chest with his arms at the ready while his feet remain solidly on the floor, this tough stance serves to remind us that painters are great fighters who size up the strength of an adversary who remains invisible to the ordinary person: nature.

Family

Next to his painting and its surrounding economic issues, family affairs were the most important part of Monet's life. Although he had an unusual and often difficult family situation for much of his life, he worked through a number of these problems and tragedies, and in fact enjoyed many years of the domestic stability that he seemed to need.

His early years as a struggling young painter were influenced by conflicts with his father, who had very little enthusiasm for his son's artistic ambitions. The two had a distant and often adversarial relationship regarding Monet's career, his affair with Camille, and financial support.

Monet's relationship with his older brother Léon was fairly normal. They kept in touch over the years, with Monet occasionally going to visit his prosperous brother at his home in Rouen or his vacation house on the Normandy coast. Léon seems to have had positive feelings about his brother Claude, as he was a witness at his wedding to Alice in 1892, and agreed to employ his son Jean during the 1890s.

There was a certain distance in many of Monet's family relationships. This, of course, is not unusual in many families, but it was probably accentuated by Monet's general self-centeredness and his driving obsession with his painting. We don't see the open affection or relaxed closeness that one would see in a more typical family situation. Monet was away for long periods, and when he was around he was often so caught up in his work that he had little time for other things.

Still, he must be described as a caring and dutiful father. Although he was very controlling and tended to want to manage his children's lives, he was a good provider and often quite generous with them. He grew especially fond of several of the Hoschedé daughters and enjoyed using them as models.

The real emotional center of Monet's life was his relationship with his second wife, Alice. Unlike his affair and marriage to Camille, his thirty-plus years with Alice gave the more mature Monet the strength and stability he needed. Their relationship was not without conflict, and the often ill-tempered and depressed Monet surely taxed the patience of the more calm and steady Alice. But they did achieve a genuine closeness. Alice was his friend, somebody he could confide in, and a very important part of his life. The influence she had on him while not generally acknowledged, was considerable.

Finances

Looking back across Monet's life, we can discern a fairly steady path of increasing economic success from his very early years when he no doubt was quite poor, through his middle years when his earnings were substantial but he claimed poverty, to his final thirty or so years when he was truly well-to-do.

His problems were mainly because of his spending, not his lack of earnings. He liked material things such as clothes, food, wine, servants, gardeners and a decent place to live. In addition, the cost of his supplies, the expenses associated with his painting excursions, and the packing and shipping of his works amounted to substantial sums. Furthermore, after about 1890 his expenditures at Giverny were extremely high. He appears to have spared no expense in building and maintaining, and then often rebuilding, his extensive gardens and water lily pond. He also expanded the house several times, and in 1915 built the huge and expensive studio to hold his monumental water lily *Decorations.*

These expenditures often went beyond his generally high but often irregular income. To fill in the gaps, he regularly begged and cajoled friends and dealers into giving him loans or advances on yet-to-be-completed paintings. He often portrayed himself, in a very whiny tone, as being in extreme poverty.

He was an honorable man, though; he always repaid his loans and fulfilled his promises of producing paintings for those who had given him advance payments. He was also often generous in helping out others in need, from fellow artists down on their luck to suffering war victims.

By the time he was forty, Monet had developed into an astute marketer of his paintings. After about 1880 he employed a variety of outlets for his works, including holding his own exhibitions, selling to private collectors and working with dealers such as Durand-Ruel and Georges Petit. In his later years he added other dealers, often playing them off against one another. He was quite sensitive to the changing demand for his paintings and would move his prices accordingly. His grasp of how the art market worked and what it wanted was extremely sophisticated.

By the last years of his life Monet was truly a wealthy man leading a very affluent life at his private estate at Giverny. He maintained a high income in these later years through a combination of selling his new works, the occasional selling off of earlier paintings he kept in inventory, and the earnings from some investments. Monet was not just the artistic leader of the Impressionists; he was also, by far, the most successful financially.

Personality and Relationships

Like many great and creative people, Monet was a complex man with often contradictory character traits. His reputation was of a loner who was often depressed, ill-tempered and moody. He cherished and needed his privacy so he could go about his work in intense solitude. When things weren't going well, he could be particularly grouchy and unpleasant. He was self-centered, very competitive and controlling, and he wouldn't stand for advice or any type of condescension. He had a strong sense of self that was both a major factor in his success and a source of arrogance and selfishness.

He was not the type of person one would think would have a lot of friends. Yet, like many strong personalities, he did attract people. Throughout his life, he had a number of enjoyable relationships and developed some lasting friendships. In his frequent periods of self-doubt and depression, he would turn to friends such as Clemenceau and Geffroy for assurance and persuasion to carry on.

A series of comments by himself, his family and some of his acquaintances gives us further insight into Monet's character. Writing to Alice in 1892, Monet described some of his traits:

> I can certainly account for my state of mind. I am a proud person with a devilish self-esteem.

His stepson Jean-Pierre recalled Monet:

> At once these villagers considered Monet a proud man—that is to say, a man with few friendly ties, who did not chat and who especially avoided gossip and useless banalities.

The American painter Lilla Cabot Perry, who knew Monet in the years 1889 through 1909, wrote a number of complimentary things about him:

> The man himself, with his rugged honesty, his disarming frankness, his warm and sensitive nature, was fully as impressive as his pictures, and from this first visit dates a friendship which led us to spend ten summers at Giverny.

> Monet was a man of his own opinions, though he always let you have yours and liked you all the better for being outspoken about them.

> In spite of his intense nature and at times rather severe aspect, he was inexpressibly kind to many a struggling, young painter. He never took any pupils, but he would have made a most inspiring master if he had been willing to teach.

> This serious, intense man had a most beautiful tenderness and love for children, birds and flowers, and this warmth of nature showed in his wonderful, warm smile, a smile no friend of his can ever forget. His fondness for flowers amounted to a passion and when he was not painting, much of his time was spent working in his garden.

The poet Maurice Rollinat summed up some of the complexities of Monet's character this way:

> Don't try to disparage yourself; you are simultaneously the absolute type of the sincere artist and the best man we have known. You always have a sympathetic word, a good smile and a kind look, even when you are most tired or most preoccupied.

Interests and Beliefs

We have very little record of what Monet really thought about subjects other than painting. His correspondence is filled mainly with talk of his work, as well as occasional references to his family. His one major interest besides painting was his gardens, which were, of course, closely related to his work.

This narrow view of the man, while not altogether inaccurate, does not give a complete picture of him. He did in fact have other interests that show up from time to time. A number of writers have mentioned stimulating sessions with Monet and other young Impressionists, sitting in cafes and discussing issues of the day. An article by Geffroy describes the scene:

> It was in the period from 1890 to 1894 that, through Monet, I met the Impressionist painters. I had the honor to be included in their monthly dinners held at the Café Riche. Besides Claude Monet, those present at the dinners were Camille Pissarro, Auguste Renoir, Alfred Sisley, Gustave Caillebotte, Doctor de Bellio, Théodore Duret, Octave Mirbeau, and sometimes Stéphane Mallarmé.
>
> These were evenings of conversation, where the events of the day were discussed with the open-mindedness of artists far removed from any official organization. I must admit that the company of Impressionists was a fairly boisterous one, and that these men, relaxing from their cares and their work, displayed the high spirit of children off from school.
>
> Like Caillebotte, Pissarro and Monet were avid readers, with a taste both refined and discerning. I remember a heated debate for and against Victor Hugo, wherein all our passions came into play, all our ardor, and all our wisdom; we left, reconciled, to go sit at some outdoor café or other and wonder at the ever-enchanting fairy-tale spectacle of Paris at night.

We can get some sense of Monet's political beliefs from his reaction to the suppression of the Commune and the Dreyfus Affair. In these incidents, Monet demonstrates a definite leaning to the left and an anti-government bias.

Monet loved books, and his large library contained works by prominent writers such as Balzac, Flaubert, Hugo, Baudelaire, Hardy, Montaigne and Dante. His regular reading included newspapers and general periodicals, as well as a large number of artistic publications. He paid particular attention to what critics were saying about him.

As he grew more famous, he attracted a number of prominent people to his circle. By age fifty or so, he could count among his friends a wide variety of leading intellectuals and writers. These relationships were important to him, and he more than held his own in their discussions.

In spite of the clear evidence that Monet had an active and sharp mind whose range of interest sometimes went beyond his own artistic world, we really know very little of his basic philosophical beliefs. We do know that he was a firm agnostic and had no time for formal religion. His lack of interest in such things is exemplified by the fact that he was many months into his project to paint the facade of the Rouen Cathedral before he even went inside the church. His strong philosophical feelings were saved for the unending wonders of nature and for capturing its beauty and mystery.

Monet's Works

Monet's output was enormous. There are over two thousand surviving oil paintings, plus some six hundred caricatures, sketches and pastels. The serenity and peacefulness he so often conveyed in his paintings do not reflect the tremendous energy, planning, frustration and plain hard work that went into them.

General Approach

Monet was not a theorist and had little time for academic approaches to art. He never really taught others what he had learned and did very little formal writing regarding technique or approach. We can, however, get a sense of his thoughts and instincts from his letters and from reports of his contemporaries. When asked to define himself as a painter in 1914, Monet replied:

> I have no idea how to answer you...since I only draw with a brush and with color, and have always refused (even when asked by my close friends) to attempt a style of work about which I know nothing...

Nature was at the center of his approach to painting. When he did give advice to artists, it was always to go back to nature and record what they saw. In the last years of his life, he again returned to this thought:

> I have always had a horror of theories...My only merit is that I have painted directly from nature, seeking to convey my impressions of her most elusive effects—

But the way Monet saw things was different. He once talked about his approach to a neighbor at Giverny:

> When you go out to paint, try to forget what objects you have before you, a tree, a house, a field or whatever. Merely think here's a little square of blue, here an oblong of pink, here a streak of yellow, and paint it just as it looks to you, the exact color and shape, until it gives you your own naive impression of the scene before you.

He also told a friend that

> He wished he had been born blind and then had suddenly gained his sight so that he could have begun to paint...without knowing what the objects were that he saw before him.

In 1912, at the age of seventy-two, he told Geffroy:

> No, I am not a great painter, nor a great poet...I only know that I do what I can to express what I feel in the presence of nature.

In spite of his simplistic advice and his hesitancy to codify or theorize about his work, Monet approached painting in a very sophisticated and innovative manner.

Out-of-door Painting

Essential to any real appreciation of Monet's work is an understanding of his commitment to painting nature out-of-doors, on location—*en pleine air.* This imperative to out-of-door painting was a central but not universal or unbroken principle of most of the Impressionist painters. For Monet in particular, though, this approach was a dominant factor. It came from his awe and respect for nature, his evolution from traditional French landscape painting, and his obligation to capture scenes or motifs in a realistic and honest way.

Monet was not a purist, however. He had studios throughout most of his career, and they became increasingly important to him as he aged and his techniques changed. What does distinguish Monet is his deep commitment to painting directly from the subject as much as possible, and his apparent pleasure in pushing through physical hardship in order to do so.

This devotion to *pleine air* and his desire to capture the particular effects of light and atmosphere on a subject caused each painting session to be quite a production. He would explore an area for the right scene, then figure out the particular viewpoint and pictorial composition that he wanted. He would then need to transport his large supply of materials, often including a number of separate canvases. Then, since he was intent on capturing specific light effects, he would often have to return day after day. The writer Guy de Maupassant described Monet working on the coast at Etretat in 1896:

> Last year, right here, I often followed Claude Monet, who was in search of impressions. Actually, he was no longer a painter but a hunter. He went along followed by children who carried his canvases, five or six canvas, all depicting the same subject at different hours of the day and with different effects.
>
> He would take them up in turn, then put them down again, depending upon the changes in the sky. Standing before his subject, he waited, watched the sun and the shadows, capturing in a few brush strokes a falling ray of light or a passing cloud and, scorning false and conventional techniques, transfer them rapidly onto canvas.
>
> In this way I saw him catch a sparkling stream of light on a white cliff and fix it in a flow of yellow tones that strangely rendered the surprising and fugitive effects of that elusive and blinding brilliance.

Monet's own words also reflect his belief in studying his subject matter first-hand. In a letter to Alice from Belle-Ile, he wrote:

> In short, I adore the sea, but I know that to do her justice you have to view her every day, at all hours, and from the same point of vantage, so as to learn how she lives.

Subject Matter

The content of Monet's paintings, as well as his techniques and approach, changed considerably over the years. He began, of course, as a landscape and seascape painter, and his early works were of fairly conventional subjects along the coast and, later, in the Barbizon area. He then moved toward depicting more contemporary scenes that might include railroads, boats or buildings. He also began dealing with more modern subjects involving real, contemporary people in specific, recognizable situations; e.g., *Luncheon on the Grass* or *Bathers at La Grenouillère.* By the early 1880s he had mainly moved away from the contemporary and man-made, and focused strongly on capturing undisturbed natural scenes. His paintings from his numerous trips to the Mediterranean, Belle-Ile, the Normandy coast and the Creuse River concentrated on flowers, waves and rocks. During the 1890s his subject matter changed again. His artistic concerns and efforts now focused on the effects of light and atmosphere on a particular subject. The exact subject matter was less important than capturing the effects of the constantly changing "envelope" surrounding the subject. Monet chose a wide variety of subjects as vehicles for his explorations—wheatstacks, Rouen Cathedral, scenes on the Seine, poplar trees, bridges and buildings in London.

After the early 1900s Monet's subjects were primarily drawn from his environment at Giverny, where he rarely painted anything except his plants and the scenes around the water lily pond. In the last years of his life, he focused even more narrowly on the pond and the lilies themselves, ending up with almost abstract works that dealt solely with the quality of the painting and had little to do with the surrounding area. They show the ending point in his evolution, as he gradually moved away from dealing with individual elements of a scene towards more refined, inwardly focused and integrated works.

Even though Monet traveled extensively during certain periods of his life, he generally painted scenes close to where he lived. When he did travel, it was to find new sensations and new challenges. But these trips were just brief interludes away from the areas along the Seine where most of his work was done.

There were times in his career when the human figure played a significant role in his works. Up until around 1880, for example, people were often important parts of his landscape paintings, helping to define their scale and space. Many paintings primarily comprised of a human figure are of Camille and Monet's son Jean. He stopped painting these in the mid-1870s. After that, his figures became subordinate to his increasing concentration on grander, natural subjects.

Monet returned to figure painting between 1886 and 1890, at the urging of some of his fellow artists. At that point he had temporarily become dissatisfied with his landscape work. Characteristically, Monet threw himself into this new endeavor. He wrote Duret in 1887:

> I'm working as never before, at some new experiments, figures in the open air as I understand them, treated like landscapes. It's an old dream that constantly plagues me in which I want to realize once and for all; but it is so difficult! In a word, I am putting a great effort into it, and I'm so involved in it that it's almost making me ill.

During this period Monet was once again challenging himself, trying to stretch. He wrote to Geffroy in 1888:

I so want to prove that I can do something different.

The result of these efforts is a very significant group of paintings of the Hoschedé daughters, shown in various scenes close to Giverny.

Still-life painting never played a major role for Monet during any period in his life. But he did, from time to time, produce some stunning canvases of flowers, fruits or game birds. Often, these were painted for practical economic reasons because he felt there was a market for them. At other times, painting still lifes provided Monet with something to do when the weather was bad and he couldn't paint out-of-doors. He did very little still-life work after the mid-1880s, as by that time he had started to occupy his bad-weather days with the finishing touches on his landscapes. Probably his most famous still lifes are a set of unusual and beautiful decorative panels for a set of doors done for Durand-Ruel in 1883–1885.

Composition

Monet, along with most of the other Impressionists, was criticized early on for paying little attention to the organization and composition of his paintings. Critics felt that he just took any arrangement that nature offered and rendered it. In reality, though, by carefully selecting his viewpoint and by deciding how the scene and the forms in it could be cut by the canvas's edge, Monet carefully constructed the composition of each of his paintings. Japanese prints were particularly influential on him in this regard. His friend Geffroy described Monet's approach:

> Very slowly and carefully Monet seeks the aspect of nature which by its arrangement, form and horizon best suits the play of light, shadow and coloring in front of him.

His stepson, Jean-Pierre Hoschedé, gave this account of how Monet selected a viewpoint:

> If, during a walk in the countryside or in his gardens, Monet stopped...screwed up his eyes, shielding his eyes with his right hand to improve his vision, then stepped back and forward, moved a little to the right and then to the left, and then continued his walk, this very often meant that he had just selected a motif.

Monet often did very rough preliminary sketches to explore potential motifs and compositional scenes. The drawings were extremely basic, with no detail, and offered very little hint of what the final painting would be. The choice of composition was not always easy for Monet, and his letters often conveyed his frustration at getting just the right pictorial formation. To others, though, he had a unique ability in this area, gaining the respect and envy of two of his fellow Impressionists. Cézanne told a friend:

> How easy it is to deform that shape. I try as hard as I can, and find it terribly difficult. Monet has that great ability—he looks, and straight away draws in proportion.

Even the egotistical Degas praised Monet:

> Everything he does is always vertical, straight away, while I take such trouble and it's still not right.

Monet's compositional approaches evolved over the years. Early in his career, he dealt more with individual elements (people, boats, buildings, etc.) in fairly simple scenes. His elements were portrayed directly, with clearly defined relationships. Later, in the 1880s, he started to blend his elements into more decorative compositions. In the 1890s and later, there is less emphasis on line and texture, and his works blend the elements closely together.

Building the Painting

From some of the partially finished canvases that exist, we can get a sense of Monet's process in working on a painting. Like others, he would start out rough, covering the canvas with simple colors and only a hint of the specific subject matter. This primary lay-in, or *ébauche,* served as the base for the painting. It was generally done fairly quickly, and directly from nature; rarely did he do any preliminary drawings on the canvas. The work would then be built up with greater contrast, more intricate brush work and much more complex use of colors. He occasionally finished a work in one setting, adding new layers of paint on top of ones not yet dry. Other paintings went through many stages and were subject to much rework over longer periods.

Fortunately, we have some very helpful contemporary descriptions of Monet's techniques. In 1880 Duret described Monet's process:

> He places a clean canvas on his easel, and briskly starts to cover it with slabs of color which correspond to the colored patches shown him by the natural scene. Often during the first session he can only make an ébauche. The next day, returning to the same spot, he adds to the first sketch and the details are brought out, the contours sharpened.

Several years later, Geffroy wrote of Monet:

> Hurriedly he covers his canvas with the dominant values, studies their gradations, contrasts them, harmonizes them.

Another description from about this time gives us insight into one of Monet's strongly held beliefs about capturing the whole scene from nature, the totality:

> The one golden rule from which Claude Monet never departs, is to work on the whole picture together, to work all over or not at all.

Monet felt that if one did not follow this rule, there could be a loss of harmony. The result would be a representation of nature as "a collection of scraps instead of as a whole." Monet himself expressed this to a friend in 1890:

> The first real look at the motif was likely to be the truest and most unprejudiced one, and...the first painting should cover as much of the canvas as possible, no matter how roughly, so as to determine at the outset the tonality of the whole.

Monet's works are generally characterized by quick, vigorous, energetic brush strokes much like Courbet's. These give his works a more active feel to them than those of, say, Renoir, who used softer and rounder strokes. This approach enabled Monet to quickly capture the particular moment before him.

One of his greatest attributes was his versatility in adapting his brush work to the task at hand. He used a number of different types of brush strokes, depending on the effect he wanted. These ranged from heavily textured, thick strokes of paint, often used early in the development of a painting, to so-called "skip strokes," where a brush was drawn lightly across a canvas, depositing paint wherever it touched. In his last years, as his eyesight failed and he was striving to convey his view of his unique water lilies, he used broad, sweeping strokes and vibrant colors.

Monet's underlying approach to color was based on his belief that forms could and should be expressed by contrast and variations of color, not by tonal gradations, and that colors owe their brightness to contrast rather than to just their inherent qualities. Added to these beliefs was Monet's acute observation of the colors of nature.

The interaction of these elements of color and brush stroke can be seen, for example, when a change occurred in Monet's paintings around 1890. At this time, Monet became interested in the atmosphere around objects—the "envelope" of interactive colored light. His brush strokes consequently changed from the stronger, energetic type to the more uniform and softer. This produced a smooth, almost opaque texture. During this period he also improvised more with colors. They became richer and more harmonious in his attempt to express the atmospheric envelope.

Monet's special abilities in the use of color and brush strokes can most clearly be seen in his paintings of water, a substance that fascinated him. He was a master at capturing its intrinsic qualities, and it was a major subject of his work throughout his life. He painted water in all of its forms. He was unmatched in his ability to portray the power of a rough sea, the tranquility of a pond or stream or the smooth flowing of a river. He was also able to capture the spray of a wave, the dampness of mist or rain and the unique qualities of snow. And his depiction of the steam from the locomotives in the *Gare St.-Lazare* paintings was revolutionary. Zola was particularly impressed with Monet's skills in this area:

> With him, water is alive, profound, and above all, real.

Berthe Morisot was similarly impressed when she said:

> Before one of Monet's pictures, I always know which way to incline my umbrella.

Manet summed up Monet's skills on this particular subject when he called Monet the "Raphael of water."

One can get a personal feel for Monet's technical skills by looking at his paintings both up very close and then at a distance. Many of his works, particularly of water, have a sheen and smoothness to them when viewed from fifteen to twenty feet away, but up close, one can see the short, often choppy strokes he used.

Productivity and Output

As we have seen, Monet had periods of discouragement and self-doubt. Occasionally, months would go by when he painted very little. But the creative flame was always there, and he would soon be re-energized, attacking his work with great focus and energy. These were periods of great productivity and, while they were exhilarating and challenging, they often left him exhausted.

A brief look at a few of these very focused efforts will give us additional insight into Monet and his works:

• In 1872, Monet's first year at Argenteuil, he completed about sixty paintings. This was more than he had done over the previous three years (1869–1871) when he was moving around between areas of France, London and Holland. This very productive period produced some of his most "classical" Impressionist canvases. Interestingly, there was a period just five years later (1877–1878) when Monet was again in Argenteuil, during which he virtually stopped painting for about nine months.

• Monet's years living in Vétheuil along the Seine from 1878 to 1881 were even more productive. He completed some three hundred works—more than during his entire seven years at Argenteuil. These work out to a rate of one every four days. The paintings were done while Monet was going through very trying financial and personal problems, including the illness and death of Camille.

• Of all of Monet's painting excursions of the 1880s, the trip to Belle-Ile on the Brittany coast in 1886 was probably the most challenging and fecund. Here he completed about forty very innovative paintings in just three months. They were done in terrible weather and unfamiliar surroundings, far away from family and friends.

• Monet's series paintings in the 1890s all represent periods of extreme focus and high productivity. For instance, his *Wheatstacks* series of some thirty paintings was mainly done in a five-to-six-month period in late 1890 and early 1891. His twenty-four-painting series of poplar trees was completed during a seven-to-eight-month period in 1891. And his thirty paintings of the façade on the Rouen Cathedral were done in two three-month periods in 1892 and 1893.

• Monet's time in London during 1899–1901, when he was sixty years old, represents his most prolific period. He went there in September 1899 after a period of over a year in which he painted very little. He stayed for six weeks in 1899 and returned during both 1900 and 1901, each time for three months. The results were nearly one hundred paintings (many of which were completed later at Giverny). This is the largest series he ever did.

Monet's energy and drive never really ceased. Except for his periodic episodes of depression, or occasional diversions because of family or business affairs, he rarely stopped painting for very long.

Other Media

Monet did very little work in media other than oil. However, there were a few occasions when other forms of expression were utilized.

Early in his career, and then again briefly in 1901, he completed several groups of pastels (drawings in chalk). Seven of them were shown in the first Impressionist exhibition in 1874. After that, he rarely worked in pastels even though the medium was well suited to quickly capturing a scene.

In his eighties, Monet claimed he had never used watercolors. However, earlier he had said that he had used them when he was in Africa as a youth in 1861–1862 and that

> At that period I considered watercolor an excellent and rapid means of rendering the "instantaneity" of light.

Over the course of his life, Monet did three very different types of drawings. As a young man, he mainly did caricatures to earn money in Le Havre. By the time he was in his early twenties, this seems to have stopped, and he devoted himself to oil painting. But as part of his preparation during certain periods, Monet made very rough pencil sketches as preliminary work on possible sites or compositional ideas. There still exist eight sketchbooks containing hundreds of these rough drawings at the Musée Marmottan in Paris.

The other class of drawings by Monet are of quite a different type—a small group of black-and-white drawings of his oil paintings. These were mostly done for publications wanting to reproduce his work. Monet considered them finished works and signed them. He did this with some reluctance, however, as he never liked to isolate drawing from color. They were done mainly in the period 1880–1892 and were soon made unnecessary by developments in photography that allowed publications to reproduce the actual paintings.

Monet's Influence and Legacy

The special exhibitions of Monet's works have been among the most popular of all time. Prices paid for his paintings, when they do come up for sale, are always in the millions of dollars. With about two thousand of his paintings in existence, his popularity is widespread. Significant collections of his work appear in most major museums, and his paintings hang in many small museums as well.

The museums with the largest number of his works are the Musée d'Orsay and the Marmottan in Paris and the Metropolitan in New York. Other significant collections can be seen in Tokyo, Boston, Chicago, Washington, D.C. and London.

Monet's effect on succeeding generations of artists has been a much-discussed and actively debated subject for years. Today, though, it is quite clear that he has had a very meaningful impact on a number of artistic developments in the twentieth century, as well as on some of the most important modern artists.

This was not always so clear, however. In the last years of the nineteenth and the early years of the twentieth century, the avant-garde artistic movements in Paris and elsewhere were moving away from what Monet was doing. Paul Gauguin and other Post-Impressionists were using hard lines and flat, evenly applied colors to define their figures. The likes of Picasso and Georges

Braque were more influenced by Cézanne, whose emphasis on form and volume led to Cubism.

However, a number of young artists who would play a significant role in twentieth-century art were strongly influenced by Monet's works around the turn of the century. For example, the great Russian abstract painter Wassily Kandinsky (1866–1944) was particularly taken by one of Monet's *Wheatstack* paintings when he saw it in Moscow in 1895:

> Suddenly, for the first time in my life, I found myself looking at a real painting...It seemed to me, that, without a catalog in my hand, it would have been impossible to recognize what the painting was meant to represent.

The work revealed to him the previously unimagined and unsurpassed power of the palette. Pointing toward the abstract, it also showed him that the object did not have to be the indispensable element in a painting.

The Dutch painter Piet Mondrian (1872–1944) was also affected in his early development by Monet's depiction of forms in his *Wheatstacks* and *Rouen Cathedral* paintings.

The whole movement toward abstract art in the mid-twentieth century owes much to Monet, particularly to his later water lily paintings. Monet, of course, was not an abstract painter. For him, his relationship to nature and his depiction of what he saw were paramount. But his sweeping brush strokes and the bright patches of colors he used to capture the very focused and isolated elements of his water lily ponds produced paintings that were on the edge of the abstract world and its disregard for a recognizable subject. It was not until the 1940s and 1950s, some twenty years after Monet's death, that the harsh style of Cubism was no longer a driving force, and artists moved toward the swirling shapes and colors reminiscent of Monet's late works. But then, in what was to be known as Abstract Expressionism, objective reality was forgotten. The inspiration was no longer nature or a specific subject but solely the artist's inner desire to structure colors and shapes as ends in themselves.

Most art critics and historians have now agreed on the major contribution Monet has made to modern art. Various authors have highlighted his influence on such successful twentieth-century artists as Matisse, Marcel Duchamp, Joan Miró and Jackson Pollock. Through his constant innovation and his unique abilities with color, brush strokes and composition, Monet is now recognized not only as the father of Impressionism, but also as an essential and important forerunner of modern art.

Monet's legacies, in addition to his some two thousand paintings, were his ingenious techniques and most importantly his role as the leader of the revolutionary Impressionists who changed the course of Western art. Through his powerful personality, his commitment and strong beliefs and his unique approach to painting, he was extremely influential on most of the leading artists who worked during the forty years around either side of the turn of the century. Similarly, as we have seen, his techniques and approaches to painting inspired others for many years after he died, even up to today.

Observations and Conclusions

My examination of Michelangelo, Beethoven and Monet has, I hope, shown that artistic greatness can come forth from very different people in a wide variety of personal circumstances and social milieux. However, there are some underlying commonalities and parallels to be found. Even with all the proper caveats and concerns about drawing conclusions from studying only three great artists, we can nevertheless get an understanding of the processes, motivations and social forces that can lead to great art.

Defining Artistic Greatness

In this book I have often used the words "creative," "great" and "genius." Let us briefly explore these three terms, and then bring them together into a definition of artistic greatness. We can then use this definition as a reference point for any observations and conclusions.

Creativity. The essence of creativity is bringing something new and unique into being. The truly creative people can't merely execute what's been done before, even if it is of high quality. They must go beyond it. By this definition, actors, musicians and artists aren't truly creative people if they just work within the established rules and norms of their art. They are practitioners, not creators. For real creativity to occur, rules must be broken, new areas explored or new standards established.

Contrary to what many people think, a creative event or work is not an individual act. There are other essential sources of input in the creative process. Mihaly Csikszentmihalyi, an expert on creativity from the University of Chicago, has advanced a theory that defines and ties together the critical elements of the creative process. He identifies three elements that are necessary for creativity:

1. The *individual* person with the talent
2. The *domain* or discipline in which the individual is working (i.e., music, painting, mathematics, etc.)
3. The surrounding *field* that passes judgment on the quality of the individual's output. Those in the field might be patrons, critics, fellow artists, experts, etc.

In his model, creativity occurs when an individual changes the rules of the domain (or creates a new domain) and this change is recognized by the field—either immediately or, as often happens, over time. Csikszentmihalyi's theory says that no matter how "talented" individuals are in an abstract sense, they are not truly creative unless they can work in a domain and produce works that are eventually valued and judged within a relevant field.

This model is helpful in thinking about our three artists. I'd argue that Renaissance Florence was not just a unique coming together of talented artisans, but a period when the domains (painting and sculpture) were organized and codified and the field (patrons, the city of Florence, guilds, the Church) was involved and supportive. Hence, had Michelangelo lived in deepest Siberia, with no established tradition of art and no body of interested patrons, he may well have never been recognized as a creative genius. Similarly, the established domain in which Beethoven worked (eighteenth-century Classical music) and the active field of patrons, critics and knowledgeable audiences that he had were necessary for his innovative and unique musical talent to be recognized. The same can be said for Monet, as he was a participant in the well-established and popular domain of French painting and was able to be judged by a knowledgeable (albeit sometimes conservative) field of interested art connoisseurs, gallery owners, critics and fellow artists.

Genius. The concept of genius focuses more on the creators, and their unusual intellectual capacities, than on the creative acts they may perform. Creativity is necessary for genius, but not sufficient. The real genius's creativity must *dramatically* break old rules and bring forth *dramatically* unprecedented works and ideas that did not exist before. Geniuses change history with their extraordinary powers of invention. They are the ones with the real breakthroughs.

No clear definition exists on what a genius is. The various attempts to define it use words such as "extraordinary," "unusual," "transcendent" and "original." Geniuses have the ability to juxtapose ideas, make unique connections and organize their thoughts in unexpected ways. Their abilities to create new visions and new domains make them rare, admired, sometimes eccentric and often misunderstood.

Because of their extraordinary innovations, each of our three artists has been recognized as a genius. Each produced works that broke significant new ground, made people think differently about art and made history by changing the direction of his art form in ways that still affect it today.

Greatness. For our purposes, greatness has to do with the remarkable skills and the extraordinary creative output of an artist who has withstood the test of time. Greatness also relates to a person's strength of character. Great persons in history stand out because of not only what they did, but also who they were as individuals. When we talk of greatness, we talk of excellence, importance, remarkableness, preeminent qualities, outstanding abilities and paramount achievements. It means the exceptional—the very few who stand out and make a difference over the long term.

The three artists we have examined can all clearly be described as great. Even though they worked in environments of intense artistic competitiveness, with many other talented artists close by, they clearly stood out because of their extraordinary skills and output.

The concepts of creativity, genius and greatness obviously overlap and often merge. What we are seeking for our purpose is a concept of artistic greatness that encompasses elements from all three terms. I suggest that the critical elements of artistic greatness are these:

- Mastery, at the highest level, of the basic skills of an art form
- Creation of change in the domain, taking the art form in new directions
- Significant artistic output of the highest quality over many years
- Major influence on other artists

- Broad and positive recognition of the quality of the artist's work by those in the field, and eventually by a meaningful portion of the general public
- Significant influence on artistic matters through their work, their strength and their commitment

Significant Parallels

Let us now explore in more detail the common characteristics, experiences, social forces and work habits of these artists, in order to glean additional insight into the subject of artistic greatness.

• All exhibited unusual artistic skills and a strong interest in expressing them while they were very young. In spite of some parental resistance in the cases of Michelangelo and Monet (but not Beethoven), they all quickly found an outlet and a supportive environment for their youthful, raw talent. While the artists appear to have had relatively normal childhoods, their interest in their art forms quickly emerged as a major part of their lives. By the time they were in their early teens, they had in one way or another become fully committed to developing their artistic skills.

Each came in contact at an early age with a mentor who both directed and inspired him. This relationship further solidified each artist's commitment and desire to pursue his work, and helped him to build the strong artistic self-confidence that was an important part of his make-up throughout the rest of his life. In Michelangelo's case, his mentors were the Florentine fresco painter, Domenico Ghirlandaio, in whose workshop he apprenticed, and Lorenzo de' Medici, who brought Michelangelo into his stimulating household when he was only fourteen years old. For Beethoven, the role was played by his teacher, Christian Neefe, and to some extent by his influential first patron, Count von Waldstein. For the young Monet it was the painter Eugène Boudin, who exposed him to, and then instructed him in, the basics of out-of-door oil painting.

Thus, by their late teens, all three of our artists had spent considerable time developing their basic skills, had received encouragement and positive feedback regarding their talents, and somehow knew that pursuing their artistic drives would be a big part of their lives.

• A crucial element in the development of Michelangelo, Beethoven and Monet was their early mastery of the rudimentary skills and techniques in their art forms. Although each of them liked to experiment and try something new, their early years were dominated not by doing "creative" things but by the hard work of learning from and about earlier artists and by developing their talents in using the fundamental building blocks of their trades. For Michelangelo this meant hours of sketching the works of Giotto, Masaccio and others and learning the techniques of fresco painting from Ghirlandaio. Beethoven spent much of his youth practicing the piano, taking instructions on a number of other instruments and receiving training in the basics of composition. Monet's early years were spent drawing, and he often studied the works of the excellent French painters of the Realist, Romantic and Barbizon schools.

Even though all three showed creative and innovative impulses early in their careers, their significant breakthroughs generally came later, after they had mastered the basics of their domains. It's clear that for even the greatest artists, it is only after building a strong foundation that the real creativity and innovation occurs. Although Michelangelo completed his beautiful and unique first *Pietà* at about age twenty-four, he had by this time become a wonderful draftsman and had spent countless hours learning the essentials of working with marble.

• For these artists, working in their art forms was an obsession, the central driving force throughout their lives. Their work required both an underlying commitment and an extremely high degree of focus and discipline. Success didn't happen through occasional efforts or sparks of inspiration. Constant work, experimentation, learning and persistence were necessary. This passionate focus on their work tended to dominate their lifestyles and their relationships.

• All three artists were also very egocentric. Their world revolved around their artistic work, and they expected the worlds of their families and acquaintances to revolve around them. All of them had regular periods of withdrawal and isolation when they were immersed in their work. They also had periods of depression and moodiness when things weren't going well. And all three were rather solitary in general.

While each of the three did develop some other interests, even these tended to be related to their art or its subject matter. Michelangelo, for instance, was a student of anatomy and a deeply religious man. These interests informed most of his work. Beethoven's love of nature and the out-of-doors became an integral part of his composing habits and occasionally the programmatic inspiration for his compositions. Monet's love of gardening, of course, became intimately connected with the major subject matter of his works over the last twenty years of his life.

• All of these artists had a need for some close connections with others. Although they were loners and very self-centered, they needed some relationships to reaffirm themselves and receive the closeness that they needed as human beings.

Interestingly, for all three of these artists this generally wasn't provided by parents or siblings. Michelangelo's mother died when he was only six, and his relationship with his father, although lengthy, was filled with conflict and stress. He never did get on very well with his brothers and was reasonably close to just one of them. It was only with his nephew, Lionardo, that he seemed to achieve a sense of family, and this occurred at a late age. Even then the relationship was dominated by Michelangelo's interference in the young man's life. Since Michelangelo never married, his most significant emotional attachments occurred outside of a family setting. He had several warm friendships with a few of the men who helped him manage his affairs. In addition, he had a strong but platonic friendship with Vittoria Colonna. And, of course, he had very strong feelings for the young man he so admired, Tommaso di Cavalieri. He also likely had some homosexual relationships, but there is little evidence that any of them were deeply emotional attachments, with the exception of Cavalieri.

Beethoven also did not find the closeness he desired in his immediate family. Times at home were often difficult and stressful for him, and his relationship with his father was particularly strained. Even as a youth, he attached himself to other families, where he found a more nurturing environment. By the time he was twenty-two, both his parents were dead. He was somewhat close to his two younger brothers, but much of their relationship was contentious and argumentative. Beethoven's attempts to find intimacy with women failed. Only with his "Immortal Beloved" did he get close, and that passed quickly. Like Michelangelo, he spent considerable time and emotional energy in his conflict-filled relationship with his nephew Karl. He did, however, manage to develop some warm and relatively close relationships with some friends and patrons.

Monet, too, had a difficult and cool relationship with his father, who was not at all supportive of his artistic interests. His mother, who died when he was sixteen, was more sympathetic, but she doesn't seem to have played a major role in his development. It was his aunt who gave him the advocacy and artistic encouragement that he needed as a young man. Because of his strong personality and good looks, Monet always had people around him, but he generally remained somewhat detached. His first marriage, to Camille, provided him with some emotional support, but he never really seemed to be deeply committed to her. It was only in his later years with his second wife, Alice, and their blended families that he built the close family ties that proved to be important to him. And as he aged, male friendships became more significant to him; he developed several with special meaning, including one with the French statesman Georges Clemenceau.

Thus we see these great artists as essentially private men who often had difficulty building close emotional ties. They came from not particularly warm or nurturing families, and they struggled to build relationships that at least partially met their needs. They all had powerful personalities and a strong set of beliefs and values. They attracted people, and many found them fascinating. The few who did become friends of these artists were very loyal and wanted to be of service. But to be a friend of any of the three great artists, one had to be extremely tolerant and understanding of their moods, their drive and the fact that nothing was more important to them than their work.

• All of these three artists possessed a compelling drive for growth, change and ongoing improvement in their work. They never stopped learning and experimenting. They were never satisfied and were always looking ahead to what else or what next they should be doing. They had an uneasiness about their work and were very critical of themselves. With individual works they were often dissatisfied, and they were constantly revising, fixing, redoing, reworking. They considered many of their most admired works unfinished and not quite right.

The change and innovation they achieved is clear from a historical perspective. But the achievement was not regular or constant in the shorter term. They went through periods of setbacks and frustrations and occasionally even doubted their own greatness. However, they were driven to innovate, to do novel things and to constantly work on the new challenges they created for themselves.

• Some of the most important and inventive work of these artists was done when they were quite old. They all kept pushing themselves to the very end. Michelangelo's final pietà, on which he was working up until a few days before he died, is his most abstract and "modern" work. His exceptional architectural designs for St. Peter's, as well as some of his later drawings, are also among his most innovative creations. In spite of ill health and deafness, Beethoven's very late compositions, particularly the *Missa Solemnis,* the ninth symphony and the late string quartets, are the most complex and original of his works. At the end of Monet's life he was breaking new ground with his unique and almost abstract paintings of water lilies.

• A common element among these three artists was their ability to overcome obstacles as they relentlessly pursued their art. As men of great courage and fortitude, they kept working through both real and perceived problems. Michelangelo, for example, was often frustrated by his patrons and was regularly pulled off projects before they were finished. Several times he also felt his life was threatened. Beethoven was constantly worried about his living conditions, his family, his frustrating love life, his financial security and his place in society. Monet, too, had his problems of poverty, rejection and the death of his first wife and his oldest son.

All three artists amazed their contemporaries with their strength in dealing with their severe physical health problems. Michelangelo was often quite ill during the last part of his life and also suffered some injuries. But his work always continued. Beethoven, of course, was essentially deaf for the last twenty years of his life, and a number of his highly innovative works were composed during times of serious illness. Failing eyesight and, eventually, near-blindness did not prevent Monet from conceptualizing and then completing his monumental *Water Lilies* paintings in his last years. A great inner strength enabled each artist to dig down deep, gather his energies and rise to the challenge.

• Michelangelo, Beethoven and Monet were all psychologically uneasy men. They were eccentric, restless, impatient, rarely satisfied for long and constantly thinking ahead to the next challenge. Out of this turmoil and unrest came creative tensions that were a driving force behind their productivity and inventiveness.

None of our three artists was mentally ill in any clinical sense. But all were men of strong intelligence whose minds were regularly involved in an uneasy struggle to grapple with the unending artistic challenges they created. They all experienced significant periods of mental turmoil, and they wrote and talked about these struggles. They seem to have had very few periods of contentment or serenity.

• In his own way, each artist had a sense of (and a reverence for) a greater being or spiritual force. This served as both an inspiration and a moral or spiritual reference point. In Michelangelo's case it was his strong belief in God and the teachings and dogma of the Catholic Church, as well as the basic ideas of humanism, with its focus on the importance of human beings. For Beethoven it was his belief in truth, virtue and the ideals of the Enlightenment. (Later in his life, Beethoven became more interested in religion and seemed to want to learn about some of the various faiths.) Monet was an agnostic, but even he was in awe of the great force and sacredness of nature. Indeed, his work revolved around it. For Monet, nature had a far greater and deeper meaning than just a source of beautiful subject matter for his paintings.

• In spite of the sometimes sophisticated and intellectual aspects of their work, and the considerable complexities of their personalities, there was a certain basic commonness about all three artists. They all came from relatively plain backgrounds, and they enjoyed much in life that was quite simple, such as good food and wine or gossipy conversation.

• Each artist had a special affection for the countryside and seemed to experience renewal by spending time outside of the city. Throughout the early part of his life, Michelangelo went to Carrara for weeks at a time to get to the source of his marble and to mix with the local workmen. Beethoven thrived in the countryside and escaped there every summer. And Monet regularly returned to elemental nature through his many trips to rural France, especially to the Normandy coast.

• All three men were happiest when they were at home or in familiar circumstances. Michelangelo spent almost all his time in the areas of Florence and Rome and never did leave the Italian peninsula. Beethoven spent all his adult years in and around Vienna, with only occasional side trips into nearby Bohemia or Hungary. He never even returned to his native Bonn. Although Monet did travel throughout France and to London, Holland, Norway, Italy and Spain, he was always anxious to get back home, especially to Giverny. All three valued the simple things in life, and even though they all ended up rich and famous, none lived an extravagant lifestyle (with the exception of Monet in his later years).

• Despite their frequent statements that money didn't matter to them, each artist did spend considerable time on his finances. All were quite astute about money matters and took an active role in negotiations with patrons, publishers or galleries. The correspondence of all three is filled with issues regarding payments, banking, contracts, fees, etc. They were all quite good at it and, as we have seen, they made substantial amounts of money.

• None of these three artists was a teacher in the traditional sense. Instead, they all focused their energies on their own work and innovation instead of formally passing on their knowledge and experiences to others. Michelangelo did have assistants who helped him out and who no doubt learned a lot from him. But he was not the leader of any defined school and preferred to work alone. He had no *bottega* (school/studio) where young artisans came for training, as was then customary.

Beethoven worked by himself and had little, if any, interest in teaching others. He had a few students from time to time, but it was not a priority in his life, and his writings occasionally expressed his dislike of giving lessons.

Monet, too, had little interest in passing along his knowledge or techniques. He loathed attempts to codify or categorize his work and generally wasn't interested in working with young artists. Even when young painters came to Giverny to be near him, he had very little time for them.

• Michelangelo, Beethoven and Monet all appeared on the scene during periods of great artistic activity. Each society they lived in was supportive of their particular art form. All three artists studied and benefited greatly from the unusually talented artists who had recently preceded them and, in some cases, were their contemporaries. The art of previous generations was easily available to them. They were thus part of a tradition, and their early works very strongly reflect the style and techniques of their predecessors.

• In all three cases, these artists' art forms had reached a state of some maturity and were ripe for change and innovation. The work of core Renaissance artists such as Donatello, Botticelli and Brunelleschi, the classical compositions of Mozart and Haydn, and the realist painting of Corot and the Barbizon school were all highly developed, forming a solid base for further invention. Michelangelo, Beethoven and Monet appeared at the right time to move beyond that base in new directions and new standards of quality.

Each of the three is now recognized as a key participant and a driving force in a critical turning point of his art form. We now see Michelangelo as a central player in moving from the mid- (classical) Renaissance to the magnificent harmony and symmetry of the High Renaissance and then to the more emotional style of Mannerism. Beethoven was the critical bridge between the tightly structured Classical musical style and the passionate, expansive, grander Romantic style. Monet is recognized as the leader of the Impressionists, who dramatically broke away from the traditions of official French art and opened up painting with their unique use of color and light.

• Each of the three had an active and financially capable patronage system as a market for his work. This was important not just for financial reasons but also for recognition and critical response. Michelangelo and Beethoven very quickly tied into the patronage system—Michelangelo with the Church and the Republic of Florence, and Beethoven with the minor nobles of Vienna who showed off their wealth by commissioning music. For Monet, success came a bit later in life, but even early on he had at least the potential of exhibiting at the official Salon as a motivating force.

• These three artists lived in times of great societal change. Things were moving at a fast pace, and new forces and discoveries were causing people to look at things in different ways. This sense of living in a time of significant transition encouraged greater experimentation as well as a greater acceptance of what was new and innovative.

The major forces of change in Michelangelo's life came from the 1527 sack of Rome and the Lutheran Reformation, which shook the very foundations of the Catholic Church. The invention of printing, the discovery of ancient Greek and Roman writings, the opening up of the New World and the constant warfare with invading European armies also added to the sense of rapid transformation taking place in society. For Beethoven, profound change came in the wake of the French Revolution, which questioned and then rejected the divine right of royalty that had ruled Europe for hundreds of years. Napoleon was also an agent of extreme disruption and alteration. His wars reordered Europe and brought into question the basic relationships that had existed on the continent for centuries. In Monet's time, we see major transformations in technology (trains, cars, photography), lifestyle (the rebuilding of Paris) and people's basic outlook on life (Darwin's *The Origin of Species*).

• Great intellectual ferment took place during the lives of all these artists. The powerful ideals of humanism (for Michelangelo), the Enlightenment (for Beethoven), and nationalism, scientific realism and liberalism (for Monet) were deeply influential on the artistic world of their times. In some cases, these movements also offered subject matter and emotional inspiration for the artists. The intense humanness of many of his figures in both sculpture and painting reflects Michelangelo's interest in humanism. Beethoven was deeply impacted by the Enlightenment, and many of his heroic, grand, uplifting compositions reflect this. For Monet, we see a focus on his beloved France and very realistic depictions of ordinary sights in that country. There is none of the noble or idealized portrayal of earlier times.

• All three men lived through and were touched by significant wars. During Michelangelo's life, fairly constant battles raged around him. Napoleon's wars directly affected Beethoven several times in his life. And Monet was shaken by the Franco-Prussian War of 1870 and its bloody aftermath. He was also affected by World War I, which at times was fought just a few miles from his home in Giverny.

• Each artist spent a good part of his life under dictatorial and repressive political systems. Michelangelo lived through a series of violent Florentine regimes, as well as several tyrannical popes. Beethoven's Vienna was ruled as a police state under the Hapsburgs. Monet's early formative years—up to 1870—were spent under the dictatorial and repressive rule of Napoleon III's Second Empire.

• All three artists had the ability and determination to operate somewhat on the edge of the existing artistic system, or even, at times, outside of it. Because of their skills, their self-confidence and their aggressiveness, they all maneuvered themselves into positions where they could operate more independently than others, be more innovative and have more control over their own work. All played significant roles in redefining their professions, from artisans/servants/tradesmen with little control over what they did toward complete independence and art for art's sake.

Because of Michelangelo's widely recognized skills and his strong personality, he had a much greater degree of freedom in choosing subject matter and deciding on interpretation than did his predecessors and contemporaries, who tended to do what they were told. Beethoven gained a great deal of autonomy early on by building his career around many different patrons and by putting on independent concerts for himself. Beethoven, who usually was able to write what he wanted and find a market for it, was one of the first composers to work successfully this way throughout most of his career. In Monet's case, early in his career he felt the need to establish a path to the public that was outside the official system of the Salon. This allowed him to paint with more freedom and feel less constrained by what he believed would be accepted. Eventually, he was completely free of the dictates of the official art world.

• Michelangelo, Beethoven and Monet were all men with a high energy level and a great capacity for hard work. They were able to throw themselves completely into their art and keep going well beyond what most others thought possible. Michelangelo's feat of working on the Sistine ceiling, under extremely harsh conditions for days on end, constitutes one of the great individual accomplishments in Western art. Beethoven could work for hours on his compositions, often skipping meals and losing track of other obligations. Monet was known for his energetic pursuit of finding just the right location to paint and then spending hours or days there, often under extremely difficult conditions.

Typically, after their periods of high energy and fanatical focus, each artist would step back for a period to regroup. But then he would soon be at it again, working furiously and amazing those around him with his seemingly endless source of energy. (Interestingly, all three men often talked proudly of their own artistic efforts and how hard they labored. They were not at all modest about the efforts they put into their work.)

• Perhaps the most important common trait among these three artists was their ability to visualize and conceptualize the whole of a work. They were always driving toward an inner vision of a complete and final creative product, and were able to keep that vision in mind as they labored through the many details and intricacies of their creations. All three were able to construct very complex works, with many components and multiple themes that they blended into works that have clarity, unity and wholeness. It is this very special ability to make a conceptualized, visionary and powerful total work out of many complex and well-constructed parts in new and innovative ways that leads to great art.

Concluding Thoughts

We have clearly learned that it takes more than raw talent and intelligence to achieve artistic greatness. It also requires an understanding of and respect for an art form's heritage, a mastery of difficult technical skills and an environment that encourages and eventually rewards excellence. Artistic greatness also requires—even demands—strong commitment, focus and discipline.

However, I believe there is even more to the creation of great art than I have discussed here. There are additional elements and dimensions that go beyond the scope of this exploration and probably beyond what can be conceptually discussed and understood.

Great art can be described, analyzed and certainly appreciated, but I do not believe it can ever be fully explained. There are special aspects of great art and those that create it that involve an almost mysterious coming together of abilities and thought processes that occur somewhere in the mind of the artist. We can feel this, for example, when everything comes together in an opera. In those moments all the elements—orchestra, soloist, chorus, the dramatic action, the setting—fuse into a glorious, unique and transcendental experience. One senses these special faculties similarly when surrounded by Monet's *Water Lilies* or when overwhelmed by the grandeur of the many elements of the Sistine Chapel. It can also occur in the quiet contemplation of a single painting or in the reflective listening to a piano sonata.

Within the great artistic geniuses, it is the unique combinations of the subconscious thought process that juxtapose and integrate ideas and techniques in new ways that lead to breakthrough creativity and works that push art in new directions. Though some have tried, this deep level of man's mental processes, and the inspiring creations it produces, have not yet been fathomed. This, in my opinion, is good. Part of the enjoyment of art, even after we have learned about the artists and the influences in their lives, is the mystery and the sense of wonderment and unexplainability that surrounds the masterpiece.

What does all this study of artistic greatness mean for us? It means we must be tolerant and sympathetic to the difficulties that are associated with the creation of great art. We must remember that significant creative efforts will challenge the established norms and are likely to make us uncomfortable. Often both the work and the artist are likely to seem eccentric or strange. During the creative process, the only ones who may understand and can visualize the work are the artists themselves. Tolerance, patience and forbearance are called for as we experience new and puzzling art works. If the basic artistic skills are there and the artists are committed and serious about their work, then we must not rush to judgment.

The potential for greatness is around us. History tells us so. It may come from surprising places as media and technology change. It could emerge from films, videos or new audio technologies. It may also come from the mind of the solitary composer working out new musical forms on the piano. Who knows who will set the standards for the next generation? As they say, only time will tell. Our commitment, though, must always be to keep our eyes, our ears and our minds open.

Bibliography

Michelangelo

Barolsky, Paul. *The Faun in the Garden.* University Park, Penn.: Penn State University Press, 1994.

Brandes, Georg. *Michelangelo: His Life, His Times, His Era.* 2nd ed, rev. Translated and with a foreword by Heinz Norden. Frederick Ungar Publishing Company, 1967.

Brucker, Gene A. *Renaissance Florence.* Berkeley, Calif.: University of California Press, 1969.

Burckhardt, Jacob. *The Civilization of the Renaissance in Italy.* 2nd ed. Translated by S. G. C. Middlemore. Introduction by Peter Burke. New York: Penguin Classic, 1990.

Burke, Peter. *The Italian Renaissance: Culture and Society in Italy.* Princeton, N.J.: Princeton University Press, 1987.

Cole, Bruce. *The Renaissance Artist at Work: From Pisano to Titian.* New York: Harper & Row, 1983.

Condivi, Ascanio. *Michelangelo: Life, Letters, and Poetry.* Translated and edited by George Bow with Peter Porter. Oxford and New York: Oxford University Press, 1987.

Fergonzi et al. *Rodin and Michelangelo.* Philadelphia: Philadelphia Museum of Art, 1997.

Gage, John. *J. M. W. Turner: A Wonderful Range of Mind.* New Haven, Conn.: Yale University Press, 1987.

Gilbert, Creighton. *Michelangelo: On and Off the Sistine Ceiling.* New York: George Braziller, Inc., 1994.

Girard, Xavier. *Matisse: The Wonder of Color.* New York: Harry N. Abrams, Inc., 1994.

Goodman, Anthony and Angus Mackay. *The Impact of Humanism on Western Europe.* London: Longman Group U.K. Ltd., 1990.

Hale, J. R. *Renaissance Europe.* Berkeley, Calif.: University of California Press, 1977.

Hay, Denys. *The Italian Renaissance: Its Historical Background.* Cambridge and New York: Cambridge University Press, 1977.

Hearder, Harry. *Italy: A Short History.* Cambridge and New York: Cambridge University Press, 1990.

Hearder, H. and D. P. Waley, D. P. *A Short History of Italy from Classical Times to the Present Day.* Cambridge: Cambridge University Press, 1986.

Heusinger, Lutz. *Michelangelo: Complete Works.* Special ed. for the Vatican museums and galleries. Florence: Scala, 1984.

Hibbard, Howard. *Michelangelo.* 2nd edition. New York: Harper & Row, 1974.

Hibbert, Christopher. *The House of Medici: Its Rise and Fall.* New York: William Morrow and Co., Inc., 1980.

Hirst, Michael et al. *The Sistine Chapel: A Glorious Restoration.* New York: Harry N. Abrams, Inc., 1994.

Kristeller, Paul Oskar. *Renaissance Thought and the Arts.* Princeton, N.J.: Princeton University Press, 1990.

Letts, Rosa Maria. *The Cambridge Introduction to Art: The Renaissance.* Cambridge and New York: Cambridge University Press, 1981.

Liebert, Robert S., M.D. *Michelangelo: A Psychoanalytic Study of His Life and Images.* New Haven, Conn.: Yale University Press, 1983.

Murray, Linda. *The High Renaissance and Mannerism.* New York: Oxford University Press, 1977.

————. *Michelangelo.* New York: Thames and Hudson, Inc., 1985.

Murray, Peter and Linda. *The Art of the Renaissance.* New York: Oxford University Press, 1963.

Plumb, J. H. *The Penguin Book of the Renaissance.* New York: Penguin Books, 1964.

Porter, Peter and George Bull. *Selected Poems of Michelangelo.* Oxford and New York: Oxford University Press, 1987.

Ramsden, E. H. *The Letters of Michelangelo.* 2 vols. Translated from the original Tuscan. Stanford, Calif.: Stanford University Press, 1963.

Vasari, Giorgio. *The Lives of the Artists.* Translated by George Bull. New York: Penguin Books, 1965.

Wallace, William E. *Leonardo, Michelangelo and Raphael in Renaissance Florence from 1500 to 1508.* Washington, D.C.: Georgetown University Press, 1992.

———. "Miscellanea Curiositae Michelangelae: A Steep Tariff, A Half Dozen Horses and Yards of Taffeta." *Renaissance Quarterly* 47, no.2 (summer 1994): 330–50.

———. *Michelangelo at San Lorenzo: The Genius as Entrepreneur.* Cambridge and New York: Cambridge University Press, 1994.

Beethoven

Ammer, Christine. *The HarperCollins Dictionary of Music.* 2nd ed., rev. New York: HarperCollins Publishers, 1991.

Autexier, Philippe A. *Beethoven: The Composer As Hero.* New York: Harry N. Abrams, Inc., 1992.

Black, Jeremy. *Eighteenth-Century Europe, 1700–1789.* New York: St. Martin's Press, 1990.

Breunig, Charles. *The Age of Revolution and Reaction, 1789–1850.* 2nd ed. New York: W. W. Norton and Company, 1977.

Cooper, Barry. *Beethoven and the Creative Process.* Oxford and New York: Oxford University Press, 1990.

———. *The Beethoven Compendium.* London: Thames and Hudson, Ltd., 1991.

Downs, Philip G. *Classical Music: The Era of Haydn, Mozart and Beethoven.* New York: W. W. Norton and Company, 1992.

Forbes, Elliot, ed. *Thayer's Life of Beethoven.* 2 vols. Princeton, N.J.: Princeton University Press, 1967.

Grout, Donald Jay. *A History of Western Music.* 3rd ed. New York: W. W. Norton and Company, 1980.

Hamburger, Michael. *Beethoven: Letters, Journals and Conversations.* London: Thames and Hudson, Ltd., 1951.

Hampson, Norman. *The Enlightenment and Evaluation of its Assumptions, Attitude and Values.* Hammondsworth and New York: Penguin Books, 1982.

Hofmann, Paul. *The Viennese: Splendor, Twilight and Exile.* New York: Anchor Books, 1988.

Kerman, Joseph and Alan Tyson. *The New Grove Beethoven.* New York: W. W. Norton and Company, 1983.

Kerst, Friedrich and Henry Edward Krehbeil, eds. Beethoven: *The Man the Artist, As Revealed In His Own Words.* Mineola, N.Y.: Dover Publications, Inc., 1964.

Kirchner, Walther. *Western Civilization from 1500.* 3rd ed. New York: HarperCollins Publishers, 1991.

Landon, H. C. Robbins, ed. *Beethoven: His Life, Work and World.* London: Thames and Hudson, Ltd., 1992.

Matthews, Denis. *Beethoven.* New York: Vintage Books, 1988.

McLeish, Kenneth and Valerie. The Listener's Guide to Classical Music. Thorndike, Maine: G. K. Hall and Company, 1986.

Miller, Hugh M. and Dale Cockrell. *History of Western Music.* New York: HarperCollins Publishers, 1991.

Mordden, Ethan. *A Guide to Orchestral Music.* New York: Oxford University Press, 1980.

Osborne, Charles. *The Dictionary of Composers.* Marlboro, N.J.: Taplinger Publishing Company, Inc., 1981.

Phillips-Matz, Mary Jane. *Verdi: A Biography.* New York: Oxford University Press, 1993.

Pugnetti, Gino. *Beethoven.* New York: Elite Publishing Corp., 1965.

Rushton, Julian. *Classical Music: A Concise History from Gluck to Beethoven.* London: Thames and Hudson, Ltd., 1986.

Solomon, Maynard. *Beethoven.* New York: Schirmer Books, 1977.

———. *Beethoven Essays.* Cambridge, Mass.: Harvard University Press, 1988.

Sullivan, J. W. N. *Beethoven: His Spiritual Development.* New York: Vintage Books, 1960.

Monet

Adams, Steven. *The Impressionists.* Philadelphia: Running Press, 1990.

Barnes, Rachel. *Monet by Monet.* New York: Alfred A. Knopf, 1990.

Blunden, Maria and Godfrey. *Impressionists and Impressionism.* Translated by James Emmons. New York: Rizzoli, 1980.

Bomford, Kirby and Roy Leighton, eds. *Impressionism.* London: National Gallery, in association with Yale University Press, 1990.

Cobban, Alfred. *A History of Modern France, Vol. 3, 1871–1962.* New York: Penguin Books, 1965.

Denvir, Bernard. *The Thames and Hudson Encyclopaedia of Impressionism.* London: Thames and Hudson, Ltd., 1990.

———. *The Impressionists at First Hand.* New York: Thames and Hudson, Ltd., 1991.

Forge, Andrew. *Monet.* Chicago: Art Institute of Chicago, 1995.

Friedrich, Otto. *Olympia: Paris in the Age of Manet.* New York: Simon & Schuster, 1992.

Gordon, Robert and Andrew Forge. *Monet.* New York: Abradale Press, 1989.

Hanson, Lawrence and Elisabeth Hanson. *Impressionism: Golden Decade, 1872–1882.* Austin, Tex.: Holt, Rinehart and Winston, 1961.

Heinrich, Christoph. *Claude Monet, 1840–1926.* Köln: Benedikt Taschen, 1994.

Herbert, Robert L. *Impressionism: Art, Leisure and Parisian Society.* New Haven, Conn.: Yale University Press, 1991.

House, John. *Monet: Nature into Art.* New Haven, Conn.: Yale University Press, 1989.

Howard, Michael. *The History of Impressionism.* New York: Museum of Modern Art, 1973.

Kirchner, Walther. *Western Civilization from 1500.* 3rd ed. New York: HarperCollins, 1991.

Levine, Steven Z. *Claude Monet.* New York: Rizzoli, 1994.

———. *Monet, Narcissus and Self-Reflection.* Chicago: University of Chicago Press, 1994.

Mühlberger, Richard. *What Makes a Monet a Monet?* New York: Metropolitan Museum of Art/Viking, 1993.

Nochlin, Linda, ed. *Impressionism and Post-Impressionism, 1874–1904.* Englewood Cliffs, N.J.: Prentice Hall, 1966.

Patin, Sylvie. *Monet: The Ultimate Impressionist.* New York: Harry Abrams, Inc., 1993.

Pool, Phoebe. *Impressionism.* London: Thames and Hudson, Ltd., 1988.

Reynolds, Donald. *The Nineteenth Century.* Cambridge: Cambridge University Press, 1985.

Rich, Norman. *The Age of Nationalism and Reform, 1850–1890.* 2nd ed. New York: W. W. Norton & Company, 1977.

Sagner-Düchting, Karin. *Monet, 1840–1926.* Köln: Benedikt Taschen, 1990.

Shirer, William L. *The Collapse of the Third Republic.* New York: Simon & Schuster, 1969.

Spate, Virginia. *Claude Monet: Life and Work.* New York: Rizzoli, 1992.

Sproccati, Sandro, ed. *A Guide to Art.* Translated from the Italian by Geofrrey Culverwell and others. New York: Harry N. Abrams, Inc., 1992.

Stuckey, Charles F. *Claude Monet: 1840–1926.* New York and Chicago, Thames and Hudson, Art Institute of Chicago, 1995.

————. *Monet: A Retrospective.* New York: Park Lane, 1986.

Taillandier, Yvon. *Monet.* Translated from the French by A. P. H. Hamilton. New York: Crown, 1993.

Taylor, John Russell. *The Life and Art of Claude Monet.* New York and Avenel, N.J.: Crescent Books, 1995.

Tucker, Paul Hayes. *Claude Monet: Life and Art.* New Haven, Conn.: Yale University Press, 1995.

————. *Monet in the '90s: The Series Paintings.* Boston and New Haven, Conn.: Museum of Fine Arts, Yale University Press, 1989.

Weber, Eugen. *France: Fin de Siécle.* Cambridge, Mass.: Belknap Press/Harvard, 1986.

Weekes, C. P. *Camille: A Study of Claude Monet.* London: Sidgwick & Jackson Ltd., 1962.

Welton, Jude. *Impressionism.* New York: Dorling Kindersley, 1993.

————. *Monet.* New York: Dorling Kindersley, 1992.

Wilson, Michael. *The Impressionists.* Oxford: Phaidon Press, Ltd., 1983.

General

Gardner, Howard. *Creating Minds.* New York: Basic Book's, 1993.

Ghiselin, Brewster. *The Creative Process.* Berkeley, Calif.: University of California Press, 1952.

Rothenberg, Albert. *Creativity and Madness.* Baltimore: Johns Hopkins University Press, 1990.

To order additional copies of this book, please send full amount plus $4.00 for postage and handling for the first book and 50¢ for each additional book.

Send orders to:

Galde Press, Inc.
PO Box 460
Lakeville, Minnesota 55044–0460

Credit card orders call 1–800–777–3454
Phone (612) 891–5991 • Fax (612) 891–6091
Visit our website at http://www.galdepress.com

Write for our free catalog.